# Supporting Development in Internationally Adopted Children

# Supporting Development in Internationally Adopted Children

by

**Deborah A. Hwa-Froelich, Ph.D., CCC-SLP**
Saint Louis University, Missouri

Baltimore • London • Sydney

**Paul H. Brookes Publishing Co.**
Post Office Box 10624
Baltimore, Maryland 21285-0624
USA

www.brookespublishing.com

Typeset by BLPS Content Connections, LLC, Chilton, Wisconsin.
Manufactured in the United States of America by
Sheridan Books, Inc., Chelsea, Michigan.

The individuals and situations/descriptions in this book are composites
based on the authors' experiences. In all instances, names and identifying
details have been changed to protect confidentiality.

**Library of Congress Cataloging-in-Publication Data**
Hwa-Froelich, Deborah A.
Supporting development in internationally adopted children / by Deborah A.
Hwa-Froelich. -- 1st ed.
    p.   cm.
Includes bibliographical references and index.
ISBN-13:  978-1-59857-191-2 (pbk.)
ISBN-10:  1-59857-191-5 (pbk.)
1.  Adopted children.  2.  Child development.  3.  Child care.  I.  Title.

HV875.S87   2012
362.734--dc23          2011035999

British Cataloguing in Publication data are available from the British Library.


2015   2014   2013   2012   2011

10    9    8    7    6    5    4    3    2    1

# Contents

About the Author ................................................................................vii
About the Contributors.........................................................................ix
Foreword     *Carol Westby*..................................................................xi
Foreword     *Femmie Juffer* ...........................................................xvii
Acknowledgments ..........................................................................xxiii

1    Theoretical Foundations for the Development of
     Internationally Adopted Children
     *Deborah A. Hwa-Froelich* .......................................................1

2    Physical Growth, Health, and Motor Development
     *Jennifer S. Ladage and Sarah E. Harris*..............................21

3    Social-Emotional and Relationship Development
     *Samantha L. Wilson* ..............................................................59

4    Cognitive Development
     *Samantha L. Wilson* ..............................................................85

5    Inhibition, Self-Regulation, Attention, and Memory
     Development
     *Deborah A. Hwa-Froelich* ...................................................107

6    Hearing, Speech, and Feeding Development
     *Deborah A. Hwa-Froelich* ...................................................133

7    Prelinguistic, Receptive, and Expressive Language
     Development
     *Deborah A. Hwa-Froelich* ...................................................149

8    Social Communication Development
     *Deborah A. Hwa-Froelich* ...................................................177

9    Intervention Strategies
     *Deborah A. Hwa-Froelich, Samantha L. Wilson, Sarah E.
     Harris, and Jennifer S. Ladage* ...........................................205

Index ................................................................................................233

# About the Author

**Deborah A. Hwa-Froelich, Ph.D., CCC-SLP,** Professor and Director of the International Adoption Clinic, 3750 Lindell Boulevard, 12 McGannon Hall, St. Louis, Missouri 63108-3412

In addition to her work as Professor in the Department of Communication Sciences and Disorders at Saint Louis University, Dr. Hwa-Froelich is the founder of the International Adoption Clinic (IAC). The IAC is a developmental clinic specializing in providing intervention services for internationally adopted children and their families. The clinic is an outgrowth of her longitudinal research documenting postadoption English language acquisition, as well as memory, social, and emotional development of internationally adopted children. She has also studied the influence of culture, poverty, maternal–child interactions, maternal mental health, and disrupted development on children's learning.

Dr. Hwa-Froelich holds a master's degree in speech-language pathology from the University of Kansas, a graduate endorsement in early childhood special education from the University of Colorado, and a doctorate in communication disorders and sciences from Wichita State University in Kansas. She has published and presented extensively on the topic of international adoption development, child development, and the effects of cultural and linguistic diversity on communication development and disorders.

A recipient of the Angel in Adoption Award from the U.S. Congressional Coalition on Adoption Institute, Dr. Hwa-Froelich also received the Louis M. DiCarlo Award for Clinical Achievement from the American Speech-Language-Hearing Foundation, the Diversity Champion Award from the American Speech-Language-Hearing Association (ASHA), and the Missouri Speech-Language-Hearing Association's Outstanding Clinician of the Year Award. She formerly served as the editor for *Perspectives of Communication Disorders in Culturally and Linguistically Diverse Populations for ASHA's Special Interest Division 14* and is a member of the Council for Exceptional Children and Division of Early Childhood.

# About the Contributors

**Sarah E. Harris, O.T.D., OTR/L,** Pediatric Occupational Therapist, Howard Park Center, St. Louis, Missouri

Ms. Harris, a licensed and registered pediatric occupational therapist, lives and works in St. Louis, Missouri. Working with adopted children and their families continues to be the most rewarding aspect of her practice. She has participated in multiple international aide trips and most recently spent 10 months working in Eastern Ukrainian orphanages as a Fulbright Fellow. In addition to her work as a therapist, Ms. Harris currently serves as secretary on the Creighton University Alumni Advisory Board.

**Jennifer S. Ladage, M.D.,** Assistant Professor of Pediatrics, Saint Louis University, 1465 S. Grand, St. Louis, Missouri 63104

In addition to her work as Assistant Professor, Dr. Ladage serves as director of the *F.A.C.E.S. Clinic* at SSM Cardinal Glennon Children's Medical Center, a clinic she founded in 1999 to address the medical needs of internationally adopted children. She is a member of the American Academy of Pediatrics and the *AAP's Council on Foster Care, Adoption, and Kinship Care.* Dr. Ladage is the mother of three internationally adopted children.

**Samantha L. Wilson, Ph.D.,** Assistant Professor of Pediatrics, Children's Hospital of Wisconsin, Child Development Center–International Adoption Clinic, Post Office Box 1997, MS 744, Milwaukee, Wisconsin 53201

Dr. Wilson is Assistant Professor of Pediatrics at the Medical College of Wisconsin and serves as the staff psychologist within the International Adoption Clinic at Children's Hospital of Wisconsin. In this position, she provides immediate postadoption support as well as psychoeducational assessment and therapeutic intervention for internationally adopted children and their families. Dr. Wilson has published numerous articles on the subjects of adoption, institutional care, attachment, and early child development.

# Foreword    Carol Westby

*Child abuse casts a shadow the length of a lifetime.*

Herbert Ward

*There can be no keener revelation of a society's soul than the way in which it treats its children.*

Nelson Mandela

*Storytelling is the thread which is woven deep in our lives, our conscious, our humanity. It has the power to bring understanding amongst the peoples of the world. Tell and listen.*

Antonio Rocha

In *Supporting Development in Internationally Adopted Children*, Dr. Deborah Hwa-Froelich and her colleagues have produced a compelling and comprehensive account of the experiences, strengths, and needs of internationally adopted children. Since 1971, approximately 450,000 international children have been adopted by U.S. citizens. Although these children typically show growth and developmental delays upon arrival in the United States, the majority of them display remarkable catch-up. Yet a significant number of them are at risk for a variety of health, social, and learning difficulties. Many professionals have limited experience with this group of children. They encounter only a few internationally adopted children; and the children they do encounter are often adopted from different countries at differing ages. As a consequence, it is difficult for most professionals to gain sufficient personal experience to learn the patterns of development in internationally adopted children. Furthermore, the research on internationally adopted children is carried out by professionals from many disciplines, making it difficult to locate the information in any one place. The authors of this book bring a wealth of knowledge on the topic of internationally adopted children. They represent multiple disciplines and have heard the stories of hundreds of internationally adopted children adopted at various ages from many different countries.

United States citizens started adopting children from other countries in substantial numbers after World War II. Many of the children adopted were European and Japanese war orphans. Additional adoptions followed the Korean War (1950–1953) and the war in Vietnam (1954–1975). Many of these children had been fathered by U.S. military personnel and were ostracized because of their biracial identity. By the last decade of the 20th century, the number of internationally adopted children increased exponentially and the reasons for international adoptions changed. Desperate poverty and social upheaval became critical factors in the adoption of children from Latin America, the former Soviet Union, and Eastern Europe. In China, government population-control policies contributed to abandonment of infant girls and overcrowded orphanages, factors in the government's decision to facilitate international adoptions. Many of these children adopted in the latter part of the 20th century and early 21st century exhibited different patterns of development compared with those adopted following war.

Mainstream North Americans have typically believed that children are highly malleable and that a loving family can compensate for any early difficulties a young child experienced. Adoption of thousands of Romanian orphans after the fall of the Ceauşescu regime in 1989 revealed this was not the case. Under Nicolae Ceauşescu, both abortion and contraception were forbidden, leading to a rise in birth rates. This resulted in many children being abandoned, then being joined in orphanages by persons with disabilities and mental illnesses. Together these vulnerable groups were subjected to institutionalized neglect and abuse, including physical and sexual abuse and use of drugs to control their behavior. Nearly 20 years of research that followed children from Romanian orphanages has documented that although the majority of children significantly improved in all aspects of physical, cognitive, language, and social-emotional development, large numbers of them continued to exhibit delays and disorders that warranted attention and intervention. Similar results have been found for children adopted from other countries.

Educational programs have often not addressed how to handle the needs of internationally adopted children. These children are often denied special education services under the Individuals with Disabilities Education Act (IDEA) because of misinterpretation of the law and lack of understanding of the developmental trajectories of the children. Internationally adopted children are often treated as bilingual English language learners (ELLs). However, internationally adopted children acquire English much differently than typical bilingual ELL students. Internationally adopted children are rarely bilingual. Unlike bilingual ELL children who are learning a second language in child care centers and schools while continuing to interact with family members in their first language at home, internationally adopted children are typically faced with abrupt loss of their first language and the immediate need to acquire a new language. The patterns of loss of a first language and acquisition of English as a second language differ between ELL children and internationally adopted children.

Dr. Hwa-Froelich has fashioned a unique formatting of this volume's chapters, creating an interaction between storytelling and informational text. Although we learn best through narrative, professional or academic books typically employ an expository style, presenting information in a dense, decontextualized manner. All the authors in this book contextualize content by beginning each chapter with a story of an internationally adopted child. They then provide a comprehensive review of the literature on all developmental topics (physical growth and motor development; social-emotional and relationship development; cognitive development; inhibition, self-regulation, attention and memory development; hearing, speech, and feeding development; prelinguistic, receptive, and expressive language development; and social communication development). In an implications section that follows a literature review, each author returns to the child's story and demonstrates how knowledge from the literature was used to assess and provide appropriate interventions for the child. In this way, they demonstrate the child's resilience and adaptations and their use of the research knowledge for problem solving, interpreting the child's behaviors, and developing recommendations. Many Native American cultures view stories as a source of healing. Leslie Marmon Silko, a member of the Laguna Pueblo, writes in the introduction to her book, *Ceremony*, "I will tell you something about stories, [he said]. They aren't just entertainment. Don't be fooled. They are all we have, you see. All we have to fight off illness and death" (p. 2). By hearing the stories that Dr. Hwa-Froelich and her colleagues tell, professionals will have the resources to facilitate healing of children who have experienced abuse, neglect, and other traumas.

The authors end each chapter with a summary of key points and, based on research data, they provide recommendations for when a child should be referred for evaluation or intervention. These recommendations will be invaluable for professionals faced with what to do with a particular child. Because so few developmental data have been available on internationally adopted children, it has been very easy to overrefer or underrefer these children for interventions. Often school testing considers primarily or only speech, language, and cognitive abilities. These are areas that internationally adopted children are likely to show the most apparent catch-up. This does not mean, however, that they have no educational and social needs. Prenatal and postnatal experiences are disruptive not only of these skills, but also of more basic skills such as attachment, social-emotional/theory of mind development, attention, working memory, and self-regulation—behaviors that are not typically assessed but influence social and academic performance.

As the social-emotional and attachment disorders of a number of internationally adopted children were becoming recognized, researchers were gaining an understanding of the importance of attunement and attachment between infants and toddlers and their caregivers and how this led to understanding of the minds of others and effective communicative interactions (Fogel & Thelen, 1987; Legerstee, 2005). Other researchers exploring attention deficit–hyperactivity disorder (ADHD; Barkley, 1997) and executive function (Lyon & Krasnegor, 1996) were discovering neurological bases and environmental factors that contribute to focused attention, self-regulation, and efficient working memory. Dr. Hwa-Froelich and her colleagues effectively apply this research to the assessment and intervention of internationally adopted children.

At the same time that professionals were recognizing the multisystem effects of prenatal and postnatal experiences on internationally adopted children, researchers in child language and child motor development were acknowledging the complexity of developmental processes in typical children. They reconceptualized theories of acquisition and development. Earlier theories of development focused on either a genetic or neurobiological basis of development or a social interactionist/ environmental basis of development—and both of these perspectives typically viewed development as linear. In the 1990s, researchers in a variety of areas of child development proposed connectionist models and dynamic systems framework to explain the interaction of multiple factors on development (MacWhinney, 1999; Smith & Thelen, 1993). These models or frameworks acknowledged the interactions of the children's biological and genetic makeups with their environmental experiences. And rather than the components interacting in a linear manner, they interacted in a heterarchical manner; that is, there is interaction across levels that results in the development of integrated neural networks of associations. Nelson and Arkenberg (2008) referred to this as a "dynamic tricky mix of development,"(p. 315) because genetic, biological, and environmental factors interact in different ways for each child. Hence, according to a connectionist or dynamic systems framework, there are multiple routes to development. Dynamic systems theory provided a mechanism for explaining the multiple, complex delays and disorders exhibited among internationally adopted children and the marked variability among children, even when they seemed to have had similar preadoptive experiences.

This book will become essential reading for all persons working with internationally adopted children and their families. Although intended for professionals who work with internationally adopted children, the book has relevance for those who work with all adopted children and those who work with children in foster care, children from high-risk families due to poverty or drug use, or children who spend much of their waking hours in child care facilities of questionable quality. In terms of neglect, abuse, drug exposure, multiple caregivers, and change of caregivers, many of these children share experiences with internationally adopted children; for example,

> Marisol is a 9-month-old girl in a child care center. The center meets the state guidelines for caregiver–child ratio. All caregivers have had to attend a 45-hour course focusing on health and safety issues, but the caregivers are required only to have a GED (high school graduate equivalency degree), and they have no specific training in child development. The caregivers view Marisol as clingy and wanting attention. They don't want to encourage this, so they leave her sitting by herself in a bouncy chair for several hours a day, interacting with her primarily to feed her or change her.
>
> Thirty-month-old Isaiah and his four-year-old brother have recently been placed with their maternal grandmother after they were found left alone by their mother, a drug user. A 6-month-old sibling was placed in a foster home because the grandmother said she could not manage all three children. The grandmother is diabetic and appears depressed. She has little energy to interact with the children. The home is cluttered and usually dark. Isaiah uses only a few single words. He is very active, has limited attention, and resists redirection.

Children such as these are in environments that are similar to those of many internationally adopted children, and they exhibit many of the physical, cognitive, language, social-emotional, and attention difficulties often associated with internationally adopted children. The knowledge that has been gained as a result of the tragic experiences of many internationally adopted children can be used to improve environments for all children so that they develop into strong, healthy adults.

Frederick Douglass said, "It is easier to build strong children than to repair broken men." Through the stories and research Dr. Hwa-Froelich and her colleagues share, they provide guidance for us to build strong children with happy stories to tell.

*Carol Westby, Ph.D.*
*Speech-Language-Literacy Consultant*
*Bilingual Multicultural Services*
*Albuquerque, New Mexico*

## REFERENCES

Barkley, R.A. (1997). *ADHD and the nature of self-control.* New York: Guilford Press.

Fogel, A., & Thelen, E. (1987). Development of early expressive and communicative action: Reinterpreting the evidence from a dynamic systems perspective. *Developmental Psychology, 23,* 747–761.

Legerstee, M. (2005). *Infants sense of people: Precursors to theory of mind.* New York: Cambridge University Press.

Lyon, G.R., & Krasnegor, N.A. (Eds.). (1996). *Attention, memory, and executive function.* Baltimore: Paul H. Brookes Publishing Co.

MacWhinney, B. (Ed.). (1999). *The emergence of language.* Mahwah, NJ: Lawrence Erlbaum Associates.

Nelson, K.E., & Arkenberg, M.E. (2008). Language and reading development reflect dynamic mixes of learning conditions. In M. Mody & E.R. Silliman (Eds.), *Brain, behavior, and learning in language and reading disorders* (pp. 315–348). New York: Guilford Press.

Silko, L.M. (1977). *Ceremony.* New York: Viking.

Smith, L.B., & Thelen, E. (Eds.) (1993). *A dynamic systems approach to development: Applications.* Cambridge, MA: MIT Press.

# Foreword    Femmie Juffer

## The Many Faces of International Adoption: A Gallery of Experiences

International adoption has many faces: a boy from Russia adopted in the United States of America, a girl from China in an adoptive home in Canada, a toddler with special needs who came from India to the Netherlands, and two siblings who were adopted simultaneously from South America to Spain. The many faces of international adoption not only include the infants, toddlers, and preschool children just before and after their adoption, but also the school-age children, adolescents, and (young) adults they become after spending their childhood years in the adoptive home.

International adoption has a history of more than 50 years and has developed from a rare phenomenon to a well-known and sometimes highly debated form of alternative care for children without parental care in their own country. Decades of developments also mean that the many faces of international adoption have formed a fast-growing gallery of experiences, knowledge, and insights. The face of international adoption definitely has changed from a perhaps naïve baby face to a more mature adult face: The field has moved from personal, individual experiences shared by adoptive families to widely recognized clinical practice and evidence-based knowledge from adoption research. A few pictures from this gallery of experiences will be depicted here.

## The Internationally Adopted Child in the Eye of Scientists and Adoptive Families

Adoption researchers and adoptive parents often differ in how they perceive the development of internationally adopted children because their goals and perspectives can vary widely. The scientist usually prefers valid findings based on representative adoption samples and evidence-based outcomes that can be generalized to new groups of adopted children. The view of such an adoption researcher is broad: sizeable samples, homogeneous groups, general statements, traceable trends, and research-informed decisions and predictions. Scientists often see adoption as a "natural experiment" of "nature and nurture," because adopted children are reared by genetically unrelated parents and bring their own genes into the adoptive household.

Adoptive parents approach the adopted child's development from quite a different angle: How should we support our child with his or her specific delays and needs? How can our adopted child's problems be recognized and treated? Does our child need therapy or special education? Adoptive parents often search for practical help and suggestions about how to parent a child who has suffered from, for example, prenatal alcohol or drug abuse, malnutrition, institutional deprivation, separations, and losses. Generally these parents are oriented not toward the general but to the individual level, and they are interested in clinical and practical solutions.

Although the different opinions of scientists and parents may collide and sometimes indeed do, there are exceptions to this rule and examples of how these divergent goals can be reconciled. Translational and clinical researchers can make an effort to make scientific knowledge available for individual families. They can try to communicate empirical outcomes in a way that parents, as well as professionals helping families, can understand and use these findings. A merit of this volume is that the two different viewpoints of scientists and parents elegantly converge: The book offers a wealth of scientific knowledge and evidence from numerous adoption studies, but it also offers lively and realistic case studies of individual children, illustrations, examples, and key points for practical use.

## From Risk to Recovery

In the public opinion, there are mixed views of adoption, ranging from overly positive ones, such as picturing adoptive parents as altruistic saviors of needy children, to overly negative views, depicting adopted children as disturbed or criminal and adoptive parents as fraudulent and selfish (Juffer et al., 2012; Kline, Chatterjee, & Karel, 2009). Realistic images of adoption are sometimes hard to get; and for the media, all too often the rule is that good news is no news.

Adoption research also started with a one-sided view of adoption. In the first years of adoption research, the focus was primarily on risks (Palacios & Brodzinsky, 2010). Adopted children were compared with nonadopted children, and risk ratios and overrepresentations were computed. Although adopted children indeed are at risk of, for example, presenting more behavior problems and clinical referrals (Juffer & Van IJzendoorn, 2005), the focus in these older studies was on highlighting how impaired adopted children with disabilities were compared with their non-adopted peers and classmates. Usually not much attention was given to the background of adopted children's problems, and comparisons with children with similar histories of early adversity were not made.

In later years, the focus switched from risks to recovery processes in adopted children, and their resilience and catch-up growth were emphasized (Palacios & Brodzinsky, 2010; Van IJzendoorn & Juffer, 2006).

Renewed attention was paid to their backgrounds, and comparisons between adopted children and nonadopted children who had to remain in institutional care were seen as highly valuable and relevant. This second wave of research revealed that adopted children show a remarkable and surprising catch-up growth after adoption. Compared to the effects of common early childhood interventions (such as Head Start or comparable enrichment programs), adoption appeared to be an even more effective intervention in children's lives (Bakermans-Kranenburg, Van IJzendoorn, & Juffer, 2008).

According to Palacios and Brodzinsky (2010), the latest trend in adoption research is a focus on recovery processes and mechanisms and an interest in the question of how children may be differentially affected by adoption based on their preadoption background experiences or their genetic makeup. As an example, adopted children with foster care experiences in China outperformed children with institutional care experiences in China with respect to their mental and motor development after adoption, and they showed a larger increase in responsiveness in parent–child interaction (Van den Dries, Juffer, Van IJzendoorn, & Bakermans-Kranenburg, 2010; Van den Dries, Juffer, Van IJzendoorn, Bakermans-Kranenburg, & Alink, in press). This study also revealed the deteriorating effects of institutional deprivation on children's cognitive and social-emotional development, as has been established in numerous studies.

The information in this volume shows a balanced view of adopted children's development. The author and contributors have succeeded in bringing together realistic information about the risks, challenges, and problems involved in adoption, while also paying considerable attention to adopted children's resilience and the recovery processes after adoption.

## Disentangling the Effects of Adoption and Deprivation

For professionals and adoptive families, it is often hard to disentangle the effects of adoption per se and the (long-term) consequences of preadoption deprivation and trauma. Meta-analytical studies have shown that early adoption (and thus less deprivation) generally is associated with a more complete catch-up and better outcomes after adoptive placement compared with later adoptions. However, even early adoption (before the first birthday) does not guarantee full catch-up, and substantial delays can be found in insecure attachment disorganization and school achievement (Van IJzendoorn & Juffer, 2006). In this book the reader can find a state-of-the-art overview of what (institutional) deprivation does to children and how parents and professionals can address adopted children's needs, delays, and difficulties.

Longitudinal adoption studies can add to the body of adoption research and be particularly helpful in disentangling the role of prolonged, cumulative deprivation and adoption per se without such experiences of deprivation. Longitudinal studies that examine the effects of deprivation (e.g., the English and Romanian Adoptee Study), effects of adoption and deprivation (e.g., the Dutch Rotterdam longitudinal cohort study), and effects of adoption without deprivation (the Dutch Leiden longitudinal study) were compared (Juffer et al., 2012). The studies examining effects of deprivation alone or deprivation and adoption together revealed problems and delays in most domains of child development, whereas the one study that included early adopted children who did not suffer from severe institutional deprivation showed a far more positive picture. The children in this study were followed from infancy to adolescence, and they showed normative development in the areas of attachment, social, emotional, and cognitive development. The only exception was found in their elevated rates of behavior problems and internalizing (e.g., anxious behavior) as well as externalizing (e.g., aggressive behavior) problems (Juffer et al., 2012). This may indicate that most problems and delays presented by adopted children and adolescents may be associated with their preadoption experiences of institutional deprivation and lack of adequate stimulation and personal attention. Nevertheless, some difficulties—particularly behavior problems during middle childhood and adolescence—may be related to adoption itself, for example to the child's perception and emotions about being adopted and looking different (Juffer & Tieman, 2009).

## Growing Up Adopted

The ever-growing gallery of experiences in international adoption will show more and new faces in the near future. The boy from Russia who was adopted in the United States may become a teenager who is not at all interested in his roots in Russia. The girl adopted from China may visit her country of origin during her preadolescence years, which may motivate her to take Chinese classes back in Canada. The Indian toddler with special needs who was adopted in the Netherlands may partially overcome her delays in childhood and as an adult start a romantic relationship and have children of her own. Her adoptive parents will hope to be the proud grandparents of her children, but they and the young mother-to-be may have questions about possible genetic vulnerabilities transmitted from her unknown birth family. Unfortunately, as searching is not possible in her case, questions will remain unanswered. Finally, the two adopted siblings in Spain may decide as young adults to search for their birth family, and they may succeed in being reunited with their relatives in South America. They may then face the puzzling task of how to establish a relationship with birth relatives who are genetically related to them but with whom they do not share a common history.

These examples illustrate that adoption is a lifelong process, and being adopted as well as long-term consequences of early life experiences (including deprivation) may be important for the life of adopted children, adolescents, and (young) adults.

International adoption has definitely left its childhood. Numerous children have been internationally adopted among more than 100 countries, and a new generation of adult adoptees are now integrating personal experiences of adoption into their lives. The fruit of more than half a century of international adoption has resulted in many invaluable insights and knowledge. It is imperative to use these insights to help (new) adopted children and to support their adoptive parents. This book makes a unique and important contribution to the field by bringing together evidence from adoption research as well as lively case studies and illustrations from (clinical) practice.

*Femmie Juffer*
*Professor of Adoption Studies*
*Centre for Child and Family Studies*
*Leiden University*
*The Netherlands*

# REFERENCES

Bakermans-Kranenburg, M. J., Van IJzendoorn, M.H., & Juffer, F. (2008). Earlier is better: A meta-analysis of 70 years of interventions improving cognitive development in institutionalized children. *Monographs of the Society for Research of Child Development, 73,* 279–293.

Juffer, F., Palacios, J., LeMare, L., Sonuga-Barke, E., Tieman, W., Bakermans-Kranenburg, M.J. et al. (2012). Development of adopted children with histories of early adversity. In R. B. McCall, M. H. Van IJzendoorn, F. Juffer, V. K. Groza, & C. J. Groark (Eds.), Children without permanent parental care: Research, practice, and policy. *Monographs of the Society for Research of Child Development.*

Juffer, F., & Tieman, W. (2009). Being adopted. Internationally adopted children's interest and feelings. *International Social Work, 52*(5), 635–647.

Juffer, F., & Van IJzendoorn, M. H. (2005). Behavior problems and mental health referrals of international adoptees: A meta-analysis. *Journal of the American Medical Association, 293,* 2501–2515.

Kline, S.L., Chatterjee, K., & Karel, A.I. (2009). Healthy depictions? Depicting adoption and adoption news events on broadcast news. *Journal of Health Communication, 14,* 56–69.

Palacios, J. & Brodzinsky, D. (2010). Adoption research: Trends, topics, outcomes. *International Journal of Behavioral Development, 34,* 270–284.

Van den Dries, L., Juffer, F., Van IJzendoorn, M. H., & Bakermans-Kranenburg, M. J. (2010). Infants' physical and cognitive development after international adoption from foster care or institutions in China. *Journal of Developmental & Behavioral Pediatrics, 31,* 144–150.

Van den Dries, L., Juffer, F., Van IJzendoorn, M. H., Bakermans-Kranenburg, M.J., & Alink, L. R. A. (In press). Infants' responsiveness, attachment, and indiscriminate friendliness after international adoption from institutions or foster care in China: Application of Emotional Availability Scales to adoptive families. *Development & Psychopathology.*

Van IJzendoorn, M. H., & Juffer, F. (2006). The Emanuel Miller Memorial Lecture 2006: Adoption as intervention. Meta-analytic evidence for massive catch-up and plasticity in physical, socio-emotional, and cognitive development. *Journal of Child Psychology and Psychiatry, 47,* 1228–1245.

# Acknowledgments

This book has been a passion of mine for several years and I am indebted to so many people who contributed and helped me through the process. First and foremost, I am grateful to the children—and their families—who so willingly gave their time to allow me to measure their development over the years. Their anonymous contributions are described throughout this book. I am also grateful to Drs. Samantha L. Wilson, Jennifer S. Ladage, and Sarah E. Harris, who contributed three outstanding chapters and coauthored a fourth. Dr. Wilson spent much time reviewing and commenting on the chapter about inhibition, self-regulation, attention, and memory. Her knowledge and expertise are much appreciated. I also would like to mention the financial support received from the Saint Louis University Beaumont fund and the Regionwise grant funding provided by the Danforth Foundation. The funding helped support some of the research reported in this book.

There were many students through the years, too many to list, who helped me collect the information included in this book. Their work is greatly appreciated. I want to acknowledge the time and energy several students spent conducting literature searches; revising, reviewing, editing, and analyzing text; and completing myriad tasks that led to the publication of this book: Jenna Roselman Becker, Kristal Schuette, Janel Golden, Jamie Brockmeier, Megan Knaeble, and Hannah Sensintaffer.

I owe a debt of gratitude to my friend, Angie Burda, and my husband, Dana, who encouraged and supported me throughout this journey. Angie provided a never-ending supply of encouragement and advice during this process and I could not have completed this book without her. Finally, I would like to thank Dana, who patiently waited countless times while I finished writing a paragraph, a page, or a chapter. I would not have been able to finish this book without his support.

*For all the children of the world, who deserve
to be loved, and for the families who love them*

# 1

# Theoretical Foundations for the Development of Internationally Adopted Children

*Deborah A. Hwa-Froelich*

*"Internationally adopted children provide a model of the impact of early adversity on developmental processes and the capacity of children to recover from early adversity when their social and physical context radically changes."*

(Gunnar, Bruce, & Grotevant, 2000, p. 678)

Andrew was adopted from Kazakhstan at 7 months of age and was the second child his parents adopted from Eastern Europe. He was born in a hospital and transferred to an orphanage after a few days. His adoptive parents described the orphanage as crowded with two to four infants in each crib and as many as 20 different caregivers interacting with the infants. Andrew was described as having above-average health, mild motor delays, and a generally happy disposition. Six months later, at 13 months of age, Andrew's parents reported concerns with his swallowing, sensitivity to sticky textures and loud noises, and a high activity level. His early childhood assessment revealed normal hearing acuity and above-average English vocabulary comprehension. Andrew also had borderline scores in prelinguistic and symbolic behavioral development, a high activity level, tactile aversion to sticky textures, delayed chewing and swallowing development with a hypersensitive gag reflex, and oral sensitivity to sticky foods.

Andrew began to receive special education services for oral motor development related to chewing and swallowing, as well as sensory integration therapy (SIT). By 2 years, 7 months of age, Andrew had speech and receptive and expressive language skills above the average range compared with English-speaking peers. He also had age-appropriate and functional feeding development and had learned to cope with his sensitivity to textures and loud noises. Andrew continued to have behavioral issues of overactivity, physical aggression, and tantrums. When Andrew was 3 years, 10 months old, his mother reported that his behaviors improved when they stayed at home and after Andrew was

1

placed on a special diet to remove heavy metals. According to his parents, a therapist recommended that Andrew have his hair analyzed for heavy metal exposure. An alternate
health provider completed the hair analysis and reported high levels of aluminum and
cadmium. Andrew was placed on a special diet, was given special vitamins, and received
saunas and footbaths to detoxify his body. Another therapist recommended auditory
integration therapy (AIT). In spite of these interventions, Andrew's overactivity and inattention adversely affected his performance on developmental measures. For example,
his receptive and expressive language scores were now below average and his selective
attention, short-term memory, and ability to understand others' perspectives were also
developmentally delayed.

Andrew is an example of an internationally adopted child who displays individual variations in development. Andrew's parents are similar
to many parents seeking myriad therapies and treatments to help their
children. It is because of Andrew and other internationally adopted children that I opened the International Adoption Clinic (IAC) at Saint Louis
University and began documenting the development of internationally
adopted children. I have evaluated many children who demonstrate mild
to no developmental delays at the time of adoption and continue to develop as their typically developing nonadopted peers do. I have also seen
children who initially demonstrate significant developmental delays and
health issues but eventually catch up with nonadopted peers. In addition,
there are children who initially demonstrate few, if any, developmental
delays but later demonstrate behaviors that negatively affect their academic and social performance. In the cases of persisting delays or unex-
plainable problems, parents seek clinical and medical practitioners who
may recommend traditional and nontraditional treatments or therapeutic
interventions. Some of these treatments or interventions may be needed,
but some children may develop typically without any intervention. At the
same time, some of the treatments children receive are evidence based,
whereas others are not.

Clinical and medical practitioners may overrefer internationally
adopted children for early intervention services. Glennen and Masters
(2002) found that in a sample of 130 infants and toddlers, 59% of internationally adopted children had one to three diagnoses such as attention-
deficit/hyperactivity disorder (ADHD), speech and/or language disorder,
or reactive attachment disorder before 3 years of age. Following 46 of
the original 130 children, Glennen and Bright (2005) found that between
6.6 and 9.1 years of age, children with multiple diagnoses decreased from
45.4% to 22.8%, diagnoses of speech-language delay or disorder decreased from 47.3% to 11.4%, but diagnoses of ADHD increased from
11.4% to 25%. It is unclear whether these enrollment statistics reflect
actual prevalence of these disorders, misreferral, or accurate diagnoses.

When inattention or overactive behaviors persist, parents and/or
practitioners may seek or recommend nontraditional interventions that

have not been researched or proven to be efficacious. As in Andrew's case, although oral motor and swallowing interventions have been found to be effective (Sheppard, 2008; Wheeler-Hegland et al., 2009), neither hair analysis, detoxification diets, SIT, nor AIT interventions are supported by the American Medical Association or the American Speech-Language-Hearing Association (ASHA, 2003; Seidel, Kreutzer, Smith, McNeel, & Gilliss, 2001). Seidel and colleagues reported that hair analyses to determine exposure to toxins were unreliable. A few studies using single subjects or small samples found that SIT had a positive effect on children's behavior regulation. In a study of seven children with pervasive developmental delay and mental retardation, children's self-injurious and self-stimulating behaviors declined an hour after SIT over a 4-week time period (Smith, Press, Koenig, & Kinnealey, 2005). The authors suggest that SIT may help children reduce self-stimulating and self-injurious behaviors, which in turn facilitates their attention needed for learning. Due to the small sample size from the same institutional environment, however, their results may not be representative or generalized to children similar to Andrew.

Tochel (2003) completed a systematic review of randomized controlled trial studies on the effect of SIT and AIT. Although only four studies on AIT and one study on SIT were reviewed, neither intervention was found to be more effective than listening to music. In addition, in meta-analyses of sensory integration therapy studies, researchers found no support that SIT was any more effective than other alternative treatment approaches for children with motor or learning disabilities (Dawson & Watling, 2000; Hoehn & Baumeister, 1994; Kaplan, Polatajko, & Faris, 1993; Vargas & Camilli, 1999; Wilson, Kaplan, Fellowes, Gruchy, & Faris, 1992). Andrew's aggressive behaviors may have been related to a need for sensory stimulation, and SIT may have helped Andrew reduce his aggressive behaviors, but he continues to display overactivity, inattention, and tantrums in spite of the specialized diets, detoxification methods, and AIT (for a review refer to Chapter 2). Thus Andrew and his parents expended time and energy seeking and receiving assessments and interventions that were not supported by research evidence. It is important for medical and clinical practitioners to be aware of evidence-based interventions so they can make appropriate recommendations and referrals. The purpose of this book is to provide evidence-based information on typical development, referral indicators, and appropriate referral sources for internationally adopted children.

## HISTORY OF INTERNATIONAL ADOPTION

Children were initially adopted from abroad following World War II and the Korean War. These adoptions included children from Germany, Austria, Japan, and South Korea. During the late 1970s and early 1980s, China instituted its One Child policy, and with a cultural preference for males, large numbers of female infants were placed in Chinese orphanages (Hesketh, Lu, & Xing, 2005). When the Romanian Revolution and the breakup of the Soviet Union occurred between 1989 and 1991, Romanian orphanages were also overpopulated with children (Ladage, 2009; Maclean, 2003; Mason & Narad, 2005a). As a result, during the 1990s, Romania, Russia, and China became the top countries from which children were adopted into the United States. Over the last decade, more children have been adopted from Guatemala, Kazakhstan, and Ethiopia, in addition to Russia and China (Ladage, 2009).

International adoptions have steadily increased since the 1950s, when children were often adopted from Korea. By 2004, the number of annual adoptions of children from different countries reached an estimated 45,000 worldwide (Selman, 2009). The growth and popularity of international adoption was also reflected in the United States. From 1971 to 2001, 265,677 children from different countries were adopted into the United States (Adoption.com, 2004; Adoption Institute, 2004). Almost the same number of children were adopted from abroad into the United States over the last 10 years. From 1998 to 2008 the number of children adopted from abroad into the United States ranged from 15,583 to 22,884 annually, with a total of 216,000 children (U.S. Department of State, 2009). Most of these children were adopted from China, Russia, and Guatemala.

U.S. families adopt children from abroad 4 to 16 times more than families from other countries (Hellerstedt et al., 2008). Compared with live births, the choice of adoption is increasing. For example, in 2003 the United States received approximately 21,600 internationally adopted children, which is 5.1 per 1,000 births. In contrast, in 2003, Sweden, Norway, and Spain received almost twice as many adoptees (11.4, 13.5, and 10.4) per 1,000 births (Van IJzendoorn & Juffer, 2006, p. 1228). The number of adoptions around the world fell by 17% during 2004 and 2007 in the United States, Australia, the Netherlands, and the Nordic countries, but increased in Italy, France, and Belgium (Selman, 2009).

Most internationally adopted children are adopted before the age of 2 years. In a recent Minnesota survey of 1,834 parents who adopted 2,291 children from abroad between 1990 and 1998, 64% of the children were adopted before 12 months of age, 17% were adopted between 12 and 23 months, 11% were adopted between 24 and 59 months of age, and 8% were adopted at age 5 or older (Hellerstedt et al., 2008). The majority of these children were adopted from institutions as opposed to foster care.

As the number of adopted children increases, the need for information about their development and appropriate services also grows. The majority of research studies on international adoption include children adopted from South Korea or Romania. Although the outcomes for children adopted from South Korea have been generally positive (Clark & Hanisee, 1982; Frydman & Lynn, 1989), the same is not true for children adopted from Romania.

The early 1990 media coverage of Romanian orphanages revealed the dire conditions in which the children were housed. Many of these institutions did not have the economic resources to provide adequate nutrition, clothing, medical care, or nurturance. Staff were poorly trained and charged with the care of large numbers of children, sometimes 1 adult to 10 or 60 children (Johnson, 2000; Johnson et al., 1992). Parents, including U.S. citizens, who adopted children from Romania had little to no knowledge of the effects these conditions had on the children. When problems developed and persisted, parents sought help from many different practitioners. For example, when Andrew continued to demonstrate overactivity, tantrums, and aggressive behaviors, his parents sought help from pediatricians, occupational therapists, speech-language pathologists, family therapists, and alternative health providers. In response to children and families similar to Andrew's, adoption medicine has become a new specialty and several adoption clinics have opened across the nation. In St. Louis, Missouri alone, two medical clinics and one developmental clinic devoted to meeting the health and developmental needs of internationally adopted children have opened since 2000. Clinical experiences have led me and many other colleagues to study and document internationally adopted children's development following exposure to early adversity.

The purpose of this chapter is to explain the adaptation and resilience of internationally adopted children in spite of their exposure to early adversity according to developmental theory.

## EARLY ADVERSITY

Historically, institutional care has had profound negative effects on adopted children's growth and development compared with nonadopted peers (Gunnar, Bruce, & Grotevant, 2000; Maclean, 2003; Sigal, Perry, Rossignol, & Ouimet, 2003). Even when their basic biological needs are met, the lack of social interaction and stimulation negatively affects children's cognitive, social, and language development (Maclean, 2003; Sigal et al., 2003; Tizard & Joseph, 1970). In addition, when children in foster care experience more transitions from caregivers (such as leaving the care of the birth mother to an orphanage, to a foster parent, back to the orphanage, and then finally to an adoptive parent), similar findings such as cognitive, social, and linguistic developmental delays are evident (Pears & Fisher, 2005).

For children living in institutions in other countries, information about their biological parents and prenatal care may be missing or incomplete. This is particularly true for children adopted from China, where pregnancies may be unreported or hidden until the gender and health of the infant are determined and then infants are *found* in crowded public places before being placed in orphanage care. Children from Eastern European institutions are often 1) from a lower socioeconomic background; 2) the product of a third or fourth pregnancy; 3) exposed to tobacco, alcohol, or other substances; 4) born premature or small for gestational age; or 5) removed from parental abusive or neglected care and placed in the orphanage (Johnson, 2000; Ladage, 2009; Mason & Narad, 2005a).

The quality and type of care after birth and prior to international adoption vary within and across countries. From clinical data, Miller (2005) reported that quality of care is variable across both Asian and Eastern European orphanages. Countries with few economic resources may expend less financial support for children living in state-run institutions, resulting in a lack of nutrition, adequate medical care, and opportunities to explore their environment or interact with toys and adults (Johnson, 2000). Caregivers who work in orphanages may be responsible for caring for several children at a time, may not direct their discourse directly to children, or may not have the educational knowledge or training to provide a vocabulary-rich conversation with each child. In his literature review of Eastern European orphanage care and educational training of Baby Home directors and staff, Johnson (2000) reported that training focused on health care rather than child development. Children in Baby Homes received basic care to meet their biological needs, but social, educational, and language stimulation were not emphasized. As in Andrew's experience, children were confined to cribs, and sometimes one to three infants were placed together in each crib. Children were expected to learn to feed themselves, and often bottles were propped in the crib or given to the infants to hold by themselves (Johnson, 2000; Miller, 2005).

Consequently, children adopted from Eastern European countries and China initially demonstrate significant growth and developmental delays (cognitive, speech-language, social-emotional, and motor), infectious diseases (tuberculosis, hepatitis B and C, HIV, and others), anemia, and elevated lead and thyroid levels. Vision, hearing, and dental impairments are often untreated (Albers, Johnson, Hostetter, Iverson, & Miller, 1997; Johnson, 2000; Miller & Hendrie, 2000; Morison, Ames, & Chisholm, 1995; Rutter & the English and Romanian Adoptees Study Team, 1998). Children adopted from Guatemalan orphanages and foster care demonstrate similar but less severe growth and developmental delays (Miller, Chan, Comfort, & Tirella, 2005). Guatemalan children who were placed in foster care performed better than those living in institutional care. These risk factors and their effects on development and learning will be discussed in more detail in subsequent chapters.

Children adopted from different countries may experience several transitions and live in several different settings. Hellerstadt et al. (2008) found that for internationally adopted children in Minnesota, 1) 52% lived in one setting, 2) 2% in family care, 3) 19% in foster care, and 4) 34% in institutional care. Forty-eight percent had experienced multiple settings prior to adoption. From my own experience with the IAC at

Saint Louis University, parents adopting children from Eastern European countries, China, Korea, and Guatemala have reported preadoption experiences that range from foster care, institutional and family or foster care, or hospital or institutional care only. Thus, internationally adopted children may have been exposed to adverse conditions prior to adoption: 1) malnutrition, 2) limited medical care, 3) little stimulation, and 4) limited or disrupted social interaction from multiple transitions. In spite of these circumstances, these children have demonstrated amazing recovery and resilience postadoption.

## ADAPTATION POSTADOPTION

Several studies have reported positive postadoption outcomes for internationally adopted children. For example, in a study following postadoption growth in domestically adopted Greek children between the adopted ages of 3–36 months, weight and height in the adopted children at 2 years postadoption were not significantly different than nonadopted peers (Tsitsikas, Coulacoglou, Mitsotakis, & Driva, 1988). Thus children benefit from improved nutrition and care and may catch up in physical growth. In a meta-analysis of more than 27 studies with more than 3,000 adopted children, children adopted before 12 months of age were found to be similar in height and weight to nonadopted peers (Van IJzendoorn & Juffer, 2006). When compared in late adolescence and early adulthood, however, the adopted children were shorter in stature and weight (Van IJzendoorn, Bakermans-Kranenburg, & Juffer, 2007). Children who remained in institutional care longer suffered from a lack of social nurturance and interaction that resulted in growth retardation and short stature. Catch-up in head circumference was not as dramatic as stature and weight. These growth effects may be due to multiple factors, including 1) inadequate maternal nutrition during pregnancy, 2) premature birth, 3) exposure to drugs and/or alcohol, 4) medical illness, or 5) severe social neglect. Length or duration of exposure to adverse environments may result in an atypical stress response in institutionalized children. This response, as well as the other adverse factors, may have a negative impact on puberty and long-term physical growth (Mason & Narad, 2005b; Teilmann, Pedersen, Skakkebaek, & Jensen, 2006).

Although internationally adopted children have less secure and more disorganized attachments than their nonadopted peers, their attachments and security are far better than that of their peers who remain in institutional care. From a meta-analysis of 10 studies involving more than 400 adopted children, 47% were securely attached compared with 67% of samples of children living with biological families (Van IJzendoorn, Goldberg, Kroonenberg, & Frenkel, 1992). Children adopted before 12 months of age seem to almost catch up in attachment with their peers who live with their biological families (Van IJzendoorn & Juffer, 2006).

Children adopted after 12 months of age remain less secure and have poorer attachment relationships than children adopted at earlier ages and peers in biological families.

In other areas of development such as cognition, language, school achievement, and self-esteem, minor differences (small effect size) between adopted and nonadopted children on performance outcomes were found among internationally adopted children, domestically adopted children, and children living with their biological families. Forty-two studies of more than 6,000 adopted children were included in a meta-analysis of intelligence quotients (IQ) in which adopted children had slightly lower IQ scores (small effect size). This was also true for language development across 14 studies with more than 15,000 participants. No differences were found between domestically and internationally adopted children. In a comparison of eight studies with more than 13,000 children, internationally adopted children seemed to have more learning problems. Adopted children were more often referred for special education services than nonadopted peers, yet no differences in self-esteem were found among internationally adopted children, domestically adopted children, and non-adopted peers in a meta-analysis of more than 80 studies including more than 40,000 children. Age of adoption was related to school achievement outcomes, in that children adopted before 12 months of age caught up with nonadopted peers. Because children who were adopted at ages older than 12 months had poorer school achievement and age of adoption was not related to IQ scores, this phenomenon may represent a disconnect between IQ scores and measures of academic achievement.

Upon review of 101 studies with more than 25,000 adopted children and 80,000 nonadopted children, the authors also found small differences with little effect on outcomes between the groups for internalizing, externalizing, and total behavior problems as a measure of adaptive behavior. Internationally adopted children were overrepresented in receiving mental health services compared with nonadopted peers. Domestically adopted children received more mental health services than internationally adopted children. However, these group differences may reflect differences in the parents' attitudes toward mental health services rather than children's actual need for these services.

In conclusion, adopted children demonstrate amazing resilience and adaptation. Early adoption, before 12 months of age, results in more positive developmental outcomes in physical growth, attachment security, and school achievement. However, age of adoption does not seem to have an impact on IQ scores, language development, adaptation, or self-esteem. Overall, adopted children have more positive outcomes than children who remain in institutional care. Children adopted at older ages may be at risk of continued developmental delays and less complete catch-up depending on the quality of their preadoption care and exposure to severe neglect, abuse, or malnutrition prior to adoption (Van IJzendoorn & Juffer, 2006).

Odenstad et al. (2008) analyzed a national cohort study of data of more than 390,000 Swedish nonadopted men and more than 2,200 internationally adopted men to see whether the quality of institutional care influenced later developmental outcomes for internationally adopted children regardless of adoption age. The reasons for the study were based on the diversity of social conditions across countries of origin. These social conditions affect the health and prenatal care pregnant women obtain, as well as the care infants or children placed in institutional care receive. In addition, these conditions may affect the reasons why biological parents decide to place their children in institutional care. Children adopted from countries with better health care and economic conditions, such as Korea, tend to have better cognitive development, academic achievement, and social adjustment outcomes than children adopted from countries with less developed infrastructures, such as Russia (Clark & Hanisee, 1982; Dalen, 2001; Frydman & Lynn, 1989; Kvifte Andresen, 1992; Wickes & Slate, 1996). Most of the South Korean children adopted during the 1970s were born to unmarried mothers, and due to sociocultural stigmas against single parents, many children were placed in institutional or foster care. This is a more positive reason for adoption than reasons of poverty, mental illness, or abusive and/ or neglectful parenting. In addition, South Korea has developed quality care guidelines that require adoption agencies to have well-educated and qualified staff (counselors, nurses, psychologists, and physicians) and has established preadoptive foster care homes (Odenstad et al., 2008).

In the Odenstad et al. (2008) study, the group of adopted adults from Korea were compared with adults adopted from other countries (India, Thailand, Chile, Ethiopia, Columbia, and Sri Lanka) and nonadopted Swedish adults. Regardless of age of adoption, the adults who were adopted from Korea had higher global and verbal mean IQ scores than the adults adopted from other countries and nonadopted Swedish peers. The cognitive test scores of those adults adopted from other countries were significantly lower than nonadopted peers and the adults who were adopted from Korea, and age of adoption was negatively correlated to IQ scores for the adults adopted from countries other than Korea. In other words, if children were adopted before 4 years of age from countries other than Korea, IQ scores were higher than if children were adopted at 6 years of age or older. Age of adoption was not correlated with IQ scores for the adults adopted from Korea.

What these studies may tell us is that if preadoption care is "good enough" (Odenstad et al., 2008, p. 1812), internationally adopted children have better chances of developmental success regardless of the age of adoption. If, however, institutional care is of poor quality, children adopted at earlier ages may still have positive chances of overcoming exposure to adverse environments. In particular, physical growth, attachment security, and school achievement seem to be more sensitive to quality of preadoption care than IQ scores, language development, self-esteem, and adaptation.

Given the findings from the meta-analyses and this large population study, what developmental theories help explain developmental delays and developmental catch-up in internationally adopted children? As in the case of Andrew, what theoretical explanation can we offer for the individual and unique behavior profile Andrew displays?

## THEORIES OF DEVELOPMENT

Although Andrew was adopted before the age of 12 months and was in good health at the time of adoption, he continues to have social and emotional behaviors that affect his developmental competence. He demonstrates a mixed picture of resilience to early adversity. His physical growth, motor development, attachment security, cognitive development, and communication at 2 years postadoption were comparable to same-age peers. Yet, in spite of these developmental advantages, he continued to struggle with attention, activity level, and emotion regulation. These challenges began to affect his performance on cognitively challenging tasks such as drawing inferences or interpreting deceptive messages. How can we explain this picture of developmental outcome and resilience?

Resilience is a process of recovery from adversity that can be affected by the type and number of experiences and the individual interpretation or reaction to these experiences over time (*Merriam-Webster Online Dictionary*, 2009). This recovery process is correlated with having average or higher cognitive ability, self-esteem, self-efficacy, and competence in solving and planning for potential problems. In addition, if children have emotional ties with a caregiver and/or an external support system that positively reinforces competence and provides a sense of confidence, these tend to be protective factors for resilience (Rutter, 2000; Rutter et al., 2000). By this definition, the theories that support an intact neurological system interacting within a stimulating environment and a positive social support system should explain Andrew's performance, yet he continues to demonstrate poor emotional regulation and inattentive behaviors that affect his learning.

## Epigenetic and Dynamic Systems Theories

Epigenetic theory and dynamic systems theory (DST) may offer logical explanations for Andrew's developmental outcomes. Epigenetic theory involves changes in gene expression as a result of interactions with an environment, or gene x environment interaction (Van de Vijver, Van Speybroeck, & de Waele, 2002).

According to epigenetic theory, children who may have a neurotypical genetic structure may develop atypically when exposed to early adverse environments such as institutional environments. This theory offers a general explanation for the diverse individual developmental outcomes of internationally adopted children.

Similarly, according to DST, humans are inherently developmentally complex systems in which multifaceted interactions with elements of the system can result in many different developmental outcomes. DST, which is closely related to connectionist theory (described later) and epigenetic theory (Thelen & Bates, 2003; Van de Vijver et al., 2002), emerged from studies of complex systems in biology, physics, and psychology and recently has been discussed as a theory to explain motor development (Thelen & Smith, 1994), emotional development and self-organization (Lewis & Granic, 2000), and language development and disorders (De Bot, Lowie, & Verspoor, 2007; Kohnert, 2008). Through dynamic stable processes of development, the organism goes through transitions in which the system destabilizes and reorganizes in systematic ways. Variables affecting change are interrelated with other variables. Constraints in dynamic systems may include initial structure of the system, such as neurobiological development, exposure to experience-expectant (e.g., age-appropriate) and experience-dependent (e.g., nurturing) events in the environment, and early foundations of self-organization development reflective of both neurobiological and environmental factors (Lewis, 1997).

Human development is a nonlinear emergent process in which self-organization may occur around attractor states formed from previous experiences or knowledge. Unstable systems require less energy to change, whereas stable systems need more energy to change. An example of this would be children who experience an environment lacking in stimulation. They have a stable system with attractor states drawn toward a static nonstimulating environment. Consequently, they will need more energy (attention, memory, motivation, and processing speed) to transition and function within a novel, dynamic environment. Because of the high degree of freedom among variables and constraints, development is a mix of indeterminism and determinism resulting in large differences in developmental outcomes. Thus development is not always predictable in a simple linear way (Fogel, Lyra, & Valsiner, 1997).

Principles of general systems theory are 1) systems are complex in that they contain many interdependent parts that influence one another dynamically; 2) systems are organized where their behavior is more than the sum of their parts and their relationships but may reflect the effects of history, efficiency, energy, and other factors; 3) systems self-organize and stabilize over time by the unique individual transactions between the individual and its relationships; 4) systems demonstrate equifinality in that many different processes can lead to a similar system organization; and 5) systems create independent but related hierarchical patterns as a result of dynamics of the system (Fogel, 1993). The greater the flexibility of the system, the greater the chance the system can make use of available resources to adjust to changes.

DST helps explain the reported developmental outcomes of internationally adopted children because it supports the findings that less exposure to institutional environments or "good enough" care results in more positive developmental outcomes. It also provides an explanation of how early adversity differentially affects self-organization and is related to attractor states, which may vary with each child. The numerous variables, as well as the multiple ways humans self-organize, may explain the variability in individual developmental outcomes regardless of age of adoption. In Andrew's case, he is able to maintain self-regulation and attention when he is allowed to spend quiet, uninterrupted time in a predictable environment. Quiet, predictable, and nonstimulating environments may be an attractor state for Andrew's self-organization. Thus, when he encounters novel stimuli or changes within his environment, he appears to need more energy to focus attention and regulate his emotions.

Both epigenetic and dynamic systems theories explain individual developmental variations that can result from genes interacting with variables in the environment, which in turn results in diverse developmental outcomes. And these theories support several other developmental theories, too, such as cognitive and social constructivism and connectionist theories.

## Cognitive and Social Constructivism

Piaget (1970) believed that children's development was influenced by their interaction with the physical environment. As children explore and interact with objects, they develop patterns of interaction that are modified as they progress through different stages of development (schemas). These stages include 1) sensorimotor (birth to 2 years), 2) preoperational (2–7 years), 3) concrete operations (7–11 years), and 4) formal operations (11+ years). As children gather information about their environment, they assimilate that information into existing cognitive knowledge or accommodate new and different information by expanding or changing what they already know. For example, during the sensorimotor stage, children learn about objects and their environment through their senses of touch, smell, taste, hearing, and sight. During the preoperational stage, children begin to represent objects with symbols such as language, but they continue to think and act concretely. In other words, for a number of objects to be the same, they must be presented in the same arrangement. During the concrete and formal operations stages, children begin to think logically in more than one dimension. Later they think abstractly and plan ahead.

Other constructivist theorists believed that cognitive construction occurred within social and cultural contexts in which adults mediated children's learning (Hobson, 2004; Vygotsky, 1986). Vygotsky believed that adults guide children to create a zone of proximal development—what the child can do with adult help and what the child can do alone. From this theoretical viewpoint, interaction with the environment is guided and mediated through social interactions to enable children to learn from developmentally supported experiences.

For the majority of neurologically intact internationally adopted children who are adopted early or received "good enough" preadoptive care, these theories generally support positive recovery and developmental outcomes. If internationally adopted children are provided adequate nutrition, stimulation, and nurturance during their preadoptive care or early after adoption (adopted before 12 months old), they are able to catch up with nonadopted peers. Yet there is a significant subset of this population similar to Andrew who do not.

## Information Processing and Connectionism

Information processing theory involves three stages of interaction with information: 1) sensory memory stage, 2) short-term or working memory stage, and 3) long-term memory stage (Atkinson & Shiffrin, 1968). In the sensory memory stage, when individuals process information, they may perceive information in a bidirectional manner (bottom-up and top-down manner). Bottom-up processing occurs when individuals encounter information in their environment, and they perceive, attend, and appraise the emotional value of the information. In top-down processing, individuals, perceive, attend, appraise, and compare the information they encounter with long-term memories associated with or similar to the information.

In addition to information processing theory, parallel-distributed processing and connectionist theories have emerged. According to parallel-distributed processing theory, different memory sections of the brain process information simultaneously (Rumelhart & McClelland, 1986). Connectionist theorists extend this theory to say that memory is stored in multiple locations in the brain in the form of neural networks. These neural networks are formed by activation of neural synapses that simultaneously receive and send information. The strength of these connections is based on learning or experiences that become recognized neural network patterns in memory, retrieval, and generalization of new information or contexts.

These theories are generally founded on four assumptions. First, the brain has capacity limitations that constrain the amount it can process, the speed at which it can process, and its efficiency for processing. Second, there is a process manager or executive function that manages information processing to encode, transform, process, store, retrieve, and use information. Third, processing is bidirectional as described above. And fourth, there are genetic predispositions to processing information in specific ways.

Neurobiological development research is better explained through these theories. For example, researchers have found higher cortisol hormone levels in children adopted from institutions than nonadopted children or children in foster care (Gunnar & Kertes, 2005). Cortisol is one of the major stress-related hormones in the body and is correlated with poor cognitive and emotional functioning (Ladage, 2009; Mason & Narad, 2005a, 2005b). Higher cortisol levels may affect neurological growth and development in young children. Chugani et al. (2001) conducted a study using positron emission tomography on 10 children approximately 8 years old adopted from Romania. They found reduced activity in the orbitofrontal cortex, infralimbic cortex, and medial temporal lobe, areas that may be involved with higher cognition, emotion, and emotion regulation. Marshall, Fox, and the BEIP Core Group (2004) used electroencephalographic techniques on a sample of 216 infants and toddlers living in an institution in Bucharest, Romania and compared these results with 72 age-and gender-matched never-institutionalized children. They found differences in the posterior scalp and the temporal and frontal lobe regions. These findings are similar to electroencephalogram studies of children from abused or neglected backgrounds and children with learning disorders such as ADHD. Thus, children who do not receive age-appropriate or adult-mediated experiences may not develop the neural networks to process information needed for academic achievement. However, in spite of these findings, there is considerable heterogeneity in postadoption outcomes.

In conclusion, these theories presuppose that, dependent upon developmentally and socially appropriate experiences during a sensitive period of development, children should universally develop enough memory and knowledge to function adequately. In contrast, children who are not exposed to stimuli or experiences do not develop neural connections to build the needed neural networks for memory and knowledge. The wide range of variability in positive outcomes in internationally adopted children does not support this theory. Rutter, O'Connor, and the ERA Team (2004) reported that in spite of the fact that most of the Romanian children who were adopted after 6 months of age did not catch up to nonadopted children or domestically adopted children, some showed no measurable impairment and others continued to show recovery and improvement several years following adoption. These findings provide evidence against the idea of permanent and irreversible damage to neural connections caused by severe deprivation and adversity during the early years. Thus, dependent upon individual factors such as cognition, interpretation, and reaction to environmental variables, as well as differences in duration and intensity of adverse early care, postadoption development can vary significantly.

## ▼▼▼ IMPLICATIONS

There are many variables to consider when working with internationally adopted children. Practitioners need access to detailed evidence-based descriptions of the average development of adopted children after adoption. In addition, they need to know what outcomes are referral indicators for further assessment or treatment, as well as which practitioners are appropriate resources for future service provision. First and foremost, the health and physical growth of children should be evaluated immediately.

Jennifer S. Ladage, M.D., FACS, a board-certified pediatrician who is a member of the American Academy of Pediatrics' Section on Adoption and Foster Care, and Sarah Harris, O.T.D., OTR/L, describe the health, growth, and motor developmental risks, typical developmental outcomes, and referral indicators in Chapter 2. Samantha L. Wilson, Ph.D. a clinical psychologist who has conducted research and clinical treatment with internationally adopted children, describes social-emotional and cognitive development in Chapters 3 and 4. In Chapter 5, I discuss inhibition, self-regulation, attention, and memory; in Chapter 6, hearing, speech, and feeding development; in Chapter 7, general language development; and in Chapter 8, social communication development. Chapter 9 includes contributions from all four authors on intervention strategies for children who have been adopted. Each chapter highlights referral indicators and appropriate referral resources.

## KEY POINTS

▶ Parents and practitioners need to know evidence-based information about the development of internationally adopted children as well as available efficacious interventions to help them.

▶ Adopted children have better outcomes than peers who remain in institutional care or who experience multiple transitions in preadoptive care.

▶ Internationally adopted children demonstrate longitudinal postadoption progress, resilience, and variability.

▶ The earlier children are adopted from adverse environments, the better the outcome.

▶ Age of adoption is not a factor if children are adopted from environments providing "good enough" care.

▶ Dynamic systems theory helps explain the nonlinear developmental outcomes in internationally adopted children.

## REFERRAL INDICATORS

▶ For initial medical assessments, a pediatrician with knowledge and skills in adoption medicine is recommended. http://www.aap.org/sections/adoption/SOAFCAdoptionDirectory2.pdf

▶ For developmental concerns, a developmental assessment by professionals with expertise in internationally adopted children is recommended. http://www.comeunoity.com/adoption/health/clinics.html

## REFERENCES

Adoption Institute. (2004). *International adoption facts*. Retrieved May 31, 2011, from http://www.adoptioninstitute.org/FactOverview/internationl_print.html

Adoption. com. (2004). *Introduction to international adoption*. Retrieved May 31, 2011 from http://adopting.adoption.com/child/introduction-to-international-adoption.html

Albers, L.H., Johnson, D.E., Hostetter, M.K., Iverson, S., & Miller, L.C. (1997). Health of children adopted from the former Soviet Union and Eastern Europe. Comparison with preadoptive medical records. *Journal of the American Medical Association, 278*(11), 922–924. Retrieved May 31, 2011, from http://www.peds.umn.edu/iac/prod/groups/med/@pub/@med/documents/asset/med_49294.pdf

American Speech-Language-Hearing Association. (2003). *EBP Compendium: Summary of systematic review*. Retrieved May 31, 2011, from http://www.asha.org/Members/ebp/compendium/reviews/Sensory-or-Auditory-Integration-Therapy-for-Children-with-Autistic-Spectrum-Disorders.htm

Atkinson, R., & Shiffrin, R. (1968). Human memory: A proposed system and its control processes. In K. Spence & J. Spence (Eds.). *The psychology of learning and motivation: Advances in research and theory* (Vol. 2, pp. 89–195). New York: Academic Press.

Chugani, H.T., Behen, M.E., Muzik, O., Juhasz, C., Nagy, F., & Chugani, D.C. (2001). Local brain functional activity following early deprivation: A study of postinstitutionalized Romanian orphans. *Neuroimage, 14*, 1290–1301.

Clark, E.A., & Hanisee, J. (1982). Intellectual and adaptive performance of Asian children in adoptive American settings. *Developmental Psychology, 18*(4), 595–599.

Dalen, M. (2001). School performances among internationally adopted children in Norway. *Adoption Quarterly, 5*, 39–58.

Dawson, G., & Watling, R. (2000). Interventions to facilitate auditory, visual, and motor integration in autism: A review of the evidence. *Journal of Autism and Developmental Disorders, 30*(5), 415–421.

De Bot, K., Lowie, W., & Verspoor, M. (2007). A dynamic systems approach to second language acquisition. *Bilingualism: Language and Cognition, 10*(1), 7–21.

Fogel, A. (1993). *Developing through relationships. Origins of communication, self, and culture.* Chicago: University of Chicago Press.

Fogel, A., Layra, M.C.D.P., & Valsiner, J. (1997). Introduction: Perspectives on indeterminism and development. In. A. Fogel, M.C.D.P. Lyra, & J. Valsiner (Eds.). *Dynamics and indeterminism in developmental and social processes* (pp. 1–10). Mahwah, NJ: Lawrence Erlbaum.

Frydman, M., & Lynn, R. (1989). The intelligence of Korean children adopted in Belgium. *Personality and Individual Differences, 10*(12), 1323–1325.

Glennen, S., & Bright, B.J. (2005). Five years later: Language in school-age internationally adopted children. *Seminars in Speech and Language, 26*(1), 86–101.

Glennen, S., & Masters, G. (2002). Typical and atypical language development in infants and toddlers adopted from Eastern Europe. *American Journal of Speech-Language Pathology, 11*, 417–433.

Gunnar, M.R., Bruce, J., & Grotevant, H.D. (2000). International adoption of institutionally reared children: Research and policy. *Development and Psychopathology, 12*, 677–693.

Gunnar, M.R., & Kertes, D.A. (2005). Prenatal and postnatal risks to neurobiological development. In D.M. Brodzinsky & J. Palacios (Eds.) *Psychological issues in adoption: Research and practice. Advances in applied developmental psychology* (Vol. 24, pp. 47–65). New York: Prager.

Hellerstedt, W.L., Madsen, N.J., Gunnar, M.R., Grotevant, H.D., Lee, R.M., & Johnson, D.E. (2008). The international adoption project: Population-based surveillance of Minnesota parents who adopted children internationally. *Maternal Child Health Journal, 12*(2), 162–171.

Hesketh, T., Lu, L., & Xing, Z.W. (2005). The effect of China's one-child family policy after 25 years. *The New England Journal of Medicine, 353*(11), 1171–1176.

Hobson, P. (2004). *The cradle of thought. Exploring the origins of thinking.* Oxford, NY: Oxford University Press.

Hoehn, T.P., & Baumeister, A.A. (1994). A critique of the application of sensory integration therapy to children with learning disabilities. *Journal of Learning Disabilities, 27*(6), 338–350.

Johnson, D.E. (2000). Medical and developmental sequelae of early childhood institutionalization in Eastern European adoptees. In C.A. Nelson (Ed)., *The Minnesota symposia on child psychology: The effects of early adversity on neurobehavioral development* (Vol. 31, pp. 113–162). Mahwah, NJ: Lawrence Erlbaum Associates.

Johnson, D.E., Miller, L.C., Iverson, S., Thomas, W., Franchino, B., Dole, K., et al. (1992). The health of children adopted from Romania. *Journal of the American Medical Association, 268*(24), 3446-3451.

Kaplan, B.J., Polatajko, H.J., & Faris, P.D. (1993). Reexamination of sensory integration treatment. *Journal of Learning Disabilities, 26*(5), 342–347.

Kohnert, K. (2008). *Language disorders in bilingual children and adults*. San Diego: Plural.

Kvifte Andresen, I.L. (1992). Behavioral and school adjustment of 12-13 year old internationally adopted children in Norway. *Journal of Child Psychology and Psychiatry and Allied Disciplines, 33*, 427–439.

Ladage, J.S. (2009). Medical issues in international adoption and their influence on language development. *Topics in Language Disorders, 21*, 6–17.

Lewis, M.D. (1997). Personality self-organization: Cascading constraints on cognition-emotion interaction. In. A. Fogel, M.C.D.P. Lyra, & J. Valsiner (Eds.). *Dynamics and indeterminism in developmental and social processes* (pp. 193–216). Mahwah, NJ: Lawrence Erlbaum Associates.

Lewis, M.D., & Granic, I. (2000). *Emotion development and self-organization. Dynamic systems approaches to emotional development*. In M.I. Hoffman & C. Shantz (Series Eds.), *Cambridge studies in social emotional development*. New York: Cambridge University Press.

Maclean, K. (2003). The impact of institutionalization on child development. *Development and Psychopathology, 15*, 853–884.

Marshall, P.J., Fox, N.A., & The BEIP Core Group. (2004). A comparison of the electroencephalogram between institutionalized and community children in Romania. *Journal of Cognitive Neuroscience, 16*, 1327–1338.

Mason, P., & Narad, C. (2005a). International adoption: A health and developmental prospective. *Seminars in Speech and Language, 26*(1), 1–9.

Mason, P., & Narad, C. (2005b). Long-term growth and puberty concerns in international adoptees. *Pediatric Clinics of North America, 52*, 1351–1368.

Miller, L. (2005). *The handbook of international adoption medicine* (pp. 45–66). New York: Oxford University Press.

Miller, L., Chan, W., Comfort, K., & Tirella, L. (2005). Health of children adopted from Guatemala: Comparison of orphanage and foster care. *Pediatrics, 115*(6), e710–e717. Retrieved May 31, 2011, from http://www.pediatrics.org/cgi/

Miller, L., & Hendrie, N. (2000). Health of children adopted from China. *Pediatrics, 105*(6): 76–87. Retrieved May 31, 2011, from http://pediatrics.aappublications.org/cgi/content/full/105/6/e76

Morison, S.J., Ames, E.W., & Chisholm, K. (1995). The development of children adopted from Romanian orphanages. *Merrill-Palmer Quarterly, 41*, 411–430.

Odenstad, A., Hjern, A., Lindblad, F., Rasmussen, F., Vinnerljung, B., & Dalen, M. (2008). Does age at adoption and geographic origin matter? A national cohort study of cognitive test performance in adult inter-country adoptees. *Psychological Medicine, 38*, 1803–1814.

Pears, K., & Fisher, P.A. (2005). Developmental, cognitive and neuropsychological functioning in preschool-aged foster children: Associations with prior maltreatment and placement history. *Journal of Developmental and Behavioral Pediatrics, 26*, 112–122.

Piaget, J. (1970). *The science of education and the psychology of the child*. New York: Grossman.

Resilience. (2009). In *Merriam-Webster Online Dictionary*. Retrieved May 31, 2011, from http://www.merriam-webster.com/dictionary/resilience

Rumelhart, D., & McClelland, J. (Eds.). (1986). *Parallel distributed processing: Explorations in the microstructure of cognition*. Cambridge, MA: MIT Press.

Rutter, M. (2000). Resilience reconsidered: Conceptual considerations, empirical findings, and policy implications. In J.P. Shonkoff & S.J. Meisels (Eds.), *Handbook of early childhood intervention* (2nd ed., pp. 651–682). New York: Cambridge University Press.

Rutter, M., & the English and Romanian Adoptees Study Team. (1998). Developmental catch-up and delay, following adoption after severe global early privation. *Journal of Child Psychology and Psychiatry, 39*, 465–476.

Rutter, M., O'Connor, T., Beckett, C., Castle, J., Croft, C., Dunn, J., et al. (2000). Recovery and deficit following early deprivation. In P. Selman & P. Selman (Eds.). *Intercountry adoption: Developments, trends and perspectives* (pp. 107–125). London: British Agencies for Adoption & Fostering.

Rutter, M., O'Connor, T.G., & the English and Romanian Adoptees (ERA) Study Team. (2004). Are there biological programming effects for psychological development? Findings from a study of Romanian adoptees. *Developmental Psychology, 40*(1), 81–94.

Seidel, S., Kreutzer, R., Smith, D., McNeel, S., & Gilliss, D. (2001). Assessment of commercial laboratories performing hair mineral analysis. *Journal of the American Medical Association, 285*(1), 67–72.

Selman, P. (2009). The rise and fall of intercountry adoption in the 21st century. *International Social Work, 52*, 575–594.

Sheppard, J.J. (2008). Using motor learning approaches in treating swallowing and feeding disorders: A review. *Language, Speech and Hearing Services in Schools, 39*, 227–236.

Sigal, J.J., Perry, J.C., Rossignol, M., & Ouimet, M.C. (2003). Unwanted infants: Psychological and physical consequences of inadequate orphanage care 50 years later. *American Journal of Orthopsychiatry, 73*(1), 3–12.

Smith, S.A., Press, B., Koenig, K.P., & Kinnealey, M. (2005). Effects of sensory integration intervention on self-stimulating and self-injurious behaviors. *American Journal of Occupational Therapy, 59*(4), 418–425.

Teilmann, G., Pedersen, C.B., Skakkebaek, N.E., & Jensen, T.K. (2006). Increased risk of precocious puberty in internationally adopted children in Denmark. *Pediatrics, 118*, e391–e399.

Thelen, E., & Bates, E. (2003). Connectionism and dynamic systems: Are they really different? *Developmental Science, 6*(4), 378–391.

Thelen, E. & Smith, L.B. (1994). *A dynamic systems approach to the development of cognition and action*. Cambridge, MA: MIT Press.

Tizard, B., & Joseph, A. (1970). Cognitive development of young children in residential care: A study of children aged 24 months. *Journal of Child Psychology and Psychiatry, 11*, 177–186.

Tochel, C. (2003). Sensory or auditory integration therapy for children with autistic spectrum disorders. In Bazian Ltd., (Ed). *STEER: Succinct and timely evaluated evidence reviews, 3*(17). London: Wessex Institute for Health Research and Development, University of Southampton and Bazian, Ltd. Retrieved May 31, 2011, from http://www.wihrd.soton.ac.uk/projx/signpost/steers/STEER_2003%2817%29.pdf

Tsitsikas, H., Coulacoglou, C., Mitsotakis, P., & Driva, A. (1988). A follow-up study of adopted children. In E. Hibbs (Ed.), *Children and families* (pp. 401–414). New York: International University Press.

U.S. Department of State. (2009). *Total adoptions to the United States*. Retrieved May 31, 2011, from http://adoptionblog.his.com/news/total_chart.html

Van de Vijver, G., Van Speybroeck, L., & de Waele, D. (2002). Epigenetics: A challenge for genetics, evolution, and development? *Annals New York Academy of Sciences, 981*, 1–6.

Van IJzendoorn, M.H., Bakermans-Kranenburg, M.J., & Juffer, F. (2007). Plasticity of growth in height, weight, and head circumference: Meta-analytic evidence of massive catch-up after international adoption. *Journal of Developmental Behavior and Pediatrics, 28*, 334–343.

Van IJzendoorn, M.H., Goldberg, S., Kroonenberg, P.M., & Frenkel, O.J. (1992). The relative effects of maternal and child problems on the quality of attachment: A meta-analysis of attachment in clinical samples. *Child Development, 63*, 840–858.

Van IJzendoorn, M.H., & Juffer, F. (2006). The Emanual Miller Memorial Lecture 2006: Adoption as intervention. Meta-analytic evidence for massive catch-up and plasticity in physical, socio-emotional, and cognitive development. *Journal of Child Psychology and Psychiatry, 47*(12), 1228–1245.

Vargas S., & Camilli, G. (1999). A meta-analysis of research on sensory integration treatment. *American Journal of Occupational Therapy, 53*, 189–198.

Vygotsky, L. (1986). *Thought and language* (A. Kozulin, Trans.). London: MIT Press. (Original work published 1934).

Wheeler-Hegland, J., Ashford, J., Frymark, T., McCabe, D., Mullen, R., Musson, N., et al. (2009). Evidence-based systematic review: Oropharyngeal dysphagia behaviorial treatments. Part II-impact of dysphagia treatments on normal swallow function. *Journal of Rehabilitation Research and Development, 46*(2), 185–194. Retrieved May 31, 2011, from: http://www.rehab.research.va.gov/jour/09/46/2/pdf/page185.pdf

Wickes, K.L., & Slate, J.R. (1996). Transracial adoption of Koreans: A preliminary study of adjustment. *International Journal for the Advancement of Counseling, 19*, 187–195.

Wilson, B.N., Kaplan, B. J., Fellowes, S., Gruchy, C., & Faris, P. (1992). The efficacy of sensory integration treatment compared to tutoring. *Physical and Occupational Therapy in Pediatrics 12*(1), 1–36.

# 2

# Physical Growth, Health, and Motor Development

**Jennifer S. Ladage and Sarah E. Harris**

*"Here, invisible yet strong, was the taboo of the old life."*

(William Golding, *Lord of the Flies,* 1954, p. 67).

## ▼▼▼ STEPHEN

Stephen was a 21-month-old boy who was adopted at 20 months and seen at an international adoption clinic for a medical evaluation. Stephen's parents reported that Stephen was born to a 32-year-old Russian mother known to abuse alcohol and intravenous drugs. He was born in her home after 35 weeks gestation, and he weighed 4 pounds. His mother had not received any prenatal care. Maternal rights were relinquished at the time of birth, and Stephen was placed in the orphanage at 2 months of age. According to orphanage records, Stephen was tested for human immunodeficiency virus (HIV), syphilis, and hepatitis B, and the test results were negative. Stephen tested positive for hepatitis C at birth and at 6 months of age, but test results for hepatitis C were negative at 12 and 15 months of age. He was otherwise reported to be healthy.

Stephen's adoptive parents described him as a very challenging toddler. They explained that he was demanding, overly active, difficult to redirect, and had no apparent fears. His parents also noted several behaviors that they considered odd. Stephen held ice cubes in his hands for extended periods of time and did not express pain after he licked the door of a hot oven. He covered his ears and rocked when loud noises came unexpectedly. He liked to wear a coat even when the outside temperature was 90 degrees or more. He loved bath time to the extent that he would throw a fit when his parents took him out of the bathtub. While Stephen's appetite was excessive, he would not eat any food with a crunchy or chewy texture. He hoarded food in his cheeks before eventually spitting it out

21

of his mouth. At times, his parents found unchewed meat that Stephen held in his cheeks hours after the meal was over. Although his parents reported that he would make eye contact and snuggle, they were able to hold him for no more than a few seconds because of his overactive and impulsive behaviors.

During the clinical evaluation, Stephen demonstrated mild global delays. His gross and fine motor skills were consistent with 12-month-old children (developmental quotient, DQ = 57%), and his language and social skills were consistent with children 14 months of age (DQ = 66%). Upon physical examination, Stephen's length, weight, and head circumference plotted below the 3rd percentile: his length plotted 3.0 standard deviations below the mean, his weight, 3.5 standard deviations below the mean, and his head circumference, 4.0 standard deviations below the mean. Stephen appeared small and thin for his age. He had flattening of the back of his head on the left side. His right eye intermittently deviated inwards. His philtrum, the grooved area beneath his nose, was smooth, and he had a thin upper lip. The remainder of his physical exam was within normal limits. Laboratory screening for hepatitis C, hepatitis B, and HIV were negative. Screening for syphilis, however, was positive. Stephen underwent a spinal tap to rule out neurosyphilis and received three weekly intramuscular injections of penicillin. Stephen's final diagnoses included congenital syphilis, fetal alcohol syndrome, body mass index 3.5 standard deviations below the mean, right esotropia (lazy eye), and sensory integration dysfunction.

After a brief inpatient stay to address malnutrition and failure to thrive, Stephen was referred for an outpatient occupational therapy evaluation with a therapist experienced in the care of international adoptees. Stephen's parents reported their main concerns were that 1) he would rarely sit still and finish a full meal; 2) when they played with him, he always preferred active, roughhousing play and he had a hard time calming down afterward; and 3) when overly stimulated or frustrated, he had a tendency to become aggressive (biting, hitting, and pinching) and was unresponsive to his parents' strategies to interrupt the behaviors. After starting twice-weekly occupational therapy treatments at the family's home, Stephen began to show marked improvements in visual attention span and his ability to sit still. He also began a protocol to address tactile defensiveness (resistance to touch). Finally, Stephen's parents reported the greatest help was the therapist's guidance in teaching them to recognize Stephen's responses to sensory experiences. Stephen's father, in particular, learned how to help Stephen wind down after rough play by giving calming, deep pressure input and using a soft, low tone of voice to indicate a change in activity level (e.g., using whispered communication, modeling, and encouraging Stephen to crawl slowly on the ground). Stephen continues to demonstrate residual issues that may be related to his complex diagnoses and early life experiences, but his parents feel they have learned how to understand him and how to support him more effectively.

## ▼▼▼ CAITLYN

Caitlyn was a 12-month-old girl who was adopted from China at the age of 11 months. She was seen at an international adoption clinic for a medical evaluation shortly after her arrival to the United States. In China, she was found outside the gates of the local social welfare institute and subsequently placed in the orphanage for care at an estimated age of 1 week. She was reported to be healthy in the orphanage. Her growth parameters from an evaluation at 3 months old reported her length to be at the 50th percentile, her weight at the 25th percentile, and her head circumference between the 25th to 50th percentiles.

After she was adopted, Caitlyn's parents reported several physical and behavioral observations. They noticed that her right foot was often held in a turned-in position. They hypothesized her abnormal foot position was related to being restrained to her bed in the orphanage for significant lengths of time. They reported circumferential bruising around both ankles as well as linear markings on her hips from breakdown of her skin superimposed on bruising. Although the right foot still turned inward, the lesions had healed significantly in the 2 to 3 weeks between her adoption and her medical evaluation. Caitlyn's parents reported that it could take up to 1½ hours for her to fall asleep and she generally woke up crying at least two times per night. Caitlyn's appetite was described as very good, but not excessive. She pushed food away when she was full. She made eye contact, sought comfort and affection from her parents, and had no history of repetitive or self-stimulating behaviors.

Caitlyn's physical exam revealed deceleration in her growth from the time of adoption to the medical evaluation. Her length had fallen to the 10th percentile, her weight to the 5th percentile, and her head circumference to the 25th percentile. Her weight at the medical evaluation, however, had increased a little more than 1 pound from the measurement obtained 3 weeks earlier at her visa exit examination in China. Caitlyn underwent evaluation for infectious diseases and for malnutrition. Laboratory studies demonstrated low ferritin levels indicating iron deficiency and an elevated thyroid-stimulating hormone, suggesting iodine deficiency. Both deficiencies corrected with appropriate supplementation to her diet. Caitlyn's developmental milestones were judged to be age appropriate for social, language, and fine motor skills. However, her gross motor skills were delayed and demonstrated abilities consistent with 7 months of age (DQ = 58%). She would, however, become highly anxious when her mother left the room. After 6 months living with her adoptive family, Caitlyn's growth parameters all plotted around the 50th percentile, her development was age appropriate, and she was sleeping through the night.

## ▼▼▼ ERIC

Eric was a 10-month-old boy who was adopted from Ethiopia. He was seen for a medical evaluation within 2 weeks of his arrival to the United States. He had been placed in the orphanage at approximately 6 months old. His birth mother relinquished her maternal rights because she was unable to financially provide for her son after the death of her husband. Her husband had died of HIV-related complications shortly after the birth of their son. An Ethiopian court reviewed Eric's case for adoption and his birth date had been legally assigned along with other children's cases that were reviewed at the same time. Eric was evaluated upon admission to the orphanage and his height, weight, and head circumference plotted at the 3rd percentile, or approximately 2 standard deviations below the mean.

Upon Eric's arrival at his new home, his parents reported that Eric had a large appetite and would not stop eating until the food was either gone or removed from the table. He preferred pastas, breads, and rice and would eat any quantity given to him. He refused milk and dairy products and was very picky regarding the meats and vegetables he would eat. His parents reported that he had several bowel movements daily and passed what seemed to be an extraordinary amount of foul-smelling gas. Some stools were watery whereas others tended to be hard and difficult to pass; his parents attributed this to changes in his diet.

At the time of his medical evaluation after arrival in the United States, his length measured at the 10th percentile (approximately 1.5 standard deviations below the mean), his weight approximated the 50th percentile (at the mean), and his head circumference plotted at the 25th percentile, 1 standard deviation below the mean. During his physical exam, diffuse crusting was observed on his scalp consistent with tinea capitis (or ring worm) and his abdomen was distended. Laboratory testing confirmed positive stool cultures for giardia, and test results for HIV, syphilis, hepatitis B, and hepatitis C were all negative. Following treatment for ringworm and giardia infection, his scalp, distended abdomen, and irregular bowel movements were resolved.

Eric's developmental evaluation revealed fine and gross motor skills consistent with a 16-month-old child, social skills consistent with a 15-month-old child, and language skills consistent with a 14-month-old child—all developmental quotients exceeding the 100th percentile and even approaching the 200th percentile. He had 12 teeth including 8 incisors and 4 molars present in his mouth. A bone age radiograph, obtained to assess bone maturation, was consistent with a chronological age of 15 months.

Approximately 12 months after adoption, Eric demonstrated interval growth, development, and bone age consistent with a child 6 to 8 months older than 22 months. Although the difference in age was significant at the time, Eric's parents agreed that advancing his assigned birth date would not afford him any long-term advantages and may potentially add to insecurities surrounding his identity when he is older. With the assistance of an adoption medicine physician, they made the decision to not reassign his birth date.

Stephen, Caitlyn, and Eric are not extraordinary examples of a few, isolated adoption stories. They collectively represent the characteristic physical state of the health of internationally adopted children after experiencing myriad adverse variables early in life. Their stories exemplify the genetic predispositions, prenatal factors, and deprived circumstances present during the most critical years of early childhood development and the detrimental effects that may remain long after the adversity is removed. As these case examples demonstrate, multiple variables result in unique and varied developmental outcomes. These examples provide further support for a dynamic systems theory (DST, see Chapter 1 for a review) of development after exposure to different kinds of early care. DST can be used to understand why the consequences of delays in this developmental area can be varied and unpredictable and why experts continue to disagree on etiology or treatment for delays in internationally adopted children.

No child's exposure to sensory or motor experiences will be identical; thus, every child's development will be different and dependent upon his or her unique experiences. The growth and physical health of children vary, even among children housed within the same institution, due to individual prenatal and genetic influences that further delineate a child's unique experience. Although motor skill and sensory processing development as well as physical health are discussed in separate sections, it is important to recognize that these systems are irrevocably intertwined and that delays in one area will affect the other. Furthermore, physical growth and sensorimotor development are strongly connected with cognitive, self-care, and social-emotional development. Readers are urged to recognize the complexity of the interactions among these areas of development. This chapter will focus specifically on the impact of negative early life experiences on the physical development of the child adopted from abroad and the potential long-term impact on the child's growth, motor development, and overall health. In the following sections, we will discuss the typical progression of physical development and then discuss the developmental presentation of international adoptees.

## TYPICAL NEUROBIOLOGICAL, PHYSICAL GROWTH, AND MOTOR DEVELOPMENT

To understand how negative early life experiences can influence growth and development, it is important to first discuss what is typical physical growth. This is a critical gauge of childhood health and development.

## Typical Growth

Growth is an indispensible tool for assessing a child's current health, normal growth (including fetal growth), long-term health, and risk for development of certain diseases such as type II diabetes mellitus, obesity, hypertension, and cardiovascular disease (Neumann, Gewa, & Bwibo, 2004; Zhang, Merialdi, Platt, & Kramer, 2010). Growth is determined by changes in height (or length), weight, and head circumference measurements and deviations in growth are identified within populations when any of these parameters fall outside of the established normal distribution ranges for that population. Fetal weight and crown-to-rump lengths can be measured and compared against population norms as early as 8 weeks gestation (Needlman, 2007). Head circumference is monitored because it is a direct reflection of brain growth.

The most significant growth of any individual occurs prior to birth, following conception, as a single cell is transformed into a unique human being. Intrauterine growth is characterized during the first 16 weeks of gestation by cellular replication and enlargement. The single cell formed at conception implants and develops into three primary distinct germ layers within 3 weeks, by which time a primitive heart and nervous system structures can be identified. By weeks 4–8, cells are differentiating into tissues and organ systems that will perform specialized tasks. During these weeks, the brain is marked by rapid growth. In addition, precursors of skeletal muscles and vertebrae appear along with brachial arches that will form the jaw, palate, external ear, and other head and neck structures. Rudiments of all major organ systems will develop by the end of the 8th week. Cell replication and enlargement diminish during weeks 16–32 as differentiation and specialization accelerate. A full range of neonatal movements such as breathing, swallowing, eye opening, and the grasp reflex are present by midgestation, or 20 weeks. From 32–40 weeks, growth is characterized by the accrual of fat, protein, iron, and calcium. During this phase, it is expected that the fetus will triple his or her weight and double in length (Needlman, 2007).

Unlike any other organ system in the body, the sensitive period for brain growth and central nervous system (CNS) development extends from a critical period in the first 3–5 weeks until 1–2 years beyond birth. The gross structures of the brain and nervous system are formed by 8 weeks' gestation. Cell replication and enlargement proceed, along with differentiation, to specialized cells such as neurons, astrocytes, oligodendroctyes, and ependymal cells. Additional processes being accomplished either simultaneously or sequentially include synaptogenesis (the formation of connections among nerve cells), migration (movement of cells), and myelinization (the addition of insulation to a nerve cell to allow a more rapid propagation of the nervous impulse). Cell replication and enlargement in the CNS peaks around 18–20 weeks' gestation and again around 3 weeks of postnatal life. Myelinization peaks around 4–5 months after birth but continues until a child is 2 years old. CNS growth and development proceed at a rapid rate so that by the time of birth, the brain comprises 100 billion neurons and by 3 years old, each neuron will have an average of 15,000 synapses. The rapid pace of brain growth and development makes it particularly vulnerable to teratogenic and hypoxic influences (Needleman, 2007). Teratogens include alcohol, illicit drugs, medications like antiseizure drugs, or infections like syphilis, rubella, cytomegalovirus (CMV) etc., and environmental exposure to lead or other heavy metals, which can disturb embryonic or fetal development. Hypoxia refers to an insufficient supply of oxygen that may lead to an insult or damage to the brain. Two possible causes of hypoxia could include maternal smoking and trauma inflicted to the mother or fetus during pregnancy.

Intrauterine growth and development can be influenced by many fetal and maternal factors. Fetal factors known to have a negative effect on growth include multiple gestations, chromosomal defects, fetal and placental malformations, and acquired infections. Maternal factors are extensive but include maternal age, previous parity, chronic untreated medical conditions including mental health disorders, malnutrition, infectious diseases, environmental exposures to heavy metals, radiation, or other toxins, and finally the ingestion, inhalation, or inoculation of toxins including alcohol, tobacco, illicit drugs, and prescription medications (Needlman, 2007; Schwartz, 2000).

Disruptions during the first 16 weeks of gestation tend to lead to symmetric intrauterine growth retardation (IUGR), meaning that an infant's weight, length, and head circumference will be affected proportionately. Disruption in growth during the third trimester, when fat and protein accretion is taking place, will generally result in asymmetric IUGR. In asymmetric IUGR, the infant's weight is predictably the parameter most deviated from normal values, and the head circumference characteristically is spared. An infant with IUGR is also frequently referred to in the medical literature as being small for gestational age (SGA), which is generally defined as an infant's weight, length, and/or head circumference measured at birth at or below 2 standard deviations below the mean. It is important to note that interruptions in fetal growth at any phase will place a child at risk for subsequent postnatal growth abnormalities (Schwartz, 2000).

Any maternal or fetal factor that interrupts the normal growth and developmental process in the first 16 weeks of gestation will have the greatest effect on the tissue or organ system experiencing the most rapid cell replication and enlargement. Each organ system has defined periods of vulnerability when it is most sensitive to teratogens and other factors. Major morphological abnormalities are more likely to result from exposures during an organ system's highly sensitive period that generally falls within the first 3–8 weeks of gestation. Less sensitive periods can extend out to 16 weeks of gestation and until birth for the eyes, ears, teeth, and external genitalia (Needlman, 2007).

## Neurobiological Development

Human beings possess the most complex brain and nervous system of all the creatures in the animal kingdom. Although the human sense of hearing may not be as acute as that of a deer and human vision may not be as keen as an eagle's, the integration and cognitive processing that occurs in the human brain after receiving information from the senses is by far the most complex. The main task of the nervous system is to receive information from the outside world through sensory receptors, and then analyze it and produce an appropriate motor action in answer to the information received (Blumenfeld, 2002; Gartner & Patestas, 2003).

The nervous system has three main parts that work together to accomplish this task at lightning speed: 1) the peripheral nervous system (PNS), 2) the autonomic nervous system (ANS), and 3) the centralized nervous system (CNS). The PNS is made up of the nerves that travel through the muscles and some organs. The ANS is comprised of the nerves that travel through organs necessary for sustaining life. It sends the involuntary and automatic messages to keep the lungs breathing, heart pumping, and digestive system moving. Finally, the CNS includes the brain and spinal cord, the thick collection of nervous tissue that runs from the brain down to the tailbone and that is protected by the vertebral column (Gartner & Patestas, 2003).

There are more than 100 billion neurons that send messages via the spinal cord, transmitting sensory information to the brain to be processed and sending motor action messages to tell the muscles and limbs how to react. Each neuron consists of three parts: 1) a cell body with a nucleus, 2) short dendrites that reach like small branches to connect to other dendrites, and 3) a long "tail" called the axon. Some axons have a myelin sheath that surrounds it to insulate and protect it. The myelin sheath allows common (or instinctive) neural connections to travel quickly and efficiently, thus decreasing the effort the brain has to use to process something it is already familiar with (Blumenfeld, 2002; Gartner & Patestas, 2003). When certain receipt and action patterns are repeated, it gets easier for the brain and body to complete them with less conscious thought. This is one main reason why top athletes repeatedly practice their swinging and throwing techniques. They try to create what is commonly referred to as muscle memory. Neurologically, this means that the neural connections for that motor action are defined and well protected. Similarly, other connections may fade if not repeated. It seems that the process of strengthening and fading varies from one part of the brain to another. This may be why individuals can still ride a bike after years of absence from the activity (hence the expression "like riding a bike") but after a year of not practicing a foreign language, it may be impossible to retrieve the information (hence the expression "if you don't use it, you lose it").

## Typical Development of Posture and Gross and Fine Motor Skills

The first 4 years of life are vital in the development of the motor cortex and cerebellum. These are responsible for motor movements and processing. When babies are born, the motor-control centers of the brain are primitive, waiting to be shaped by the future interactions children will have with their environment (Nichols, 2005). Development proceeds in a stepwise manner, with stability first emerging from the core of the body. As the core muscles become stable, children are free to exercise coordinated movements involving several different muscle groups, and then finally, they are able to refine their movements to perform the delicate precise tasks that depend on prerequisite core stability (Nichols, 2005). By understanding the complexity and sensitivity of the developmental process, it is possible to explore stages at which the effects of early deprivation are too profound to allow for full recovery.

Postural control, or the ability to maintain an upright position against gravity, is a prerequisite for the typical development of all motor skills, including smooth and precise dexterity of the hands. The development of stabilizing musculature of the trunk and abdomen is the foundation for postural control (Nichols, 2005). Think of the body as a camera tripod, on top of which sits the head, capturing a picture of the world. If a camera tripod has one leg that is shaky or uneven, or if the neck of the tripod tips backward every few minutes, it would be quite a challenge to steady it to get a good shot. The same is true for the human body. If the core structure and support for the head is not solid, it can be very difficult to manage the irregularities and changes in terrain without losing focus of the more important object of interest. For example, if the musculature around the pelvis is not well developed, it can be difficult for children to maintain a seated position or to stand upright comfortably for an extended period. Energy that could be devoted to higher cognitive functions is relegated instead to keep the body in a stable position. In general, postural stability develops in a predictable pattern but is subject to environmental conditions. Jantz, Blosser, and Fruechting (1997) found that infants who slept on their stomachs tended to roll from prone to supine—stomach to back—earlier, and infants who slept on their backs tended to roll from supine to prone earlier. Thus, the authors suggested that the time a child spends in either position influences the emergence of rolling direction. Further evidence suggesting that practice and experience influence emergence of motor skills can be found in a study by Vereijken and Thelen (1997) who reported that infants who practiced stepping during the age range of 3–7 months demonstrated an increase in stepping behavior. These findings support a connection between early experiences and neuromotor development.

As postural control progresses, so too does attainment of motor milestones. Meeting motor milestones (rolling, sitting, crawling, walking) within normal age ranges demonstrates a vital progression of brain development and interaction between sensory processing and motor responses. During the first 4 years of life, children attain skills that contribute to an independent life by mastering the ability to move about and interact with the environment. Renowned developmental psychologist Jean Piaget (1954) theorized that intrinsically motivated and self-produced movement is a fundamental building block for knowledge. Such movement represents a complete coordination of the senses with motor movements and higher cognitive functions such as memory, curiosity, persistence, and bonding.

Although there is individual variation in attainment of these milestones, the following progression is generally understood as typical. First, babies learn to roll from side to supine, from prone to supine, and then back and forth in either direction (Nichols, 2005). By 6 months old, babies challenge gravity by pushing down through the arms when prone on their stomachs and lifting their heads up to pivot and observe the world. By 8 months old, babies creep, begin to move into an all-fours position, and sit. Soon, babies crawl on all fours and move toward objects of interest.

By the 9th or 10th month, babies begin to stand up and cruise along furniture, taking steps while holding on to their caregivers' hands (Nichols, 2005). The average age of independent walking is 11.2 months (Bly, 1994; Cech & Martin, 1995). By the 15th month, they run, albeit unsteadily, and by 18 months old they kick a ball. After the second birthday, they walk the stairs without help and by 2½ years old, they can stand on one foot. At 3½ years old, they can hop on one foot and by 4½ years old, they learn to skip and take running leaps (Ireton, 2005a, 2005b).

Fine motor skill, or dexterity, refers to the coordination of the small muscles in the hands to complete controlled and precise movements that involve manipulation of objects in the environment. The basic components of fine motor skill are reach, grasp, carry, voluntary release of an object, in-hand manipulation, and bilateral hand use (Exner, 2005). Although there is variation in what is considered typical developmental attainment of fine motor milestones, the following is a progression of skills that is generally accepted by developmental specialists and pediatricians. At 4 months old, babies are grasping objects and bringing these to their mouths. The grasp pattern at this stage is primitive, involves the whole palm and all fingers, and is facilitated by the residual grasping reflex (Folio & Fewell, 2002). By 6 months old, babies can transfer an object from one hand to the other. At 7 months old, they can feed themselves a cracker. By 10 months old, they can pick up smaller things using their thumb and either one or two other fingers. This is known as the pincer grasp and is an important precursor for later tool use (Folio & Fewell, 2002). At 13 months old, they are holding a cup independently, and 2 months later, they can feed themselves with a spoon and scribble back and forth with a drawing utensil. By 28 months old, typically developing children are able to scribble in circular motion, and by 3 years old, they can snip paper with scissors. By the time children are 4½ years old, they can fasten buttons and zippers (Ireton, 2005a, 2005b).

In recent years, developmental specialists have looked to DST to better understand the individual differences in milestone attainment. Instead of a straight-forward hierarchical progression of nervous system development, DST acknowledges the importance of body mass, muscle strength and tone, sensory system function, and environmental barriers in a child's motor development (Nichols, 2005). This view helps one understand the interdependent nature of all aspects of development. The next section provides background on typical development of the sensory processing domain of physical development.

## Typical Development of Sensory Processing and Integration

At every moment, a child's body is receiving information about the external world through sensory receptors: eyes, ears, mouth, nose, skin, muscles, and the equilibrium fluid in the inner ears. The receipt and processing of this information is necessary for human beings to be able to safely and appropriately interact with the world. Dr. A. Jean Ayres (1964, 1979) described the process of sensory integration as the useful synthesis of sensory information from the environment to produce an adaptive response, usually in the form of a voluntary motor action. Ayres (1960) theorized that motor learning was influenced by and potentially dependent upon incoming sensory messages. She also wrote that the abilities to focus, maintain attention, and regulate arousal level were in part dependent upon the way that the nervous system responded to touch and other sensations (Ayres, 1964).

Typical sensory processing begins to develop even before a child is born. In the womb, fetuses demonstrate primitive avoidance and protective reactions by arching toward or away from tactile stimulation (Parham & Mailloux, 2005). As soon as a child is born, sensation processing contributes to bonding and attachment between children and familiar caregivers. Infants very early on can recognize patterns and similarities in voice, facial features, and touch of a familiar caregiver (Williamson & Anzalone, 2001). This demonstrates early processing and integration of auditory, visual, and tactile sensations. Along with taste and smell, most people are familiar with the senses of sight, hearing, and touch. However, two less commonly known senses that are actually more dominant in infancy than any other sense are proprioception and vestibular. Proprioception is the sensation of the interaction between muscles and joints and the relationship between parts of the body and the environment. The vestibular, or sense of movement and balance, consists of three semicircular canals in the inner ear and is responsible for the sensation of the direction of the head in space (Ayres, 1979; see also Stock-Kranowitz, 2005). These two senses are the most developed in infancy whereas, initially, visual and auditory processing are largely immature.

During the first 6 months of life, infants become increasingly aware of the world around them. The integration of visual, proprioceptive, and vestibular sensory information helps to govern adaptive motor responses with progressive complexity and voluntary control. As was discussed in a previous section, infants possess an inner drive to move against gravity in several predictable developmental postures. As the child attempts to move against gravity, there is sensory feedback that helps the lateral vestibulospinal tract in the spinal cord mature (Parham & Mailloux, 2005). Furthermore, as a child develops a memory bank about attempted motor actions, future attempts become increasingly mediated by cognitive processes. Thus, the more the child moves, the more sensory experiences accrue and the child remembers the movements resulting in success and those that did not. This process is known as praxis, or motor planning (Ayres, 1985; see also May-Benson & Cermak, 2007). Also during the first 6 months, there is development in the hands related to a refining tactile sense. Children begin to manipulate objects with simple grasp patterns (using the entire hand) and they can voluntarily study objects visually by holding them at the middle of the body. This budding connection between the visual systems and tactile manipulation in the hands is the foundation for hand–eye coordination.

The major development during the latter 6 months of a child's first year of life involves the increasing voluntary ability to move and explore the environment. The proprioceptive sense develops as an infant practices fitting into various sized spaces with his or her body. Children learn to recognize the boundaries of their bodies and the relationship between parts of the body and the external world. This constant practice keeps a child's body busy and helps regulate attention and activity level (Ayres, 1979; see also Williamson & Anzalone, 2001). Tactile refinement is evident as children are able to manipulate smaller objects and isolate use of two or three fingers demonstrating a pincer grasp generally at 10 months old (Folio & Fewell, 2002). Also at this stage, auditory information integrates with tactile and proprioceptive information around the mouth and children begin to make simple consonant-vowel-sound repetitions. At the end of this stage, children become independent when feeding, a milestone that represents coordination of proprioception, visual, and tactile movement of jaw and tongue muscles to move food, the correct placement of food from hand to mouth, and the management of more complex textures. In addition, there is involvement from smell and taste receptors. Emergent self-feeding represents an important rite of passage for children in that it is an occupation with a strong link to social and cultural meaning.

In the second year of life, the visual-proprioceptive-vestibular triangle of sensory integration rapidly develops as children practice dynamic balance and gain fluidity through repeated practice of motor actions. The most complex aspect of motor planning, ideation, is emerging during this year (Ayres, 1979). Toddlers show signs that they are thinking about how to accomplish a voluntary motor action. Whether contemplating taking steps on uneven ground or figuring out how to crouch under a chair to retrieve a favorite toy, you can see the gears turning in their heads as they visualize a plan and move systematically to achieve a particular goal. If a plan does not work the first time, and very often it doesn't, children can revise their plans and try again until successful. The increased mastery of voluntary movement is related to the child's development of an individual sense of self (Piaget, 1954).

During the ages of 3 to 7, the trajectory of sensory processing development depends largely upon individual experience. At this stage, sensations integrate to allow children to perform cognitive functions with increasing complexity. Children begin to show selective attention to sensations that relate to the task at hand and can ignore sensations that are superfluous. For example, they can 1) ignore the brief discomfort of a shirt tag and focus on the teacher giving instructions, 2) notice facial expressions and gestures from peers and learn to understand the meaning of these cues for social interaction, 3) share toys, follow rules, empathize and be flexible, and 4) make adaptations throughout life to compensate for new challenges and situations.

In summary, the previous sections described physical development in typically developing children. Sensory processing and voluntary motor skills are interconnected and development of these domains is particularly sensitive to children's early experiences. When the typical developmental process is affected by genetic, prenatal, or environmental factors, or a combination thereof, the effect can be profound. Early adversity and poor health—common conditions for the internationally adopted child—can leave an immeasurable and sometimes insurmountable impression. The preadoption circumstances that may contribute to short- and long-term consequences will be described followed by a discussion of the specific health and development of internationally adopted children.

## PREADOPTION FACTORS AND HEALTH STATUS OF INTERNATIONALLY ADOPTED CHILDREN

In recent years, international adoption specialists have made great strides in documenting and reporting on the health status and development of children residing in orphanages. Although small sample sizes limit the ability to generalize findings for many of these reports, they begin to give us an empirical picture of the effects of preadoption conditions on children's futures. First, we will examine the factors that influence children's physical growth, health, and ultimately, their development. Second, we will review what is already known regarding physical and motor development in internationally adopted children.

### Prenatal and Perinatal Factors

A number of factors have been reported as possible prenatal contributors to developmental delays in internationally adopted children. These include existing genetic factors, prenatal toxin exposures (drugs, alcohol, tobacco, and other toxins) (Miller, 2005a), maternal stress, and a lack of prenatal medical, pharmacological, and nutritional care (Miller, et al., 2006).

Fetal alcohol syndrome caused by maternal consumption of alcohol during fetal gestation is most commonly documented in children adopted from Russia, Ukraine, and other parts of Eastern Europe (Davies & Bledsloe, 2005; Johnson, 2000). It has been reported, however, in cases from nearly every sending country (Miller, 2005a). Children diagnosed with a fetal alcohol spectrum disorder (FASD) have growth deficiencies, characteristic craniofacial malformations, and CNS dysfunction (Davies & Bledsloe, 2005). Notable CNS impairments include hyperactivity, poor social skills, attention deficits, and sensory processing issues including visuospatial and perceptual problems and problems with visual, auditory, and vestibular processing (Church & Abel, 1998).

Many birth mothers have been impoverished, single women who have been sexually promiscuous or have engaged in prostitution—circumstances that place them at risk for contracting sexually transmitted infections including syphilis, herpes, hepatitis B, and HIV (Ladage, 2009; Miller, 2000). Drug use places mothers at additional risk for hepatitis C and HIV infection. Birth mothers who are reported to have one of these infections must be considered at risk for other sexually transmitted infections, as sexually transmitted infections are often diagnosed together. In a study of the health of children in Ethiopia, more than 50% of children were true orphans, mainly due to the death of both parents related to complications of HIV (Miller, Tseng, Tirella, Chan, & Feig, 2008). Jenista (2000) found that maternal syphilis was diagnosed in 14% of birth mothers during pregnancy in a retrospective chart review of 2,814 pre-adoption medical record reviews, 88% completed on children being considered for adoption from Russia and other Eastern European countries, and 12% from African and Asian countries; however, this is likely an underestimation because many of the medical records did not contain any maternal history. In the case of Chinese adoptions, children are often found and subsequently taken to an orphanage. Thus, no information about the birth parents is available (Miller, 2005a).

Maternal malnutrition is the most common contributing factor to infant and maternal iron deficiency and affects an estimated 30%–50% of pregnancies in developing countries (Lozoff & Georgieff, 2006). In addition to inadequate iron in the mother's diet, fetal iron deficiency is compounded when fetal demands increase due to untreated maternal conditions that result in chronic fetal hypoxia such as diabetes mellitus and hypertension. Lozoff and Georgieff reported on two studies of full-term babies born in developing countries with evidence of iron deficiency at the time of birth that link fetal and neonatal iron deficiency to greater infant irritability. Poorer iron status at birth was correlated with higher levels of infant irritability and lower levels of alertness and ability to be soothed (Lozoff & Georgieff, 2006). It is easy to postulate that infants who are more difficult to soothe may further limit their already inadequate interaction with caregivers. In addition, a 5-year longitudinal study of fetal iron deficiency predicted poorer auditory comprehension of language, fine motor skills, and self-regulation (Lozoff & Georgieff, 2006).

After birth and before they are placed in an orphanage, children can experience significant adversity while they are in the care of their birth families. Parental alcohol or drug abuse, parental mental health disorders, evidence of physical abuse, severe neglect, and/or abandonment of the children are all frequently cited as reasons for termination of parental rights and placement of a child into the orphanage (Jenista, 2000). Of the 193 children residing in Russian orphanages whose health and development were evaluated, 96% were placed in orphanages because of termination of parental rights, relinquishment, abandonment, or parental imprisonment. Only four were true orphans (both parents deceased). Seventy-eight percent of these children lived in multiple places before placement in an orphanage (Miller et al., 2007).

## Infectious Disease Factors

Internationally adopted children living in orphanages or with foster care families are also at increased risk for acquisition of infectious diseases. Some infectious diseases are directly associated with developmental delays. While specific infectious diseases may vary in prevalence by the country of origin, no internationally adopted child is completely immune. Infections such as stool parasites, syphilis, hepatitis B, HIV, and tuberculosis have been described in internationally adopted children since the 1980s (Hostetter, Iverson, Dole, & Johnson, 1989; Jenista & Chapman, 1987) and reconfirmed as significant risks in more recent studies (Aronson, 2000; Miller, 2005b; Miller et al., 2008; Miller & Hendrie, 2000; Saiman et al., 2001). As stated previously, many of these infections are contracted from the children's birth mothers either during the pregnancy, at the time of delivery, or through breast-feeding—a risk mainly for children from African countries. Syphilis remains a risk to all internationally adopted children because it is observed worldwide with national prevalence varying from 2.5% to 17.4% (Chakraborty & Luck, 2008). Children in Eastern European countries, particularly Russia, are at high risk due to the 40-fold increase in the rate of syphilis that occurred throughout the 1990s (Aronson, 2000). This increase is reflected in the statistic that more than 30% of preadoption, Eastern European medical records mention maternal syphilis during pregnancy (Aronson, 2000) and 15%–20% indicate a history of congenital syphilis in the adopted child (Alber, Johnson, Hostetter, Iverson, & Miller, 1997). Children adopted from countries outside of Eastern Europe are at risk as well. Miller (2005b) found internationally adopted children with undiagnosed and untreated congenital syphilis were more likely to have originated from China and the United States. Surprisingly, the diagnosis of syphilis only continues to be made in approximately 1% of U.S. adopted children when evaluated after adoption (Aronson, 2000). Syphilis, when left untreated, may result in neurosyphilis (infection of the CNS), developmental delays, cognitive impairment, and even dementia (Lane & Oates, 1988). Congenital syphilis is more common in infants who are more often born to young, unmarried mothers from low socioeconomic backgrounds, especially when these infants are also born premature and small for gestational age (Lane & Oates, 1988).

HIV infection has long been recognized as a risk for internationally adopted children and is often the source of greatest concern for many adoptive parents. Although the prevalence of infection in internationally adopted children is very low, cases have been reported in children from Russia, Romania, Vietnam, and Cambodia. In a study of 7,299 adopted children brought to the United States during the period of 1990 through 2002 and evaluated in 1 of 17 international adoption clinics, 12 children, or 0.16%, were infected with HIV (Miller, 2005b). In addition to these countries, Haiti, Kazakhstan, and many African nations also frequently report maternal HIV infection in preadoption medical records and should be considered at high risk among these countries of origin (Ladage, 2009). Features of HIV infection can mimic or overlap with malnutrition and institutional sequelae presenting as developmental delays, failure to thrive, anemia, recurrent infections, and common skin infections such as scabies and molluscum contagiosum, a viral infection of the skin or mucous membranes. Discerning the etiology of these conditions can be difficult, if not impossible, and underscore the importance of appropriate laboratory screening (Miller, 2005b).

Not all infectious diseases are directly linked to developmental delays. However, untreated chronic medical diseases have been documented as a risk factor that increases the likelihood of growth failure and developmental delays in institutionalized children (Miller, 2000). Infections recognized in internationally adopted children that are included in this category are a) hepatitis B, b) hepatitis C, and c) tuberculosis. Stadler, Mezoff, and Staat (2008) reported a hepatitis B infection prevalence of 4% in 1,282 children examined at their international adoption clinic between November 1999 and October 2006, including 1.1% that demonstrated active or chronic infection. Similarly, the Centers for Disease Control Committee on the Infectious Disease Report indicated the overall prevalence of hepatitis B in internationally adopted children has remained around 3%–5% (American Academy of Pediatrics [AAP], 2009; Miller, 2005b; Saiman et al, 2001). Hepatitis C infection is significantly less prevalent, being observed in less than 1% of internationally adopted children (Miller, 2005b). Miller (2005b) reported that although hepatitis C is found worldwide, only 26, or 1.3%, of 1,932 international adoptees from many placing countries were identified as being exposed to hepatitis C infection. Johnson (2000) indicates that approximately 1% of 357 Chinese adoptees were documented to be infected with hepatitis C compared with 3.5% of adoptees with hepatitis B. Aronson reported 2 out of 129 children assessed in an international adoption clinic in Boston between 1989 and 1993 were found to have active hepatitis C infection, as were five children adopted from an orphanage in Yangzhou, China, in 1995 (Aronson, 2000). Although the prevalence is very low, maternal hepatitis C infection has been frequently observed in the medical records of children from the countries of the former Soviet Union. It should be noted that because IV drug use is a risk factor for hepatitis C and HIV infection, it is common for users to be infected with both.

Latent (inactive) tuberculosis infection has also been well documented in internationally adopted children. Saiman and colleagues (2001) reported that 19% of 404 children tested in their retrospective cohort study of 504 internationally adopted children were positive (reaction 10mm or greater) when tested with tuberculin skin tests. All children with positive skin tests had a negative chest x ray indicating they did not demonstrate evidence of active disease. Miller and colleagues report a tuberculosis infection prevalence of 3.5% in children in Chinese orphanages (Miller & Hendrie, 2000), 7% in children adopted from Guatemala (Miller, Chan, Comfort et al, 2005), and 18% in children who were adopted from Ethiopia (Miller, Tseng, Tirella, Chan, & Feig, 2008). Mandalakas and colleagues (2007) conducted a retrospective chart review on 880 children adopted from abroad from 1986 to 2001 and reported 12% of the children had evidence of tuberculosis infection. In addition, the odds of infection increased with the age of the child at adoption. In this chart review, the authors noted that 33% of children had evidence of either chronic or acute malnutrition and were therefore at considerable risk for progression of tuberculosis disease. They also noted tuberculin skin response was not associated with birth region, supporting that this is not a disease isolated to any one country or geographical region.

## Other Medical Factors

Issues related to determination of age have been well documented in the international adoption population throughout the past 2 decades (Ladage, 2009). Children in Chinese orphanages have nearly all been abandoned and are often found without documentation of their date of birth. Consequently, birth dates are assigned upon admission to the orphanage. Although the percentile of children placed in orphanages in other countries due to abandonment is significantly lower, it remains a common reason for institutionalization. Issues surrounding age assignment have continued to rise with the number of children adopted from African nations because many of them do not commemorate birthdays in the same manner as in the United States. As a result, children are often arbitrarily assigned birth dates by the government in court proceedings as part of the adoption process. Many families adopting from Ethiopia have reported that all the children being processed by the courts at the same time as their child were assigned identical birth dates even though the children had visibly different chronological ages. Age determination may not be as significant an issue for younger infants, but in older children it can be particularly difficult, especially when making decisions for school placement. Age determination may be aided by examining physical growth, development, dentition, and bone-age radiographs that look at bone maturation. However, all of these may be significantly delayed at the point of adoption due to malnutrition, chronic disease, and deprivation. It is best to closely follow the progression of growth and development of a child during the first year following adoption. Extreme caution and compelling reasons should be provided before birth dates are adjusted.

Records of immunizations are often lacking or have inadequate documentation in institutionalized children. Even when age-appropriate vaccines are administered, children may fail to mount a sufficient immune response because their immune system may be suppressed due to malnutrition or psychosocial deprivation. Likewise, inadequate responses may be secondary to receiving improper dosages or expired vaccines given at inappropriate intervals (Aronson, 2000; Ladage, 2009). In a retrospective cohort study of a sample 504 children (71% were girls; 88% resided in orphanages) adopted from 16 countries with a mean age of 19 months, Schulte and colleagues (2002) found that only 35% of children had immunization records. Of those children with records, 94% of the records were considered valid by U.S. standards. Two thirds were reported to be up-to-date in at least one vaccine series, indicating that one third of the children were not current in any of the series (Schulte et al., 2002). An Italian study examined the immunization status of 70 children, including the children's level of protection to polio virus types 1, 2, and 3, tetanus, diphtheria, pertussis, measles, mumps, rubella, and hepatitis B (Viviano et al., 2006). The authors concluded,

> Internationally adopted children should be tested for their immunization status on arrival in the adopting country because they are not protected in a sufficient way against vaccine preventable diseases and their preadoptive immunization records sometimes are lacking and frequently are scarcely reliable (Viviano et al., 2006, p. 4138).

## ENVIRONMENTAL FACTORS

It is still not fully understood exactly how environmental deprivation and major shifts in early caregiving environments translate into physical abnormalities and delays, but one theory being investigated by researchers is the mechanism of the hypothalamic pituitary adrenal (HPA) stress axis (Mason & Narad, 2005). The HPA stress axis regulates the production of stress hormones, particularly cortisol, and this production increases under adverse conditions. Animal studies involving this axis have shown that it has significant influence on physical growth (Armario, Castellanos, & Balasch, 1984; Armario, Lopez–Calderon, Jolin, & Castellanos, 1986; Brown & Martin, 1974).

Few studies that investigate the lasting effects of changes in the HPA axis have been completed with internationally adopted children. One study that took cortisol measurements of children 6½ years after adoption found that cortisol levels remained higher in children who lived in orphanages longer than in children who were adopted early (Gunner, Morison, Chisholm,

& Schuder, 2001). Persistent elevations of cortisol or stress hormone production in children may down regulate or turn off the production of the growth hormone. In addition to poor growth, abnormally high levels of cortisol have been associated with poor cognitive function and emotional regulation. This early evidence may be the key to understanding the residual problems internationally adopted children sometimes demonstrate in the areas of cognitive, behavioral, and emotional development (Mason & Narad, 2005). In Chapters 5 and 8, there are in-depth discussions of the influence of the HPA axis and early stress on executive functioning, attention, memory, and social-emotional development. More research is needed to study the long-term effect of early adversity on cortisol.

Malnutrition after birth also contributes to delays in physical growth (height, weight, head circumference) and development. Chronic protein and calorie malnutrition is defined in terms of stunting or linear growth retardation (a height of 2 or more standard deviations below the mean). It is estimated that 40% of the children in the world are stunted and this is due primarily to insufficient intake of calories, protein, and micronutrients including iodine, zinc, vitamin D, and calcium (Neumann, et al., 2004). Stunting has been associated in childhood with motor retardation and poorer school performance. Likewise, iron deficiency, estimated to affect more than 50% of children worldwide, is associated with developmental delays (Neumann et al, 2004). Lozoff and Georgieff (2006) reported that 16 different studies completed in various countries around the world on infants 6 to 24 months old have shown children in the general pediatric population with iron deficiency anemia have poorer cognitive, motor, and social-emotional functioning compared with those who are not iron deficient. Nine of these studies included follow-up of these infants who ranged from posttreatment (3 months) to adolescence and observed persistence of poorer functioning in these domains attributable to chronic severe iron deficiency or iron deficiency anemia. One of the follow-up studies completed on full-term infants, born in Costa Rica without any other identifiable medical condition except iron deficiency, demonstrated persistent motor differences and more grade repetition, anxiety, depression, social problems, and inattention compared with their non-iron deficient peers even at 19 years of age, despite having received appropriate treatment to correct their anemia (Lozoff & Georgieff, 2006).

Micronutrient deficiencies prior to placement have been documented in internationally adopted children. Johnson (2000) reported that iron deficiency along with iodine deficiency has been documented in 12%–20% of internationally adopted children. Miller and Hendrie (2000) evaluated 452 children adopted from China and found 35% were diagnosed with anemia and 10% with abnormal thyroid test. Although these conditions are often attributed to iron and iodine deficiency respectively, the authors do not comment on the specific etiologies in this group of children. Similarly, in children adopted from Guatemala, 30% of 103 children were found to be anemic (Miller et al., 2005). Miller and colleagues (2007) document in a retrospective chart review of 193 healthy, institutionalized children residing in Murmansk, Russia, that 6% of those children, ranging in age from 2 to 72 months old, were diagnosed with anemia and 21% with vitamin D–deficiency rickets. Likewise, three children between the ages of 29 to 39 months old adopted from the former Soviet Union were found to have unusual radiological findings consistent with vitamin D–deficiency rickets. These children had heights documented shortly after placement, measuring below the 5th percentile for their age.

In addition, malnutrition can manifest as behaviors that limit the child in attaining age-appropriate motor milestones and cognition. For example, Barnes (1976) described malnourished children as apathetic and avoidant of new experiences; they often had extreme reactions to stimuli and showed less locomotor activity. He also wrote that malnourished children demonstrated decreased curiosity to explore their environment, which in turn impacted the learning potential that occurred during a crucial developmental window. These characteristics may affect a child's ability to procure more attention or larger portions or additional helpings of food, as well as develop foraging or scavenging behaviors especially needed for survival and learning.

## CULTURAL FACTORS

An examination of the trends of sending countries (countries from which children are adopted) throughout the past several decades reveals that as political and societal attitudes affect the countries that U.S. families most frequently adopt from, there are differences in the medical needs of arriving children. For example, when the majority of adoptees were of Korean descent and were relinquished for adoption by relatively healthy women stigmatized by single parenthood, most of the children had been raised in foster homes and had received adequate medical care (Johnson, 2005). These children had relatively few health issues as compared with children involved in the next significant U.S. trend in international adoption, children from Russian and Chinese orphanages. Many of these children had been neglected or abandoned by mothers who had experienced poor or no prenatal care, drug and alcohol abuse, and malnutrition (Johnson, 2002). The children of these mothers were then placed in institutional care, compounding their fragile predispositions. The recent rise in adoptions from Africa can be attributed in part to high mortality rates from HIV (Miller et al., 2008). Many otherwise healthy African children are becoming true orphans or are given up for adoption because of the imminent death of one or both parents (Ladage, 2009; Miller et al., 2008). These children often demonstrate fewer growth and developmental delays (Miller et al., 2008).

Though this ebb and flow is likely to continue in future years, it is unlikely that international adoption will cease to be a viable solution to the problem of children in need of permanent homes. However, as sending countries develop in-country foster care systems, the prevalence of medical problems and developmental delays are likely to increase in future international adoptees. In support of this prediction, Johnson (2005) writes:

> Because those adopting domestically in placing countries share a preference for younger healthy children, those available for international adoption in the future are likely to be older and to have special needs. As the risk of medical, developmental, and behavioral challenges increase, adoption must continue to be child centered but not blind to the desires, and particularly the abilities, of potential adoptive families (Johnson, 2005, p. 1240).

## PREADOPTION FACTORS AND MOTOR DEVELOPMENT

Caregiver interactions can have a profound impact on child development in nearly all domains including sensorimotor development. In some orphanages, caregivers must devise means to increase efficiency in order to care for each child, sometimes resulting in detrimental consequences. In an orphanage environment, children may have limited, impersonal, and even abusive interactions with caregivers (Johnson et al., 1992; Ladage, 2009; Miller, 2000) and are often cared for by multiple caregivers (Miller, 2000).

Adoptive parents have repeatedly described feeding practices during postplacement evaluations throughout the past 10–15 years. One common practice in some crowded orphanages is to prop bottles up in cribs so that children can eat without assistance (Johnson, 2000; Ladage, 2009). This practice decreases the physical touch children receive and also has an adverse effect on normal progression of independent feeding skills. Children may also be fed by bottle instead of taught to feed themselves from a plate with their fingers or utensils. Other children, as observed in orphanages in Russia and other Eastern European countries, are force-fed by caregivers or are rushed to eat quickly in limited periods of time, even when the food offered is too hot to eat. Children have also been expected to feed themselves with utensils as early as 15 months old. Food has been limited to a pureed and soft consistency that limits opportunity to chew and develop oral muscle tone and lateral tongue movements. These circumstances may predispose the child to the development of aversions to oral textures and underdeveloped chewing skills and can lead to malnutrition and growth failure (also see Chapter 6).

Infants in Chinese orphanages are frequently heavily bundled while lying in cribs and toddlers may be restrained with straps tied around the ankles and hips. These practices are usually done as protective measures to keep children both warm and safe in the crib or bed. While these children can present with gross motor delays due to the lack of opportunity to move, the delays have been clinically observed to generally resolve quickly on their own when children are provided opportunities for movement and exploration.

Another common practice in China reported by parents and clinically observed is to place children in "split" pants with openings for urination and bowel movements so that children do not remain in wet clothing if they urinate or have a bowel movement away from the toilet. In Russia and other Eastern European countries, children may sit on toilet chairs for extended periods several times a day to wait for them to urinate and defecate (Miller, 2005c). These children awaiting adoption have been described as potty trained when actually they have never learned to communicate the urge to go. After adoption, when they no longer sit on the potty chair for 30–40 minutes at a time, accidents occur (Miller, 2005c).

## DEVELOPMENT IN INTERNATIONALLY ADOPTED CHILDREN

Developmental delays, including motor developmental delays, have been well documented in internationally adopted children both from measures standardized in the United States and clinical observation and by retrospective review of in-country records. Prevalence, severity, and type of delay are often connected with children's preadoptive environment (orphanage or foster care) and with country of origin. Environmental and cultural factors likely play a role in these outcomes.

Johnson and colleagues (1992) conducted a study on the health and development of children who were adopted from Romania and evaluated at U.S. international adoption medical specialist clinics. Sixty-five children were included in the study (2:1 female-to-male ratio). Two thirds of the children resided in orphanages prior to arrival in the United States and age at arrival ranged from 6 weeks to 73 months old. Seventy-one percent were evaluated within 3 weeks of arrival. Of the original children studied, 61 were evaluated for developmental level by occupational therapists on staff at the clinics. Assessments were made based on clinical observation and parent report, as standardized assessments were not considered to be valid for the population. Most children demonstrated delays in various developmental areas. Of the children 66 months old and younger (n=20), 13 were within normal limits. For children from birth to 12 months of age (n=10), 3 were within normal limits. For children 12 to 24 months old (n=10), 1 was within normal limits, and for children 30 to 73 months of age (n=21), only 2 were within normal limits. The majority of children who were assessed as performing within normal limits were very young or had lived with birth families prior to adoption. Delays reported included abnormal muscle tone, decreased visual attention, gross and fine motor delays, abnormal social-emotional behaviors, and decreased strength and endurance.

Children adopted from China initially demonstrated several areas of developmental delay. Miller and Hendrie (2000) completed a retrospective chart review of 192 children adopted from China. The children were seen for clinical evaluation following adoption at an international adoption specialty clinic in the United States. Approximately 188 of the 192 children in the group were female with an age range of 2–149 months (mean age 15.7 ± 17.5 months) at time of evaluation. Eighty-eight percent were seen within 2 months of arrival. A pediatrician and an occupational therapist specializing in development evaluated children in this group. Development was evaluated across seven domains: 1) fine motor, 2) gross motor, 3) social-emotional, 4) cognitive, 5) receptive language, 6) expressive language, and 7) activities of daily living. Instruments used included the Peabody Developmental Motor Scales (Folio & Fewell, 2002) and the University of Michigan Early Intervention Developmental Profile (Schafer & Moersch, 1981). From this initial clinical evaluation, 55% of children had delays in gross motor skills, 49% in fine motor skills, 32% in cognitive skills, 43% in language skills, 28% in self-care skills, and 30% in activities of daily living. Approximately 44% demonstrated global delays (delays in three or more domains). Delays in both language skills and activities of daily living directly correlated with length of institutionalization in an orphanage. Furthermore, the authors commented on the irregularities and inaccuracies of diagnoses found in original medical records or reported by orphanage staff. Often, children were labeled as having special needs when they had minor and fixable issues such as head flattening or hemangiomas (benign vascular growths). In addition, a small number of the most severely developmentally delayed children evaluated in this study were originally offered to their adoptive parents as healthy children (Miller & Hendrie, 2000).

In another retrospective study, the development of children adopted from Guatemala was examined. Miller, Chan, Comfort, and Tirella (2005) examined the health and development of 103 Guatemalan children (55 male, 48 female, mean age at evaluation 18.6 ± 20.52 months) adopted by parents in the United States. The authors examined data collected from evaluation of adoptees seen at an international adoption specialty clinic shortly after adoption. For comparison, 50 of the original 103 children were case matched to investigate variations in outcomes for children with different preadoptive conditions. Twenty-five children resided in orphanages prior to placement and the other 25 resided in foster care. Children in foster care showed better overall physical growth and cognitive scores. Most children in both groups were performing well (80%–92% of expected performance in all domains), but 14% had developmental delays in three or more domains. Delays were defined as scores of less than 66% on standardized tests. Approximately 87% of children were evaluated within the first 4 months postadoption, 71% within the first 2 months. Developmental delays did not correlate with age of arrival or location of residence prior to adoption. For children under 2 years of age at arrival, developmental scores for cognition, language, and activities of daily living were inversely correlated with age at adoption. Thus, children who were adopted earlier had higher scores, and the longer they waited for adoption, the more they fell behind typically developing peers.

Continuing a line of research on health and development of internationally adopted children, Miller, Tseng, Tirella, Chan, and Feig (2008) reported data from a retrospective chart review of adoptees from Ethiopia and Eritrea. Study participants included 50 children (26 female, 24 male) adopted by U.S. families at a mean age of 4 years old (age range 3 months to 15 years, 1 month; 62% were under 4 years old). Seventy-two percent of children were evaluated within 3 weeks of arrival in the United States. Developmental assessment was completed as described in the previous two studies with the addition of two tests for academic readiness of older children, the Wide Range Achievement test (Wilkinson, 1993) and the Beery-Buktenica Developmental Test of Visual-Motor Integration (Beery, Buktenica, & Beery, 2005). Eighty-six percent of children were performing at the expected age level for fine motor, gross motor, and cognitive skills. In fact, 58% of children scored average or better for fine motor skills. No children were identified as having global delays, and behavior problems reported by parents were minimal and resolved quickly. The authors stated that differences between outcomes for these children and children in studies from other parts of the world could reflect that 50% of these children were true orphans (both parents deceased, usually from HIV) and 55% had been living with relatives prior to adoption.

In summary, studies of children from multiple sending countries, before and after adoption, report a strong trend in the presence of developmental delays, among them, gross and fine motor delays. It is important to note that these studies did not include follow-up data to determine whether these children's development improved after adoption when their nutrition, social stimulation, and care would have dramatically changed.

## SENSORY PROCESSING OF INTERNATIONALLY ADOPTED CHILDREN

Sensory processing is connected to many developmental domains that are often delayed in institutionalized children. Research has documented that sensory experiences in orphanages are infrequent and of low quality (Casler, 1975). Provence and Lipton (1962) described an interconnection between voluntary motor actions and sensory input in institutionalized children. The authors used the term *action unit* to describe a voluntary attempt at a motor action guided by sensory information. They suggested that the infrequency of self-initiated, precise motor movements observed in the study group were connected to a lack of sensory experiences in the deprived living environment. Other, more recent studies, have begun to highlight differences in sensory processing in internationally adopted children as compared with nonadopted peers and to adopted peers with varied lengths of institutionalization (Cermak & Daunhauer,

1997; Lin, Cermak, Coster, & Miller, 2005). Notably, a number of studies conducted throughout the years have discussed the prevalence of behavior concerns such as inattention, hyperactivity, self-stimulatory behaviors, and emotional reactivity in internationally adopted children (Kreppner, O'Connor, Rutter, & the English and Romanian Adoptees Study team, 2001; Rutter et al., 1999; Verhulst, Althaus, & Versluis-den Beiman, 1990a, 1990b, 1990c). All of these are behaviors that may be related to sensory processing dysfunction.

Lin et al. (2005) examined the relationship between length of institutionalization and sensory processing dysfunction in children adopted from Eastern Europe. The majority of children were originally from Romania and Russia, but the study also included one child each from Hungary, Moldova, Latvia, Kazakhstan, and Albania. They compared 30 children with longer institutionalization histories (mean = 34 months) with 30 children institutionalized for a shorter time (mean = 3 months). The former group scored lower (indicating greater dysfunction) on the sensory integration and praxis test (SIPT) (Ayres, 1989) in vestibular–proprioceptive, visual, and praxis areas. The group who resided longer in institutional settings also displayed behaviors indicative of sensory modulation dysfunction (SMD) more frequently. Sensory modulation refers to the ability to accurately adjust the degree and intensity of a voluntary response to sensory input in accordance with the demands of the task (Miller, Anzalone, Lane, Cermak, & Osten, 2007); children with SMD often push too hard, squeeze too tight, or move too quickly or slowly than is necessary. The group who spent less time in institutional settings scored within the average to low-average range as compared with the SIPT's normative samples. Thus, those children who were institutionalized for less than 6 months had scores similar to family-reared children for all 17 of the SIPT tests for sensory processing and integration.

Cermak and Daunhauer (1997) compared children adopted from Romania (n=73) to typically developing peers in the United States (n=72) for differences in sensory processing and related behaviors. For the Romanian subjects, the mean length of institutionalization was 13 months, the mean length of time spent with adoptive families was 42 months, and the mean age of the children at the time of this study was 56.3 months. The mean age for children in the control group was 55 months. Parents completed surveys with questions regarding six sensory processing domains (including touch, avoids movement, seeks movement, vision, and audition) and five behavioral domains (including activity level, feeding, organization, and social-emotional). An example of a movement avoidance question is, "Does your child become anxious when his or her feet leave the ground?" (p. 504, table 2). An example of a feeding domain question is, "Does your child have difficulty eating food with lumps (i.e. chunky soups)?" (p. 504, table 2). The Romanian adoptees demonstrated greater dysfunction in five of six sensory processing domains and four of five behavioral domains.

Some studies have reported behaviors indicative of a form of sensory processing dysfunction known as tactile defensiveness in Romanian adoptees (Cermak, 1994; Haradon et al., 1994). Ayres (1964) described tactile defensiveness as a fear response out of proportion to the sensory stimuli. Children who are described as tactile defensive may avoid many normal childhood experiences, such as going barefoot, swimming, roughhousing with peers or parents, and getting dirty. They may also demonstrate aggressive behaviors such as hitting or shoving others who have gotten too close to them. This may have negative outcomes on the bonding process between parent and child (Cermak & Daunhauer, 1997).

Some studies reported autistic-like behaviors that may be related to sensory dysfunction. For example, Rutter et al. (1999) examined the occurrence of autistic patterns in children who were deprived early in life while living in institutions in Romania. Random sampling was used to select a group of 165 children adopted from Romania to the United Kingdom before the age of 42 months. This particular study focused on 11 children who had been identified as having "autistic features" (p. 537). In 7 of those 11 children, a preoccupation with sensations was observed (i.e., liking the feel of men's moustaches or liking to feel textures on one's face and/or lips). The children were also observed to have unusual or absent communication and stereotyped behaviors (rocking, spinning), features characteristic of autism spectrum disorders. Out of the 111 representative sample, 6% overall were found to have a pattern of behavior similar to autistic children. Hoksbergen, ter Laak, Rijk, van Dijkum, and Stoutjesdijk (2005) reported similar results on a study of Romanian children (44 male, 36 female) adopted by Dutch parents. Of 80 children studied, 13 (16%) were found to exhibit symptoms within the autistic range. The children in the study had largely resided in orphanages from birth and were on average 2 years, 10 months old when adopted. The average age at the time of the study was 8 years old. All of the research in this area documents sensory processing in children adopted from Eastern European countries; more research is needed to determine if findings are similar for children from orphanage environments in other countries.

In summary, the evidence throughout the past 30 years overwhelmingly supports that children who are raised in deprived environments early in life demonstrate significant delays in motor development both before and immediately after adoption (Jenista & Chapman, 1987; Miller & Hendrie, 2000; Van IJzendoorn & Juffer, 2006). Emerging research suggests the same is true of sensory processing development (Cermak & Daunhauer, 1997; Jirikowic, Carmichael, & Kartin, 2008; Lin et al., 2005). It is important to recognize that research on sensorimotor development is limited, has included children residing in an orphanage at the time of evaluation, and does not exclusively reflect those children adopted by U.S. parents. In addition, children who are adopted may represent the healthiest of children raised in orphanages (Miller & Hendrie, 2000). Once adopted, life circumstances vastly improve, and research has shown that children demonstrate resilience and positive adaptation over time.

## RESILIENCE IN PHYSICAL GROWTH AND MOTOR DEVELOPMENT

Despite the prevalence of developmental delays in many international adoptees, most children make rapid gains after adoption. There have been several well-designed studies tracking the baseline growth and development of Romanian adoptees and following their development over time. Johnson and colleagues (1992) reported one 16-month-old child with initial global developmental delays who demonstrated catch-up of 6–10 months in a period of just 3½ months. In two studies, one from the United Kingdom (Kreppner et al., 2007; O'Connor et al, 2000; Rutter & the English and Romanian Adoptees Study Team, 1998; Rutter et al., 1999) and another from British Columbia (Ames, 1997), both comparing Romanian adoptees to control groups of biologically born children from the country of origin, marked delays in physical growth and development at arrival resolved over time. In the United Kingdom study, 59% of Romanian children (n=144) had a Denver developmental quotient score of under 50 (indicating significant impairment) at arrival and another 15% had scores placing them in the mildly impaired range. There were 58 children at arrival with height and weight measurements 1.5 standard deviations below the mean for a U.K. population. In many cases, birth parent information (height and weight) was unknown, so comparison to a U.K. population was the only measure available. All Romanian children in the study had been reared in institutions from infancy for durations extending up to 42 months. In the study from British Columbia, every child demonstrated some delay and 78% were delayed in all areas assessed (fine and gross motor skills, personal, social, and language) at arrival.

Children in the study group from British Columbia demonstrated average catch-up of 2 developmental quotient points per month during the first year of placement with adoptive families. All children in the study group from the United Kingdom demonstrated marked catch-up in weight and head circumference. Notably, for all children institutionalized for 6–24 months, catch-up in weight was complete by follow-up evaluation at 6 years of age. Those institutionalized for longer than 24 months demonstrated similar but incomplete catch-up. Catch-up for head circumference, however, was incomplete for all children and stayed approximately 1.5 standard deviations below the mean despite duration of institutionalization. Authors asserted that catch-up in head circumference, therefore, could not be fully attributed to improved nutri-tion and body growth (O'Connor et al., 2000). In both studies there was evidence of a dose-dependent response to the effects of early deprivation; children who were institutionalized for shorter durations demonstrated the most complete catch-up in comparison to mother country born peers. This pattern was true even for the developmental areas in which none of the children demonstrated complete catch-up; children institution-alized for shorter duration still showed the greatest degree of recovery (Ames, 1997; O'Connor et al., 2000, Rutter & the English and Romanian Adoptees Study Team, 1998).

Resilience in children adopted from adverse early living conditions is still not fully understood and more studies from other countries are needed, but many theorize that the adoption event itself stimulates brain development in a number of ways. Researchers studying motor skill relearning after brain injury in both animal and human models have identified the remarkable ability of intact brain tissue to be functionally modified during the recovery process (Nudo, 1998). This is a process known as brain plasticity (Barinaga, 1994), cortical plasticity (Nudo, 1998), or cortical reorganization (Liepert, Bauder, Miltner, Taub, & Weiller, 2000). Whichever label is used, the meaning is the same; brain tissue can modify itself, particularly during recovery from brain injury. Some have suggested that islands of recovery are possible even many years after injury (Johansson, 2000). Others have documented the im-portance of a guided rehabilitation program in supporting the sponta-neous recovery that the body begins on its own to help an individual recover to the highest degree (Liepert et al., 2000; Nudo, 1998; Nudo, Wise, SiFuentes, & Milliken, 1996).

In the infant brain, neural connections are constantly emerging, evolving and fading away as the child has new experiences. Stronger pathways try to forge themselves and others begin to fade from lack of need or use. This process, referred to as pruning, explains why French children end up with a strong pathway for making a rolled *r* sound and Japanese children do not because of the absence of an *r* sound in the Japanese language (Stock-Kranowitz, 2005). The previously discussed research on plasticity, and the potential for recovery after injury, offers an interesting method to understand the rapid rate of catch-up and resilience that internationally adopted children generally display. This is an area of inquiry that deserves more attention, as it holds remarkable importance in the development of intervention methods that would maximize growth and developmental catch-up following adoption.

Van IJzendoorn and Juffer (2006) described a model of rapid catch-up and neuro-plasticity that has been documented in international adoptees after placement with adoptive families. In a meta-analysis of more than 270 studies that included more than 230,000 adopted and nonadopted children from various countries and preadoption backgrounds, the authors concluded that the act of adoption itself is a successful intervention leading to rapid catch-up. In their described model, physical growth is the first area of catch-up attained. However, they also reported that the more time children spent in institutional care, the more their physical growth lagged behind their nonadopted peers. In a subsequent meta-analysis by Van IJzendoorn, Bakersmans-Kranenburg, and Juffer (2007) of 33 papers examining 122 studies, internationally adopted children showed impressive and almost complete catch-up growth in height and weight after adoption except children adopted at 9 years of age or older, but these findings were speculated to be confounded by precocious puberty. Catch-up of head circumference growth was much slower and remained incomplete regardless of duration of institutionalization and age at adoption.

Following physical catch-up, children make gains in both cognition and attachment that the authors attribute to the development of basic trust. They conclude that for some children, particularly those adopted after spending less than 1 year in a nonpermanent, deprived care environment, the catch-up can be full and swift. For others, though, the long-term consequences of early neglect, deprivation, and trauma may resurface throughout the lifespan as issues about self-esteem, trust, and maladaptive behaviors.

While the majority of children demonstrate incredible catch-up in all or many areas of development, some do not. It is still unclear to researchers and adoption-care professionals why some children do not demonstrate the resilience that their peers do. Miller (2005c) wrote that motor delays often resolved quickly whereas language and cognitive delays took longer. It seems to be true that after a certain age, some degree of development cannot be regained no matter the richness of the postplacement conditions. This is not to suggest that parents should not continue to try and give their adoptive children every chance to grow and learn, rather it is simply important that adoptive parents understand the limitations that early deprivation can place on children's abilities to achieve milestones that same-age, nonadopted peers meet. This is when it can be highly beneficial to seek an evaluation with professionals with expertise in the care of internationally adopted children.

## ▼▼▼ IMPLICATIONS

A primary goal of an international adoption professional should be to help potential adoptive parents make informed decisions about whether they have the resources—emotional, social, spiritual, financial, and otherwise—to parent a certain child. For example, Johnson and Dole (1999) wrote, "While some parents may have both the desire and resources to successfully bring a special-needs child into their family, others do not" (p. 36). Weitzman and Albers (2005) suggested that adoptive parents of children who have had adverse early experiences must be extraordinarily good parents in order to help their children navigate the complex issues surrounding their early lives. There are data that highlight a higher than normal level of stress among some adoptive parents, particularly those dealing with children with special needs and children with difficult behaviors (McGlone, Santos, Kazama, Fong, & Mueller, 2002). It is the challenge of the international adoption and professional communities to organize and provide adequate support to adoptive families so that even children who require more than good enough parenting are able to thrive along with their other family members.

Stephen, Caitlyn, and Eric demonstrate many of the physical health complexities that have been discussed in this chapter and hopefully illuminate how important it is to have a comprehensive medical evaluation soon after adoption by professionals knowledgeable in the issues that impact the health and development of children adopted abroad. The postadoption evaluation of an internationally adopted child by a private physician specialist or by an interdisciplinary team is often a long and detailed visit during which the physician or team tries to piece together as much accurate information about the child's history and current health status as possible. It is absolutely essential to bring to this evaluation all preadoption medical reports, including birth country immunization records. Without this information, the physician or team cannot appropriately assess the child's specific growth pattern and individual risk factors for nutritional deficiencies and infectious diseases. Likewise, decisions cannot be made regarding whether it is necessary to restart age-appropriate vaccinations or check blood levels for protective antibodies so that in-country immunizations can be accepted.

Recommendations for screening of medical conditions and infectious diseases in internationally adopted children can be found in the *American Academy of Pediatrics' Red Book: Report of the Committee on Infectious Diseases, 28th Edition* (AAP, 2009). The recommendations include general screening for all children as well as specific recommendations for certain countries or geographical areas. It is important to recognize that because many of the screening tests are for infectious diseases or medical conditions that may be silent, it is essential to screen a child who appears healthy and shows no signs of an infectious disease, untreated medical conditions, growth failure, or developmental delay. Although most infants born with untreated congenital syphilis will be symptomatic at birth or in the weeks or months immediately following birth, syphilis can remain latent for years. Likewise, if HIV infection has not become symptomatic in the first 2 years of life, it may remain silent until the child's elementary or preteen years. Most children who acquire hepatitis B and C infection from their birth mothers will remain asymptomatic until early adulthood. Screening is crucial for all children adopted abroad.

Interdisciplinary developmental evaluations by professionals with international adoption experience are also recommended. These evaluations can be provided through international adoption clinics, early childhood special education teams, or school-based special education teams (Dole, 2005). It is recommended that these evaluations occur soon after adoption so that if services are needed, they can be provided as soon as possible. There are, however, some indications that a referral to early intervention services; direct occupational, physical, or speech therapy; or a clinical or developmental psychologist is warranted immediately. If the child is younger than 2 years old, the following are risk factors that should alert the need for immediate referral: 1) a diagnosis known to affect development (Down syndrome, cerebral palsy, fetal alcohol syndrome, etc.),

2) absent or poor eye contact, 3) history of abuse, 4) limited or absent vocalizations, and 5) a medical condition known to affect development (club feet, malnutrition, abnormal vision and/or hearing, etc.). If the child is older than 2 years old, the aforementioned conditions apply, with the addition of the following: 1) aggressive or violent behaviors, 2) learning disabilities, 3) indiscriminate friendliness, 4) language delays in native tongue, and/or 5) poor attention span (Johnson & Dole, 1999). It is common, however, for children to undergo a period of disruption as they adjust to a new time zone, new foods and living conditions, and new interaction with a family unit. It is important that the evaluation team takes this into consideration when making diagnoses and further referrals. If the child is lacking in any area of development, the evaluating physician or therapist may give the family an individualized plan designed to help the child catch up and may suggest a follow-up evaluation in 3–6 months if the child does not show improvement. Johnson and Dole used the term *watchful waiting* to describe the attitude that health professionals ought to take when completing developmental screens during the initial postadoption evaluation.

Watchful waiting can be helpful and necessary in other scenarios as well; consider the case about Eric. It is important to recognize that the professionals who evaluated Eric understood the special circumstances involved with the care of an internationally adopted child. His advanced motor skills could have been praised and the cause of those scores overlooked until much later, when an inaccurate age assignment may reveal itself in other ways. Just as evidence of significant delays should be suspect, so too should evidence of significantly high achievement. This is not to suggest that adoptive parents should not have high hopes for their child, but to caution that results of developmental screenings can yield important information to help parents understand their child's development.

## KEY POINTS

▶ Parents and practitioners need to be aware of significant health concerns of internationally adopted children, including: growth and nutritional deficiencies, infectious diseases, developmental delays, environmental exposures, and immunization status.

▶ It is paramount that the internationally adopted child is appropriately screened upon arrival to the United States. A practitioner with expertise and experience in adoption medicine best performs the postadoption evaluation.

▶ All internationally adopted children should be screened for infectious diseases and undiagnosed medical conditions because many diseases can be silent for months and even years after adoption.

▶ Many internationally adopted children will experience rapid catch-up in growth and development in the 6–12 months following adoption and will therefore have increased nutritional requirements. Failure to recognize these needs may be detrimental to their health and development. Additional research is critical in this area.

▶ Developmental screening tools can be helpful when identifying areas of development to monitor. Areas of development that were initially observed as low may quickly resolve as the child adjusts.

## REFERRAL INDICATORS

▶ Primary care physicians can reference the American Academy of Pediatrics, Medical Evaluation of Internationally Adopted Children for Infectious Diseases in L.K. Pickering, C.J. Baker, D.W. Kimberlin, S.S. Long, (Eds.), *Red Book: 2009 Report of the Committee on Infectious Diseases* 28th ed., for a more in-depth postadoption evaluation, and when the primary care physician is not knowledgeable or unwilling to complete the recommended screening, consultation with an adoption medical specialist or specialty team is indicated.

▶ Children with growth parameters, particularly length-to-weight ratios and/or body mass indices that remain below the 3rd percentile at 6 months after adoption, and children who at any time have weight-to-length ratios and/or body mass indices that are declining, should be evaluated by a physician or medical team with expertise in internationally adopted children. If adoption medicine professionals are not available, other qualified pediatric subspecialists such as endocrinologists, infectious disease specialists, or gastroenterologists can be sought for support.

▶ If a child is adopted with a diagnosis known to affect development (Down syndrome, cerebral palsy, fetal alcohol syndrome, etc.), referral to appropriate medical subspecialists and therapists (geneticists, endocrinologists, occupational therapists, physical therapists, speech–language therapists) is indicated.

▶ If the following conditions persist longer than 6 months after living with the adoptive family, referral to an occupational therapist specializing in pediatric care is indicated for a sensory evaluation: absent or poor eye contact, repetitive self-stimulatory behaviors, poor attention span, clumsiness that interferes with daily activity, and delays of 50% or more in gross motor, fine motor, or self-care development.

▶ Most states have an affordable early intervention program for children younger than 3 years of age. Internationally adopted children who demonstrate delays of 50% or greater in two or more areas of development are generally eligible to receive therapy through these programs. In some states, children with developmental delays of 30% or greater will qualify for services. Many of these programs are accessed through local school districts.

## REFERENCES

Albers, L.H., Johnson, D.E., Hostetter, M.K., Iverson, S., & Miller, L.C. (1997). Health of children adopted from the former Soviet Union and Eastern Europe:

Comparison with pre–adoptive medical records. *The Journal of the American Medical Association*, 278, 922–924. Retrieved June 2, 2011, from http://jama.ama-assn.org/content/278/11/922.full.pdf

American Academy of Pediatrics. (2009). Medical evaluation of internationally adopted children for infectious diseases. In L.K. Pickering, C.J. Baker, D.W. Kimberlin, S.S. Long (Eds.), *Red book: 2009 Report of the committee on infectious diseases* (28th ed., pp. 177–184). Elk Grove Village, IL: American Academy of Pediatrics.

Ames, E.W. (1997). *The development of Romanian orphanage children adopted to Canada.* Burnaby, BC: Simon Fraser University.

Armario, A., Castellanos, J.M., & Balasch, J. (1984). Adaptation of anterior pituitary hormones to chronic noise stress in male rats. *Behavioral and Neural Biology, 41,* 71–76.

Armario, A., Lopez-Calderon, A., Jolin, T., & Castellanos, J.M. (1986). Sensitivity of anterior pituitary hormones to graded levels of psychological stress. *Life Sciences, 39,* 471–475.

Aronson, J. (2000). Medical evaluation and infectious considerations on arrival. *Pediatric Annals, 29,* 218–223.

Ayres, A.J. (1960). Occupational therapy for motor disorders resulting from impairment of the central nervous system. *Rehabilitation Literature, 21,* 302–310.

Ayres, A.J. (1964). Tactile functions: Their relation to hyperactive and perceptual motor behavior. *American Journal of Occupational Therapy, 18,* 6–11.

Ayres, A.J. (1979). *Sensory integration and the child.* Los Angeles, CA: Western Psychological Services.

Ayres, A.J. (1985). *Developmental dyspraxia and adult–onset apraxia.* Torrance, CA: Sensory Integration International.

Ayres, A.J. (1989). *Sensory integration and praxis tests (Manual).* Los Angeles, CA: Western Psychological Services.

Barinaga, M. (1994). Watching the brain remake itself. *Science, 266,* 1475–1476.

Barnes, R.H. (1976). Dual role of environmental deprivation and malnutrition in retarding intellectual development. *A. G. Hogan Memorial Lecture: American Journal of Clinical Nutrition, 29,* 912–917. Retrieved June 2, 2011, from http://www.ajcn.org/content/29/8/912.full.pdf+html

Beery, K.E., Buktenica, N., & Beery, N.A. (2005). *BEERY™ VMI (The Beery-Buktenica developmental test of visual–motor integration), 5th ed.* Eagan, MN: Pearson Assessments.

Blumenfeld, H. (2002). *Neuroanatomy through clinical cases.* Sunderland, MA: Sinauer Associates.

Bly, L. (1994). *Motor skills acquisition in the first year.* Tucson, AZ: Therapy Skill Builders.

Brown, G.M., & Martin, J.B. (1974). Corticosterone, prolactin, and growth hormone responses to handling and new environment in the rat. *Psychosomatic Medicine, 36,* 241–247. Retrieved June 2, 2011, from http://www.psychosomaticmedicine.org/content/36/3/241.full.pdf

Casler, L. (1975). Supplementary auditory and vestibular stimulation: Effects on institutionalized infants. *Journal of Experimental Child Psychology, 19,* 456–463.

Cech, D., & Martin, A. (1995). *Functional movement development across the life span.* Philadelphia: W.B. Saunders.

Cermak, S.A. (1994). Romanian children demonstrate sensory defensiveness. *Attachments, 1,* 5–6.

Cermak, S.A., & Daunhauer, L.A. (1997). Sensory processing in the postinstitutionalized child, *American Journal of Occupational Therapy, 51,* 500–507.

Chakraborty, R., & Luck, S. (2008). Syphilis is on the increase: The implications for child health. *Archives of Disease in Childhood, 93,* 105–109.

Church, M.W., & Abel, E.L. (1998). Fetal alcohol syndrome: Hearing, speech, language, and vestibular disorders. *Obstetrics and Gynecology Clinics of North America, 25-85.*

Davies, J., & Bledsoe, J.(2005). Prenatal alcohol and drug exposures in adoption. *Pediatric Clinics of North America, 52,* 1369–1393.

Davies, P.L., & Gavin, W.J. (2007). Validating the diagnosis of sensory processing disorders using EEG technology. *American Journal of Occupational Therapy, 61,* 176–189. Retrieved June 2, 2011, from http://www.spdfoundation.net/pdf/davies_gavin.pdf

Dole, K. (2005). Education and internationally adopted children: Working collaboratively with schools. *Pediatric Clinics of North America, 52,* 1445–1461.

Exner, C.E. (2005). Development of hand skills. In J. Case-Smith (Ed.), *Occupational therapy for children, 4th ed.* (pp. 289–328). St. Louis: Mosby.

Folio, M.R., & Fewell, R.R. (2002). *Peabody developmental motor scales. 2nd ed.* New York: Riverside Publishers.

Gartner, L.P., & Patestas, M.A. (2003). *Essentials of neuroanatomy. 2nd ed.* Baltimore, MD: Jen House Publishing Company.

Gunner, M.R., Morison, S.K., Chisholm, K., & Schuder, M. (2001). Salivary cortisol levels in children adopted from Romanian orphanages. *Development and Psychopathology, 13*, 611–628.

Haradon, G., Bascom, B., Dragomir, C., & Scripcaru, V. (1994). Sensory functions of institutionalized Romanian infants: A pilot study. *Occupational Therapy International, 1*, 250–260.

Hoksbergen, R., ter Laak, J., Rijk, K., van Dijkum, C., & Stoutjesdijk, F. (2005). Post-institutional autistic syndrome in Romanian adoptees. *Journal of Autism and Developmental Disorders, 35*, 615–623.

Hostetter, M.K., Iverson, S., Dole, K., & Johnson, D. (1989). Unsuspected infectious diseases and other medical diagnoses in the evaluation of internationally adopted children. *Pediatrics, 83*, 559–564.

Ireton, H.R. (2005a). *Child development chart: First five years.* Retrieved June 2, 2011, from http://www.richmondchildrenfirst.ca/parents/child_development_chart.pdf

Ireton, H.R. (2005b). *Infant development chart: First 18 months.* Retrieved June 3, 2011, from http://www.childdevrev.com/page7/page16/assets/IDIChart.pdf

Jantz, J., Blosser, C., & Fruechting, L. (1997). A motor milestone change noted with a change in sleep position. *Archives of Pediatric and Adolescent Medicine, 151*, 565–568.

Jenista, J.A. (2000). Pre-adoption review of medical records. *Pediatric Annals, 29*, 212–215.

Jenista, J.A., & Chapman, D. (1987). Medical problems of foreign-born adopted children. *American Journal of Diseases of Children, 141*, 298–302.

Jirikowiz, T., Carmichael Olson, H., & Kartin, D. (2008). Sensory processing, school performance, and adaptive behavior of young school-age children with fetal alcohol spectrum disorders. *Physical and Occupational Therapy in Pediatrics, 28*, 117–136.

Johansson, B.B. (2000). Brain plasticity and stroke rehabilitation: The Willis lecture. *Stroke, 31*, 223–230.

Johnson, D.E. (2000). Long-term medical issues in international adoptees. *Pediatric Annals, 29*, 234–241. Retrieved June 2, 2011, from http://www.peds.umn.edu/iac/prod/groups/med/@pub/@med/documents/asset/med_49462.pdf

Johnson, D.E. (2002). Adoption and the effect on children's development. *Early Human Development, 68*, 39–54.

Johnson, D.E. (2005). International adoption: What is fact, what is fiction, and what is the future? *Pediatric Clinics of North America, 52*, 1221–1246.

Johnson, D.E., & Dole, K. (1999). International adoptions: Implications for early intervention. *Infants and Young Children, 11*, 34–45. Retrieved June 2, 2011, from http://www.peds.umn.edu/iac/prod/groups/med/@pub/@med/documents/asset/med_49295.pdf

Johnson, D.E., Miller, L.C., Iverson, S., Thomas, W., Franchino, B., Dole, K., et al. (1992). The health of children adopted from Romania. *The Journal of the American Medical Association, 268*, 3446–3451.

Kreppner, M., O'Connor, T.G., Rutter, M., & the English and Romanian Adoptees Study Team. (2001). Can inattention/overactivity be an institutional deprivation syndrome? *Journal of Abnormal Child Psychology, 29*(6), 513–518.

Kreppner, J.M., Rutter, M., Beckett, C., Castle, J., Colvert, E., Groothues, et al. (2007). Normality and impairment following profound early institutional deprivation: A longitudinal follow-up into early adolescence. *Developmental Psychology, 43*, 931–946.

Ladage, J.S. (2009). Medical issues in international adoption and their influence on language development. *Topics in Language Disorders, 29*(1), 6–17.

Lane, G.K., & Oates, R.K. (1988). Congenital syphilis has not disappeared. *The Medical Journal of Australia, 15*(148), 171–174.

Leipert, J., Bauder, H., Miltner, W.H.R., Taub, E., & Weiller, C. (2000). Treatment-induced cortical reorganization after stroke in humans. *Stroke, 31*, 1210–1216. Retrieved June 2, 2011, from http://stroke.ahajournals.org/cgi/content/full/strokeaha;31/6/1210

Lin, S.H., Cermak, S., Coster, W.J., & Miller, L. (2005). The relationship between length of institutionalization and sensory integration in children adopted from Eastern Europe. *American Journal of Occupational Therapy, 59*, 139–147.

Lozoff, B., & Georgieff, M. (2006). Iron deficiency and brain development. *Seminars in Pediatric Neurology, 13*, 158–165.

McGlone, K., Santos, L., Kazama, L., Fong, R., & Mueller, C. (2002). Psychological stress in adoptive parents of special-needs children. *Child Welfare, 81*(2), 151–171.

Mandalakas, A.M., Kirchner, H.L., Iverson, S., Chesney, M., Spencer, M.J., Sidler, A., et al. (2007). Predictors of mycobacterium tuberculosis infection in international adoptees. *Pediatrics, 120*, e610–e616.

Mason, P., & Narad, C. (2005). International adoption: A health and developmental prospective. *Seminars in Speech and Language, 26*(1), 1–9.

May-Benson, T. A., & Cermak, S. A. (2007). Development of an assessment for ideational praxis. *American Journal of Occupational Therapy, 61*, 148–153. Retrieved June 2, 2011, from http://www.spdfoundation.net/pdf/may-benson_cermak.pdf

Miller, L.C. (2000). Initial assessment of growth, development, and the effects of institutionalization in internationally adopted children. *Pediatric Annals, 29*, 224–232.

Miller, L.C. (2005a). *The handbook of international adoption medicine: A guide for physicians, parents, and providers.* New York: Oxford University Press.

Miller, L.C. (2005b). International adoption: Infectious diseases issues. *Clinical Infectious Diseases, 40*, 286–293.

Miller, L.C. (2005c). Immediate behavioral and developmental considerations for internationally adopted children transitioning to families. *Pediatric Clinics of North America, 52*, 1311–1330.

Miller, L.C., Chan, W., Comfort, K., & Tirella, L. (2005). Health of children adopted from Guatemala: Comparison of orphanage and foster care. *Pediatrics, 115*, e710–e717.

Miller, L.C., Chan, W., Litvinova, A., Rubin, A., Comfort, K., Tirella, L., et al. (2006). Fetal alcohol spectrum disorders in children residing in Russian orphanages: A phenotypic survey. *Alcoholism: Clinical and Experimental Research, 30*(3), 531–538.

Miller, L.C., Chan, W., Litvinova, A., Rubin, A., Tirella, L., & Cermak, S. (2007). Medical diagnosis and growth of children residing in Russian orphanages. *Acta Paediatrica, 96*, 1765–1769.

Miller, L.C., & Hendrie, N.W. (2000). Health of children adopted from China. *Pediatrics, 105*, e1–e6.

Miller, L.C., Tseng, B., Tirella, L.G., Chan, W., & Feig, E. (2008). Health of children adopted from Ethiopia. *Maternal Child Health Journal, 12*, 599–605.

Miller, L.J., Anzalone, M.E., Lane, S.J., Cermak, S.A., & Osten, E.T. (2007). Concept evolution in sensory integration: A proposed nosology for diagnosis. *American Journal of Occupational Therapy. 61*, 135–140. Retrieved June 2, 2011, from http://www.spdfoundation.net/pdf/Miller_Anzalone.pdf

Needlman, R. (2007). Growth and development. In R.E. Bherman, R.M. Kliegman, & H.B. Jenson (Eds.), *Nelson textbook of pediatrics, 16th ed.* (pp. 23–30). Philadelphia: Saunders.

Neumann, C.G., Gewa, C., & Bwibo, N.O., (2004). Child nutrition in developing countries. *Pediatric Annals, 33*, 658–674. Retrieved June 2, 2011, from http://www.ph.ucla.edu/epi/faculty/detels/ph150/Neumann_Malnutrition.pdf

Nichols, D.S. (2005). Development of postural control. In J. Case-Smith (Ed.), *Occupational therapy for children, 4th ed.* (pp. 266–288). St. Louis: Mosby.

Nudo, R.J. (1998). Role of cortical plasticity in motor recovery after stroke. *Neurology Report, 22*(2), 61–67.

Nudo, R.J., Wise, B.M., SiFuentes, F., & Milliken, G.W. (1996). Neural substrates for the effects of rehabilitative training on motor recovery after ischemic infarct. *Science, 272*, 1791–1794.

O'Connor, T.G., Rutter, M., Beckett, C., Keaveney, L., Kreppner, J.M., & the English and Romanian Adoptees Study Team. (2000). The effects of global severe privation on cognitive competence: Extension and longitudinal follow-up. *Child Development, 71,* 376–390.

Parham, L.D., & Mailloux, Z. (2005). Sensory integration. In J. Case-Smith (Ed.), *Occupational therapy for children, 4th ed.* (pp. 289–328). St. Louis: Mosby.

Piaget, J. (1954). *The construction of reality in the child.* New York: Basic Books.

Provence, S., & Lipton, R. C. (1962). *Infants in institutions: A comparison of their development with family-reared infants during the first year of life.* New York: International Universities Press.

Rutter, M., Andersen-Wood, L., Beckett, C., Bredenkamp, D., Castle, J., et al. (1999). Quasi-autistic patterns following severe early global privation. *Journal of Child Psychology and Psychiatry, 40,* 537–549.

Rutter, M., & the English and Romanian Adoptees Study Team. (1998). Developmental catch-up, and deficit, following adoption after severe global early privation. *Journal of Child Psychiatry, 39,* 465–476.

Saiman, L., Aronson, J., Zhou, J., Gomez-Duarte, C., Gabriel, P.S., et al. (2001). Prevalence of infectious diseases among internationally adopted children. *Pediatrics, 108,* 608–612.

Schafer, D., & Moersch, M. (1981). *The early intervention development profile: Developmental programming for infants and young children.* Ann Arbor, MI: University of Michigan Press.

Schulte, J.M., Maloney, S., Aronson, J., San Gabriel, P., Zhou, J., & Saiman, L. (2002). Evaluating acceptability and completeness of overseas immunization records of internationally adopted children. *Pediatrics, 109,* E22. Retrieved June 2, 2011, from http://www.orphandoctor.com/medical/currentresearch/evaluation.html

Schwartz, I.D. (2000). Failure to thrive: An old nemesis in the new millennium. *Pediatrics in review, 21,* 257–264.

Stadler, L.P., Mezoff, A.G., & Staat, M.A. (2008). Hepatitis B virus screening for internationally adopted children. *Pediatrics, 122,* 1223–1228.

Stock-Kranowitz, C. (2005). *The out of sync child.* New York: The Berkley Publishing Group.

Van IJzendoorn, M.H., Bakersman-Kranenburg, M.J. & Juffer, F. (2007). Plasticity of growth in height, weight, and head circumference: Meta-analytic evidence for massive catch-up and plasticity in physical, socio-emotional, and cognitive development. *Journal of Developmental & Behavioral Pediatrics, 28,* 334–343.

Van IJzendoorn, M.H., & Juffer, F. (2006). The Emanuel Miller memorial lecture 2006: Adoption as intervention. Meta-analytic evidence for massive catch-up and plasticity in physical, socio-emotional, and cognitive development. *Journal of Child Psychology and Psychiatry, 47,* 1228–1245.

Vereijken, B., & Thelen, E. (1997). Training infant treadmill stepping: The role of individual pattern stability. *Developmental Psychobiology, 30,* 89–102.

Verhulst, F.C., Althaus, M., & Versluis-den Bieman, H. (1990a). Problem behavior in international adoptees: I. An epidemiological study. *Journal of the American Academy of Child and Adolescent Psychiatry, 29,* 94–103.

Verhulst, F.C., Althaus, M., & Versluis-den Bieman, H. (1990b). Problem behavior in international adoptees: II. Age at placement. *Journal of the American Academy of Child and Adolescent Psychiatry, 29,* 104–111.

Verhulst, F.C., Althaus, M., & Versluis-den Bieman, H. (1990c). Problem behavior in international adoptees: III. Diagnosis of child psychiatric disorders. *Journal of the American Academy of Child and Adolescent Psychiatry, 29,* 420–428.

Viviano, E., Cataldo, F., Accomando, S., Firenze, A., Valenti, R.M., & Romano, N. (2006). Immunization status of internationally adopted children in Italy. *Vaccine, 24*(19), 4138–4143.

Weitzman, C., & Albers, L. (2005). Long-term developmental, behavioral, and attachment outcomes after international adoption. *Pediatric Clinics of North America, 52,* 1395–1419.

Wilkinson, G.S. (1993). *Wide range achievement test.* Wilmington, DE: Jastak Associates.

Williamson, G.G., & Anzalone, M.E. (2001). *Sensory integration and self regulation in infants and toddlers: Helping very young children interact with their environment.* Washington, D.C.: Zero to Three.

Zhang, J., Merialdi, M., Platt, L.D., & Kramer, M.S. (2010). Defining normal and abnormal fetal growth: Promises and challenges. *American Journal of Obstetrics & Gynecology, 202,* 522–528.

# 3

# Social-Emotional and Relationship Development

## Samantha L. Wilson

---

*"A relationship with a caregiver who is available and responsive to helping the child navigate the demands of development over time is likely to be the most important factor influencing a young child's ability to achieve positive outcomes, maintain competent functioning under stress, and recover from traumatic experiences."*

Zeanah & Doyle Zeanah (2001, p. 17)

---

Patrick was a 7-year-old first grader who resided with both parents and an older sister. He was adopted at 25 months of age from orphanage care in Russia. Little information was known about his prenatal/birth experiences or orphanage history.

At the time of adoption, Patrick appeared healthy, although his parents reported immediate concerns with regard to his hypervigilance, aggression, and avoidance of physical contact. Patrick's parents initially described him as shaky and scared; he often tensed his body when approached by others and actively refused physical comfort by squirming out of his parents' hugs. In the months following adoption, family and peer interactions were overwhelmingly negative and his parents were increasingly distressed by Patrick's aggressive behavior and generally negative mood.

Within 6 months of adoption, the family initiated therapy with a mental health clinician, who was well versed in postinstitutionalized behavior and development. The family remained in contact with this clinician during the subsequent 20 months, during which time Patrick's parents learned to better understand and appropriately respond to his behavior. They became increasingly more competent in redirecting or preventing aggressive behavior. Family-based intervention was eventually supplemented with psychiatric care. When he entered school, Patrick regularly took stimulant medication to reduce impulsive behaviors. He also participated in about 30 hours of neurofeedback (a type of alternative intervention that sought to teach him increased control over his brain's activity). From his parents' perspective, there was little to no direct behavioral improvement following this intervention.

Despite behavioral gains, 5 years after adoption, Patrick's affect remained generally neutral; he smiled minimally and rarely sought to share enjoyment with others. His play interests were described as "more aggressive" than other children his age (e.g., excessive focus on fires and swords).

Patrick's teacher described him as "a nice kid" and indicated that he generally worked hard in class. Nonetheless, his impulsive behavior concerned her; she indicated that she had removed the scissors within the classroom due to concerns about his impulsivity (not necessarily due to fear of overt aggression). An individualized education program (IEP) was developed to provide increased classroom support with regard to behavior regulation (e.g., increased adult assistance during classroom transitions, an incentive system to promote positive behavior). Patrick responded well to this system and, over the course of the school year, significant improvement was reported with regard to his reduced impulsive behavior, increased independence during transitions, and appropriate engagement with learning and peers.

Patrick's postadoption aggressive behavior and limited emotional expression are reflections of delays in social-emotional development. As will be explored in this chapter, many children who have experienc ed prolonged psychological deprivation (i.e., lack of warm, sensitive caregiving) enter adoptive homes with myriad confusing (and at times scary) behavior. The presence of a stable, empathic caregiver in the early years has been increasingly recognized as vital to a young child's behavior regulation and social-emotional development. For many internationally adopted children, such a caregiver is not readily (or consistently) available. Thus children enter adoptive homes without a strong foundation for emotion regulation or positive social interactions. This chapter will highlight the range of social-emotional outcomes for internationally adopted children and aspects of postadoption interactions that ultimately form the basis for their improved social-emotional development.

## TYPICAL SOCIAL-EMOTIONAL DEVELOPMENT

The infant–caregiver relationship has long been recognized as crucial to a child's social-emotional functioning and later personality development (Lieberman & Zeanah, 1995). In an ideal situation, a child spends his or her early years in close connection with caregivers who provide security, affection, nurturance, and stimulation (Cohen & Kaufmann, 2005). The inability to form this relationship can result in failure to thrive during infancy, insecure attachment, aggression or withdrawal, low motivation, and interpersonal difficulties (for reviews, see Lyons-Ruth, Zeanah, & Benoit, 1996; Wilson, 2001). Child neglect and early deprivation undermine the formation of this relationship (Hildyard & Wolfe, 2002).

Unfortunately, such conditions are commonly suspected or confirmed in the early experiences of internationally adopted children, warranting special postadoption support for children and families.

## Child–Caregiver Relationships

The innate drive for social relationships is strong because the alleviation of internal needs relies almost exclusively on other people in the first years of life. *Attachment* refers to an emotional connection between a child and a more powerful adult (e.g., caregiver) that is enduring and provides the child with an identified person from whom to derive comfort and safety (Cassidy, 1999). Although a comprehensive description of attachment theory is beyond the scope of this chapter (see Marvin & Britner, 1999), an introductory outline is provided to serve as a basis from which to understand the emerging social-emotional development within adoptive families. It has been presumed that infants are biologically wired from birth to signal and interact with others (Bowlby, 1969). Thus, attachment describes the biological drive for an infant to seek proximity and reassurance in times of stress from an identified attachment figure in order to ensure safety (Hoffman, Marvin, Cooper, & Powell, 2006). Along with the provision of safety, the presence of an attachment figure fosters a child's exploration, play, and social behaviors (Bretherton & Munholland, 1999), providing the basis of later learning. Consistent with information processing theory (see Chapter 1), the infant's expectations of a caregiver are presumably wired into the brain as a part of the neural networks that are regularly activated in that caregiver's presence. Thus, by the end of an infant's first year, based on repeated interactions, he or she begins to anticipate the primary caregiver's response to bids for comfort and engagement and to act in accordance with these emerging expectations (Egeland, Weinfield, Bosquet, & Cheng, 2000).

Thousands of times throughout an infant's life, he or she experiences a state of arousal (e.g., hunger, discomfort, pain, fear) and signals a caregiver to alleviate the distress. The consistency with which the caregiver responds has an impact on the child's physiological arousal and ultimately forms the basis by which the infant learns about the world and the people within it. All infants who have stable caregivers form attachment relationships within the first year, yet individual differences in the unique dyadic history create differences in the quality of the attachment and can lead to different social-emotional outcomes.

## Secure Attachment

Preferably, an infant's primary caregivers adjust their interactions to appropriately modulate the infant's internal arousal on a consistent basis. That is, a caregiver successfully decodes the infant's cues, determines the nature of the distress, and intervenes to return the infant to a state of contented, physiological calm. When the infant is calm, active exploration and learning (the basis of optimal brain development, see Chapter 4) are more likely to occur. The repeated experience of the caregiver as a consistent, available source of comfort over time forms the basis of a *secure* attachment pattern (Ainsworth, Blehar, Waters, & Wall, 1978). In the context of a secure attachment relationship, the infant will continue to seek that person when distressed and be soothed in the context of relational interactions with that person.

Secure attachment is generally evident within the first 12 months of life if the child has a consistent caregiver. It is associated with a high degree of caregiver sensitivity and responsiveness, that is, attunement (Isabella, 1993). In the context of secure attachment, the child derives comfort and enjoyment from the caregiver; subsequently, the child is secure enough to explore the environment in the caregiver's presence, knowing that the caregiver is available to alleviate distress as it arises. When confronted by a potential stressor (e.g., an unfamiliar person or environmental change), the child increases contact with the caregiver (e.g., eye contact or increased proximity) and assesses the caregiver's response. In times of overt distress or fear, the child shows a marked preference for the caregiver over a less familiar adult. The caregiver is effectively able to soothe and regulate the child's emotional reaction and return the child to a contented, exploratory state (Sroufe & Waters, 1977).

To say a child has a secure attachment pattern is to presume that the child has developed an expectation that the caregiver is safe and physically/emotionally available. As such, secure attachment is a behavioral representation that the child has experienced numerous repetitions of comfort and calm in the historical interactions with the caregiver. But, caregivers are not perfectly accurate in deciphering their children's needs at *all* times, nor should they be expected to be; there are many expectable (and appropriate) missteps in dyadic communication. These missteps, in and of themselves, are not inherently problematic and in fact provide the child with mild, tolerable frustrations that allow him or her to increase regulatory coping. In most cases, a competent (i.e., "good enough") caregiver recognizes the miscues and works to repair them quickly. What is important for the development of secure attachment is that, from the child's perspective, the majority of dyadic interactions are experienced as generally positive and supportive (Crockenberg & Leerkes, 1999).

Children receive enormous social feedback in the context of warm, early relationships. By the nature of secure attachments, children have increased face-to-face interactions, which provide the basis of facial processing and the later ability to recognize emotional states in others. Emotionally, a history of attuned caregiving provides the child with a sense of the world as predictable and manageable. In this manner, the earliest relational interactions are the foundation through which the presence of other people becomes perceived as pleasant and enjoyable, affecting later social connectedness.

## Patterns of Insecure Attachment

Unfortunately, some early caregivers chronically overstimulate their children, neglect their internal states, or are strikingly inconsistent/ ineffective in their interactions. This is the basis for *insecure* attachment patterns. Due to a historical inability to derive consistent comfort from the caregiver, a child identified with an insecure attachment pattern is unsure (i.e., insecure) about his or her safety even in the caregiver's presence (Lieberman & Zeanah, 1995). Children with an *insecure/avoidant* pattern of attachment show a marked avoidance of the caregiver and little emotional reciprocity and tend to show minimal behavioral cues when under stress. Children with an *insecure/resistant* pattern of attachment tend to be exceptionally inhibited in normative exploratory (i.e., play) behaviors and ambivalent in their cues to the caregiver during times of distress. In general, insecure attachment (either avoidant or resistant) is associated with historically lower (or inconsistent) levels of caregiver sensitivity/responsiveness. Children with insecure attachment patterns are less likely to meaningfully explore their environments and have greater difficulty regulating their emotional responses (Sroufe, 1997) than do children with secure attachment relationships.

Perhaps the most problematic insecure attachment pattern is the *disorganized* pattern (Main & Solomon, 1986). The term *disorganized* is used because children have not developed a coherent strategy for coping with environmental stressors and are unable to gain access to the caregiver for comfort in some cases because the caregiver is the source of distress. Children classified with disorganized attachment patterns exhibit contradictory behavior (e.g., intense displays of distress while walking *away* from the caregiver) and may demonstrate overt fear toward the caregiver. Exploration in the caregiver's presence tends to be frenetic (e.g., wild and uncontrolled) with little to no positive interactions. Such a pattern has been highly correlated with frightening or abusive behavior on the part of the caregiver (Green & Goldwyn, 2002). A disorganized attachment pattern is problematic because it represents a child's habitual experience of the caregiver (and by extension, people in general) as overtly nonresponsive (at best) or hurtful (at worst). This attachment pattern has been most consistently linked to later psychopathology within the child (Solomon & George, 1999).

Children who lack warm early relationships may approach others with a combination of ignorance, apprehension, or indifference. Other people have not been paired with pleasure or comfort, and the world is perceived as overwhelming and chaotic. As such, children with insecure attachments represent a graded continuum of attachment problems, with varying degrees of adjustment. And although insecure attachment does not necessarily demonstrate a clinical disorder per se, it tends to be overrepresented in high-risk samples (Zeanah, 2000). In fact, insecure attachment is a significant risk factor in the later development of ambivalent relationships and negative mood states (Noshpitz, Flaherty, & Sarles, 1997). Although outcomes from insecure attachment are less optimal, they are not invariably pathological.

## Attachment and Emotion Regulation

Emotional development is inextricably entwined with early attachment relationships. Not only do emotions emerge in a social context, but self-regulation emerges in the context of caregiving relationships (Sroufe, 1997). Through the attentive presence of the caregiver as indicated within a secure attachment relationship, the child's developing brain becomes more adept at tolerating and regulating high arousal and emotional reactions (Schore, 2001). Specifically, infants in secure relationships experience an externally supported coordination of the autonomic nervous system, which permits physiological balance to be reestablished following stress (Egeland et al., 2000). Over time, the child is increasingly able to tolerate environmental stressors without a resulting elevation in his or her stress response system; that is, he or she remains physiologically calm in the face of stress (see Figure 3.1). Thus, attachment not only regulates a

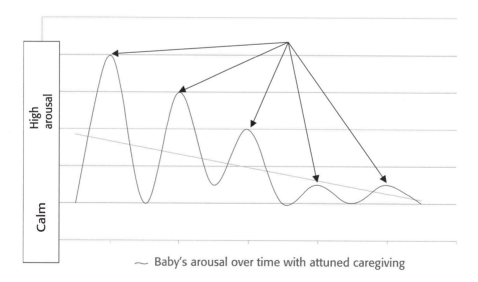

~ Baby's arousal over time with attuned caregiving

**Figure 3.1.**   Demonstration of a child's physiological arousal in the context of attuned caregiving. As the caregiver responds with appropriate care to the child's needs (see arrows), the child returns to a calm state of physiological arousal. (From Perry, B.D. [2009, October]. *The impact of trauma and neglect on the developing child.* Plenary session at the Midwest Conference on Child Sexual Abuse, Madison, WI; adapted by permission.)

child's exploration but is also the means through which the child develops a stress and emotion regulation system, or lack thereof.

Infants with insecure attachment patterns have experienced inconsistent care that can include both under- and overarousal, leading to poor organization of the autonomic nervous system (Egeland et al., 2000). When early caregivers are unreliable or unable to bring relief to the infant, he or she is unable to return to a state of physiological calm or regulate the internal reaction to stress. In severe cases of maltreatment, the caregiver might actually be the cause of the infant's physiological distress, creating an inexplicable bind for the developing infant: The source of distress and comfort are the same. The child does not benefit from external support to regulate arousal, and over time his or her physiological system becomes more reactive and susceptible to overload in the face of even "minor" environmental stressors (see Figure 3.2).

A child like Patrick who develops in the context of inconsistent or neglectful caregiving relationships remains in an elevated physiological state that negatively affects emotion regulation, social connectedness, and stress tolerance. Most problematic is the fact that the brain becomes wired in a "use-dependent" fashion; thus the more a child remains in a state of hyper- or hypoarousal, the more persistent neurological patterns become (Perry, Pollard, Blakley, Baker, & Vigilante, 1995). In other words, ineffective regulatory patterns are in essence "wired" into the

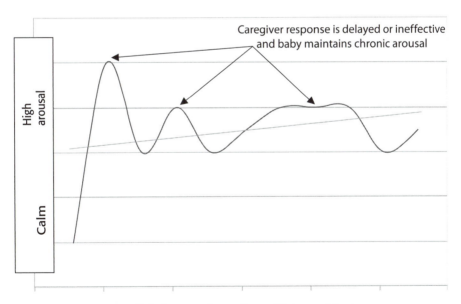

Caregiver response is delayed or ineffective and baby maintains chronic arousal

High arousal

Calm

⌒ Baby's arousal over time with inconsistent care

**Figure 3.2.** Demonstration of a child's physiological arousal in the context of inconsistent caregiving. As the caregiver's response is delayed or ineffective, the child stays at a high level of physiological arousal (see arrows). (From Perry, B.D. [2009, October]. *The Impact of Trauma and Neglect on the Developing Child.* Plenary session at the Midwest Conference on Child Sexual Abuse, Madison, WI; adapted with permission.)

brain over repeated experiences (consistent with information processing theory as described in Chapter 1), creating later problematic response patterns to stress. Furthermore, when the brain is bathed in stress-induced hormones, learning is limited. Consequently, children with this type of attachment pattern are likely to be delayed in their learning (unable to explore their environment in a meaningful manner), stunted in their growth (due to neuroendocrine response in the face of chronic stress), and somewhat disconnected from or excessively fearful of others in their environment.

Children with such caregiving experiences are easily overwhelmed by environmental stress. Consequently, in response to perceived stress, they tend to withdraw from the environment (e.g., stare blankly) or act out in uncontrolled bursts of behavior (e.g., tantrums or aggression). In Patrick's case, even when placed in a context of supportive care within his new family, his physiology had already been established to promote high reactivity to environmental stress or change; he had little to no internal resources to return himself to a state of calm.

## EFFECTS OF PREADOPTIVE ENVIRONMENT ON SOCIAL-EMOTIONAL DEVELOPMENT

For internationally adopted children, early caregivers include nonparental adults within orphanage care centers or foster care homes. As with parents, the consistency with which these early caregivers interact with children in warm, supportive ways is related to optimal early development (Phillips & Adams, 2001). Although individual variation occurs, data suggest that the social deprivation within orphanages is profound and has an impact on a child's social-emotional development. For example, in one study infants in orphanage care were noted to spend the majority (i.e., 65%) of time alone (Tirella et al., 2007). In another study children experienced an estimated 60–100 different caregivers by 24 months of age (St. Petersburg–USA Orphanage Research Team, 2005).

Such structural limitations within orphanage settings are thought to underlie subsequent problems in attachment formation (and later social interactions, emotion regulation, and behavioral adjustment). In fact secure attachment patterns are rarely noted between children and their orphanage caregivers. In contrast to the relatively lower incidence among the general population ($\approx$10%), disorganized attachment is exceptionally common ($\approx$70%) in samples of children within orphanages in the context of their presumed primary caregiver relationship (van den Dries, Juffer, Van IJzendoorn, & Bakermans-Kranenburg, 2009). This corresponds with the high rate noted among children who have experienced significant maltreatment (Cicchetti, Rogosch, & Toth, 2006) and represents a significant risk factor in the lives of internationally adopted children, the majority of whom are adopted from orphanage care.

Increasingly there is evidence that family-based foster care supports improved social-emotional and behavioral functioning for children who would have otherwise remained in orphanage care (Smyke, Zeanah, Fox, & Nelson, 2009). However, research within the U.S. foster care system has documented exacerbation of problematic behavior in the context of foster care (Lawrence, Carlson, & Egeland, 2006). It is unclear whether or not conflicting data are related to variation in comparison samples or differences in the purpose of the particular foster care system under review. Participation in U.S.–based foster care follows substantiated abuse/neglect to protect the child from later abuse, whereas foster care throughout other parts of the world is more often developed for (and funded by) international adoption.

## POSTADOPTION SOCIAL-EMOTIONAL DEVELOPMENT

Given stability of interpersonal interactions and environmental constancy, attachment patterns in children raised by their biological families are generally stable over time. However, in the case of internationally adopted children, consistency of environment and relationships is not presumed, and the variation between the pre- and postadoptive environment can be extreme. This provides a unique avenue for families to create opportunities for new (hopefully secure) attachment relationships. Due to the nature of family disruption (that preceded a child's availability for adoption), orphanage experience (and its potentially incongruent or inconsistent caregiving), and possible experience of neglect/abuse, early nurturing experiences are less likely to occur for children who are ultimately adopted into a permanent family. That is not to say that all children are destined to form insecure attachments with their new parents, but parents will need to appreciate children's early relational experiences to understand their initial relational behaviors within the new family as well as their emerging ability to tolerate stress.

Consistent with catch-up growth often reported following alleviation of malnutrition and social-emotional deprivation, children have the capacity to demonstrate positive recovery in the development of secure attachment. Although cases of children with severe behaviors and extreme limitations in social relationships have garnered increased media attention, it is important to remember that they do not reflect the majority of family experiences. In general, there is a spectrum of relational concern for internationally-adopted children.

Meta-analytic findings on attachment behavior have demonstrated that over time, adopted children were as securely attached as nonadopted children raised with their biological parents (van den Dries et al., 2009). Furthermore, it was noted that children within adoptive families had a remarkably lower rate of disorganized attachment ($\approx$30%) than those observed within orphanage settings ($\approx$70%). This discrepancy represents "an impressive although incomplete catch-up after...placement" (p. 417) within an adoptive family. These meta-analytic data support the view that later corrective attachment experiences can remediate early deprivation and support the potential for the establishment of secure attachment within new caregiver relationships. Children adopted from Asian countries showed a similar percentage of secure attachment patterns than nonadopted children, whereas children from Eastern European countries showed a lower percentage of secure attachment relative to nonadopted children. Age was noted to be a potential moderator for attachment security; children adopted before 12 months of age were more likely to demonstrate secure attachment patterns. Because all children in the study adopted from Asian countries entered their new families before 12 months of age, the authors were unable to separate the potential influence from region of origin (i.e., Asia versus Eastern Europe) from that associated with age at adoption.

Even in the context of emerging relationships with primary caregivers, internationally adopted children (especially those with relatively longer periods of orphanage care) have been noted to demonstrate disinhibited social behavior with unfamiliar adults (O'Connor, Bredenkamp, Rutter, & the English and Romanian Adoptees [ERA] Study Team, 1999). That is, they are more likely to seek out and willingly leave with an unfamiliar adult. Such social behaviors are presumed to be superficial and nonreciprocal, perhaps marking aberrant social behavior that places a child at risk for later social difficulties (O'Connor, Rutter, & the ERA Study Team, 2000; Rutter et al., 2007a). This behavior has *not* been linked with insecure attachment relationships; that is, disinhibited behaviors have been noted to occur even in the context of secure attachment within the primary caregiving relationship (Bruce, Tarullo, & Gunnar, 2009; Zeanah, 2000). Although previously believed to have arisen as an adaptive response to a previous lack of individualized care (e.g., Chisholm, Carter, Ames, & Morison, 1995), disinhibited behavior has been equally reported for children adopted from international foster care (presumably where the child would have experienced more individualized care) *and* for those adopted from orphanages (Bruce et al., 2009). Nonetheless, a sizable portion of children (i.e., 35% of the children adopted from institutional care and 52% of the children adopted from international foster care) showed *no* disinhibited social behavior. When present, disinhibited behavior has been found to be unrelated to parent-reported degree of deprivation, cognitive functioning, or developmental delay; it more likely occurred within a context of overall poor inhibitory control (Bruce et al., 2009). Thus, disinhibited social behavior has been more recently conceptualized as a social cognitive concern combined with an insatiable desire for social contact and impairments in inhibitory control (Gunnar, 2010). The important message within the context of emerging attachment relationships is the understanding that disinhibited social behavior is not invariably a reflection of poor attachment to the child's parent(s).

## POSTADOPTION BEHAVIORAL OUTCOMES

Many factors contribute to a child's long-term behavioral adjustment follow-ing international adoption, including genetic contribution; extent/duration of preadoptive adversity; the child's developmental, language, and emo-tional status at the time of adoption; postadoption developmental trajec-tory; and family and community resources following adoption (Weitzman & Albers, 2005). Although developmental delays and behavioral concerns often coincide, developmental delays often show dramatic improvement in the initial time period following adoption after living in a stable set-ting (see Chapter 3). Conversely, behavioral concerns (when present at adoption) tend to persist over time within the adoptive family (Wilson & Weaver, 2009).

In the initial 6–12 months following adoption, feeding problems (e.g., developmentally inappropriate refusal of solid foods or overeating/hoarding) and stereotyped behavior (e.g., rocking) are often observed in internationally adopted children and most commonly in children adopted from orphanage care (Fisher, Ames, Chisholm, & Savoie, 1997; Weitzman & Albers, 2005). Self-stimulatory and self-aggressive behav-iors are also frequently observed during the initial 6 months following adoption. The majority of these behaviors often subside within the first year of adoption as children develop new ways to regulate internal states and stimulate their senses. For some children, however, such atypical behaviors persist for years, with their duration associated with the length of orphanage care (Beckett et al., 2002).

Early adversity, such as poverty, family disruption, and/or orphanage care, that is a part of the history for many internationally adopted chil-dren represents a developmental stressor that is a substantial risk for later mental health problems (Teicher et al., 2010). A wide range of psychiatric disorders (e.g., mood concerns, substance abuse, behavioral dysfunction) seems to arise as a consequence of childhood adversities, such as abuse, witnessing domestic violence, neglect, or deprivation (Anda et al., 2006); as such, there is little specificity to the myriad problems children can experi-ence following early adverse experiences. Even when children are removed from the context of early adversity, risk for later mental health concerns re-mains (van der Vegt et al., 2009). This is partly due to the brain adaptations that occur following early adversity: smaller hippocampus (implicated in long-term memory), synaptic reduction in areas responsible for planning and problem solving, changes in the corpus callosum (which has an impact on brain efficiency and cross-hemispheric connections), and brain wave abnormalities (for a review see Teicher, Tomoda, & Andersen, 2006). Fur-thermore, early neglect has been shown to affect the growth and differen-tiation of the right prefrontal cortex (Faber, 2000), which is presumed to underlie later difficulty in social relatedness and reduction in appropriate exploration. Long-term presence of stress-related hormones (e.g., cortisol, vasopressin, adrenalin) can lead to collective alterations in brain functioning and information processing (Teicher et al., 2006). These brain changes have an impact on the eventual behavioral outcomes for internationally adopted children in ways we are only just beginning to understand.

The ERA Study is one of the largest cohorts of internationally adopted children (i.e., from Romania into the United Kingdom) that provides some insight into the long-term trajectory of behavioral adjustment and psychosocial functioning for internationally adopted children (Beckett et al., 2002; Castle et al., 1999; Kreppner et al., 2010; Kreppner, O'Connor, & Rutter, 2001; O'Connor et al., 2000; Rutter & the ERA Study Team, 1998; Rutter, Kreppner, & O'Connor, 2001; Rutter, O'Connor, & the ERA Study Team, 2004; Sonuga-Barke, Schlotz, & Kreppner, 2010). This study has monitored postadoption development and behavioral adjustment for a subset of Romanian children who were adopted into U.K. families at various developmental ages and compared their behavior/learning with domestically adopted children within the United Kingdom and nonadopted community children.

By age 6 years (2–4 years postadoption), 70% of the children who were adopted prior to 6 months of age showed typical psychosocial functioning with regard to attachment, minimal (if any) atypical behaviors, appropriate peer interactions, and behavioral compliance, which is a proportion comparable to the sample of U.K. children who were not adopted (Rutter et al., 2001). Nearly 25% of those children adopted from institutions after age 2 showed typical functioning across domains; thus, some children with presumably the greatest degree of early adversity (indexed by length of orphanage care) seemed to be functioning typically by age 6 years. Relational problems (e.g., indiscriminate engagement with strangers) and quasi-autistic behaviors (e.g., repetitive behaviors) were the most prominent behavioral concerns. Length of orphanage care was strongly associated with ratings of inattention/overactivity. Inattention/overactivity is the "common cold" of mental health and can be the overt display of numerous underlying concerns: learning problems, cognitive concerns, language impairments, limited memory capacity, poor emotion regulation, and social stress. In short, there is considerable heterogeneity of behavioral sequelae observed in internationally adopted children (Rutter et al., 2001).

By age 11, about a third of children adopted after 6 months of age received ongoing care from a mental health specialist (Castle et al., 2006). This rate was significantly higher than that noted for children adopted from Romania before 6 months of age (15%) or those adopted from within the United Kingdom (11%). Of those receiving ongoing mental health care, about 60% were predominantly for atypical social relatedness, inattention, or overactivity; another 20% received care for notable concerns with conduct or emotional distress. Thus, despite at least 7 years of enriched postadoptive environment, about half of the children with more than 6 months of orphanage deprivation continued to show multiple impairments (Kreppner et al., 2007), with a sizable proportion receiving mental health services. Consistent with other groups of internationally adopted children (especially children adopted from Eastern Europe, see Lindblad, Weitoft, & Hjern, 2010), externalizing behaviors tended to be predominant concerns.

To date, the ERA Study findings provide the most comprehensive assessment of the long-term behavioral functioning of internationally adopted children. However, the sample includes only children adopted from Romania. It is plausible that findings would be similar for children adopted from other countries with similar experiences of adverse pre-adoptive care, but as yet longitudinal research with children adopted from other countries is limited.

For a subset of people adopted internationally, problems with emotion regulation, mood concerns (e.g., depression, anxiety), and interpersonal relatedness emerge for the first time during adolescence and persist during adulthood (Hjern, Lindblad, & Vinnerljung, 2002; van der Vegt et al., 2009). A slight increase in suicidality has also been noted for a cohort of adolescents adopted as children from Asia and Latin America into Sweden (Hjern, Linblad, & Vinnerljung, 2002). Increased problematic behavior during adolescence may reflect increased complexity of identity development (e.g., "Who am I?") that emerges during adolescence and early adulthood. This aspect of self-understanding is complicated for adoptees as they recognize differences (e.g., physical appearance, ethnic/cultural origins, disabilities, or talents) from their adoptive parents (Grotevant, 1997; Grotevant, Dunbar, Kohler, & Lash Esau, 2000) and perhaps from their adoptive culture. Adolescents who are better able to explain, account for, and understand their preadoptive experiences and ways that they connect to the culture at large are "presumably associated with psychological well-being and resilience" (Grotevant, 1997, p.11).

Internationally adopted children and adolescents have been noted to be overrepresented among those receiving inpatient or outpatient mental health services (Castle et al., 2006) and are referred for mental health services at increased rates compared with nonadopted peers (Juffer & Van IJzendoorn, 2005). Whereas statistics such as these have invariably been construed as indicative of psychological risk on the part of adoptees, Warren (1992) noted a referral bias following normative behavior issues. Specifically, internationally adopted children were more likely to be referred to mental health services for behavior that was relatively normative—(and not generally in need of additional support). Also, because international adoption requires relatively higher family income, increased access to care may facilitate increased rates of referral.

Although internationally adopted children have been noted to have increased rates of behavioral concerns relative to nonadopted peers, such concerns appear to be relevant only for a subset of children and are not inevitable for all. The vast majority of internationally adopted children function well (Bimmel, Juffer, Van IJzendoorn, & Bakermans-Kranenburg, 2003;

Juffer and Van IJzendoorn, 2005). Although adoption of older children can be successful, the older a child is at the time of adoption, the greater the risk for later behavioral concerns or poor social adjustment.

## FACTORS AFFECTING OVERALL ADJUSTMENT AFTER ADOPTION

Although internationally adopted children are often thought to be at higher risk for attachment concerns, entry into a safe, stable home with a consistent caregiver often permits the formation of a secure attachment within the new family. In fact, children in adoptive families are noted to have similar rates of secure attachment (60%–70%) at rates similar to the general population (van den Dries et al., 2009). Although the process by which children integrate into their new family has been less routinely researched, optimal adjustment and social-emotional development are likely a result of numerous child- and parent-related factors.

### Child Factors

When children enter a new family, their behavior bears the stamp of previous experiences. Those who received attentive caregiving in their preadoptive environment are more likely to have appropriate developmental progression, display better behavior regulation, be better able to regulate their stress response, and (following acclimatization) interact with their new parents in positive, meaningful ways. These factors allow the children to communicate internal needs in a more coherent fashion to elicit parental response and support as needed. Assuming the parents are receptive and responsive to the children's cues, a secure attachment relationship with the new caregivers would be expected over time.

However, children who experienced deprivation, abuse, and/or neglect in their preadoptive environment are more likely to have developmental delays, disorganized or confusing behavior, poor physiological regulation, high emotional reactivity, and avoidant or aggressive interactions with their new parents. Even for caregivers who enter new relationships with knowledge and sensitivity to work toward secure attachments with children, child behaviors following neglect, deprivation, or abuse can be complex, confusing, and/or contradictory. When children's signals are subtle or difficult to interpret, the parents' ability to respond in a sensitive manner is compromised (Juffer, Van IJzendoorn, & Bakermans-Kranenburg, 2008). In some cases, new parents may find themselves poorly equipped to respond to their children's emotional distance, refusal to seek comfort, lack of preference for them, sudden mood shifts, noncompliance, or aggression (Lieberman, 2003). This is presumed to be a partial explanation for the sensationalized (although thankfully rare) reports of children being relinquished, abandoned, or harmed by their adoptive parents within a few months/years of adoption.

## Parent Factors

Parenthood requires a major adjustment of time, finances, family roles, and emotional resources. Although parental stress is normative and often unavoidable, high levels of stress affect the quality and sensitivity of parental responses (Judge, 2003). Some of the unique needs of internationally adopted children (e.g., developmental delays, medical illness, and behavioral concerns) are generally recognized to increase a parents' perception of stress (Deater-Deckard, 2004). Parenting a child with an orphanage history and/or problematic behavior (versus isolated cognitive or motor delays) has been correlated with increased perception of parental stress relative to age-/gender-matched nonadopted peers (Judge, 2003; Mainemer, Gilman, & Ames, 1998).

Although adults who adopt internationally tend to be informed and educated (which buffer perceived stress), there are unique aspects to adoptive family formation that may contribute distinctive parental stress (Miller, 2005b). Specifically, adoptive families may have to address infertility, creation of a multiracial family, disclosure of adoptive status, concerns/questions about biological origins, scrutiny by adoption agencies, and the variable and unpredictable time leading to the adoption. Similarly, as with all parents, they nonetheless hold expectations for their new child that may be mismatched with the child's emerging capacity. There is likely variability in how adults adapt to and cope with these issues that could lead to different levels of parental stress within adoptive families.

Variable rates of parental stress have been noted between mothers and fathers (Judge, 2003; Wilson, 2006). Although samples have been small, fathers have tended to report slightly increased rates of stress after adoption compared with mothers, related primarily to the child's behavior. In other studies, parental stress following adoption has been noted to be relatively low (Judge, 2004). At what point the perception of parental stress impedes attuned caregiving within international families is speculative. However, increased stress and problematic adjustment have been correlated with increased rates of postadoption depression (Payne, Fields, Meuchel, Jaffe, & Jha, 2010).

Although research regarding postadoptive depression is relatively new (Miller, 2005a), rates of significant depressive symptoms have ranged from 15% to 30% of parents in the first year following adoption (Gair, 1999; Payne et al., 2010; Senecky et al., 2009). When new parents express negative reactions following adoption (e.g., feeling overwhelmed or disillusioned), they may receive less psychosocial support from previous support systems. Specifically, extended social networks may have difficulty acknowledging or validating those emotions, in essence saying, "They asked for this, so how can they complain?" (Weitzman & Albers, 2005, p. 1415).

During a nationwide survey of parent beliefs and expectations, investigators noted that a large percentage (40%) of parents, in general, expected children to exert significant self-control by age 3; for example, they expected them to ask for help when frustrated in lieu of crying, with about 20% holding this expectation for their 2-year-old (Lerner & Ciervo, 2010). Two thirds of the parents did not believe that young infants would be affected by the parent/caregiver mood or able to experience sadness or fear. Together, these reflect a general disregard for the emotional life of a developing infant/toddler and a general myth of presumed behavioral/emotional control for young children. In the context of adoption, such misconceptions can lead to greater parental stress and may lead new parents to underestimate their children's internal world and subsequent emotional needs within the new family. Such concerns were highlighted by Lieberman (2003), who documented four prevalent themes upon treatment-seeking families within 6 months of adoption: 1) distress about the child's behavior; 2) minimization of the child's expressions of anxiety; 3) missed signs of the child's preference for them; and 4) misattributions of parental rejection during times of child noncompliance or temper tantrums. These themes represent areas of support and education that could be provided proactively to adoptive parents to support their initial transition to parenthood (both in a general sense and with specific regard to adoption).

High degrees of responsiveness and sensitivity have been noted to have a strong influence on promoting optimal child behavior within biologically related families. Rates of responsiveness and sensitivity demonstrated by adoptive parents have generally been noted to be consistent with or somewhat higher relative to income-/education-matched parents with biologically related offspring (Chatham, Tarullo, & Gunnar, 2007). As with biologically related families, parent sensitivity has been related to higher rates of secure attachment and subsequently improved child behavior within adoptive families (Bakermans-Kranenburg, Van IJzendoorn, & Juffer, 2003; Juffer, Hoksbergen, Riksen-Walraven, & Kohnstamm, 1997; Stams, Juffer, & Van IJzendoorn, 2002). However, Castle, Beckett, Rutter, and Sonuga-Barke (2010) noted that long-term variation in child behavior outcomes "was not systematically [associated] with variations in the quality of rearing in the adoptive families" (p. 184) in the ERA Study. Thus, whereas certain elements of parenting (e.g., sensitivity) are likely necessary, they may, at times, be insufficient to promote universally positive child outcomes for children with unknown developmental histories.

## SCREENING FOR SOCIAL-EMOTIONAL AND BEHAVIORAL CONCERNS

Attachment relationships do not exist in isolation and thus are best assessed within an interactive context. As such, the gold standard for assessing attachment relationships has been the "Strange Situation" (Zeanah, 2008). The Strange Situation (Ainsworth et al., 1978) is a 20-minute procedure that consists of two brief child–caregiver separations intended to promote mild stress for the infant/toddler. The child's behavior during reunions provides an example of the child's expectations of the caregiver (a proxy for his or her interactional history) in terms of availability and capability to regulate the child's distress following separation. As such, classification of the attachment relationship is based on children's behaviors both within dyadic interactions with their caregivers as well as their reactions to the increasing stress, with particular attention to behavior toward their caregivers during the reunion episodes. Children who demonstrate contentment/exploration in the caregivers' presence and effective use of the caregivers for support and comfort following distress are considered to have a secure attachment relationship. Children who are unable to explore in the caregivers' presence, avoid the caregivers, or are unable to be soothed following distress demonstrate one of the insecure attachment patterns.

Because the Strange Situation is a specialized procedure that requires extensive training and expertise, it is often outside of the scope of many professionals who serve families who have adopted internationally. Similarly, it is only validated for use with young children (i.e., toddlers). Extension of this practice for older children and adolescents would be inappropriate; e.g., what behaviors would be expected for a 12-year-old to demonstrate appropriate exploration and comfort seeking to define secure attachment? Although there are rating scales available that purportedly assess attachment behaviors for older children and adolescents, such rating scales minimally distinguish between co-occurring mental health conditions and often overendorse "attachment-related" problems. Even developmental attachment research has no substantially validated measures of attachment in middle childhood or early adolescence, leaving the question of what constitutes clinical disorders of attachment for older children less clear (Chaffin et al., 2006). In short, rating scales of the attachment relationship are generally not well standardized and often of little benefit.

Assessment of children with presumed relational impairments should be completed by trained individuals who can rule out competing diagnostic concerns such as a neurological condition (e.g., autism), pervasive developmental delay, genetic syndrome, temperamental variation, or a stress reaction that may have an impact on perceived social relatedness. Behavioral assessment should include information about the child's social interactions over time and across situations and include information regarding interactions with multiple caregivers and peers. At any time it is important to recognize that current behaviors may be a culturally based variation (e.g., eye contact) or reflect adjustment to new or stressful circumstances. A good assessment will include information not only about the child's level of cognitive, language, and social-emotional functioning but also highlight aspects of parental and family functioning that could influence the child's behavior (either positively or negatively).

Because behavioral concerns often reflect an underlying difficulty with cognition, learning, language, or mood regulation (Weitzman & Albers, 2005), assessment by a trained mental health professional well versed in the unique complexities of internationally adopted children is encouraged to determine if the problematic behavior represents a cultural variant, temperamental trait, transitory concern, or a more long-term developmental issue (Wilson, 2009).

## ▼▼▼ IMPLICATIONS

Consistent with the research indicating increased risk with social-emotional problems for internationally adopted children, Patrick demonstrated social-emotional delays. Although Patrick's cognitive scores were generally well developed and within the average to high-average range, there was notable difficulty in the area of visual immediate memory. This was related to Patrick's great difficulty with facial recognition and facial discrimination. Such performance is not inconsistent with the behavioral concerns noted. Generally, children who have difficulty with facial recognition and facial processing demonstrate difficulties with social interactions and behavior regulation, likely related to a subtle right hemisphere dysfunction (which has been noted to be negatively affected by early adversity and deprivation).

Like many children who experience a period of relational disruption and social deprivation, Patrick showed increasing problems with behavior regulation (i.e., overactivity, noncompliance, emotion regulation, inattention, impulsivity). Some inattentive behaviors were reflective of hypervigilance given some of Patrick's early traumatic experiences. Like many children who have experienced early trauma/deprivation, Patrick became hyperaroused in group settings; that is, he was constantly looking for threats. He was often overstimulated and inattentive when he was unsure about his safety.

Patrick also processed negative intentions to benign social interactions, which both reflected and reinforced a negative mood state. This overattribution of anger has been noted in other children who experienced early orphanage care associated with deprivation (Wismer Fries & Pollak, 2004). As such, the hostility with which he viewed the world contributed to an oppositional tendency toward others in his environment. This emotional difficulty inhibited him from having more positive interactions with others, further reinforcing his limited social development.

Children learn to regulate their emotions and behavior in the context of relationships. When early relationships are inconsistent, nonexistent, or abusive, children have a far more difficult time learning to regulate their emotions. As such, Patrick's early history left him insecure and frightened in relationships, further reducing his ability to develop optimal coping skills.

Patrick's relationship with his parents emerged slowly, yet consistently, from the time of adoption. Given his history of trauma and disruptive relationships, however, Patrick often sought attention through inappropriate (and sometimes confusing) means. For example, he would climb on furniture while smiling at his parents (seemingly an effort to consistently engage them with negative behavior) but later hit them when they sought quiet playtime with him. At other times, he ran away from his parents when distressed, leading them to initially conclude that they were not needed. Furthermore, his behavior became quite dysregulated when parental attention was divided from him, albeit briefly; Patrick would scream for 45 minutes whenever his parents were engaged in adult conversation. For years postadoption Patrick required frequent consistent reassurance and positive adult attention to form the basis of emotion/behavior regulation.

Undoubtedly, there was exceptional parental stress within the first months of family adjustment. There was considerable confusion about Patrick's behavior and the perception that he "hated his new family." His parents naively (and perhaps inappropriately) expected Patrick to approach his new setting with interest and gratitude, considering the material improvement it represented over his previous experiences. Further, they had fallen in love with him during the course of their adoption process, reviewing his photos and anticipating his future, increasing the rejection they felt when his immediate behavior was not one of reciprocal affection. His initial aggression seemed erratic and unpredictable, and because his parents were the primary recipients, they felt that Patrick was targeting them as a form of rejection. They, in turn, began to withdraw from him, limiting his parent–child interactions to those times when his behavior needed to be corrected or redirected (or in the worst of situations, restrained). Dyadic interactions had become predictably tense and unpleasant for all within the family, contributing to parental stress and marital discord as adults struggled to understand the meaning behind Patrick's behavior.

Patrick's parents were reflective in their interactions and recognized the emotional toll they were feeling was only a portion of the emotional strain that Patrick had endured. They were wise in recognizing that their network of other parents provided advice that (although well intended) failed to promote any positive behavioral change within their family. Unsolicited advice such as, "He should be put in time-out when he hits to learn that hitting is unacceptable"; "He's old enough to be sleeping alone"; "I spanked my child once and he never did [insert behavior] again" were provided by family and friends in those first months. When Patrick's behavior continued to control the family emotions and his parents felt lost, they were astute enough to seek the support of a seasoned mental health clinician with extensive experience in the behavior of postinstitutionalized children.

The clinician worked initially with both parents to help them understand the impact of Patrick's early history on his current behavior. Although his exact experiences were difficult to confirm, Patrick's initial behavior reflected a child who was overwhelmed and unable to regulate his stress response. As such, he responded to the changes in his environment with a mixture of fear and intense anxiety. His response to such fear was to be aggressive (i.e., fight) or run away (i.e., flee). Helping his parents see that Patrick was not rejecting them in anger but rather that he remained in a constant state of physiological arousal (that prompted fight-or-flight responses) helped them see past the behavior and see the scared child. They further recognized the deleterious impact of discipline that relied on removal and isolation (e.g., time-out), especially in those earliest months. Patrick had learned to regulate his emotions, albeit ineffectively, in isolation already; what he needed was to learn that others in his environment were available and able to help him soothe his physiological system. That required a different parental approach than what his parents had initially practiced.

The first step to soothing his stress response and promote eventual learning was to create an environment that was structured, predictable, and nurturing—tasks all the more challenging when there is not a common language to allow the parents or child to negotiate or predict environmental changes. Parents were encouraged to keep a consistent routine of events throughout the day and to ensure that one or both parents were available to Patrick at all times to play, to comfort him, and to provide for daily necessities (i.e., food and warmth). In the earliest months, increased structure was facilitated by a visual calendar, placed at Patrick's eye level in his room. Pictures of Patrick completing the daily tasks were placed in sequence and turned over as completed so that Patrick could begin to rely on that visual calendar to predict his day. This calendar similarly served as a frequent reminder to his parents for the ongoing need for predictability and consistency.

Bedtime (often a difficult time in most families and especially fearful for children with histories of deprivation and chronic stress) was especially structured to include soothing activities to calm Patrick's hyperaroused system. His parents had to be creative to find activities that soothed Patrick; their initial attempts at holding him in their laps were met with frantic efforts to escape. Patrick, however, seemed calmed by a particular toy that his parents had brought back from Russia. His parents maintained contact with that toy, and over time Patrick began to associate them with the soothing impact of the toy. At that point he was more tolerant of physical touch and allowed his parents to stroke his hair or massage his back briefly before bed.

As these small events unfolded, moments of positive connections began to multiply. Patrick's parents were supported to see the small gains in his emerging relationship and seek patience in themselves and with Patrick in supporting new skills for him. As Patrick's physiological system began to soothe, his learning and language began to expand, providing new opportunities for Patrick to negotiate and predict his environment.

Patrick continued to become highly dysregulated in the first years, and tantrums took on an especially unique quality. His parents began to note that this too was a marker of deprivation; Patrick was unable to cope with stressors and became easily overwhelmed. His parents learned how to stay present and connected with Patrick during those times and reduce the use of isolation that only served to maintain dysregulated behavior.

His parents worked together tirelessly to remain consistently available and supportive. They sought to look beyond the frightening behavior to see the frightened child. With time, patience, and professional guidance, positive parent–child interactions became more frequent and pleasurable to Patrick and both parents. Through continuous collaboration with the school setting, which provided increased structure within the academic day, and ongoing consultation with a mental health clinician, the adults in Patrick's world were able to provide a safe environment. Patrick's oppositional behavior and aggression subsequently decreased. Medication assisted with a reduction in impulsive behavior, which facilitated an increase in positive social interactions. His parents grew to appreciate Patrick's unique strengths and used humor to maintain their own emotional regulation.

Were there not increased collaboration between critical adults, Patrick's social-emotional and behavioral concerns would have affected his engagement in the classroom and eventually his later academic development. In fact early social-emotional competence has been linked to later academic performance over and above that predicted by cognitive skills (Raver & Knitzer, 2002). His parents' resilience, resolve, and willingness to seek support contributed to a new social-emotional trajectory for Patrick.

## CONCLUSION

The adoption of children into the United States from other countries is generally quite positive and undoubtedly creates a new life trajectory for the children. Nonetheless, issues related to early deprivation and stress tolerance (or lack thereof due to the absence of regulatory systems in the preadoptive environment) are important to recognize if children are to flourish within their new environment. The emerging relationships within their families are of particular importance in this regard. It is the character of these relationships (especially that with the new parent or parents) that provide capacity for the children to explore, learn, regulate emotions, engage with others, and ultimately understand and integrate their unique adoptive history.

## *KEY POINTS*

▶ Internationally adopted children are a heterogeneous group. Those with greater degree and duration of early adversity are generally at higher risk for developmental delay, behavior problems, and attachment disturbances.

▶ Cognitive/language skills, behavioral adjustment, and social-emotional development are synergistically interrelated.

▶ Attachment is the means through which children develop a stress regulation system.

▶ Secure attachment is associated with high caregiver responsivity and optimal child development.

▶ By nature of early relational experiences, internationally adopted children can demonstrate attachment behaviors that may be confusing to new caregivers.

▶ Some social-emotional vulnerability derived from early adversity may persist in subtle or overt ways, creating lasting effects on children and families.

▶ Later experiences with sensitive, responsive caregiving can compensate for early adversity. Warm, attentive caregiving is necessary, although not always sufficient, to promote secure attachment.

▶ In some cases, specialized parenting support to address effects of trauma/deprivation on the child's relatedness and stress response can facilitate family relationships and later positive development.

▶ Early childhood mental health providers (e.g., counselor, psychologist) can assist new parents to determine whether or not unusual behaviors/development reflect a cultural variant, temperamental trait, transitory concern, or developmental issue that is more chronic.

## REFERRAL INDICATORS

The following are times when children should be referred for mental health assessment:

▶ Parent(s) report increased distress, anger, or confusion regarding the child's behavior.

▶ There is little reported (or observed) positive emotional interchange between the child and parent(s).

▶ The child seeks comfort preferentially from unfamiliar adults rather than familiar caregivers.

▶ Parent(s) indicate that the child rarely communicates a need or feeling of distress.

▶ The child demonstrates poorly regulated emotions with reduced positive affect, increased irritability, and sadness.

▶ Self-injury that is *worse* in the presence of the parent, relative to other caregivers.

▶ Levels of anxiety that impede appropriate exploration in the presence of the parent.

## REFERENCES

Ainsworth, M.D., Blehar, M.C., Waters, E., & Wall, S. (1978). *Patterns of attachment.* Mahwah NJ: Lawrence Erlbaum Associates.

Anda, R.F., Felitti, V.J., Bremner, J.D., Walker, J.D., Whitfield, C., Perry, B.D., et al. (2006). The enduring effects of abuse and related adverse experiences in childhood: The convergence of evidence from neurobiology and epidemiology. *European Archives of Psychiatry and Clinical Neuroscience, 256,* 174–186.

Bakermans-Kranenburg, M.J., Van IJzendoorn, M.H., & Juffer, F. (2003). Less is more: Meta-analyses of sensitivity and attachment interventions in early childhood. *Psychological Bulletin, 129,* 195–215.

Beckett, C., Bredenkamp, D., Castle, J., Groothues, C., O'Connor, T.G., Rutter, M., & the English and Romanian Adoptees Study Team. (2002). Behavior patterns associated with institutional deprivation: A study of children adopted from Romania. *Journal of Developmental and Behavioral Pediatrics, 23,* 297–303.

Bimmel, N., Juffer, F., Van IJzendoorn, M.H., & Bakermans-Kranenburg, M.J. (2003). Problem behavior of internationally adopted adolescents: A review and meta-analysis. *Harvard Review of Psychiatry, 11,* 64–77.

Bowlby, J. (1969). *Attachment and loss* (Vol. 1). New York: Basic Books.

Bretherton, I., & Munholland, K.A. (1999). Internal working models in attachment relationships. In J. Cassidy & P. R. Shaver (Eds.), *Handbook of attachment: Theory, research, and clinical applications* (pp. 89–111). New York: Guilford Press.

Bruce, J., Tarullo, A.R., & Gunnar, M.R. (2009). Disinhibited social behavior among internationally adopted children. *Developmental Psychopathology, 21,* 157–171.

Cassidy, J. (1999). The nature of the child's ties. In J. Cassidy & P. R. Shaver (Eds.), *Handbook of attachment: Theory, research, and clinical applications* (pp. 3–20). New York: Guilford Press.

Castle, J., Beckett, C., Rutter, M., & Sonuga-Barke, E.J. (2010). Postadoption environmental features. *Monographs of the Society for Research in Child Development, 75,* 167–186.

Castle, J., Groothues, C., Bredenkamp, D., Beckett, C., O'Connor, T., Rutter, M., & the English and Romanian Adoptees Study Team. (1999). Effects of qualities of early institutional care on cognitive attainment. *American Journal of Orthopsychiatry*, *69*, 424–437.

Castle, J., Rutter, M., Beckett, C., Colvert, E., Groothues, C., Hawkins, A., et al. (2006). Service use by families with children adopted from Romania. *Journal of Children's Services*, *1*, 5–15.

Chaffin, M., Hanson, R., Saunders, B.E., Nichols, T., Barnett, D., Zeanah, C., et al. (2006). Report of the APSAC Task Force on attachment therapy, reactive attachment disorder, and attachment problems. *Child Maltreatment 11*, 76–89.

Chatham, M.L., Tarullo, A.R., & Gunnar, M.R. (2007, March). *Predicting attachment behaviors in internationally adopted children from ratings of joint attention at 18 months.* Poster session presented at the Society for Research on Child Development, Boston.

Chisholm, K, Carter, M.C., Ames, E.W., & Morison, S.J. (1995). Attachment security and indiscriminate friendly behavior in children adopted from Romanian orphanages. *Development and Psychopathology*, *7*, 283–294.

Cicchetti, D., Rogosch, F.A., & Toth, S. (2006). Fostering secure attachment in infants in maltreating families through preventive interventions. *Development and Psychopathology*, *18*, 326–349.

Cohen, E., & Kaufmann, R. (2005). *Early childhood mental health consultation* (DHHS Pub. No. CMHS-SVP0151). Rockville, MD: Center for Mental Health Services, Substance Abuse and Mental Health Services Administration.

Crockenberg, S., & Leerkes, E. (1999). Infant social and emotional development in family context. In J. Cassidy & P.R. Shaver (Eds.), *Handbook of attachment: Theory, research, and clinical applications* (pp. 60–90). New York: Guilford Press.

Deater-Deckard, K. (2004). *Parenting stress*. New Haven: Yale University Press.

Dries, L., van den, Juffer F., Van IJzendoorn, M.H., & Bakermans-Kranenburg, M.J. (2009). Fostering security? A meta-analysis of attachment in adopted children. *Children and Youth Services Review*, *31*, 410–421.

Egeland, B., Weinfield, N.S., Bosquet, M., & Cheng, V. (2000). Remembering, repeating, and working through: Lessons from attachment-based intervention. In J. Osofsky & H. Fitzgerald (Eds.), *WAIMH Handbook of infant mental health, Vol. 4: Infant mental health in groups at high risk* (pp. 37–89). New York: Wiley.

Faber, S. (2000). Behavioral sequelae of orphanage life. *Pediatric Annals*, *29*, 242–248.

Fisher, L., Ames, E.W., Chisholm, K., & Savoie, L. (1997). Problems reported by parents of Romanian orphans adopted to British Columbia. *International Journal of Behavioral Development*, *20*, 67–82.

Gair, S. (1999). Distress and depression in new motherhood: Research with adoptive mothers highlights important contributing factors. *Child and Family Social Work*, *4*, 55–66.

Green, J., & Goldwyn, R. (2002). Annotation: Attachment disorganization and psychopathology: New findings in attachment research and their potential implications for developmental psychopathology in childhood. *Journal of Child Psychology and Psychiatry*, *43*, 835–846.

Grotevant, H.D. (1997). Coming to terms with adoption: The construction of identity from adolescence into adulthood. *Adoption Quarterly*, *1*, 3–27.

Grotevant, H.D., Dunbar, N., Kohler, J.K., & Lash Esau, A.M. (2000). Adoptive identity: How contexts within and beyond the family shape developmental pathways. *Family Relations*, *49*, 379–387.

Gunnar, M. (2010). Commentary on deprivation-specific psychological patterns: Effects of institutional deprivation. *Monographs of the Society for Research in Child Development*, *75*, 232–247.

Hildyard, K.L., & Wolfe, D.A. (2002). Child neglect: Developmental issues and outcomes. *Child Abuse & Neglect*, *26*, 679–695.

Hjern, A., Lindblad, F., & Vinnerljung, B. (2002). Suicide, psychiatric illness, and social maladjustment in intercountry adoptees in Sweden: A cohort study. *Lancet*, *360*, 443–448.

Hoffman, K.T., Marvin, R.S., Cooper, G., & Powell, B. (2006). Changing toddlers' and preschoolers' attachment classifications: The Circle of Security intervention. *Journal of Consulting and Clinical Psychology*, *74*, 1017–1026.

Isabella, R.A. (1993). Origins of attachment: Maternal interactive behaviors across the first year. *Child Development, 64,* 605–621.

Judge, S. (2003). Determinants of parental stress in families adopting children from Eastern Europe. *Family Relations, 52,* 241–248.

Judge, S. (2004). The impact of early institutionalization on child and family outcomes. *Adoption Quarterly, 7,* 31–48.

Juffer, F., Hoksbergen, R.A.C., Riksen-Walraven, J.M., & Kohnstamm, G.A. (1997). Early intervention in adoptive families: Supporting maternal sensitive responsiveness, infant-mother attachment, and infant competence. *Journal of Child Psychology and Psychiatry, 38,* 1039–1050.

Juffer, F., & Van IJzendoorn, M.H. (2005). Behavior problems and mental health referrals of international adoptees: A meta-analysis. *Journal of the American Medical Association, 293,* 2501–2515.

Juffer, F., Van IJzendoorn, M.H., & Bakermans-Kranenburg, M.J. (2008). Supporting adoptive families with video-feedback intervention. In F. Juffer, M.J. Bakermans-Kranenburg, & M.H. Van IJzendoorn (Eds.), *Promoting positive parenting* (pp. 139–154). Mahwah, NJ: Lawrence Erlbaum Associates.

Kreppner, J.M., Kumsta, R., Rutter, M., Beckett, C., Castle, J., Stevens, S., et al. (2010). Developmental course of deprivation-specific psychological patterns: Early manifestations persistence to age 15, and clinical features. *Monographs of the Society for Research in Child Development, 75,* 79–101.

Kreppner, J.M., O'Connor, T.G., & Rutter, M. (2001). Can inattention/overactivity be an institutional deprivation syndrome? *Journal of Abnormal Child Psychology, 29,* 513–529.

Kreppner, J.M., Rutter, M., Beckett, C., Castle, J., Colvert, E., Groothues, C., et al. (2007). Normality and impairment following profound early institutional deprivation: A longitudinal follow-up into early adolescence. *Developmental Psychology, 43,* 931–946.

Lawrence, C.R., Carlson, E.A., & Egeland, B. (2006). The impact of foster care on development. *Development and Psychopathology, 18,* 57–76.

Lerner, C., & Ciervo, L. (2010). Parenting young children today: What the research tells us. *Journal of Zero to Three, 30,* 4–9.

Lieberman, A.F. (2003). The treatment of attachment disorder in infancy and early childhood: Reflections from clinical intervention with later-adopted foster care children. *Attachment and Human Development, 5,* 279–282.

Lieberman, A.F., & Zeanah, C.H. (1995). Disorders of attachment in infancy. *Child and Adolescent Psychiatric Clinics of North America, 4,* 571–587.

Lindblad, F., Weitoft, G.R., & Hjern, A. (2010). ADHD in international adoptees: A national cohort study. *European Child and Adolescent Psychiatry, 19,* 37–44.

Lyons-Ruth, K., Zeanah, C.H., & Benoit, D. (1996). Disorder and risk for disorder during infancy and early toddlerhood. In E J. Mash & R.A. Barkley (Eds.), *Child psychopathology* (pp. 457–491). New York: Guilford Press.

Main, M., & Solomon, J. (1986). Discovery of an insecure-disorganized/disoriented attachment pattern. In T.B. Brazelton & M. Yogman (Eds.), *Affective development in infancy* (pp. 95–124). Norwood, NJ: Ablex.

Mainemer, H., Gilman, L.C., & Ames, E.W. (1998). Parenting stress in families adopting children from Romanian orphanages. *Journal of Family Issues, 19,* 164–180.

Marvin, R.S., & Britner, P.A. (1999). Normative development: The ontogeny of attachment. In J. Cassidy & P.R. Shaver (Eds.), *Handbook of attachment: Theory, research, and clinical applications* (pp. 44–67). New York: Guilford Press.

Miller, L.C. (2005a). Immediate behavioral and developmental considerations for internationally adopted children transitioning to families. *Pediatric Clinics of North America, 52,* 1311–1330.

Miller, L.C. (2005b). *The handbook of international adoption medicine.* New York: Oxford University Press.

Noshpitz, J.D., Flaherty, L.T., & Sarles, R.M. (Eds.). (1997). *Handbook of child and adolescent psychiatry* (Vol. 3). New York: Wiley.

O'Connor, T.G., Bredenkamp, D., Rutter, M., & the English and Romanian Adoptees Study Team. (1999). Attachment disturbances and disorders in children exposed to early severe deprivation. *Infant Mental Health Journal, 20,* 10–29.

O'Connor, T.G., Rutter, M., & the English and Romanian Adoptees Study Team. (2000). Attachment disorder behavior following early severe deprivation: Extension and longitudinal follow-up. *Journal of the American Academy of Child and Adolescent Psychiatry, 39*, 703–712.

Payne, J.L., Fields, E.S., Meuchel, J.M., Jaffe, CJ., & Jha, M. (2010). Post adoption depression. *Archives of Women's Mental Health, 13*, 147–151.

Perry, B.D. (2009, October). *The impact of trauma and neglect on the developing child.* Plenary session at the Midwest Conference on Child Sexual Abuse, Madison, WI.

Perry, B.D., Pollard, R.A., Blakley, T.L., Baker, W.L., & Vigilante, D. (1995). Childhood trauma, the neurobiology of adaptation, and "use-dependent" development of the brain: How "states" become "traits." *Infant Mental Health Journal, 16*, 271–291.

Phillips, D., & Adams, G. (2001). Child care and our youngest children. *Future of Children, 11*, 35–51.

Raver, C.C., & Knitzer J. (2002). *Ready to enter: What research tells policymakers about strategies to promote social and emotional school readiness among three- and four- year-old children. Promoting the emotional well-being of children and families, policy paper #3.* New York: National Center for Children in Poverty, Mailman School of Public Health, Columbia University.

Rutter, M., Colvert, E., Kreppner, J., Beckett, C., Castle, J., Groothues, C., et al. (2007a). Early adolescent outcomes for institutionally-deprived and non-deprived adoptees I: Disinhibited attachment. *Journal of Child Psychology and Psychiatry, 48*, 17–30.

Rutter, M., & the English and Romanian Adoptees Study Team. (1998). Developmental catch-up, and deficit, following adoption after severe global early privation. *Journal of Child Psychology and Psychiatry, 39*, 465–476.

Rutter, M., Kreppner, J.M., Croft, C., Murin, M., Colvert, E., Beckett, C., et al. (2007b). Early adolescent outcomes for institutionally deprived and non-deprived adoptees III: Quasi-autism. *Journal of Child Psychology and Psychiatry, 48*, 1200–1207.

Rutter, M.L., Kreppner, J.M., & O'Connor, T.G. (2001). Specificity and heterogeneity in children's responses to profound institutional privation. *The British Journal of Psychiatry, 179*, 97–103.

Rutter, M., O'Connor, T.G., & the English and Romanian Adoptees Study Team. (2004). Are there biological programming effects for psychological development? Findings from a study of Romanian adoptees. *Developmental Psychology, 40*, 81–94.

Schore, A.N. (2001). The effects of secure attachment relationship on right brain development, affect regulation, and infant mental health. *Infant Mental Health Journal, 22*, 7–66.

Senecky, Y., Agassi, H., Inbar, D., Horesh, N., Diamond, G., Bergman, Y.S., & Apter, A. (2009). Post-adoption depression among adoptive mothers. *Journal of Affective Disorders, 115*, 62–68.

Smyke, A.T., Zeanah, C.H., Fox, N.A., & Nelson, C.A. (2009). A new model of foster care for young children: The Bucharest Early Intervention Project. *Child Adolescent Psychiatric Clinics of North America, 18*, 721–734.

Solomon, J., & George, C. (1999). The place of disorganization in attachment theory: Linking classic observations with contemporary findings. In J. Solomon & C. George (Eds.), *Attachment disorganization* (pp. 3–32). New York: Guilford Press.

Sonuga-Barke, E., Schlotz, W., & Kreppner, J. (2010). Differentiating developmental trajectories for conduct, emotion, and peer problems following early deprivation. *Monographs of the Society for Research in Child Development, 75*, 102–124.

Sroufe, L.A. (1997). *Emotional development: The organization of emotional life in the early years.* Cambridge, UK: Cambridge University Press.

Sroufe, L.A., & Waters, E. (1977). Attachment as an organizational construct. *Child Development, 48*, 1184–1199.

St. Petersburg–USA Orphanage Research Team. (2005). Characteristics of children, caregivers, and orphanages for young children in St. Petersburg, Russian Federation [Special Issue]. *Journal of Applied Developmental Psychology: Child Abandonment, 26*, 477–506.

Stams, G.J., Juffer, F., & Van IJzendoorn, M.H. (2002). Maternal sensitivity, infant attachment, and temperament in early childhood predict adjustment in middle childhood:

The case of adopted children and their biologically unrelated parents. *Developmental Psychology, 38*, 806–821.

Teicher, M.H., Tomoda, A., & Andersen, S.L. (2006). Neurobiological consequences of early stress and childhood maltreatment: Are results from human and animal studies comparable? *Annals of the New York Academy of Sciences, 1071*, 313–323.

Teicher, M.H., Rabi, K., Sheu, Y., Seraphin, S.B., Andersen, S.L., Anderson, C.M., et al. (2010). Neurobiology of childhood trauma and adversity. In R.A. Lanius, E. Vermetten, & C. Pain (Eds.), *The impact of early life trauma on health and disease: The hidden epidemic* (pp. 112–120). London: Cambridge University.

Tirella, L.G., Chan, W., Cermak, S.A., Litvinova, A., Salas, K.C., & Miller, L.C. (2007). Time use in Russian baby homes. *Child: Care, Health and Development, 34*, 77–86.

Vegt, E.J.M., van der, Tieman, W., van der Ende, J., Ferdinand, R.F., Verhulst, F.C., & Tiemeier, H. (2009). Impact of early childhood adversities on adult psychiatric disorders: A study of international adoptees. *Social Psychiatry and Psychiatric Epidemiology, 44*, 724–731.

Warren, S.B. (1992). Lower threshold for referral for psychiatric treatment for adopted adolescents. *Journal of the American Academy of Child and Adolescent Psychiatry, 31*, 512–517.

Weitzman, C., & Albers, L. (2005). Long-term development, behavioral, and attachment outcomes after international adoption. *Pediatric Clinics of North America, 52*, 1395–1419.

Wilson, S.L. (2001). Attachment disorders: Review and current status. *Journal of Psychology, 135*, 37–51.

Wilson, S.L. (2006). *International adoption: Exploring the cognitive and motor skills acquisition of infant/toddler adoptees after arrival into the United States* (Unpublished doctoral dissertation). Saint Louis University, St. Louis.

Wilson, S.L. (2009). Attending to relationships: Attachment formation within families of internationally adopted children. *Topics in Language Disorders, 29*, 18–31.

Wilson, S.L., & Weaver, T.L. (2009). Follow-up of developmental attainment and behavioral adjustment for toddlers adopted internationally into the USA. *International Social Work, 52*, 679–694.

Wismer Fries, A.B., & Pollak, S.D. (2004). Emotion understanding in postinstitutionalized Eastern European children. *Development and Psychopathology, 16*, 355–369.

Zeanah, C.H. (2000). Disturbances of attachment in young children adopted from institutions. *Developmental and Behavioral Pediatrics, 21*, 230–236.

Zeanah, C.H. (2008). Observational procedures and psychopathology in young children. *Journal of the American Academy of Child and Adolescent Psychiatry, 47*, 611–613.

Zeanah, C.H., & Doyle Zeanah, P. (2001). Towards a definition of infant mental health. *Zero to Three, 22*, 13–20.

# 4 ◥◥◥◥

# Cognitive Development

## *Samantha L. Wilson*

*"Cognitive development is the product of two interacting influences—brain growth and experience—both of which exert their greatest impact during the first few years of life.... Experience, of course, accrues throughout life, but it is infinitely more potent in the earliest months and years, when synapses are still forming and the brain is at its height of plasticity."*

(Eliot, 2000, p. 392)

Sophie was a 9-year-old fourth grader and the youngest of three children. She and her sisters were adopted as infants from China. Sophie was 13 months old when she immigrated to the United States to join her new family.

Sophie's genetic family history was unknown. Consistent with the stories for many children adopted from China, her parents were told that she had been found in a public park within a couple days of birth. Her birth date had been estimated from the presence of the umbilical cord stump (that generally falls off within 10–21 days after birth). At the time of adoption, the orphanage staff said little about Sophie's development other than she was a "quiet" baby. Within the orphanage, Sophie was noted to be among 25 infants who received care from two to three nannies at a time, rotating every 8–10 hours. There were an estimated 100 children within the entire orphanage. Her parents recalled that the orphanage appeared "clean and well organized." Although their recollections were vague, they recalled a certain "sadness" about the orphanage as they described the bare walls and minimal number of toys available for the children.

Sophie's medical history from the time of adoption was unremarkable; her hearing and vision were measured to be within normal limits. In spite of this positive medical history, she did not verbalize for months following adoption. In fact, the onset of expressive vocalizations/speech (even relative to clinical expectations for internationally adopted children) was delayed. Sophie did not use single words until about 30 months of age. Other developmental skills were met within age expectations. At around 40 months of age, Sophie attended preschool twice weekly; by this time her speech had expanded and she was socially proficient in verbal communication. Within the preschool classroom Sophie was reported to be well engaged in learning activities and cooperative with her peers.

There were no concerns about Sophie's learning until first grade, when she was noted to be behind in reading skills. She responded well to a 3-month phonics program and received additional review in reading outside of the regular classroom. Individualized tutoring (across subjects) was maintained during second and third grades, and Sophie participated in summer school each year to review academic skills, especially math and reading. During third grade, her parents enrolled her in a specialized program in which she received individualized instruction 4 hours a week for about 6 months. Some benefit was noted from this intervention, but Sophie continued to need significant review and repetition to acquire academic information. During academic testing, even when it appeared that she knew the content, her test scores tended to be poor.

Similar to many internationally adopted children, Sophie was adopted following unknown prenatal experiences and group-based care that likely provided little opportunity for individualized attention and appropriate developmental stimulation. As will be discussed throughout this chapter, Sophie's postadoption trajectory (e.g., initial mild developmental concerns, postadoption developmental "catch-up," early academic struggles, receipt of additional educational support) is common among internationally adopted children. In some cases similar to Sophie's, cognitive concerns are relatively mild and, although distressing for the parents and occasionally the child, often respond well to individualized support. In other cases, cognition is significantly impaired and related development (e.g., language, social-emotional) is adversely affected to a similar degree. When exploring the cognitive outcomes for any one child, it is often difficult to tease apart the independent contributions of genetic loading, prenatal environment (e.g., exposure to toxins), and early infant environmental experiences (e.g., amount of stimulation, biological adaptations to early adversity) on ultimate cognitive functioning, because many of these factors are relatively unknown. This chapter will introduce the range of cognitive outcomes for internationally adopted children to illuminate the various effects on later learning and development.

## INTRODUCTION TO BRAIN DEVELOPMENT

Although development occurs throughout the lifespan, brain growth is exceptionally critical during gestation and the infant and toddler years. Although gestational brain development is largely driven by genetics, the impact of the uterine environment is still considerable. In fact, it is estimated that 20% of cognitive variance can be attributed to prenatal factors (Eliot, 2000). For example, poor maternal nutrition and the presence of toxins (e.g., alcohol) during pregnancy are known to harm the developing brain

(Tierney & Nelson, 2009), with the extent of impact presumably based on gestational timing and degree.

During early childhood, neurons, the basic building blocks of the brain, form networks to perform a certain function, such as vision (Perry, Pollard, Blakley, Baker, & Vigilante, 1995). The majority of neurons are present at birth. Quite rapidly these neurons begin to link together through the development of *synaptic connections*. These synaptic connections are generated in a use-dependent way (Perry, 2004). That is, *neurons that fire together, wire together*. Environmental experience stimulates the synapses between neurons to subsequently create patterns of neuronal activity. Within the first 2 years of life, about 1,000 trillion synaptic connections are created and account for the majority of brain growth in that time. In fact, a child forms synaptic connections at "a rate of 1.8 million new synapses per second between two months of gestation and two years after birth!" (Eliot, 2000, p. 27). However, various brain regions experience their peak of synaptic production at different times, affecting the degree of plasticity across brain areas (Tierney & Nelson, 2009). For example, the area responsible for vision reaches its synaptic peak between 4 and 8 months of age.

Following this proliferation of synaptic connections, brain regions begin a process of *neuronal pruning*. During this secondary process, synapses that are redundant or rarely activated due to low environmental stimulation atrophy; that is, *use it or lose it*. Between early childhood and adolescence, an estimated 20 billion synapses per day are eliminated to promote efficient brain functioning (Eliot, 2000). Early experiences determine which neural pathways will be maintained and which will be eliminated (Johnson, Browne, & Hamilton-Giachritsis, 2006). However, for this process to result in typical brain development, the infant "must interact with a living and responsive environment" (Balbernie, 2001, p. 239). In an ideal setting, a child's experience of the environment is mediated through an attentive, caring adult who introduces new stimuli in a manner that is gradual, predictable, and appropriate to the infant's stage of development (Perry & Pollard, 1998). Internationally adopted children may be less likely to have this buffering relationship; subsequent brain adaptations within the preadoptive environment can subsequently complicate later adjustment and learning.

Pruning (such as synaptic creation) occurs at variable rates across brain regions, leading to unique windows of time during which certain brain regions are maximally sensitive to early experiences. For example, the brain areas that process visual and auditory stimuli complete pruning between 4 and 6 years of age. Initially, infants' brains are capable of perceiving the range of sounds noted throughout the world's languages. Often within the first 6–8 months, their brains become astute at perceiving those language sounds that are present in their immediate environment. Infants who are better at deciphering sounds within their native language have better later language (and subsequent reading) skills (Kuhl, 2004). As such, later cognitive functions are dependent on these earlier aspects of brain development (Tierney & Nelson, 2009).

Once pruned, brain regions are less malleable. Thus, in the case of language perception, after 5–6 years of age, diverse language sounds are less recognizable to the auditory regions of the brain. Such is the nature of an adolescent English speaker who experiences exceptional difficulty deciphering the tonal variations between Vietnamese words…or a young adult French speaker who struggles to pronounce the "th" sound prominent in English. Together, the creation of synapses and subsequent pruning in the infant's brain allows the adaptation of the brain in response to the environment (i.e., neuroplasticity) and provides the basis for later cognitive functions.

## PREADOPTIVE ENVIRONMENT AND COGNITIVE DEVELOPMENT

### Gestational Experiences

For each of us, cognitive development is a synergistic interplay between brain structure and functioning that is affected by genetic endowment and environment and combined with experiential opportunity. For internationally adopted children, genetic potential (or vulnerability) is difficult to determine, as information about biological parents is speculative at best (Miller, 2005). Outside of clear genetic markers (e.g., fragile X, trisomy 21), conclusions about genetic determination of cognition are limited for the internationally adopted child. As such, there has been increasing exploration of the environmental and experiential aspects of cognitive development for internationally adopted children.

Poverty is presumed to be a large contributor to the placement of children within orphanages (Miller, 2005), leading to their eventual availability for adoption. Because malnutrition, toxic exposure, maternal stress, and substance use often co-occur within the context of poverty (Wood, 2003), fetal brain development is likely affected. In fact, substance use, maternal stress, and malnutrition during pregnancy have all been linked with poorer cognitive outcomes in subsequent children (Bergman, Sarkar, O'Connor, Modi, & Glover, 2007; Huizink & Mulder, 2005). For any specific child adopted internationally, however, the degree of adverse gestational impact is often unknown. (For a review of these variables, refer to Chapter 2).

### Early Care

Along with gestational vulnerability, early care experiences create a distinctive risk factor for internationally adopted children. The quality of care within preadoptive environments varies greatly, often related to sociocultural and economic indicators within the country of origin. Long-term, group-based (i.e., orphanage) care remains widely practiced worldwide; it is estimated that 65% of internationally adopted children spend the majority of their preadoptive lives within orphanage care (Johnson, 2000a). Although there is undoubtedly variation in the conditions of care (Judge, 1999), orphanages tend to be underfunded, understaffed, and ill-equipped to meet the developmental needs of the children entrusted to their care (Wilson, 2003).

Reports from various sources across different orphanages worldwide converge upon a similar description: inadequate nutrition, minimal interpersonal contact, and little-to-no sensory stimulation (e.g., Groze & Ileana, 1996; Johnson, 2000b; Kaler & Freeman, 1994; Rutter and the English and Romanian Adoptees Study Team, 1998; Zeanah et al., 2003). Because of the rapid brain development that occurs in early childhood, the developing brain is influenced by exposure to myriad stressors that are thought to increasingly co-occur with orphanage care: neglect, verbal abuse, harsh physical punishment (Teicher et al., 2010). The effects of early orphanage care are invariably connected to the degree of individual care and consistency (or lack thereof) experienced by the young child, with variations in the amount of individual care having a particular effect on later cognitive attainment (Castle et al., 1999). Although not impossible, a positive relationship between a child and an orphanage caregiver is unlikely (Zeanah, Smyke, Koga, Carlson, & the Bucharest Early Intervention Project Core Group, 2005), creating a potential risk factor for later cognitive, language, and social development of the young child (for a review see Chapter 3).

Foster care, although far from a perfect solution to the need for extrafamilial care, is presumed to provide increased levels of individual care. And in fact, children adopted from international foster care (as practiced in Guatemala, Korea, and increasingly China) have been noted to have stronger cognitive and health outcomes relative to peers adopted from orphanage care within the same country of origin (Miller, Chan, Comfort, & Tirella, 2005; Nelson et al., 2007). The Bucharest Early Intervention Project (BEIP, Zeanah et al., 2003) has provided increasing evidence for improvements noted with early foster care relative to long-term orphanage care. The BEIP followed three groups of children over time: children who remained within Romanian orphanages (where environmental input was notably low); Romanian children who were placed into foster care after an average of 22 months of orphanage care (and thus experienced improvement in the amount of environmental input); and Romanian children who never experienced orphanage care and remained with their birth families. Those children who remained in orphanage care showed stunted cognitive and physical growth with patterns of brain activity that were vastly different from those children who never experienced orphanage care (Marshall, Fox, & the BEIP Core Group, 2004). Similarly, children moved from orphanage care into foster care before 24 months showed brain patterns that were more similar to those children who never experienced orphanage care (Marshall, Reeb, Fox, & the BEIP Core Group, 2008), than did those children placed into foster care following 24 months of age. Similar trends were noted with regard to cognitive recovery (Nelson et al., 2007) and language acquisition (Windsor, Glaze, Koga, & the BEIP Core Group, 2007). Thus, foster care, and the presumed increased access to appropriate environmental stimulation and support, was linked with more positive child outcomes.

Even so, foster care may not remediate all risk factors associated with long-term orphanage care. Children adopted from foster care are likely to have been separated from their birth family due to extreme poverty. Thus, the potential remains for negative prenatal or early infant experiences prior to foster care placement that could have long-term cognitive implications. In addition, internationally adopted children may have experienced a mixture of foster and orphanage care, with unknown numbers of early care transitions that can have a negative impact on their development (Ward, 2009).

Across both foster and orphanage care, child–caregiver interactions are invariably driven by cultural factors that have an impact on the caregiver's belief system about child rearing in general and the worth of a particular child in care. However, the larger sociocultural context of foster and orphanage care remains poorly understood (Gibbons, Wilson, & Schnell, 2009); nonetheless, it is likely a contributing variable to the eventual cognitive outcomes of internationally adopted children. Within a cultural context in which children are perceived to be innocent victims of events beyond their (or their birth parents') control, such as governmental policy or a nonstigmatized death of the biological parent, care providers may be more likely to interact with children in warm, empathic ways. However, if children are perceived to need nonfamilial care due to culturally stigmatized reasons (e.g., death from AIDS or other taboo parental behavior), or they are members of a culturally oppressed ethnic group, caregivers may be more likely to shape interactions that reflect negative cultural biases. As such, perceived "undesirable" children may be less likely to receive warm, empathic care or consistent levels of appropriate social interactions, regardless of their placement within foster or orphanage care. Such variations in social interactions invariably affect brain development and later cognitive functioning, although the mechanisms responsible for this remain poorly understood and undocumented.

## Impact of Early Adversity on Brain Structure and Function

Diverse structural changes have been noted to occur in the brain following early chronic stressors (e.g., abuse, neglect). For example, animal research has demonstrated that the corpus callosum, the connective tissue that provides communication and integration between the right and left hemispheres, is negatively affected by early social isolation, with subsequent decreases directly related to poorer cognitive functioning (Sánchez, Hearn, Do, Rilling, & Herndon, 1998). Such cognitive impairments persist even after later placement in a socially enriched environment. Similar structural changes have been noted within the brains of children who have experienced early deprivation and neglect (Teicher et al., 2004) and represent a potential risk factor for children adopted from impoverished/ neglectful early care.

The cerebellum, a lower region near the brain stem, is well-known to support motor control and coordination. Increasingly it is implicated in more advanced cognitive skills such as planning, visual-spatial perception, and abstract reasoning (Schmahmann & Sherman, 1998) and has been noted to be highly susceptible to environmental influences. This area of the brain has been found to be smaller in internationally adopted children (presumably due to early deprivation associated with orphanage care), relative to matched peers without such early experiences. In addition, larger cerebellar volumes have been associated with better spatial memory and planning (Bauer, Hanson, Pierson, Davidson, & Pollak, 2009).

Along with structural variation, reduced neuronal activity was noted in the brains of children who were adopted from orphanage care in Romania and thus experienced an isolated period of environmental deprivation (Chugani et al., 2001). Following early environmental deprivation, the areas that showed the most reduction in brain activity were those associated with emotion regulation, problem solving, and impulse control.

Increasingly, neuroendocrine changes following early adversity are presumed to underlie some cognitive and behavioral outcomes. Cortisol, known as the "stress hormone," is released when the body is under stress to facilitate the fight-or-flight response. Generally, blood levels of cortisol are highest in the morning and decline over the course of the day, to relatively low levels at night. Gunnar, Morison, Chisholm, and Schuder (2001) noted that duration of early orphanage care was correlated with higher daytime levels of cortisol. Even into adulthood, individuals adopted as children following significant preadoptive adversity (e.g., severe neglect or physical abuse) were found to have abnormal daily cortisol patterns (van der Vegt, van der Ende, Kirschbaum, Verhulst, & Tiemeier, 2009). Elevations in cortisol also have been related to later cognitive impairment (De Bellis et al., 1999).

## POSTADOPTION COGNITIVE OUTCOMES

Although early risk factors, such as those identified in the preadoptive experiences of many internationally adopted children, have been shown to have an additive impact on later developmental and health outcomes, early adversity does not invariably cause irreversible damage for children.

Instead, early, stable environmental improvement can negate deleterious effects of early adversity (Colombo, de la Parra, & Lopez, 1992). In a meta-analysis of 62 studies, which included data on more than 17,000 children adopted within 17 different countries (both internationally and domestically), Van IJzendoorn, Juffer, and Klein Poelhuis (2005) noted positive gains in cognitive skills for adopted children. Specifically, adopted children were noted to have significantly stronger cognitive scores when compared with peers who remained in the preadoptive setting (e.g., orphanage care or birth family) and cognitive scores consistent with nonadopted siblings within the current adoptive family.

The English and Romanian Adoptees (ERA) Study represents the largest longitudinal cohort of internationally adopted children (i.e., from Romania into the United Kingdom) and has provided innumerable observations about the postadoption cognitive development of children. The ERA Study followed participating children into adolescence to document their cognitive and academic outcomes following a circumscribed period of orphanage care associated with high levels of environmental deprivation. At adoption, more than half of the children were within the "retarded" range on an early childhood developmental measure. Around age 4 (i.e., at least 2 years within their adoptive families), children's developmental quotient, a proxy for emerging cognitive skills, rose from 63 (extremely low) to 107 (average range), demonstrating tremendous cognitive growth (Rutter & the ERA Study Team, 1998). Others have noted this remarkable acquisition of developmental skills during the initial years following international adoption (Cohen, Lojkasek, Zadeh, Pugliese, & Kiefer, 2008; Judge, 2003; Morison & Ellwood, 2000; Pomerleau et al., 2005; Wilson & Weaver, 2009; Wilson, Weaver, Cradock, & Kuebli, 2008). It has been estimated that children demonstrate an average increase of 2 developmental quotient points per month after removal from orphanage care (Johnson, 2000a).

In the ERA Study, children adopted prior to 6 months of age had cognitive scores similar to the U.K.–based comparison sample at age 4 (Rutter & the ERA Study Team, 1998). Children with more extensive orphanage care showed dramatic (though incomplete) catch-up with regard to cognitive recovery at age 4 years. Surprisingly, weight at entry into the United Kingdom was not predictive of cognitive functioning at age 4. Hence, Rutter and the ERA Study Team (1998) concluded, "severe malnutrition…had no major continuing effect on cognitive performance after a period of at least two years rearing in an adoptive home" (p. 474). Jacobs, Miller, and Tirella (2010) similarly reported that growth parameters at arrival (i.e., height, weight, and head circumference) were unrelated to cognitive development assessed at 4–5 years of age for children adopted into the United States from primarily China, Russia, Guatemala, and Kazakhstan at an average age of 12 months.

The ERA Study Team reported that by 6 years of age there was a significant association between the age when participating children joined their U.K. families (an index of the duration of deprivation) and early childhood cognitive outcomes (O'Connor et al., 2000). Children who experienced less than 6 months of orphanage care continued to be indistinguishable from the comparison sample of U.K.–based peers, with cognitive profiles that were generally within the average range. Children who had 6–24 months of orphanage care had somewhat lower cognitive scores; children with more than 24 months of orphanage care were particularly impaired. In other words, the longer the duration of deprivation, the lower the chance that the child reached average cognitive functioning (Altemeier, 2000). Nonetheless, there was considerable variability in cognitive scores for those in the late-adopted group, with some children demonstrating normative cognitive functioning. For those children who were adopted prior to 24 months of age, increased attainment of cognitive functioning was most evident within the first 2 years of adoption. From ages 4–6, there was less increase in cognitive skills for the entire cohort, although children with the greatest impairment at age 4 showed continued cognitive gains (O'Connor, et al., 2000).

By age 11, cognitive consistency was the norm; children generally maintained their cognitive scores at comparable levels between ages 6 and 11; thus less catch-up growth was documented within the ERA Study cohort (Beckett et al., 2006). When improvements were noted, it tended to be among those children with the most significant impairments at age 6. Specifically, children with cognitive scores in the lowest 15th percentile were more likely than any other group to have documented cognitive improvement. Castle et al. (2006) reported that a portion of these gains were likely related to the fact that children with lower cognitive functioning were also the most likely to receive increased academic support and remediation. Negative cognitive effects were reported for children who experienced at least 6 months of orphanage care; surprisingly, negative impact on cognitive function did not uniformly increase with continued orphanage care beyond 6 months. In other words, just 6 months of orphanage placement was (in some cases) sufficient to lead to enduring cognitive deficits.

Following the ERA Study cohort into middle adolescence (i.e., 15–16 years of age), previously documented patterns of cognitive functioning persisted: Youth with more than 6 months of early orphanage care had significantly lower cognitive skills than youth with less than 6 months of deprivation or U.K.–based peers (Beckett, Castle, Rutter, & Sonuga-Barke, 2010). Also, as noted previously, those children with the greatest impairment in previous assessments, showed continued, albeit incomplete, cognitive improvement. Language skills at 18 months were moderately associated with later academic functioning; that is, those children with some language at 18 months were more likely to have higher standardized testing scores in English and math than those children with no language at 18 months. Surprisingly, early language functioning was not related to behavioral functioning. The researchers concluded that early deprivation exerted a lasting negative impact on multiple aspects of cognitive functioning. Nonetheless, "some dozen years after leaving institutional care, modest continuing cognitive gains are possible" (Beckett et al., 2010, p. 139).

Kreppner et al. (2007) explored the developmental pattern of cognitive functioning for those children followed as part of the ERA Study. They concluded that impairments, if present, were notable by age 6, with continuity of outcome maintained to age 11. The primary predictor of later outcome was experience of orphanage deprivation for more than 6 months in early infancy/childhood. It was noted that about 67% of children at both 6 and 11 years of age with less than 6 months of depriving orphanage care showed "normative" functioning across multiple psychosocial outcomes. There was significant heterogeneity of outcomes for those children with more than 6 months of orphanage deprivation in early childhood. About a third of the group of these children showed normative functioning at age 6 and then later at age 11. However, despite at least 7 years' enriched postadoptive environment, about half of the children with more than 6 months of orphanage deprivation continued to show multiple impairments (Kreppner et al., 2007).

Taken together, the longitudinal findings of the ERA Study indicate that the first 12 months of life can have a major impact on cognitive functioning up through adolescence; however, significant impairment is far from a universal phenomenon. Some children demonstrate normative cognitive functioning even with considerable experiences of early deprivation. For children whose cognitive impairment was initially most pronounced, there was continued, long-term improvement noted in cognitive functioning, although complete recovery was not always observed. Consistent with dynamic systems theory (see Chapter 1), complex biological-environmental interactions result in many different developmental outcomes.

The longitudinal findings of the ERA Study, although provocative and important for understanding cognitive outcomes for children adopted from Romania, may not apply to children adopted from other countries. For example, Odenstad, Hjern, Lindblad, Rasmussen, Vinnerljung, and Dalen (2008) demonstrated that for the majority of adults who were adopted into Sweden from South Korea, cognitive scores were within the average range, regardless of age at adoption. Others (e.g., Stams, Juffer, Rispens, & Hoksbergen, 2000) have highlighted the high cognitive functioning demonstrated by the majority of children adopted from South Korea. Unlike children adopted from Romania, children adopted from South Korea generally are not exposed to risk factors usually involved in international adoption (e.g., orphanage care, poor prenatal health). This may explain the robustly positive cognitive findings. Longitudinal data from other countries with more recent participation in international adoption (e.g., Guatemala, Ethiopia) are minimal, although early reports of initial developmental status are optimistic (e.g., Miller et al., 2005; Miller, Tseng, Tirella, Chan, & Feig, 2008).

Exploring the rates of identified disabilities based on findings from the 2000 U.S. Census, Kreider and Cohen (2009) documented that internationally adopted children (36% of whom were adopted from Korea, ≈25% from Central/South American countries, ≈20% from Eastern European countries, ≈12% from China and other Asian countries) had a similar proportion of documented "mental disability" (i.e., chronic problem with learning, memory, or concentration) as children adopted domestically (≈10%). However, this rate was twice that noted in the general population of youth age 5–15 (Waldrop & Stern, 2003). As expected, children who were adopted within the year they were born showed the lowest rates of disability, relative to children age 2–9 years at adoption. For reasons yet unclear, females tended to show lower rates of disability than males. There was significant variability in disability rates noted by country of origin; about 25% of children adopted from Eastern European countries or Haiti were reported to have at least one disability versus about 3% of those children adopted from Japan or China. Variability is likely affected by the culture of child welfare and preadoptive child care options available within the specific country of origin.

Although group-based differences in brain structure and functioning (as indexed by global and specific cognitive outcomes) have been documented, there remain considerable individual differences within the group of internationally adopted children. Individual variation, given similar environmental influences, likely reflects genetic, as well as experiential, factors (Kreppner et al., 2007) and is a seeming result of dynamic interactions as predicted by dynamic systems theory (DST) (see Chapter 1). Consistent with DST, Beckett et al. (2006) proposed that the heterogeneity of cognitive outcomes provided evidence that genetics made some children more or less susceptible to environmental hazards (i.e., deprivation). The innumerable gene–environment interactions remain a dynamic (and poorly understood) influence on eventual cognitive outcomes following international adoption.

## POSTADOPTION ACADEMIC PERFORMANCE

Despite evidence for continued cognitive recovery and the majority of cognitive functioning within the average range (Van IJzendoorn et al., 2005), academic performance among internationally adopted children has been noted to be somewhat lower relative to nonadopted siblings within the adoptive family (Van IJzendoorn & Juffer, 2006). In fact, 12.8% of adopted children were referred to special educational services compared with 5.5% in the nonadopted group (Van IJzendoorn et al., 2005). Academic difficulty was more salient for those children adopted after 12 months of age.

Even in the context of intact global cognitive functioning, subtle impairments continue to be documented in language, memory, and/or attention following removal from orphanage care (Behen, Helder, Rothermel, Solomon, & Chugani, 2008). Pollak et al. (2010) documented that school-age children adopted into the United States from Eastern Europe, Asia, and Latin America following at least a year of orphanage care performed more poorly on tasks of visual-spatial memory and attention than internationally adopted children with less than 4 months' orphanage care or nonadopted peers. These difficulties (even in the context of robust cognitive functioning) can negatively impact academic performance and contribute to the increased incidence of learning concerns for internationally adopted children.

## FACTORS AFFECTING COGNITIVE DEVELOPMENT AFTER ADOPTION

Although there is considerable evidence that family-based factors (e.g., income, parental education, availability of enrichment activities) are associated with a child's resulting cognitive functioning within biologically related families, such associations have been less pronounced for adoptive families. For example, using a nationally representative sample of U.S. adolescents, Neiss and Rowe (2000) matched adopted and nonadopted adolescents on gender, race, age, and parental education. Results indicated that correlations between parental education and resulting verbal reasoning skills were about .40 within biological families and about .17 within adoptive families. Within this particular sample, the birth countries of children in the adopted sample were not collected. Thus it was impossible to parcel out internationally adopted children from those adopted domestically. Nonetheless, parental education has been unrelated to the presence of a cognitive disability in internationally adopted children (Kreider & Cohen, 2009).

Along with the genetic independence between parents and children and the relative reduction in environmental risk factors within adoptive families (as a result of preadoptive screening and approval), it may be that parental factors that have been determined to be related to cognitive development in nonadopted children do not invariably apply in the same way to internationally adopted children. Many internationally adopted children have experienced some degree of deprivation and thus have "special needs" unrelated to their parents' backgrounds (Castle, Beckett, Rutter, & Sonuga-Barke, 2010).

Within the ERA Study, variation among adoptive families (e.g., education level) was largely unassociated with either the cognitive level at age 11 or in change over time from age 6. This is not to say that parental factors had no impact on cognitive functioning; the remarkable catch-up growth by age 4 attested to the powerful intervention of a stable, enriching home environment. Nonetheless, unlike findings in biologically related families, parental education generally has only a modest impact on an adopted child's eventual cognitive functioning (Van IJzendoorn et al, 2005). To date there is little to suggest that child outcomes following international adoption are invariably linked to differences within the adoptive family (Castle et al., 2010). It may be that "good enough" parenting (Winnicott, 1958) is necessary, although at times insufficient, to lead to optimal cognitive recovery following adverse early experiences. Independent of cognitive functioning, family attitudes about achievement are likely to contribute to children's ultimate academic performance (Miller, 2005), although this relationship has (as yet) been minimally explored.

## COGNITIVE ASSESSMENT FOLLOWING ADOPTION

Internationally adopted children represent a diverse background of cultural experiences, risk exposure, and developmental trajectories. A toddler adopted at 33 months of age from a government-run, understaffed orphanage and born premature with suspected prenatal alcohol exposure will have vastly different developmental, cognitive, and later academic needs than an infant born full-term and adopted at 8 months of age from a stable foster-care placement. Similarly, a 9-year-old who lived her entire life in a crowded orphanage with untreated ear infections and chronic malnutrition will have a vastly different cognitive profile and learning needs than the 10-year-old who remained with his biological family for 9 years before the unexpected death of both parents that prompted orphanage care for a year prior to adoption.

Because of the exceptional variability in risk exposure and developmental outcomes, medical clinics dedicated to serving internationally adopted children have emerged throughout the United States to provide specialized health care and support the optimal growth and resiliency of these children.[1] Many international adoption clinics utilize an interdisciplinary team to assess and support children integrating into the U.S. culture and adjusting to new families. Although some of the care provided within these clinics is consistent with general pediatric practice (e.g., discussions about medical concerns, development, and behavior), such conversations carry new meaning for the child with an undocumented (or unverified) medical history, unknown immunization status, and experience of disrupted relationships (at best) or possible neglect/abuse/trauma (at worst). These specialty clinics are often in a prime position to assess the needs of internationally adopted

---

[1]For a list of medical providers who specialize in adoption, please visit the American Academy of Pediatrics' section on Adoption and Foster Care: http://www.aap.org/sections/adoption/SOAFCAdoption Directory2.pdf

children and to support the family in identifying appropriate cognitive and academic resources.

All children should be evaluated to rule out medical or genetic conditions that may affect their development and learning. Some medical/developmental concerns that could have an impact on later cognitive functioning and learning will be evident at adoption (e.g., cleft lip and palate), whereas others might not emerge for years (e.g., fetal alcohol effects). At least initially, children who fail to show a catch-up recovery of developmental skills within the first 12–24 months of adoption may require more intensive services for a longer duration. Many developmental delays coincide with medical concerns (e.g., language delays secondary to untreated ear infections); other times, delays are the result of many cocontributing factors and require multiple interventions to support improved functioning. Acute medical conditions should be assessed and treated first before long-term intervention plans are developed.

If concerns are present for toddlers, assessments can be obtained through the state-level early intervention program. Interventions are often assigned based on the child's degree of delay. Depending on the child's time within the adoptive family, such assessments could be postponed to allow for the child's adjustment and acclimatization. In many cases, this delay of initial assessment by 3–6 months is appropriate. In other cases, in which there is a clear indicator (e.g., genetic condition) that long-term impairment is likely, such delay may be inappropriate.

School-age children are often assessed through their public school district to determine if they have a persistent disability in any of the following areas: autism, cognitive disabilities, hearing impairment, visual impairment, emotional-behavioral disabilities, "other health impairment" (e.g., cystic fibrosis, cerebral palsy), speech-language impairments (independent from English language learning), specific learning disabilities, significant developmental delay, and traumatic brain injury. In some cases (e.g., autism), children may meet criteria for services within the school without a medical diagnosis. Conversely, they may have a medical diagnosis that is not determined to have a negative impact on academic engagement, and thus these children would not qualify for services within the school. Although eligibility criteria are determined by the federal government, state-level interpretation leads to variations among states for actual provision of services (Dole, 2005).

Some families choose to obtain assessments of their children's functioning by clinicians independent of the school. Although such assessments may be helpful, they do not invariably ensure that the child will meet criteria for services within the school, and parents may find that they have to pursue services elsewhere (e.g., private agencies). In either case, due to the complexity of children's development and the myriad factors that have an impact on the development of internationally adopted children, a comprehensive assessment that includes evaluation of current cognitive skills, academic functioning, communication abilities, physical development, health or medical status, social-emotional development, and behavioral regulation will be most helpful in delineating appropriate interventions.

All assessment measures are limited in their direct application to internationally adopted children, in part because standardization samples do not include these children (e.g., those with extended histories of orphanage care or significant environmental change/disruption inherent in international adoption). Because of such concerns, developmental and early screening tools should not be used as a predictive measure unless such measures have been used and published to document postadoption development. Nonetheless, assessments (although limited in predictability for this group of children) do provide a way to introduce to parents their children's strengths and discuss normative developmental progression (Miller, 2000). Parents often find such assessments to be a worthwhile way to learn more about their children (Wilson et al., 2008). Lastly, psychoeducational assessment can provide an initial baseline to assess an individual child's rate of change and developmental progress.

In cases in which parents have concerns about their child's rate of learning or behavioral development (that may be a reflection of cognitive functioning), it may be best to return to the agency that facilitated the adoption to acquire a list of adoption-competent professionals who can assess the child and provide recommendations for intervention. Adoption-competent providers, especially those with an understanding of the impact of early adversity and stress on brain development, can help to elucidate whether a child's present concerns are due to limited English acquisition, inherent language impairment (separate from English acquisition), poor cognitive functioning, hypervigilance secondary to preadoption trauma, transitory adjustment concern, or social-emotional impairment. In Sophie's case, a thorough cognitive assessment by an interdisciplinary team at an international adoption medical clinic helped differentiate her strengths and weaknesses.

## ▼▼▼ CASE STUDY UPDATE

Sophie's trajectory was somewhat consistent with "normative" cognitive trajectories for internationally adopted children. Although initial developmental delays were noted, Sophie demonstrated positive developmental growth across areas. Relative to emerging expectations for language acquisition following international adoption (see Chapter 6), Sophie's initial English acquisition was delayed, an early precursor to potential cognitive and academic difficulties (especially reading) later on. As reported for many internationally adopted children (Van IJzendoorn et al., 2005), Sophie's academic skills lagged behind her presumed cognitive functioning. Her parents had worked both within the school and through outside private agencies to provide Sophie with numerous academic resources, leading to an only modest impact on her academic performance.

Sophie's ongoing learning concerns prompted her parents to request a comprehensive psychoeducational assessment through their local international adoption clinic. The assessment included a review of Sophie's history and evaluation of her current levels of cognitive, memory, visual-motor, attentional, and social-emotional functioning. The assessment confirmed that the majority of Sophie's cognitive scores fell within the average range. However, although global measures of cognitive functioning were intact and appropriate, subtle cognitive impairments were identified. Specifically, Sophie demonstrated a relative strength in the area of verbal skills but had significant difficulty with aspects of spatial processing. The discrepancy noted between Sophie's verbal and spatial skills was pronounced, the degree being exceptionally uncommon in the general population of all children.

Difficulty with spatial understanding and visual processing was demonstrated consistently across tests and helped to explain Sophie's ongoing academic concerns. Children with problems in visual-spatial processing have difficulty organizing math problems, finding and retaining important information in written texts, copying from the board or books, and developing automaticity and speed in writing and reading. Pollak et al. (2010) speculated that the visual-spatial difficulty they noted in their sample of internationally adopted children reflected the increased dependence of the visual system on environmental stimulation for appropriate functioning. It may have been that Sophie's early orphanage setting provided her with poor visual stimulation, that did not provide the early building blocks required for more advanced visual processing to occur later in her development.

When schoolwork is challenging for children, feelings of frustration and ineffectiveness further interfere with learning. By the time Sophie was assessed, the cumulative academic difficulty had created emotional distress; low levels of negative mood adversely affected her engagement with schoolwork. In situations in which Sophie felt pressured, she was likely to become anxious, lessening her ability to demonstrate acquired knowledge directly. Thus, a synergistic interaction of emotional distress, subtle cognitive impairments, and reduced academic acquisition was maintained.

Following the assessment, Sophie participated in occupational therapy (specific to visual-spatial–processing difficulties) for about 6 months to support improvement within this sensory system. During that time, her parents and educators coordinated to provide some modifications to reduce academic stress that had a negative impact on her academic functioning. Following this increased collaboration and specialized therapeutic intervention, Sophie's academic performance improved and her engagement with tests and homework was more appropriate. She was able to increase her skills with visual-spatial processing, although she remained somewhat behind her peers within this cognitive area. Throughout school, she continued to receive minor academic modifications (through an individualized education program) and additional educational support/review (through specialized, private tutoring), but she was generally well served within regular education classes.

Whether the isolated cognitive impairments in Sophie's case were caused by genetic factors, biological effects, or subtle influences of early adversity is difficult to determine. Nonetheless, a comprehensive assessment delineated critical cognitive areas for targeted support to facilitate her academic progression. Sophie's subsequent transition into later school years was less stressful, providing a positive trajectory for her inclusion into high school and future interest in postsecondary education.

# ▼▼▼ *IMPLICATIONS*

Internationally adopted children represent a diverse background of cultural experiences, risk exposure, and developmental trajectories. Critical factors in their eventual cognitive functioning and academic development include genetic influences, prenatal experiences, nutritional status, experience of deprivation or neglect, incidents of physical or sexual abuse, and the number and quality of preadoptive placements. Children often arrive into the United States with little or no birth information and speculative reports of preadoptive experiences. The limited historical information increases the complexity of determining what issues will influence a child's long-term cognitive and educational needs (Dole, 2005).

Although remarkable catch-up growth is expected upon adoption, cognitive recovery is not always complete and subtle impairments can persist, complicating later academic functioning. Unknown genetic factors, biological influences, preadoptive experiences, and postadoption opportunity invariably have an impact on the degree of cognitive difficulty. The most salient factor across outcome studies is the degree and duration of early adversity, often indexed by duration of early orphanage care. Children adopted prior to 6 months of age are more likely to demonstrate normative cognitive functioning and later academic performance consistent with their peers. Children adopted at later ages can certainly show normative cognitive functioning, but as a group, outcomes are more variable. Academic skills may be lower for international adoptees for myriad reasons. As such, cognitive assessment is important for children who demonstrate problems in learning.

# *KEY POINTS*

▶ Early psychosocial environment shapes biology and, thus, influences long-term cognitive outcomes.

▶ Initial cognitive impairment and subsequent catch-up vary as a function of the length and severity of psychosocial and physical deprivation experienced.

▶ Although development occurs throughout the lifespan, early childhood represents a period of time that is particularly critical to the development of a healthy brain.

▶ Higher level functions are dependent upon lower level functions, the roots developing in early childhood.

▶ Adoption into a stable home environment often results in an improvement in cognitive outcomes.

▶ Although some early insults can be remediated with environmental changes, others may be more persistent.

▶ The degree of cognitive improvement varies from child to child according to genetic influences and the effects of preadoptive experiences as well as (as yet poorly defined) aspects of the postadoption environment.

## Referral Indicators

The following reflect times when children should be referred for cognitive assessment:

▶ Developmental acquisition within 10–12 months of arrival does not demonstrate accelerated acquisition toward age-appropriate functioning.

▶ Even years after adoption, difficulties with learning or academic development warrant a full assessment to determine whether cognitive, memory, language, or emotional factors are present to the degree (or duration) that would warrant additional support.

▶ Poor school performance suggests the need for psychoeducational assessment to document the child's level of overall cognitive functioning, language capacity, memory skills, and attentional capacities.

## REFERENCES

Altemeier, W.A. (2000). Growth charts, low birth weight, and international adoption. *Pediatric Annals, 29,* 204–205.

American Academy of Pediatrics. (n.d.). *Adoption Directory.* Retrieved July 15, 2001, from http://www.aap.org/sections/adoption/SOAFCAdoptionDirectory2.pdf

Balbernie, R. (2001). Circuits and circumstances: The neurobiological consequences of early relationships and how they shape later behavior. *Journal of Child Psychotherapy, 27,* 237–255.

Bauer, P.M., Hanson, J.L., Pierson, R.K., Davidson, R.J., & Pollak, S.D. (2009). Cerebellar volume and cognitive functioning in children who experienced early deprivation. *Biological Psychiatry, 66,* 1100–1106.

Beckett, C., Castle, J., Rutter, M., & Sonuga-Barke, E.J. (2010). Institutional deprivation, specific cognitive functions, and scholastic achievement: English and Romanian Adoptee (ERA) Study findings. *Monographs of the Society for Research in Child Development, 75,* 125–142.

Beckett, C., Maughan, B., Rutter, M., Castle, J., Colvert, E., Groothues, C., et al. (2006). Do the effects of early severe deprivation on cognition persist into early adolescence? Findings from the English and Romanian Adoptees Study. *Child Development, 77,* 696–711.

Behen, M. E., Helder, E., Rothermel, R., Solomon, K., & Chugani, H.T. (2008). Incidence of specific absolute neurocognitive impairment in globally intact children with histories of early severe deprivation. *Child Neuropsychology, 14,* 453–469.

Bergman, K., Sarkar, P., O'Connor, T.G., Modi, N., & Glover, V. (2007). Maternal stress during pregnancy predicts cognitive ability and fearfulness in infancy. *Journal of the American Academy of Child and Adolescent Psychiatry, 46,* 1454–1463.

Castle, J., Beckett, C., Rutter, M., & Sonuga-Barke, E.J. (2010). Postadoption environmental factors. *Monographs of the Society for Research in Child Development, 75,* 167–186.

Castle, J., Groothues, C., Bredenkamp, D., Beckett, C., O'Connor, T., Rutter, M., et al. (1999). Effects of qualities of early institutional care on cognitive attainment. *American Journal of Orthopsychiatry, 69,* 424–437.

Castle, J., Rutter, M., Beckett, C., Colvert, E., Groothues, C., Hawkins, A., et al. (2006). Service use by families with children adopted from Romania. *Journal of Children's Services, 1,* 5–15.

Chugani, H.T., Behen, M.E., Muzik, O., Juhász, C., Nagy, F., & Chugani, D.C. (2001). Local brain functional activity following early deprivation: A study of postinstitutionalized Romanian children. *Neuroimage, 14,* 1290–1301.

Cohen, N.J., Lojkasek, M., Zadeh, Z.Y., Pugliese, M., & Kiefer, H. (2008). Children adopted from China: A prospective study of their growth and development. *Journal of Child Psychology and Psychiatry, 49,* 458–468.

Colombo, M., de la Parra, A., & Lopez, I. (1992). Intellectual and physical outcome of children undernourished in early life is influenced by later environmental conditions. *Developmental Medicine and Child Neurology, 34*, 611–622.

De Bellis, M.D., Baum, A.S., Birmaher, B., Keshaven, M.S., Eccard, C.H., Boring, A.M., et al. (1999). Developmental traumatology, part 1: Biological stress systems. *Biological Psychiatry, 9*, 1259–1270.

Dole, K. N. (2005). Education and internationally adopted children: Working collaboratively with schools. *Pediatric Clinics of North America, 52*, 1445–1461.

Eliot, L. (2000). *What's going on in there? How the brain and mind develop in the first five years of life.* New York: Bantam.

Gibbons, J.L., Wilson, S.L., & Schnell, A.M. (2009). Foster parents as a critical link and resource in international adoptions from Guatemala. *Adoption Quarterly, 12*, 59–77.

Groze, V., & Ileana, D. (1996). A follow-up study of adopted children from Romania. *Child and Adolescent Social Work, 13*, 541–565.

Gunnar, M.R., Morison, S.J., Chisholm, K., & Schuder, M. (2001). Salivary cortisol levels in children adopted from Romanian orphanages. *Development and Psychopathology, 13*, 611–628.

Huizink, A.C., & Mulder, E.J.H. (2005). Maternal smoking, drinking or cannabis use during pregnancy and neurobehavioral and cognitive functioning in human offspring. *Neuroscience and Biobehavioral Reviews, 30*, 24–41.

Jacobs, E., Miller, L.C., & Tirella, L.G. (2010). Developmental and behavioral performance of internationally adopted preschoolers. *Child Psychiatry and Human Development, 41*, 15–29.

Johnson, D. (2000a). Medical and developmental sequelae of early childhood institutionalization in Eastern European adoptees. In C.A. Nelson (Ed.), *The effects of early adversity on neurobehavioral development* (pp. 113–162). Mahwah, NJ: Lawrence Earlbaum.

Johnson, D. (2000b, October). *Perspectives on orphanage care.* Paper presented at the meeting of the Association for Treatment and Training in the Attachment of Children, Minneapolis, MN.

Johnson, R., Browne, K., & Hamilton-Giachritsis, C. (2006). Young children in institutional care at risk of harm. *Trauma, Violence, and Abuse, 7*, 34–60.

Judge, S.L. (1999). Eastern European adoptions: Current status and implications for intervention. *Topics in Early Childhood Special Education, 19*, 244–252.

Judge, S. (2003). Developmental recovery and deficit in children adopted from Eastern European Orphanages. *Child Psychiatry and Human Development, 34*, 49–62.

Kaler, S.R., & Freeman, B.J. (1994). Analysis of environmental deprivation: Cognitive and social development in Romanian orphans. *Journal of Child Psychology and Psychiatry, 35*, 769–781.

Kreider, R.M., & Cohen, P.N. (2009). Disability among internationally adopted children in the United States. *Pediatrics, 124*, 1311–1318.

Kreppner, J.M., Rutter, M., Beckett, C., Castle, J., Colvert, E., Groothues, C., et al. (2007). Normality and impairment following profound early institutional deprivation: A longitudinal follow-up into early adolescence. *Developmental Psychology, 43*, 931–946.

Kuhl, P.K. (2004). Early language acquisition: Cracking the speech code. *Nature Reviews: Neuroscience, 5*, 831–843.

Marshall, P., Fox, N.A., & the BEIP Core Group. (2004). A comparison of the electroencephalogram between institutionalized and community children in Romania. *Journal of Cognitive Neuroscience, 16*, 1327–1338.

Marshall, P., Reeb. B.C., Fox, N.A., & the BEIP Core Group. (2008). Effects of early intervention on EEG power and coherence in previously institutionalized children in Romania. *Development and Psychopathology, 20*, 861–880.

Miller, L.C. (2000). Initial assessment of growth development, and the effects of institutionalization in internationally adopted children. *Pediatric Annals, 29*, 224–241.

Miller, L.C. (2005). *The handbook of international adoption medicine.* New York: Oxford University Press.

Miller, L., Chan, W., Comfort, K., & Tirella, L. (2005). Health of children adopted from Guatemala: Comparison of orphanage and foster care. *Pediatrics, 115*, e710–e717.

Miller, L.C., Tseng, B., Tirella, L.G., Chan, W., & Feig, E. (2008). Health of children adopted from Ethiopia. *Maternal and Child Health Journal, 12*, 599–605.

Morison, S.J., & Ellwood, A.L. (2000). Resiliency in the aftermath of deprivation: A second look at the development of Romanian orphanage children. *Merrill–Palmer Quarterly, 46*, 717–737.

Neiss, M., & Rowe, D.C. (2000). Parental education and child's verbal IQ in adoptive and biological families in the National Longitudinal Study of Adolescent Health. *Behavior Genetics, 30*, 487–495.

Nelson, C.A., Zeanah, C.H., Fox, N.A., Marshall, P.J., Smyke, A., & Guthrie, D. (2007). Cognitive recovery in socially deprived young children: The Bucharest Early Intervention Project. *Science, 318*, 1937–1940.

O'Connor, T.G., Rutter, M., Beckett, C., Keaveney, L., Kreppner, J., & the ERA Study Team. (2000). The effects of global severe privation on cognitive competence: Extension and longitudinal follow-up. *Child Development, 71*, 376–390.

Odenstad, A., Hjern, A., Lindblad, F., Rasmussen, F., Vinnerljung, B., & Dalen, M. (2008). Does age at adoption and geographic origin matter? A national cohort study of cognitive test performance in adult inter-country adoptees. *Psychological Medicine, 38*, 1803–1814.

Perry, B.D. (2004). *Maltreated Children: Experience, Brain Development, and the Next Generation*. New York: W.W. Norton.

Perry, B.D., & Pollard, R.A. (1998). Homeostasis, stress, trauma and adaptation: A neurodevelopmental view of childhood trauma. *Child and Adolescent Clinics of North America, 7*, 33–51.

Perry, B.D., Pollard, R.A., Blakley, T.L., Baker, W.L., & Vigilante, D. (1995). Childhood trauma, the neurobiology of adaptation, and "use-dependent" development of the brain: How "states" become "traits." *Infant Mental Health Journal, 16*, 271–291.

Pollak, S.D., Nelson, C.A., Schlaak, M.F., Roeber, B.J., Wewerka, S.S., Wiik, K.L., et al. (2010). Neurodevelopmental effects of early deprivation in postinstitutionalized children. *Child Development, 81*, 224–236.

Pomerleau, A., Malcuit, G., Chicoine, J.F., Séguin, R., Belhumeur, C., Germain, P., et al. (2005). Health status, cognitive and motor development of young children adopted from China, East Asia, and Russia across the first six months after adoption. *International Journal of Behavioral Development, 29*, 445–457.

Rutter, M., & the English and Romanian Adoptees Study Team. (1998). Developmental catch-up, and deficit, following adoption after severe global early privation. *Journal of Child Psychology and Psychiatry, 39*, 465–476.

Sánchez, M.M., Hearn, E.F., Do, D., Rilling, J.K., & Herndon, J.G. (1998). Differential rearing affects corpus callosum size and cognitive function of rhesus monkeys. *Brain Research, 812*, 38–49.

Schmahmann, J.D., & Sherman, J.C. (1998). The cerebellar cognitive affective syndrome. *Brain, 121*, 561–579.

Stams, G.J., Juffer, F., Rispens, J., & Hoksbergen, R.A.C. (2000). The development and adjustment of 7-year-old children adopted in infancy. *Journal of Child Psychology and Psychiatry, 41*, 1025–1037.

Teicher, M.H., Dumont, N.L., Ito, Y., Vaituzis, C., Giedd, J.N., & Andersen, S.L. (2004). Childhood neglect is associated with reduced corpus callosum area. *Biological Psychiatry, 56*, 80–85.

Teicher, M.H., Rabi, K., Sheu, Y., Seraphin, S.B., Andersen, S. L., & Anderson, C.M., (2010). Neurobiology of childhood trauma and adversity. In R. A. Lanius, E. Vermetten, & C. Pain (Eds.), *The impact of early life trauma on health and disease: The hidden epidemic* (pp. 112–120). London: Cambridge University.

Tierney, A.L., & Nelson III, C.A. (2009). Brain development and the role of experience in the early years. *Journal of Zero to Three, 30*, 9–13.

Van IJzendoorn, M.H., & Juffer, F. (2006). The Emanuel Miller Memorial Lecture 2006: Adoption as intervention. Meta-analytic evidence for massive catch-up and plasticity in physical, socio-emotional, and cognitive development. *Journal of Child Psychology and Psychiatry, 47*, 1228–1245.

Van IJzendoorn, M.H., Juffer, F., & Klein Poelhuis, W. (2005). Adoption and cognitive development: A meta-analytic comparison of adopted and nonadopted children's IQ and school performance. *Psychological Bulletin, 13*, 301–316.

Vegt, E.J.M., van der, van der Ende, J., Kirschbaum, C., Verhulst, F.C., & Tiemeier, H. (2009). Early neglect and abuse predict diurnal cortisol patterns in adults: A study of international adoptees. *Psychoneuroendocrinology, 34,* 660–669.

Waldrop, J., & Stern, S.M. (2003). *Disability Status: 2000.* Washington, DC: US Census Bureau.

Ward, H. (2009). Patterns of instability: Moves within the care system, their reasons, contexts and consequences. *Children and Youth Services Review, 31,* 1113–1118.

Wilson, S.L. (2003). Post-institutionalization: The effects of early deprivation on physical, cognitive, and social development of Romanian adoptees. *Child and Adolescent Social Work, 20,* 473–483.

Wilson, S.L., & Weaver, T.L. (2009). Follow-up of developmental attainment and behavioral adjustment for toddlers adopted internationally into the USA. *International Social Work, 52,* 679–694.

Wilson, S.L., Weaver, T.L., Cradock, M.M., & Kuebli, J.E. (2008). A preliminary study of the cognitive and motor skills acquisition of young international adoptees. *Children and Youth Services Review, 30,* 585–596.

Windsor, J., Glaze, L.E., Koga, S.F., & the BEIP Core Group. (2007). Language acquisition with limited input: Romanian institution and foster care. *Journal of Speech, Language, and Hearing Research, 50,* 1365–1381.

Winnicott, D.W. (1958). *Collected papers.* London: Tavistock.

Wood, D. (2003). Effect of child and family poverty on child heath in the United States. *Pediatrics, 11,* 707–711.

Zeanah, C.H., Nelson, C.A., Fox, N.A., Smyke, A.T., Marshall, P., Parker, S., et al. (2003). Designing research to study the effects of institutionalization: The Bucharest Early Intervention Project. *Development and Psychopathology, 15,* 885–907.

Zeanah, C.H., Smyke, A.T., Koga, S., Carlson, E. & the BEIP Core Group (2005). Attachment in institutionalized and community children in Romania. *Child Development, 76,* 1015–1028.

# 5 ▼▼▼▼

# Inhibition, Self-Regulation, Attention, and Memory Development

## *Deborah A. Hwa-Froelich*

---

*"The test of a first-rate intelligence is the ability to hold two opposed ideas in the mind at the same time, and still retain the ability to function."*

F. Scott Fitzgerald (1936), *The Crack-Up*

*"The ability to focus attention on important things is a defining characteristic of intelligence."*

Robert J. Shiller, *Irrational Exuberance*

*"The memory should be specially taxed in youth, since it is then that it is strongest and most tenacious. But in choosing the things that should be committed to memory the utmost care and forethought must be exercised; as lessons well learnt in youth are never forgotten."*

Arthur Schopenhauer (1788–1860)

---

▼▼▼ Robbie was adopted from Russia at the age of 2½ years. He had spent approximately 6 months in the care of his biological mother and was placed in an orphanage at 6 months of age. His adoptive parents reported that, according to the orphanage director, Robbie's biological mother had not received prenatal care but reported a typical delivery with no complications. They described the orphanage as old but clean; Robbie lived with approximately 40 other children.

At the time of the adoption, his parents reported that Robbie was in good health. Several specialists saw him: a pediatrician with training and experience with children adopted from Eastern Europe, a dentist, and a speech-language pathologist with expertise in the development of internationally adopted children. According to his parents, Robbie seemed to be very active, was not potty-trained, and threw tantrums when "he did not have his way." Approximately 1 month after he was adopted, because both his parents worked, Robbie was placed in a child care facility 5 days a week for about 8 hours a day. Robbie was speaking some Russian and some English approximately 6 months following his adoption. Both parents reported that Robbie was hard to understand at times and that he became frustrated when they could not understand him.

Approximately 6 months after his adoption, Robbie demonstrated significant delays in receptive and expressive English language acquisition, scoring more than 2 standard deviations below published mean scores for internationally adopted children (Glennen, 2009). Audiology testing showed that Robbie had fluid in both ears and demonstrated a mild to moderate hearing loss. His symbolic play skills were at an approximate age level of 2 years, about 1 year behind his chronological age.

Robbie was reevaluated approximately 1 year later. The audiology evaluation showed that he continued to have flat tympanograms, which indicated fluid behind the tympanic membrane, or eardrum, in both ears. In spite of this, he was able to pass the hearing screening. His speech intelligibility was within normal limits for his age, but his language scores continued to be delayed compared with same-age internationally adopted children. His English receptive scores were within the reported average range for internationally adopted children, but his English expressive language performance was 2 standard deviations below average scores of Eastern European children adopted at older ages (Glennen, 2009).

Robbie's play development also reflected developmental delays. His symbolic play was limited in the number of objects selected, schemas demonstrated, and complexity of play schemas. He had difficulty thinking flexibly when new characters or problems were introduced in play themes. His parents reported an increase in inattention; Robbie's scores on the Child Behavior Checklist (Achenbach, 2000) for attention problems was in the clinical range, which was an indication he demonstrated more problems with sustained attention than other children his age. Robbie also seemed to be clumsy, shifted tasks quickly, and wandered. In addition, he was beginning to have behavior problems at the child care center and aggressive behaviors at home.

Two years after his adoption, Robbie continued to have problems. The audiology evaluation showed improvement over the past evaluations; he no longer had fluid in his ears and he passed the hearing screening. His English receptive and expressive language development, however, continued to be delayed, consistently falling 2 standard deviations below the mean for nonadopted English-speaking children and expectations for internationally adopted children. Problems with attention affected his performance on these tests and at school; poor emotion and self-regulation resulted in tantrums and physical aggression.

Soon after he was adopted, Robbie began to demonstrate signs of challenging behavior and development problems. His parents noted high activity levels and tantrums. Development specialists with expertise in international adoption observed atypical delays in English acquisition, symbolic play behavior, and inflexibility in thinking. Robbie had difficulty inhibiting his attention to distractions to selectively focus his attention on the completion of tasks. He was unable to regulate his inhibition and attention in order to solve problems, choosing to shift his attention or wander. His lack of attention and reduced self-regulation were behavioral representations of poor working memory and impaired executive function skills. These behaviors may have been related to Robbie's early experiences living in an orphanage, as some children develop a heightened sense of hypervigilance (i.e., increased arousal and responsiveness to stimuli perceived as possible threats). Hypervigilance may negatively influence children's attention, inhibition, working memory, and executive function (for a review see Schore, 2001).

*Executive function* refers to a set of mental processes that involves "inhibiting actions, restraining and delaying responses, attending selectively, setting goals, planning, and organizing, as well as maintaining and shifting set" (Singer & Bashir, 1999, p. 266). As such, executive function is integrally related to selective/focused attention and working memory (Barkley, 1996, 1997; Cowan & Alloway, 2009; Cowan & Courage, 2009; National Center for Learning Disabilities, 2005; Pennington & Ozonoff, 1996; Singer & Bashir, 1999). These mental processes appear to be correlated with mathematical ability, reading ability, verbal and nonverbal reasoning, academic achievement, communication, social skills, and emotion regulation (for a review see Bernier, Carlson, & Whipple, 2010). To have adequate executive function capacities, one must be able to selectively attend to a task, utilize working memory to delineate possible solutions, and sequence and organize the steps and materials needed to complete the task. *Working memory* is defined as "a brain system that provides temporary storage and manipulation of the information necessary for such complex cognitive tasks as language comprehension, learning, and reasoning" (Baddeley, 1992, p. 556). To selectively attend to and focus on a task, individuals must also be able to inhibit attention to distractions and regulate negative emotions such as anger, frustration, or fear to persist with barriers, problem solving, or self-monitoring and think flexibly to solve and complete the task. Consequently, inhibition and self-regulation are also needed for executive function and working memory.

Some components of executive function begin to develop in infancy (Bernier et al., 2010; Diamond, 2000; Reznick, 2009). Most of these skills continue to develop and are refined as children interact with different people, contexts, and problems. Thus, differences in adult mediation and experiences can result in different developmental outcomes that support a dynamic systems theory on developmental outcomes for internationally adopted children (for a review see Chapter 1). In Robbie's case, he struggled with maintaining selective attention and focus to persist with tasks, which resulted in shifting attention and wandering. He also had difficulty regulating his emotions when things did not go as he wished, which resulted in tantrums or aggressive behaviors (see Chapter 3). Robbie needed to learn how to inhibit distractions and negative emotions to improve his self-regulation, attention, and executive function. If he could improve his attention and self-regulation, he would perhaps more effectively use his working memory and executive function.

The purpose of this chapter is to describe 1) the development of inhibition, self-regulation, attention, and memory in children who are not adopted; 2) the effect of institutional or early adverse environments on this development; and 3) the development of inhibition, self-regulation, attention, and memory after adoption.

## DEVELOPMENT OF INHIBITION, SELF-REGULATION, ATTENTION, AND MEMORY

The research and information available about the development of inhibition, self-regulation, attention, and memory are extensive and cannot be described fully in this book. The following sections provide an abbreviated description of each area to offer a basic understanding of typical development, followed by research findings on the postadoption development of internationally adopted children.

### Development of Inhibition and Self-Regulation

Barkley (1997) believes that to be successful in inhibition, children must be able to inhibit three different types of impulses. First, they must be able to inhibit reflexive or unconscious impulses that may have direct consequences. An example of this is inhibiting the impulse to grab food within reach and eat it. Some food may be rotten or dirty, thus children must learn to inhibit this impulse and instead request or ask permission to take or eat the food. Second, they must be able to suspend an action that is ineffective. For instance, they must learn that they do not fit in all spaces and so must learn to duck when crawling or walking under tables and stop trying to squeeze their bodies into spaces where they do not fit. Third, children must learn to manage interfering sources that could disturb or damage the task at hand (Barkley, 1997). For example, they must learn that water can ruin the pages of a book, thus they must not put books in the bathtub or leave them outside in the rain.

The development of inhibition is integrally tied to the development of self-regulation and working memory. Infants are born completely dependent upon adults to accurately read their behavioral cues and thus provide appropriate care for their needs. In the beginning months of life, infants use others to assist them in regulating their discomfort, fear, or distress (see Chapter 3). Through consistent face-to-face interactions with caring adults, infants learn to infer from their caregivers' calm, positive eye gaze and soothing tone of voice that their needs will be met, and they learn to gradually inhibit negative emotions during these interactions (Bronson, 2000). For example, infants stop crying when they are picked up or when they hear their mothers' voice. As infants mature, they internalize and recall their parents' strategies and use them to help calm themselves when their parents are not present, and they become increasingly independent in regulating their emotions (Bronson, 2000). For instance, in the absence of caregivers, some infants who become distressed may use a blanket or pacifier to calm themselves.

Children learn to regulate and inhibit some of their behaviors, emotions, and arousal before they develop language (Barkley, 1997). An example of this development is when toddlers are able to inhibit impulses and initiate joint attention to check with their caregivers before engaging with a new object or person. With language development, children begin to follow directions and remember social rules in the absence of caregivers. As children move through the preschool years, they begin to internalize rules of behavior and use internal speech to regulate their behavior (Bronson, 2000; Vygotsky, 1986). For example, children may comfort themselves by talking to themselves, saying, "Mommy will be back soon." This development is strongly influenced by the attitudes and behaviors of the caregivers (Bernier et al., 2010; Bronson, 2000). Bernier and colleagues found that maternal sensitivity (parental accuracy in reading and meeting their children's cues and needs), parents' talk about mental states (talk about the emotions of parents, child, and others) when interacting with their children, and parental support for autonomy (support for children's independence and individuality) were related to their children's developing executive function abilities. More specifically, parental support for developmentally appropriate autonomy when their children were 15 months old was related to their children's working memory development at 18 months of age and executive functioning development at 26 months of age above and beyond general cognitive ability and maternal education (Bernier et al., 2010). Parental behaviors in support of autonomy included scaffolding, respect of individual differences in rate of learning, and encouragement of their children's participation and role in successful task completion. Eventually, children develop an independent system for motivating themselves and appraising their work so that they can independently analyze and synthesize their behavior prior to, during, and after completion of any task.

In conclusion, children must develop self-regulation to inhibit attention on distractions and focus attention on completion of tasks (Welsh, Pennington, & Groisser, 1991; Zelazo, Carter, Reznick, & Frye, 1997). Parenting behaviors of sensitivity, talk about mental states, and support for their children's autonomy (scaffolding, respect, and encouragement) were instrumental in the promotion of executive function development.

## Development of Attention

Infants begin to attend to objects and people in their environment immediately after birth. Between birth and 6 months of age, infants prefer to gaze at people's faces, responding to eye gaze and facial expressions, and begin to discriminate, attend to, and imitate mouth and tongue movements, as well as sounds from their native language (Legerstee, 2005; Moon, Cooper,

& Fifer, 1993; Mundy & Sigman, 2006; Nazzi, Jusczyk, & Johnson, 2000). Within 2–4 months of age, infants are able to switch their attention from one stimulus to another. Thus, attention and self-regulation (i.e., inhibition of attention from one stimulus to focus attention on another) seem to develop concurrently. This concurrent development also includes the development of memory. During this time period, infants begin to form mental representations of themselves and their primary caregivers with whom they have different and shared experiences, which enable them to move to secondary intersubjectivity (Legerstee, 2005; Mundy & Sigman, 2006).

Secondary intersubjectivity occurs when children share attention between another person and an object or event. By 8–10 months of age, infants begin to demonstrate joint attention by following the directed gaze, gesture, or head turn of their caregivers toward an object or event (Corkum & Moore, 1998; Morales, Mundy, & Rojas, 1998; Mundy & Sigman, 2006). By 10 months of age, infants react to an object or event and then share their affect by initiating joint attention with another person and regulating the other person's behavior to share attention and affect with a particular object or event (Mundy & Sigman, 2006). In essence, the child is communicating, "Do you see what I see?" or "Should I engage with this object?" Between 9 and 18 months of age, infants develop their abilities to communicate intentionally by initiating joint attention as well as initiating behaviors that attempt to regulate others' behaviors. These attention behaviors are motivated by infants' desires to share experiences, socially engage, and interact with others. These behaviors precede and develop concurrently with infants' social communication of wants and needs through coordinated joint attention, gestures, and vocalizations (Legerstee, 2005; Moses, Baldwin, Rosicky, & Tidball, 2001; Mundy & Sigman, 2006). Joint attention is related to later social competence and language development (for a review see Mundy & Sigman, 2006). Initiated joint attention and response to joint attention are related to inhibition, self-regulation, interpretation of nonverbal expression of emotions, and social cognitive development.

Inhibition and attention skills are observable in children's play, particularly in problem solving, mastery, and symbolic play. Children must inhibit negative emotions and selectively attend when solving problems. As children use trial-and-error problem-solving techniques with cause–effect toys, they must inhibit ineffective methods and refine their behaviors to fit the functions of the toy. They must also focus their attention on the parts and unique characteristics of the toy that are important for successful operation. For example, operating a pop-up toy requires various actions, sometimes pushing and other times turning or sliding different knobs and buttons. Some toys require two or three steps before they can be operated. Thus, children must inhibit ineffective strategies (e.g., banging or shaking), focus their attention, and learn a variety of successful maneuvers in a particular sequence to eventually operate a toy or solve a problem. Once children begin to demonstrate symbolic or pretend play, they must also inhibit and self-regulate to pretend to be someone else, such as a doctor, or pretend that an object represents something else, that a banana is a telephone receiver for example. By taking on a social role, children must inhibit and regulate their behavior in order to act like someone else. In addition, they must inhibit the impulse to eat the banana and instead pretend to use it as a phone.

The ability to inhibit and attend enables children to demonstrate the emerging executive function and working memory skills needed to solve problems (Brocki, Eninger, Thorell, & Bohlin, 2010; Kofler, Rapport, Bolden, Sarver, & Raiker, 2010). Brocki and colleagues found that inhibition and selective attention skills at 5 years of age predicted working memory skills at 6 years of age. Focused as opposed to divided attention was found to be essential for working memory capacity (Kofler et al., 2010). In other words, inhibition; selective, focused attention; and memory are necessary to persist and master problems.

## Development of Memory

Although researchers theorize that the firing of neurons results in the behaviors identified as attention, emotion, and memory, little is known about how this brain activity results in individual mental experiences. With that being said, the discussion of memory is based on the state of scientific and theoretical knowledge accumulated over approximately the last decade. Memory consists of knowledge gained from experiences that are accessed, manipulated, and used for present and future actions. Memories are built neurologically from the repeated and systematic patterns of firing of neurons that encode, store, and retrieve previous experiences (Siegel, 1999). Infant neurological systems are dependent upon and expect to be exposed to learning experiences to facilitate neural connectivity, coherence, and integration (see Chapter 4). Neurons that fire at the same time may develop connections that result in neural connectivity and mental associations (Siegel & Hartsell, 2003). This neural stimulation and early neuronal growth build foundations for higher and more complex cognitive thought and flexibility. Short-term memory may be represented as transient neuronal changes, whereas long-term memory may involve structural changes (Siegel, 1999).

For the purposes of this chapter, I will discuss memory generally as two major components, implicit and explicit, which in turn involve other different and overlapping memory structures. Implicit memories are represented as unconscious summaries of mental or perceptual models of an experience (e.g., procedural memories or emotional, behavioral, sensory, or physical body models), for example implicit memories for doing everyday actions such as sitting, walking, or standing (Siegel & Hartsell, 2003). Through early interactions with caregivers, infants begin to develop a sense of who is most like them, which is often encoded as implicit memories. This development can be seen in 2- to 3-month-old infants' early preferences for human interaction or interest, extended attention on humanlike stimuli such as pictures or drawings of faces, and discrimination between humans and objects (Legerstee, 2005). Within 1–3 months of birth, infants begin to model other humans through their early imitation of mouth and tongue movements. They show discrimination between human and nonhumans by their restraint in imitating an inanimate object displaying the same movements (Legerstee, 2005).

During this time infants respond to their world, gathering information about objects, humans and other animate beings, actions, emotions or mental states, and routines or events. With time infants use an abstract symbol set, or language, to communicate about this knowledge. Thus, they are building sensory and procedural (i.e., implicit) models about their world. During later infancy (starting around 9 months of age), children begin to develop object permanence. In other words, they recognize something exists, even when it is out of sight; thus, they will look for a hidden object. Furthermore, they begin to call out or cry when their parents are no longer visible, demonstrating the emerging representation of their parents. By 12–15 months of age, infants use words to represent their caregivers and express a label (*mama* or *dada*) to gain their caregivers' attention or regulate their caregivers' behaviors.

Explicit memories use the encoding processes of implicit memory and process information through the hippocampus around 18 months of age, depending on the maturation of the hippocampus (Siegel & Hartsell, 2003). This process enables the child to contextualize experiences beyond mental models to form representations of experiences. To move explicit memory from short-term storage to long-term storage involves cortical consolidation. This consolidation process is not fully understood, but one aspect of it involves rapid eye movement (REM) sleep as well as continued maturation of the frontal lobes (Siegel & Hartsell, 2003). Children also process past experiences through pretend play, which may be another aspect of cortical consolidation.

Expressive language and a sense of self begin to develop and mature between 1 and 5 years of age. These areas of development interact to enable the development of semantic memory (knowledge) and as recall for previous situations, events, or personal experiences (e.g., episodic memory or the sense of oneself and one's feelings associated with events across time). Episodic memory is facilitated through conversations between a caregiver and child, creating a narrative (i.e., declarative memories) about the child's experiences and feelings about an event (Siegel, 1999). Because most children do not explicitly recall experiences until the age of 5 years, it is hypothesized that cortical consolidation, the child's sense of self, and expressive language are mature enough by age 5 to allow for the expression of autobiographical memory (Siegel & Hartsell, 2003).

## DEVELOPMENT OF PLAY

Westby (2000) described play development across four dimensions: 1) decontextualization, 2) themes, 3) theme organization, and 4) self and other relationships. During initial stages of decontextualization, children discover objects and functions of objects. Early schemas around 5–9 months of age include exploratory behaviors such as hitting, banging, mouthing, and throwing (Linder, 2008). Children at approximately 8–12 months interact with lifelike objects and imitate functions they have experienced or observed, such as using a spoon to feed themselves (Linder, 2008; Westby, 2000). Around 2–3 years of age, children are able to decontextualize their play and use miniature replicas to represent lifelike objects, such as miniature houses, people, and cars. Eventually at approximately 3½–4 years of age, children can use language to set the scene with pretend props to substitute for real objects, such as a banana as a telephone or a hand gesture to show they are holding an imaginary phone (Linder, 2008; Westby, 2000). This dimension demonstrates use of short-term and long-term memory of objects, their functions, and ways to play with them that are not present in the immediate context using their memory of the size, shape, and function of the object.

Children also act out themes of life in their play (Lillard, 1994; Westby, 2000). Initially, between 15–24 months of age, they pretend to carry out typical daily routines such as cooking and eating. Later, between 2 and 3 years of age, they play out themes that occur often but perhaps not every day. These kinds of themes may include shopping at the grocery store or going to the doctor. Eventually, around 3–5 years of age, children act out pretend themes they have observed but not experienced such as fantasy themes (Singer, Golinkoff, & Hirsh-Pasek, 2006; Westby, 2000). For example, children may pretend to put out a fire like a firefighter or slay a pretend dragon.

These themes develop in complexity as children mature (Westby, 2000). Initially, children 17–22 months of age may use a few objects and few steps in their play. They may begin by using a spoon to feed a baby doll. Later, as they increase their memory of routines, objects, and functions, children mentally plan and sequence events, employing self-regulation, working memory, and executive function skills. Children between ages 2 and 3 years old may set the table, wake up the doll, dress the doll, and fix food on a stove to put on plates on the table before sitting down to feed the doll. When children accomplish this level of play by themselves, they are able to plan increasingly complex play episodes that combine multiple themes between 4 and 6 years of age. For example, they may combine the theme of eating breakfast with a theme of the house being on fire and a third theme that people get hurt and have to go to the hospital.

The final dimension of play development integrates social and cognitive knowledge with decontextualization, themes, and thematic organization

(Westby, 2000). Initially children pretend on themselves, such as pretending to eat or sleep. Then when they are 17–22 months old, they pretend on dolls or stuffed animals, feeding, bathing, or performing surgery on them. Children between the ages of 2 and 3 years then begin to talk to their dolls or stuffed animals and their dolls or animals talk back to them. By 3 and 4 years of age, children act out scenarios in which dolls have false beliefs, play tricks on others, and have emotions. Finally 4- to 6-year-olds learn to take on roles of other people, and their play reflects the perspective, voice, actions, and beliefs of the character they are pretending to be (Diamond, 2000; Westby, 2000). To pretend to be someone else during play requires inhibition of oneself, focused attention to pretend to be someone else, planning, setting goals, and organizing props and behavior while monitoring one's own behavior (Berk, Mann, & Ogan, 2006; Perner, 1991). Throughout play development, children are refining their skills of inhibition, self-regulation, attention, and memory.

## INFLUENCE OF EARLY ADVERSE ENVIRONMENTS

Given an intact neurological system and having one's basic biological needs met, the expectation and need for a competent and sensitive adult caregiver are essential to facilitate and nurture the development of inhibition, self-regulation, attention, and memory. Early exposure to stress, abuse, and/or neglect has negative effects on neurobiological development as well as the development of inhibition, self-regulation, attention, and memory.

### Effects on Neurobiological Development

Evidence in support of the effect of stressful environments on neuro-biological development and inhibition, self-regulation, attention, and memory can be found from animal studies (for a review see Sánchez, Ladd, & Plotsky, 2001). In animal research, developmental outcomes are worse when animals are exposed to environments with limited social contact. These animals tend to demonstrate profiles of reduced inhibition, attention, and motivation, as well as poor social behaviors similar to those observed in children exposed to abuse and/or neglect and children reared in institutional environments. These behavioral profiles include increased overactivity and stereotypical behaviors with fewer social behaviors with other animals (Sánchez et al., 2001). For example, in one study researchers increased stress for mothers of infant macaque primates by making foraging for food more difficult. This stress resulted in differences in the magnetic resonance spectroscopic imaging of the infants (Mathew et al., 2003). More specifically, 10 years after exposure to stressful rearing conditions, different ratios of cerebral metabolites and neurotransmitters were found in the anterior cingulate and medial temporal lobe. These findings were similar to clinical reports of human adolescents diagnosed with posttraumatic stress disorder (Mathew et al., 2003). In another study of rhesus monkeys raised either individually in a nursery condition or in a more naturalistic social environment, researchers found differences in the size of the corpus callosum between groups, and this persisted even after the experimental group received 6 months' exposure to a natural social environment (Sánchez, Hearn, Do, Rilling, & Herndon, 1998). These findings provide support for connectionist and social interaction theories as discussed in Chapter 1.

The majority of neurologically healthy children who are exposed to and interact with sensitive caregivers in a typical social environment become children with adequate inhibition, self-regulation, attention, and memory skills. Children who are exposed to little or disrupted social interaction, or abuse and/or severe neglect, however, often demonstrate problems with inhibition, regulation of emotional states, social-emotional behaviors, attention, and representational play behaviors (for a review see Schore, 2001). Traumatic events that occur early in children's lives affect their neurobiological development and function as well as place them at increased risk of developing mental health disorders such as personality disorders, depression, anxiety, executive function concerns, and other types of mood disorders. For example, neurobiological differences and lower levels of oxytocin hormones (associated with mediating bonding and reduction of stress) have been found in children who had experienced maltreatment and severe early neglect (Sánchez & Pollack, 2009; Schore, 2001).

## Effects on Development of Attention and Executive Function

Early exposure to adverse or poor quality care may negatively affect children's attention. In a study of 6- to 7-year-olds living in either group homes or foster families, children living in group homes had higher levels of hyperactivity and inattention, as discovered from social work case files, classroom observation, parent and teacher interviews, and teacher and parent report measures (Roy, Rutter, & Pickles, 2000). Inattention was also found to correlate with lower early reading performance (Roy & Rutter, 2006). Thus, poor quality of care and institutional care are associated with attention and inhibition problems.

Executive function development may also be affected by early adverse care or disrupted social interaction. In a study by Pears and Fisher (2005) 3- to 6-year-olds placed in foster care (99) due to abuse and/or neglect were compared with age- and socioeconomic status (SES)–matched community children (54) on general cognition, language, and neuropsychological functioning including executive function measures (Korkman, Kirk, & Kemp, 1998). Children who were placed in foster care earlier had higher executive function than children who were placed at older ages. Children with more placements over time demonstrated lower executive function scores. Thus duration of exposure to adverse early care and disrupted or inconsistent social relationships negatively affected these children's attention and executive function development (Pears & Fisher, 2005).

## Effects on Development of Play

Poor quality of care may negatively impact play development as well. In a study of 72 children between the ages of 13 and 24 months who lived with families from middle- and working-class backgrounds, researchers compared child care quality with children's play development (Howes & Matheson, 1992). They found that children who received care from centers providing above-average care, such as low child–adult ratios, demonstrated more advanced and complex play behaviors than children receiving poorer quality of care and higher child–adult ratios. In other words, although these children had not experienced abuse or neglect, the quality of their child care setting affected their play development significantly.

Children experiencing maltreatment were found to overattend to cues perceived as threatening, and children with insecure or disorganized attachment (due to abuse and/or neglect) demonstrated fewer numbers of play episodes that were of shorter duration and reduced complexity (Sánchez & Pollak, 2009). In other words, these children's memories of adverse experiences negatively affected their executive function skills to plan, organize, and carry out longer and more complex play episodes. Similar findings were reported for children receiving institutional care. In a study of 26 children between the ages of 10 and 38 months living in Romanian orphanages, cognitive and play development were measured (Daunhauer, Coster, Tickle-Degnen, & Cermak, 2010). The researchers found that the children demonstrated a range of play behaviors, from mouthing to symbolic or representational play. The oldest children (31 to 38 months of age) spent most of their time in functional play (e.g., using two objects together to appropriately hammer a peg) as opposed to symbolic play. The children's play development was largely delayed in comparison to developmental norms for U.S. children raised in their homes with their biological families from middle-income backgrounds.

In summary, several early factors could affect children's development. Early exposure to and duration of adverse care, disruption of or inconsistent social relationships, or poor quality of care may affect their inhibition, self-regulation, attention, executive function, and memory development for complex play behaviors.

## DEVELOPMENT OF INHIBITION, ATTENTION, AND MEMORY AFTER ADOPTION

As discussed in Chapters 1 and 4, outcomes following adoption were positive for most of the children who were adopted at younger ages (Juffer & Van IJzendoorn, 2005, 2009; Loman, Wiik, Frenn, Pollak, & Gunnar, 2009; Odenstad et al., 2008; Van IJzendoorn & Juffer, 2006). In general, children adopted before the age of 1 year demonstrated more complete catch-up compared with domestically adopted and nonadopted peers in most developmental areas. In addition, if children had experienced positive, stable familial care prior to being placed in institutional care, their developmental outcomes were no different than nonadopted children (Vorria, Rutter, Pickles, Wolkind, & Hobsbaum, 1998). In other words, variations in early care have long-lasting effects on developmental outcomes. These findings provide evidence in support of a dynamic system theory in developmental variations found in internationally adopted children.

In most of the research studies, global measures were used to measure longitudinal development. More specific measures may be needed to measure more subtle differences in developmental ability, such as inhibition, self-regulation, attention, executive function, working memory, and representational play (Gunnar, Bruce, & Grotevant, 2000; MacLean, 2003; Rutter et al., 2000). The following section will describe emerging research with more specific measures of cognitive abilities inherent in flexible thinking and complex cognitive functions.

## Inhibition and Attention Development After Adoption

Early studies on Romanian children adopted by families in the United Kingdom found that parents had concerns with their children who were adopted after the age of 6 months regarding attachment, regulation of emotions, and peer interactions (for a review see Gunnar et al, 2000). Canadian families who had adopted Romanian children reported similar findings. After 3 years within their families, the children had difficulty handling peers' attention toward them and demonstrated more behavioral problems, particularly attention-related problems (for a review see MacLean, 2003). Several early studies found adopted Romanian children were overly active, inattentive, and distractible. Although these behaviors improved over time, impulsivity and inattention persisted at age 11 years (Beckett et al., 2007; Kadlec & Cermak, 2002; Kreppner et al., 2007; Kreppner, O'Connor, & Rutter, 2001; Mainemer, Gilman, & Ames, 1998; MacLean, 2003; Marcovitch et al., 1997; Pollak et al., 2010; Rutter et al., 2000). These behaviors were also found to be related to indiscriminate friendliness (affection and friendliness to strangers).

Although Colvert and colleagues (2008) found increased risk for inattention, overactivity, disinhibition, and attachment in a sample of 165 Romanian adoptees, these behaviors were not related to their measures of Theory of Mind (ToM; reading the minds of themselves and others) or executive function. Colvert et al. used the Stroop test (Stroop, 1935), which measures executive skills of inhibition, cognitive flexibility, attention shift, and focused and sustained attention. However, only one measure for ToM and one for executive function were collected, which is a limitation of their findings (for information about ToM development see Chapter 8). The sample of 165 children were divided into three groups of Romanian children: 1) adopted prior to 6 months of age, 2) adopted between 6 and 24 months of age, and 3) adopted after 24 months of age. These groups were compared with a group of British children (58) who were domestically adopted prior to 6 months of age. The Romanian children who were adopted after the age of 6 months demonstrated lower levels of performance on ToM and executive function measures. In other words, the group of children who were adopted from Romania after the age of 6 months displayed disinhibition, inattention, overactivity, and indiscriminant friendliness as well as delayed ToM and executive function, yet these behaviors were not related to ToM or executive function performance. Thus, Romanian children who experienced early adverse care for 6 months or more may be a proxy for children who have experienced adverse early care in that they may be at risk of problems with inhibition, attention, activity levels, indiscriminant friendliness, ToM, and executive function. In conclusion, children experiencing adverse early care may be at risk for problems with attention and inhibition, but it is unclear whether these behaviors predict or are related to other skills such as ToM and executive function.

Given the meta-analytic studies comparing children from different countries of origin, differences in early care experiences may result in variations of developmental outcomes. Problems with attention and inhibition have been reported in studies with children adopted from several different countries of origin. In a study of 132 eight- and nine-year-olds adopted from a variety of countries (primarily Eastern Europe and Asia) by U.S. families at 1 year of age or older (up to 6.5 years of age), researchers found differences based on institutional care (Pollak et al., 2010). Comparisons included children who had experienced 1) extended exposure to institutional care, 2) foster care or adoption before 3 months of age, and 3) family care such as nonadopted children. Children were excluded if they demonstrated cognitive delays (scores $\geq 2$ standard deviations below the mean), facial symptoms of fetal alcohol syndrome (FAS; such as smooth philtrum, thin upper lip), or language delays ($\geq 2$ standard deviations below the mean on language comprehension). The institutionalized group scored lower than the other children on tests of learning and visual attention, but similarly on measures of executive function (memory results will be discussed later in this chapter), and girls performed better than boys. More specifically, children exposed to institutional care demonstrated more impulsivity and had difficulty with visual attention and matching, but they performed similarly with the other groups in auditory attention. Most of these studies recruited internationally adopted children who did not have medical diagnoses of physical disabilities or genetic or neurological problems. However, children were not excluded if they were suspected of having learning problems that may have influenced their findings.

Preliminary findings from data collected from adopted 4-year-olds who were not receiving special education services and scored within normal range in language development demonstrated no differences in inhibition (Hwa-Froelich, Roselman, & Golden, 2009). Hwa-Froelich and colleagues measured inhibition in a sample of 30 four-year-olds adopted from Eastern European and Asian countries before the age of 2 compared to an age- and SES-matched group of 27 nonadopted children. Using a simple inhibition task in which the children were asked to follow directions of one puppet but not follow the directions given by a second puppet, in preliminary analyses no statistically significant differences were found between the adopted and nonadopted groups. In addition, no differences were found between the children adopted from Eastern European countries and those adopted from Asian countries. This unpublished evidence supports the hypothesis that if internationally adopted children demonstrate development that parallels nonadopted children, they demonstrate similar inhibition skills. Earlier studies of larger samples of children recruited from the same country of origin did not control language ability and identification of special education needs. Due to the small size of this sample and the use of only one measure of inhibition, however, one cannot generalize these findings to the general population of internationally adopted children. More research with more restrictive recruitment methods is needed to study the incidence of inhibition in internationally adopted children.

Several studies included children adopted from Asian countries. Kroupina and colleagues (2003, as cited by Mundy & Sigman, 2006) studied joint attention development in a sample of children adopted from Chinese institutions by U.S. families. They found that the duration of institutional care was not related to the children's response to joint attention or initiated behavior responses to regulate caregiver behavior, but it did have a negative effect on the children's initiated joint attention development. After approximately 14 months of institutional care, the children demonstrated a decline in initiated joint attention. These findings may support the idea that there is a critical period during the first 2 years of life in which children are dependent upon expected social stimulation to develop all aspects of joint attention. However, it is important to study the development of attention behaviors after children are adopted and exposed to improved quality of care.

Adopted children's behavior has been studied through parent surveys and analysis of national registers. Gunnar, Van Dulmen, and the International Adoption Project Team (2007) conducted a parent survey with the Child Behavior Checklist (CBCL/6-18, Achenbach, 1991). The sample consisted of 1,948 children between the ages of 4 and 18 years adopted from China, Guatemala, Russia, Colombia, India, and Korea into U.S. families. Children experiencing institutional life for 4 or more months were compared with children who had experienced less than 4 months of institutional care. Overall, the majority of children who had experienced institutional care had few pervasive behavior problems. The researchers found that children who were adopted later (≥24 months), regardless of whether they had received only institutional care or less than 4 months of institutional care and mostly foster care, were at increased risk of attention problems in the clinical range. Boys and children adopted from Eastern Europe tended to have higher rates of behavior problems, which may reflect gender and cultural variables. Similar findings were reported in a Swedish national register study of children adopted by Swedish families. Linblad, Weitoft, and Hjern (2009) conducted a national cohort study of Swedish adoptees between the ages of 6 and 21 years. They found that children adopted from Eastern Europe, Middle East/Africa, and Latin America, as opposed to children adopted from the Far East or South Asia, were more frequently prescribed stimulant medication than children adopted from other countries and the general Swedish population, with children from Eastern Europe having the highest rate of stimulant prescription.

In a study including both behavioral screening and parent-report questionnaire measures, Loman and colleagues (2009) conducted a study with 269 children adopted primarily from Eastern Europe and Asia by U.S. families representing three groups: 1) postinstitutionalized children adopted at 12 months of age or older, 2) children adopted before 8 months of age experiencing less than 2 months of institutional care or who had experienced foster/relative care, and 3) nonadopted children. Children were excluded for known genetic disorders, congenital impairments, neurological conditions, and medically diagnosed FAS, and they were also screened and excluded if they demonstrated facial features associated with FAS. The parents completed a questionnaire about academic performance and service utilization. Most of the children experiencing institutional care were reported to be behind their peers in some or most school subjects and were receiving services for speech-language, learning disability, or emotional/behavior problems; children from Eastern Europe and South America were reported to receive higher rates of special education services than children adopted from African or Asian countries. These findings may be associated with problems of inhibition, attention, and/or memory.

Two survey studies, one with parents and another with schoolteachers, found higher rates of adult-reported concerns with attention and overactivity for children adopted from China by U.S. families (Tan, 2009). Tan also reported that attention problems seemed to mediate developmental delays and academic problems in children adopted from China. Tan used the CBCL/6-18 (Achenbach & Rescorla, 2001) as a survey instrument on 177 school-age children adopted from China. The checklist was used first when the children were approximately 8 years old and then again when they were approximately 11 years old. Higher ratings of attention problems at age 8 were associated with teacher-reported academic problems at age 11. In addition, Dalen and Rygvold (2006) found that hyperactivity, when associated with impulsive and inattentive behaviors, was associated with poorer educational performance in children adopted from China by Norwegian families. In a teacher-survey study of 77 children adopted from China and compared with a gender- and age-matched Norwegian peers, no differences were found between the Chinese and Norwegian groups, but more variability was found within the adopted group. This variability was explained by the teachers' judgment of the children's hyperactivity and academic language (Dalen & Rygvold, 2006). Both studies provide evidence that children adopted from China may be at risk for inattention, overactivity, and impulsivity.

To answer the question about whether internationally adopted children are at risk of inhibition and attention problems, the evidence is mixed. Although two studies report no differences in executive function or auditory attention (Hwa-Froelich et al., 2009; Pollak et al., 2010), from parent and teacher reports and behavior observation, children experiencing institutional care are rated and observed as having problems with joint attention, visual attention, learning problems, impulsivity, and overactivity across countries of origin and receiving countries (Dalen & Rygvold, 2006; Gunnar et al., 2007; Hwa-Froelich et al., 2009; Linblad et al., 2009; Loman et al., 2009; Pollak et al., 2010; Tan, 2009). Although males seem to be at greater risk, as well as children adopted from Eastern Europe and South America, the reasons for these findings are unclear.

Other factors may influence attention and inhibition. There may be cultural differences as to what is judged to be appropriate attention and activity levels between the country of origin and the receiving country. In addition to cultural differences, other unstudied variables may influence developmental outcomes for children adopted from different countries of origin who may have had different institutional experiences. More research is needed using behavioral assessment and controls to exclude children who may have a developmental delay or disorder and to control for cultural differences.

## Memory Development After Adoption

Very few studies have included measures of memory. Bos, Fox, Zeanah, and Nelson (2009) studied visual working memory and executive function in a sample of Romanian children adopted by U.K. families. They compared 8-year-olds residing in institutional care (93) and children who had been removed from institutional care and placed in foster care (48) when they were between 9 to 33 months old. Bos and colleagues administered the Cambridge Neuropsychological Test and Automated Battery (CANTAB, Cambridge Cognition). The CANTAB is a computerized neuropsychological battery developed for research, not clinical use. It consists of five subtests: 1) motor screening, 2) delayed match to sample (recognition memory), 3) paired associates learning (visual memory and learning), 4) stockings of Cambridge (spatial planning), and 5) spatial working memory (Bos et al., 2009). Their results indicated that any exposure to institutional care predicted poor performance on both working memory and executive function.

Pollak and colleagues (2010) utilized the NEPSY Developmental Neuropsychological Assessment (Korkman, Kirk, & Kemp, 1998) to measure aspects of working memory and executive function: 1) spatial working memory, 2) memory for faces, 3) a narrative memory test, 4) visual memory, 5) auditory attention and response (selective auditory attention), 6) match to sample visual search task (speed and accuracy), 7) rapid visual information processing (visual sustained attention), and 8) knock and tap test (inhibition). Recall the results of inhibition, attention, and learning for the 132 eight- and nine-year-olds adopted primarily from Eastern Europe and Asia by U.S. families that were discussed earlier. In terms of memory performance, children who were institutionalized for 12 to 78 months (1 to 6.5 years) performed less well on the spatial working memory and memory for faces tasks; no differences were found between groups on the narrative memory task. From the results of this study, children experiencing longer duration of institutional care demonstrated age-appropriate auditory memory and attention but delayed visual attention and memory and increased impulsivity (Pollak et al., 2010).

Preliminary findings for a group of 4-year-olds (32) adopted from Eastern Europe (14) and Asia (18) compared with a nonadopted peer group (31) are mixed (Hwa-Froelich et al., 2009). Although no differences were found between Eastern European and Asian adopted children, the internationally adopted children performed less well than their nonadopted U.S. peers on sentence repetition and forward digit span measures of short-term memory. On a phonological processing task often used to measure phonological short-term memory, the adopted group performed as well as the nonadopted group. Thus, internationally adopted children adopted before the age of 2 years and exposed to English for 2 to 3 years appear to demonstrate phonological short-term memory skills commensurate with nonadopted peers. They may, however, need more time to develop verbal short-term memory skills required for sentence repetition and digit span. Due to the small sample size, these results should be interpreted with caution.

In survey studies using the CBCL/6-18 (Achenbach, 1991; Achenbach & Rescorla, 2001), higher ratings of parent-reported concerns in thought problems and social concerns have been noted for adopted children (Gunnar et al., 2007; Tan, 2009). For example, Gunnar and colleagues reported these results from their survey study of 1,948 internationally adopted children (primarily Eastern European and Asian adoptees) between 4 and 18 years of age. Although it was not possible to determine whether elevated ratings of thought and social problems were clinically significant, children adopted at an older age, regardless of whether they had experienced more institutional or foster care, received higher ratings of attention, thought, and social problems. Tan also reported that his sample of 177 Chinese girls between the ages of 7 and 13 years received higher parent ratings of internalizing concerns (e.g., thought problems). These problems may be related to problems in working memory and social cognition. As children mature, they are often faced with more complex social situations and learning that require multi-modal social and cognitive processing, attention and emotional regulation, and planning and monitoring of their own responses and behaviors.

## Play Development After Adoption

Although limited, a few studies have reported findings for representational play development in internationally adopted children. Children's play, language, and cognitive development at the age of 4 years were compared in a study of 111 children adopted from Romania either within 6 months of age or between 6 and 24 months of age and 52 domestically adopted children in the United Kingdom (Kreppner, O'Connor, Dunn, Andersen-Wood, and the English and Romanian Adoptees [ERA] Study Team, 1999). The U.K. children demonstrated higher frequencies and more advanced pretend play, interactive role-play, and made more references to others' mental states than the early adopted group and the later adopted group. Children adopted from Romania at younger ages also demonstrated more advanced play development than children adopted at older ages. These differences remained after controlling for cognitive and language development but were not related to physical measures of deprivation (weight or head circumference at adoption). The authors speculated that these differences might reflect social-emotional deprivation and have implications for children's relationships with peers and social interactions in general (Kreppner et al., 1999).

Hwa-Froelich and colleagues collected a variety of assessments, including play assessments on a sample of 20 children adopted from Eastern Europe (11), Asia (8), and Guatemala (1) (Hwa-Froelich, 2007; Hwa-Froelich & Matsuo, 2010). All children were adopted by U.S. families before the age of 2 years and assessed at or before 6 months after adoption and again 12 months after adoption. Play behaviors for symbolic play, problem solving, and mastery were scored as: 1) 0 if delayed by more than 6 months, 2) 1 if delayed between 3 and 6 months, and 3) 2 if there was no delay or children scored above their chronological age. Figures 5.1 and 5.2 show the developmental profiles for the total group before 6 months and after 1 year of adoption. Figures 5.3 and 5.4 show the profiles of children adopted from Asia and children adopted from Eastern Europe prior to 6 months of adoptive care and 12 months after adoption. Approximately 1 year after adoption, children adopted from Asia displayed play skills that were largely the same as published normative ranges for U.S. children. The children adopted from Eastern Europe displayed play behaviors that were mildly delayed compared with the Asian group and test norms.

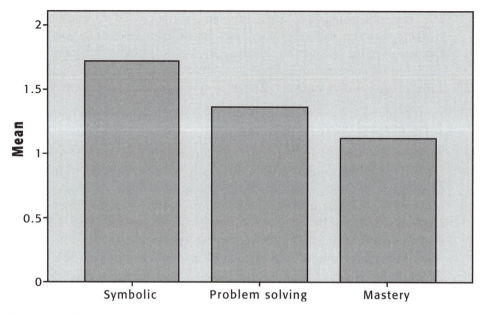

**Figure 5.1** Play behaviors at 0–6 months postadoption for total sample. These are results from an unpublished study of 20 adopted Asian, Eastern European, and Guatemalan children between the ages of 9 and 22 months. Children's play behaviors were assessed at 6 and 12 months postadoption.

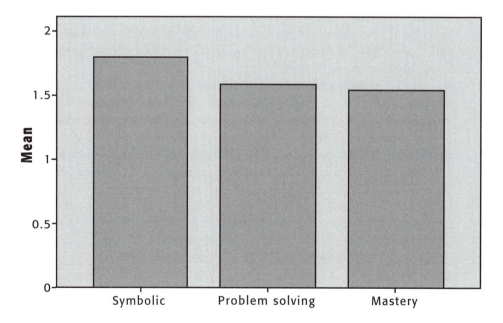

**Figure 5.2.** Play behaviors at 1 year postadoption for total sample. These are results from an unpublished study of 20 adopted Asian, Eastern European, and Guatemalan children between the ages of 9 and 22 months. Children's play behaviors were assessed at 6 and 12 months postadoption and their development was largely within normal range as compared to nonadopted developmental norms.

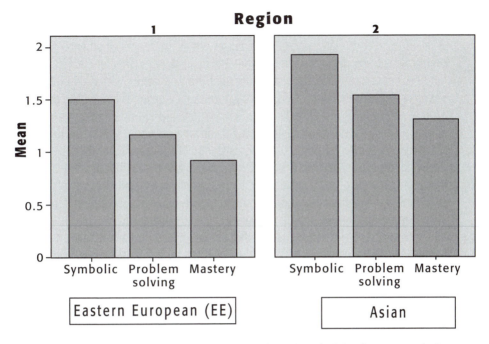

**Figure 5.3.** Play behaviors at 6 months postadoption by region of origin. These are results from an unpublished study of 20 adopted Asian, Eastern European, and Guatemalan children between the ages of 9 and 22 months. Children's play behaviors were assessed at 6 and 12 months postadoption. No statistically significant differences were found between region of origin across play behaviors.

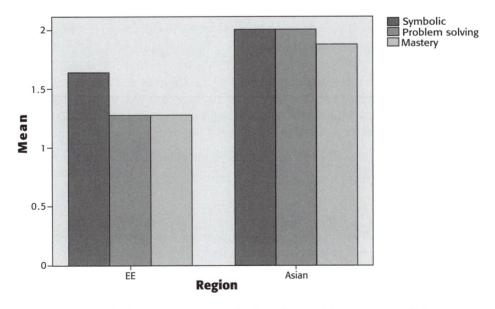

**Figure 5.4.** Play behaviors at 1 year postadoption by region of origin. These are results from an unpublished study of 20 adopted Asian, Eastern European, and Guatemalan children between the ages of 9 and 22 months. Children's play behaviors were assessed at 6 and 12 months postadoption. No statistically significant differences were found between region of origin across play behaviors at 6 or 12 months postadoption.

## ▼▼▼ *IMPLICATIONS*

Children exposed to early adverse experiences are at risk for developmental delays or problems with impulsivity, self-regulation, attention, working memory, and executive function. Robbie was evaluated early after adoption and demonstrated developmental delays in self-regulation, attention, executive function, working memory, receptive and expressive language, and symbolic play. Research findings are mixed in terms of differences based on gender and country of origin and whether visual or auditory modalities are more or less affected. Some of the research also provides evidence that males are at increased risk, as are children adopted from countries with a poor infrastructure and poor economic support for institutional care, such as Romania and other Eastern European countries, Latin American countries, and some African countries. Age of adoption seemed to be a predictor for developmental outcomes, with children adopted from Romania before 6 months of age having better developmental outcomes than Romanian children adopted after 6 months of age. For children adopted from countries other than Eastern Europe, children may have positive developmental outcomes if adopted before the age of 4 years (Odenstad et al., 2008).

This chapter provides a beginning review of the research on internationally adopted children and their developmental outcomes in attention, inhibition, regulation, memory, and play development. As discussed, some of the studies used clinically relevant measures, whereas others did not. Some of these measures involving parent and/or teacher report may be affected by cultural differences in judgment of children's behavior between the countries of origin and the receiving countries. The children's behavior may also reflect cultural differences of child rearing from their country of origin.

There is also great variability within study samples and among adopted children. This variability is most likely due to the myriad variables to which the children are exposed, as well as the individual variables within each child. For these reasons, it is advisable to assess adopted children early and often to determine whether any delays or problems are observed. Robbie was evaluated early, and, consequently, early intervention was recommended to build a strong relationship with his parents and to support his self-regulation and attention during play-based activities. Early intervention may provide children who have unique patterns of developmental risk and delay opportunities for recovery and adaptation that may help them avoid continued or later developmental delays in complex and more advanced cognitive and social skills.

## *KEY POINTS*

▶ Inhibition, self-regulation, and attention are important components of executive function, working memory, and symbolic play.

▶ Executive function and working memory are related and integrated and required for complex thinking, problem solving, symbolic play, and social interactions.

▶ Early adverse experiences such as abuse and/or neglect or poor quality of care have negative effects on neurobiological aspects, resulting in concerns with inhibition, self-regulation, attention, executive function, memory, and symbolic play development.

▶ Children exposed to institutionalized care are at risk of problems with inhibition, self-regulation, attention, executive function, working memory, and symbolic play problems and/or delays.

▶ Children adopted from countries with a poor infrastructure or weak economies with few resources to support institutional care may be at increased risk of problems with inhibition, self-regulation, attention, executive function, working memory, and symbolic play problems and/or delays.

▶ For reasons not clearly understood, male children may be at increased risk of problems with inhibition, self-regulation, attention, executive function, working memory, and symbolic play problems and/or delays.

## REFERRAL INDICATORS

An interdisciplinary team of adoption specialists should evaluate children within the first year of adoption. Children should be referred for special services if they:

▶ Display impulsivity, inattention, and/or overactivity above a clinically determined level for their developmental level

▶ Persist in exploratory play or functional use of objects during play instead of symbolic play by or after the age of 3 years

▶ Have difficulty solving problems or mastering multistep tasks by or after the age of 3 years

▶ Demonstrate problems with verbal working memory such as with forward digit span and sentence span (the ability to repeat a series of digits in order or a sentence of varying length) tasks 2 years after adoption

▶ Have difficulty with visual attention or visual memory

## REFERENCES

Achenbach, T.M. (1991). *Manual for the Child Behavior Checklist 04-18 and 199 Profile*. Burlington: University of Vermont, Department of Psychiatry.

Achenbach, T.R.L. (2000). *Manual for the ASEBA Preschool Forms & Profiles*. Burlington: University of Vermont Department of Psychiatry.

Achenbach, T.M., & Rescorla, L.A. (2001). *Manual for the ASEBA School-Aged Forms & Profiles: An integrated system of multi-informant assessment*. Burlington: University of Vermont, Research Center for Children, Youth and Families.

Baddeley, A. (1992). Working memory. *Science, 255*, 556–559.

Barkley, R.A. (1996). Linkages between attention and executive functions. In G.R. Lyon & N.A. Krasnegor (Eds.), *Attention, memory, and executive function* (pp. 307–325). Baltimore: Paul H. Brookes Publishing Co.

Barkley, R.A. (1997). Behavioral inhibition, sustained attention, and executive functions: Constructing a unifying theory of ADHD. *Psychological Bulletin, 121*, 65–94.

Beckett, C., Maughan, B., Rutter, M., Castle, J., Colvert, E., Groothues, C., et al. (2007). Scholastic attainment following severe early institutional deprivation: A study of children adopted from Romania. *Journal of Abnormal Child Psychology, 35*, 1063–1073.

Berk, L.E., Mann, T.D., & Ogan, A.T. (2006). Make-believe play: Wellspring for development of self-regulation. In D.G. Singer, R.M. Golinkoff, & K. Hirsh-Pasek (Eds.), *Play=learning*. Oxford: Oxford University Press.

Bernier, A., Carlson, S.M., & Whipple, N. (2010). From external regulation to self-regulation: Early parenting precursors of young children's executive functioning. *Child Development, 81*(1), 326–339.

Bos, K.J., Fox, N., Zeanah, C.H., & Nelson, III, C.A. (2009). Effects of early psychosocial deprivation on the development of working memory and executive function. *Frontiers in Behavioral Neuroscience, 3*(16).

Brocki, K.C., Eninger, L., Thorell, L.B., & Bohlin, G. (2010). Interrelations between executive function and symptoms of hyperactivity/impulsivity and inattention in preschoolers: A two year longitudinal study. *Journal of Abnormal Child Psychology, 38*, 163–171.

Bronson, M.B. (2000). *Self-regulation in early childhood*. New York: Guilford.

Colvert, E., Rutter, M., Kreppner, J., Beckett, C., Castle, J., Groothues, C., et al. (2008). Do theory of mind and executive function deficits underlie the adverse outcomes associated with profound early deprivation?: Findings from the English and Romanian adoptees study. *Journal of Abnormal Child Psychology, 36*, 1057–1068.

Corkum, V., & Moore, C. (1998). The origins of joint visual attention in infants. *Developmental Psychology, 34*(1), 28–38.

Cowan, N., & Alloway, T. (2009). Development of working memory in childhood. In N. Cowan & M.L. Courage (Eds.), *The development of memory in infancy and childhood* (pp. 303–341). New York: Psychology Press.

Cowan, N., & Courage, M.L. (Eds.). (2009). *The development of memory in infancy and childhood*. New York: Psychology Press.

Dalen, M., & Rygvold, A.L. (2006). Educational achievement in adopted children from China. *Adoption Quarterly, 9*(4), 45–58.

Daunhauer, L.A., Coster, W.J., Tickel-Degnen, L., & Cermak, S.A. (2010). Play and cognition among young children reared in an institution. *Physical & Occupational Therapy in Pediatrics, 30*(2), 83–97.

Diamond, A. (2000). The early development of executive functions. In E. Bialystok, & F.I.M. Craik (Eds.), *Lifespan cognition: Mechanisms of change* (pp. 70–95). New York: Oxford University Press.

Glennen, S. (2009). Speech and language guidelines for children adopted from abroad at older ages. *Topics in Language Disorders, 29*(1), 50–64.

Gunnar, M.R., Bruce, J., & Grotevant, H.D. (2000). International adoption of institutionally reared children: Research and policy. *Development and Psychopathology, 12*, 677–693.

Gunnar, M.R., Van Dulmen, M.H.M., & the International Adoption Project Team (2007). Behavior problems in postinstitutionalized internationally adopted children. *Development and Psychopathology, 19*, 129–148.

Howes, C., & Matheson, C.C. (1992). Sequences in the development of competent play with peers: Social and pretend play. *Developmental Psychology, 28*(5), 961–974.

Hwa-Froelich, D.A. (2007, November). *Internationally adopted children: Regional variations*. Presentation at the American Speech-Language-Hearing Association annual conference, Boston.

Hwa-Froelich, D.A., & Matsuo, H. (2010). Communication development and differences in children adopted from China and Eastern Europe. *Language, Speech, and Hearing Services in Schools, 41*, 1–18.

Hwa-Froelich, D.A., Roselman, J., & Golden, J. (2009, November). *Executive function and verbal working memory in children adopted from abroad*. Poster presentation at the American Speech-Language-Hearing Association, New Orleans.

Juffer, F., & Van IJzendoorn, M.H. (2005). Behavior problems and mental health referrals of international adoptees. A meta-analysis. *Journal of the American Medical Association, 293*(20), 2501–2515.

Juffer, F., & Van IJzendoorn, M.H. (2009). International adoption comes of age: Development of international adoptees from a longitudinal and meta-analytic perspective. In G.M. Wroebel & G. Neil (Eds.), *International advances in adoption research for practice* (pp. 169–192). London: John Wiley & Sons.

Kadlec, M.B., & Cermak, S.A. (2002). Activity level, organization and social-emotional behaviors in post-institutionalized children. *Adoption Quarterly, 6*(2), 43–57.

Kofler, M.J., Rapport, M.D., Bolden, J., Sarver, D.E., & Raiker, J.S. (2010). ADHD and working memory: The impact of central executive deficits and exceeding storage/rehearsal capacity on observed inattentive behavior. *Journal of Abnormal Child Psychology, 38*, 149–161.

Korkman, M., Kirk, U., & Kemp, S. (1998). *NEPSY: A developmental neuropsychological assessment manual.* San Antonio, TX: Psychological Corporation.

Kreppner, J.M., O'Connor, T.G., Dunn, J., Andersen-Wood, L., & the English and Romanian Adoptees (ERA) Study Team. (1999). The pretend and social role play of children exposed to early severe deprivation. *British Journal of Developmental Psychology, 17,* 319–332.

Kreppner, J.M., O'Connor, T.G., & Rutter, M. (2001). Can inattention/overactivity be an institutional deprivation syndrome? *Journal of Abnormal Child Psychology, 29,* 513–528.

Kreppner, J.M., Rutter, M., Beckett, C., Castle, J., Colvert, E., Groothues, C., et al. (2007). Normality and impairment following profound early institutional deprivation: A longitudinal follow-up into early adolescence. *Developmental Psychology, 43*(4), 931–946.

Kroupina, M., Kuefner, D., Iverson, S., & Johnson, D. (April, 2003). *Joint attention skills of post-institutionalized children.* Poster presented at the Society for Research in Child Development. Tampa, FL.

Legerstee, M. (2005). *Infants' sense of people.* New York: Cambridge University Press.

Lillard, A. (1994). Making sense of pretense. In C. Lewis, & P. Mitchell (Eds.), *Children's early understanding of mind. Origins and development* (pp. 211–234). Hillsdale, NJ: Lawrence Erlbaum Associates.

Linblad, F., Hjern, A., & Vinnerljung, B. (2003). Intercountry adopted children as young adults—a Swedish cohort study. *American Journal of Orthopsychiatry, 73*(2), 190–202.

Linblad, F., Weitoft, G.R., & Hjern, A. (2010). ADHD in international adoptees: A national cohort study. *European Child and Adolescent Psychiatry, 19,* 37-44.

Linder, T. (2008). *Transdisciplinary play-based assessment* (2nd ed). Baltimore: Paul H. Brookes Publishing Co.

Loman, M.M., Wiik, K.L., Frenn, K.A., Pollak, S.D., & Gunnar, M.R. (2009). Postinstitutioinalized children's development: Growth, cognitive, and language outcomes. *Journal of Developmental & Behavioral Pediatrics, 30*(0), 426–434.

MacLean, K. (2003). The impact of institutionalization on child development. *Development and Psychopathology, 15*(4), 853–884.

Mainemer, H., Gilman, L.C., & Ames, F.W. (1998). Parenting stress in families adopting children from Romanian orphanages. *Journal of Family Issues,19,* 164–180.

Marcovitch, S., Goldberg, S., Gold, A., Washington, J., Wasson, C., Krekewich, K., et al. (1997). Determinants of behavioral problems in Romanian children adopted to Ontario. *International Journal of Behavioral Development, 20,* 17–31.

Mathew, S.J., Shungu, D.C., Mao, X., Smith, E.L.P., Perera, G.M., Kegele, L.S., et al. (2003). A magnetic resonance spectroscopic imaging study of adult nonhuman primates exposed to early-life stressors. *Biological Psychiatry, 54,* 727–735.

Moon, C., Cooper, R.P., & Fifer, W.P. (1993). Two-day-olds prefer their native language. *Infant behavior and development, 16,* 495–500.

Morales, M., Mundy, P., & Rojas, J. (1998). Following the direction of gaze and language development in 6-month-olds. *Infant Behavior & Development, 21*(2), 373–377.

Moses, L.J., Baldwin, D., Rosicky, J.G., & Tidball, G. (2001). Evidence for referential understanding in the emotions domain at twelve and eighteen months. *Child Development, 72*(3), 718–735.

Mundy, P., & Sigman, M. (2006). Joint attention, social competence, and developmental psychopathology. In D. Cicchetti & D.J. Cohen (Eds.), *Developmental psychopathology* (pp. 293–332). Hoboken, NJ: Wiley & Sons.

National Center for Learning Disabilities (NCLD). (2005). *Executive function fact sheet.* Retrieved July 15, 2011, from http://www.nldline.com/xf_fact_sheet.htm

Nazzi, T., Jusczyk, P.W., & Johnson, E.K. (2000). Language discrimination by English-learning 5-month-olds: Effects of rhythm and familiarity. *Journal of Memory and Language, 43,* 1–19.

Odenstad, A., Hjern, A., Lindblad, F., Rasmussen, F., Vinnerljung, B., & Dalen, M. (2008). Does age at adoption and geographic origin matter? A national cohort study of cognitive test performance in adult inter-country adoptees. *Psychological Medicine, 38,* 1803–1814.

Pears, K., & Fisher, P.A. (2005). Developmental, cognitive, and neuropsychological functioning in preschool-aged foster children: Associations with prior maltreatment and placement history. *Developmental and Behavioral Pediatrics, 26*(2), 112–122.

Pennington, B.F., & Ozonoff, S. (1996). Executive functions and developmental psychopathology. *Journal of Child Psychology and Psychiatry, 37*, 51–87.

Perner, J. (1991). *Understanding the representational mind.* Cambridge, MA: MIT Press.

Pollak, S.D., Nelson, C.A., Schlaak, M.F., Roeber, B.J., Wewerka, S.S., Wiik, K.L., et al. (2010). Neurodevelopmental effects of early deprivation in postinstitutionalized children. *Child Development, 81*(1), 224–236.

Reznick, J.S. (2009). Working memory in infants and toddlers. In N. Cowan & M.L. Courage (Eds.), *The development of memory in infancy and childhood* (pp. 303–341). New York: Psychology Press.

Roy, P., & Rutter, M. (2006). Institutional care: Associations between inattention and early reading performance. *Journal of Child Psychology and Psychiatry, 47*(5), 480–487.

Roy, P., Rutter, M., & Pickles, A. (2000). Institutional care: Risk from family background or pattern of rearing? *Journal of Child Psychology and Psychiatry, 41*(2), 139–149.

Rutter, M., O'Connor, T., Beckett, C., Castle, J., Croft, C., Dunn, J., et al. (2000). Recovery and deficit following profound early deprivation. In P. Selman (Ed.), *Intercountry adoption: Developments, trends, and perspectives* (pp. 107–125). London: British Agencies for Adoption and Fostering.

Sánchez, M.M., Hearn, E.F., Do, D., Rilling, J.K., & Herndon, J.G. (1998). Differential rearing affects corpus callosum size and cognitive function of rhesus monkeys. *Brain Research, 812*, 38–49.

Sánchez, M.M., Ladd, C.O., & Plotsky, P.M. (2001). Early adverse experience as a developmental risk factor for later psychopathology: Evidence from rodent and primate models. *Development and Psychopathology, 13*, 419–449.

Sánchez, M., & Pollak, S.D. (2009). Socioemotional development following early abuse and neglect. Challenges and insights from translational research. In M. de Hoon & M.R. Gunnar (Eds.), *Handbook of developmental social neuroscience* (pp. 497–520). New York: Guilford.

Schore, A.N. (2001). The effects of early relational trauma on right brain development, affect regulation, and infant mental health. *Infant Mental Health, 22*(1), 201–269.

Siegel, D.J. (1999). *The developing mind.* New York: Guilford Press.

Siegel, D.J., & Hartsell, M. (2003). *Parenting from the inside out.* New York: Tarcher/Penguin.

Singer, B.D., & Bashir, A.S. (1999). What are executive functions and self-regulation and what do they have to do with language-learning disorders? *Language, Speech, and Hearing Services in Schools, 30*, 265–273.

Singer, D.G., Golinkoff, R.M., & Hirsh-Pasek, K. (2006). *Play=learning.* Oxford: Oxford University Press.

Stroop, J.R. (1935). Studies of interference in serial verbal reactions. *Journal of Experimental Psychology, 18*, 643–666.

Tan, T.X. (2009). School-age adopted Chinese girls' behavioral adjustment, academic performance, and social skills: Longitudinal results. *American Journal of Orthopsychiatry, 79*(2), 244–251.

Van IJzendoorn, M.H., & Juffer, F. (2006). The Emanual Miller Memorial Lecture 2006: Adoption as intervention. Meta-analytic evidence for massive catch-up and plasticity in physical, socio-emotional, and cognitive development. *Journal of Child Psychology and Psychiatry, 47*(12), 1228–1245.

Van IJzendoorn, M.H., & Juffer, F. (2009). International adoption comes of age: International adoptees from a longitudinal and meta-analytical perspective. In G.M. Wrobel & E. Neil (Eds.), *International advances in adoption research for practice* (pp. 189–192). Malden, MA: Wiley.

Vorria, P., Rutter, M., Pickles, A., Wolkind, S., & Hobsbaum, A. (1998). A comparative study of Greek children in long-term residential group care and in two-parent families: II. Possible mediating mechanisms. *Journal of Child Psychology and Psychiatry, 39*, 237–245.

Vygotsky, L. (1986). *Thought and language.* (A. Kozulin, Trans.). London: MIT Press. (Original work published in 1934).

Welsh, M.C., Pennington, B.F., & Groisser, D.B. (1991). A normative-developmental study of executive function: A window on prefrontal function in children. *Developmental Neuropsychology, 7*(2), 1331–1349.

Westby, C.E. (2000). A scale for assessing development of children's play. In K. Gitlin-Weiner, A. Sandgund, & C. Schaefer (Eds.), *Play diagnosis and assessment* (pp. 15–57). New York: Wiley.

Zelazo, P.D., Carter, A., Reznick, J.S., & Frye, D. (1997). Early development of executive function: A problem-solving framework. *Review of General Psychology, 1*(2), 198–226.

# 6

# Hearing, Speech, and Feeding Development

## *Deborah A. Hwa-Froelich*

---

*"Through seven figures come sensations for a man; there is hearing for sounds, sight for the visible, nostril for smell, tongue for pleasant or unpleasant tastes, mouth for speech, body for touch, passages outwards and inwards for hot or cold breath. Through these come knowledge or lack of it."*

Hippocrates *Regimen,* in *Hippocrates,* (Trans.), W.H.S. Jones (1931), (Vol. 4, p. 261). (Original work authored 400 B.C.).

---

Bella was adopted from China as the fourth child, into a family with four daughters, all adopted from China. She was approximately 5 months old when she was found and placed in care. She experienced Chinese orphanage and foster care until she was adopted at 3 years, 6 months of age. Prenatal, birth, or developmental information, prior to adoption, was not provided. Foster parents reported that Bella attended a preschool program in China and spoke very little when she was in their care. It is unknown how much time Bella spent in an orphanage or in foster care in China.

Bella's parents reported generally positive health and developmental outcomes following her adoption and said that she had enjoyed good health during the 10 months prior to the evaluation. The parents reported that Bella had one ear infection since adoption with no recurrence thereafter. The family had observed that Bella had some difficulty calming herself when tired or upset and would typically cry for long periods of time or until she fell asleep. They also reported that Bella learned English more slowly than her other adopted sisters. Bella expressed some words only to stop using them in the future, and she expressed little functional communication. The parents reported that early childhood education professionals believed Bella's communication difficulties to be typical examples of second language learning and that Bella did not need special education services.

Approximately 10 months after she was adopted and at 4 years, 6 months of age, Bella demonstrated hearing, speech, language, and symbolic play developmental delays compared with other internationally adopted children. Although Bella passed the hearing screening, she often did not alert, attend, or shift attention from visual to auditory stimuli. In addition, Bella did not consistently respond to her name or environmental sounds such as a knock on the door or whistling.

Bella's speech intelligibility was fair but negatively affected by her phonological patterns. Most of her phonological patterns were not related to first language interference. She demonstrated initial consonant deletion /j/, /p/, /k/, /r/; initial syllable deletion; fronting (d/t for medial and final k); and labilization of /b/ for /n/. Some of her processes may have been related to first-language interference such as final consonant deletion /r/, /s/, cluster reduction, and strident substitution *sh* for /s/.

Bella also demonstrated receptive, expressive, and pragmatic language delays. Her adoptive mother reported that Bella comprehended 185 words with a better understanding of verbs than nouns and all functional phrases listed in the MacArthur Communicative Developmental Inventory: Words and Gestures (CDI–WG). In addition, Bella expressed only 41 English words. During an assessment, Bella followed simple, one-step directions relying on visual cues; expressed two- to three-word utterances to request, comment, reject, and initiate social interaction; and did not answer *what* or *where* questions. These communication behaviors placed Bella at an approximate language age of 12–18 months, and her development after adoption was delayed compared with typically developing children adopted from China. In the area of symbolic play, Bella demonstrated limited and delayed play behaviors. Bella preferred to play with puzzles and other visually attractive toys such as sorting by color and playing with kitchen toys or a doctor kit. She typically combined two toys in dramatic play and linked three steps but did not link multiple themes (e.g., using a stethoscope with a doll, giving the doll medicine and a bandage). Her play behaviors placed her at a developmental level of a 24- to 30-month-old.

Bella is an example of an internationally adopted child who was adopted at an older age and had learned some Chinese. Approximately 46% of all internationally adopted children are adopted at ages younger than 12 months; 43% are adopted between 1 and 4 years old; 8% are between 5 and 9 years old; and 3% are adopted when they are older than 9 (Evan B. Donaldson Adoption Institute, 2002). Thus, approximately 54% of internationally adopted children are adopted at ages older than 1 year. In a population survey study of more than 4,000 internationally adopted children adopted between 1990 and 1998 residing in Minnesota, 64% of the children were adopted before 12 months of age, 28% were between 12 and 59 months of age, and 8% were older than 5 years old (Hellerstadt et al, 2008). Since the *Hague Convention on Protection of Children and Co-operation in Respect of Inter-country Adoption* or the *Hague Adoption Convention* (1993) was enforced in 1995, more safeguards for the protection of children have delayed adoption procedures, resulting in children adopted at older ages. Consequently, they are at various stages of development when they arrive and begin immersion into their adopted language and country. In addition to being older at the time of adoption, these children may have had more varied preadoption experiences than children adopted before 12 months old. These variations may result in unique developmental profiles for different children, providing evidence in support of dynamic systems theory (for a review see Chapter 1).

Bella's age at the time of immigration and complex developmental profile also confused early education and special education practitioners. Children placed in domestic foster care as opposed to institutional care tend to catch up with nonadopted community peers in receptive language and cognition (Nelson, III et al., 2007; Windsor, Glaze, & Koga, 2008). In spite of receiving increased social and environmental stimulation from living with a foster family and attending a Chinese preschool program, Bella demonstrated delays in hearing, speech, language, and play development. In addition, her speech and phonological patterns were not reflective of first-language interference. Practitioners need to know the typical hearing and speech development patterns for internationally adopted children in order to be able to discriminate between children with and without developmental delays. The purpose of this chapter is to describe typical and atypical hearing, speech, and feeding development of internationally adopted children. Typical receptive and expressive language development will be discussed in Chapter 7.

## FACTORS AFFECTING HEARING, SPEECH, AND FEEDING DEVELOPMENT

### Hearing Development

Auditory systems develop rapidly during the first year of life in healthy, typically developing, nonadopted children. The inner ear and central pathways are developed at birth. The inner ear consists of the cochlea, three semicircular canals, and the vestibule, which are responsible for transmission of sound to the eighth cranial nerve and responsible for interpretation of balance and movement. The brain stem contains the efferent and afferent nerves to and from the auditory cortex that is fully developed by 2–3 years of age and is responsible for processing auditory information. Infants are born with a fully functional auditory system. Auditory sensitivity toward frequency or pitch variations, particularly in relation to speech frequencies (between 500 and 1500 hertz), develops during the first year of life. Infants have hearing loudness thresholds comparable to adult listeners ranging between 3 and 25 decibels (Sininger, Doyle, & Moore, 1999). Localization of sound origins is highly dependent upon hearing and vision experiences and corresponds with motor development of head turning. Infants must be able to hear a sound within the radius of their head, turn to integrate the auditory and visual feedback loop, and learn what object or being is making a particular sound. Localization abilities develop dramatically during the first year of life and reach adult-like performance by age 5 (Sininger et al., 1999).

Hearing loss from a sensorineural or conductive loss during the first 2 years of life can adversely affect development of the auditory cortex and processing of sound. Sensorinueral hearing loss is loss associated with dysfunction of the inner ear, the eighth cranial nerve, or the auditory cortex. Causes of sensorineural hearing loss can be due to 1) genetics, 2) a birth defect, 3) an infection, or 4) prolonged exposure to high levels of noise (Stach & Ramachandran, 2008). A *conductive loss* is a hearing loss that occurs as a result of outer or middle ear dysfunction. The outer ear consists of the pinna and the ear canal, also known as the auditory meatus. The middle ear consists of the air-filled area behind the tympanic membrane, or eardrum, containing three bony ossicles (malleus, incus, and stapedius) attached to the oval window leading to the inner ear. These ossicles translate sound vibrations from the tympanic membrane into fluid waves in the fluid-filled semicircular canals. The eustachian tube opens into the middle ear and equalizes air pressure in the middle ear (Sininger et al., 1999). Conductive hearing loss can occur due to excessive ear wax, scarred or perforated tympanic membranes, or recurrent and untreated otitis media. Early detection and treatment of hearing loss, to allow typical exposure and perception of auditory stimuli, can lead to improved hearing development. Early auditory development is dependent upon an infant's perception of and exposure to auditory and speech experiences and early treatment of hearing loss (Sininger et al.,1999).

A history of recurrent ear infections may place children at risk for poor developmental outcomes. Some researchers have reported that children with histories of middle ear infections perform lower on intelligence tests compared with children without a history of ear infections. Others have found that children who suffered from otits media had poorer verbal and auditory perception but better visual sequential memory (Klein, 1984). These studies were conducted on typically developing children whose ear infections were diagnosed and treated. Developmental outcomes may be worse for children whose ear infections were not diagnosed or treated, which is often the case for children living in institutions (Johnson, 2000; Miller, 2005).

## Speech Perception Development

It is well documented that infants attend and begin to learn speech sounds early in life. Infants respond more to vowel sounds than to tones and remember previously heard speech sounds within 24 hours of birth (Sininger et al., 1999). Researchers have found that 6- to 9-month-old infants use phonotactic patterns to discern words in running speech (Friederici & Wessels, 1993; Mattys et al., 1999). In addition, early speech perception performance at 6 months of age has been found to predict language development at 2 years of age (Tsao, Liu, & Kuhl, 2004). Tsao and colleagues argued that having more advanced phonetic perception assists infants in detecting phonetic word differences and accelerates language learning. Although the infants in these studies were exposed to only one language, these findings show that early exposure to speech is important for speech perception development and is also important for later language development. These findings support the social interaction and connectionist theories of development, in that children need to be exposed to social interactions after birth for speech and language learning and neurobiological development.

In studies of children exposed to different language stimuli, children demonstrate native language preferences at early ages. Infants as young as 2 days old show preferences for native language sounds and melodies over foreign ones if the languages of choice are from significantly different origins (Moon, Cooper, & Fifer, 1993). For example, infants discriminate between the rhythmically different Japanese and English languages but not between German and English languages (Nazzi, Bertoncini, & Mehler, 1998; Nazzi, Jusczyk, & Johnson, 2000). Discrimination between similar languages, however, develops by 4–5 months of age (Bosch & Sebastian-Galles, 1997). By 6–12 months of age, infants show a decreased perception of foreign languages and an increased perception of native language stimuli (Kuhl, Tsao, & Liu, 2003). Speech perception of the languages children hear affects their linguistic representations and they no longer attend to speech stimuli outside of this representation by 12 months of age (Werker & Polka, 1993; Werker & Tees, 1984). It is typical for internationally adopted children to be exposed to one language, their birth language, and then be removed from it. When they are adopted, the children may be exposed to similar or different phonologies, syllable structures, and morphological structures than their birth language.

## Speech Development

To develop speech perception and expression, children need to be exposed to adult language models. Children living in institutional care receive less social interaction and verbal stimulation. Consequently, their speech and language development is often delayed. In an early study by Brodbeck and Irwin (1946), 94 children between birth to 6 months of age living in an institution displayed less crying, fewer different types of vocalizations, and fewer consonants and vowels than children residing with their families.

For typically developing nonadopted infants, speech development follows a predictable pattern. Specific monolingual English developmental milestones for vowel, consonant, and consonant cluster productions are available from multiple publications. It is not my intent to review these specific developmental milestones, but to provide a brief general overview of speech development. Infants develop in a linear progression from 1) reflexive crying and vegetative sounds at birth to 2 months old, 2) cooing and laughter from 2 to 4 months old, 3) vocal play from 4 to 6 months old, 4) canonical babbling around 6 months of age or older, and 5) jargon and meaningful speech from 10 to 18 months old (Bauman-Waengler, 2009; Ferguson, Menn, & Stoel-Gammon, 1992).

Articulation development begins with vowel then consonant production. The first consonants to develop are labials (made with the lips), followed by front and back plosives such as /p/, /t/, and /k/. As children continue to develop more plosive sounds, fricatives such as /f/ and /s/ begin to develop (Bauman-Waengler, 2009). More than 90% of all consonant, vowel, and consonant cluster productions should be produced accurately by the time children are 6 years old (James, van Doorn, & McLeod, 2002). Children 4 years old and older should be at least 90% intelligible in all productions (Gordon-Brannan, 1994).

Phonological development should be adult-like by 5–8 years old (Bauman-Waengler, 2009; James, 2001). Children naturally simplify speech productions through predictable processes and have been documented to inhibit use of these processes by certain ages. For example, reduplication of syllables such as *wawa* for *water* occurs prior to 1 year of age but is no longer produced by 18–21 months of age. Final consonant deletion (*my shoe* for *my shoes*) disappears around 3 years of age, whereas weak or unstressed syllable deletion (*telphone* for *telephone*) is inhibited by age 4 years. Cluster reduction (*swirl* for *squirrel*) and epenthesis (insertion of sounds such as *puhleaz* for *please*) may continue to be evident in 8-year-old children (Bauman-Waengler, 2009).

Bilingual speech development, while different, is similar to monolingual development. Simultaneous bilingual speech development is more similar to monolingual speech development than sequential bilingual speech development. Sequential bilingual language learners often produce second language (L2) errors that resemble monolingual speakers with specific language impairment (Gildersleeve-Neumann, Kester, Davis, & Peña, 2008; McLeod, 2007). First-language (L1) interference of the L2 or other language learning can affect vowel, consonant, consonant cluster productions, and phonological processes. If L1 is similar to their L2, children acquire L2 more easily. Dulay and Burt (1974) found that children who speak Chinese were less accurate in expressing English morphemes than children who speak Spanish. L1 was more similar to L2 for the Spanish speakers than the Chinese speakers. When comparing Russian and Chinese with English, consonant clusters, syllabic stress in multisyllabic words, and inflectional morphemes are common in the English and Russian languages but not in the Chinese language (Borras & Christian, 1971; Shi, 2002; So, 2007; Thelin, 1975; Townsend, 1968; Wright, 2005; Zhu, 2007). Thus, consonant clusters, multisyllabic words, syllabic stress, and inflectional morphemes are difficult for Chinese speakers learning English (Cheng, 1991). Given that Russian shares certain key characteristics with English that Chinese lacks, it is possible that these characteristics might facilitate ease of acquisition in those shared domains.

## Feeding Development

The development of suck, swallow, and feeding follows predictable stages. During the first few months of life, infants demonstrate several oral reflexes such as a rooting, suck, swallow, and tongue-thrust reflexes (Morris & Klein, 2000). Although they demonstrate a weak lip closure and poor control of their heads, necks, and trunks, infants suck and swallow liquids readily and push solids out of their mouths. By 4–5 months of life, infants lose the suck and tongue-thrust reflexes and begin to intentionally suck. Warning signs of feeding problems include 1) coughing or choking, 2) frequent spitting up, 3) recurring respiratory infections and pneumonia, 4) gurgling, hoarse, or breathy voice, and 5) unusual behaviors during feeding such as body stiffening, lack of alertness, feeding times lasting more than 30 minutes, and/or lack of weight gain (Wolf & Glass, 1992).

From 5 to 8 months old, infants begin to swallow cereals and pureed foods. They may demonstrate up-and-down munching patterns, some tongue lateralization, longer suck and swallow sequences when drinking, visual perception of and oral motor preparation for a spoon, and retraction of the upper lip after being fed with a spoon. These developmental behaviors improve and develop over the next 3 months to the point that infants demonstrate phasic biting and can hold onto a cookie or cracker with their mouth. Lateralization and beginning rotary chewing may occur during this time as well, and lips begin to remove food from a spoon with little remaining food residue left on the spoon (Morris & Klein, 2000). Possible warning signs of feeding difficulty include 1) coughing, gagging, or throwing up after meals, 2) stuffing or pocketing food in the mouth for long periods of time, 3) food or liquid leaking from the mouth, 4) aversion to different food textures, and 5) prolonged eating times (Wolf & Glass, 1992).

From 1 to 2 years of age, infants and toddlers continue to refine their biting, chewing, and swallowing behaviors until, by 3 years of age, they develop completely functional feeding skills. After 1 year, toddlers can tolerate ground, mashed, or chopped food and can bite soft cookies or crackers. Although their rotary chew is becoming more refined, they may still lose some liquid or food while chewing. The suck-and-swallow sequence has improved, although toddlers will occasionally cough when drinking too quickly. These problems are usually resolved by the time toddlers are 2 or 3 years old (Morris & Klein, 2000). If children continue to exhibit problems while eating, such as the problems listed above, they should be referred to a speech-language pathologist.

Some problems with eating are associated with psychological issues. These eating disorders include anorexia nervosa, binge eating, and bulimia nervosa. Anorexia nervosa is a type of eating disorder associated with extreme weight loss and self-starvation. Another type of eating disorder is binge eating, which is recurrent uncontrollable overeating without other compensatory strategies for eating. Bulimia nervosa involves binging followed by forcing oneself to throw up after eating (NEDA, 2009). When children demonstrate these kinds of eating disorders, they should be referred to a clinical psychologist with experience treating eating disorders. While these developmental patterns and possible disorders in hearing, speech perception, speech, and feeding development are based on children living with their biological families, internationally adopted children may have similar developmental, medical, or psychological issues related to hearing, speech, and feeding development.

## HEARING AND MIDDLE EAR HEALTH OF INTERNATIONALLY ADOPTED CHILDREN

Medical systems and quality of medical care for institutionalized children vary across countries. For example, immunizations against diseases affecting hearing, such as the measles, mumps, and rubella vaccinations, are administered inconsistently (Johnson, 2000). Otitis media, unsuspected hearing loss, ear tags, and respiratory infections are often undetected and untreated (Johnson, 2000; Johnson & Dole, 1999; McGuinness & Dyer, 2006; Miller 2005; Miller & Hendrie, 2000). Cleft palates are often unrepaired, or in some countries only the cleft lips are repaired to make the children appear physically pleasing for adoption (Bledsoe & Johnston, 2004; Miller, 2005). In general, the longer children remain in poor quality institutional care, the poorer the health, growth, and developmental outcomes (Johnson, 2000; McGuinness & Dyer, 2006; Odenstad et al., 2008; Van IJzendoorn, & Juffer, 2006). As a result, children residing in orphanages and newly adopted children demonstrate reduced physical height, reduced weight and head circumference, and developmental delays. They are also prone to infectious diseases and multiple health issues, including but not exclusive to, dental caries, undetected chronic otitis media and hearing loss, respiratory infections, feeding problems, and strabismus (Johnson, 2000; Miller 2005; Miller & Hendrie, 2000).

In addition to the high risk factors discussed above, little auditory and visual stimulation are provided in institutions. Although play materials are given to these institutions, they are often only displayed to visitors and the children rarely interact with them. Children may be medicated to induce sleep, and many of the children have never left the orphanage from the time they were placed (Bledsoe & Johnston, 2004; Johnson, 2000). As in Bella's case, children may pass hearing screenings but may not respond typically to environmental or verbal stimuli. Bella may not have developed the auditory or visual-feedback loop to localize or attend to meaningful sounds. Sounds in her preadoption life may have been perceived, but without adult mentoring, these sounds became background noise with little or no meaning.

Because children living in orphanages are not treated for ear infections or respiratory infections, they often become accustomed to the discomfort and may not complain about or show behaviors related to ear or respiratory discomfort. Therefore, parents are often unaware when their children have an infection. In spite of the fact that hearing issues may be over-looked initially, after adoption, children with chronic otitis media appear to recover well with treatment. In a study of 28 internationally adopted children from Eastern Europe, China, Korea, and Guatemala, only five children failed the hearing screening (25%) due to otitis media. By 1 year following adoption, all had resolved their otitis media and passed hearing screenings (Hwa-Froelich et al., 2006). Through the International Adoption Clinic at Saint Louis University, it is common to see children with undetected hearing loss sometimes 1–2 years after their adoption. Either the pediatrician did not conduct a hearing screening with audiometry and tympanometry, or the parents assumed the children's hearing was normal. It is highly recommended that both hearing and vision screenings be completed as soon as possible after the child is adopted and that hearing screenings occur regularly and frequently (Schulte & Springer, 2005; Stauffer, Kamat, & Walker, 2002).

## SPEECH DEVELOPMENT OF INTERNATIONALLY ADOPTED CHILDREN

Internationally adopted children represent a different kind of English language learner (ELL) and are often adopted by families who do not speak their birth language. Thus, the children cannot use their birth language to assist them in learning their adopted language. Consequently, internationally adopted children stop listening to and speaking their birth language and begin listening to and speaking their new adopted language. This situation leads to birth language attrition and rapid learning of the adopted language (Nicoladis & Grabois, 2002; Pallier et al., 2003). In addition, because of varied early experiences, internationally adopted children demonstrate different developmental trajectories than children living with their biological families. Most internationally adopted children before the age of 6 years learn English rapidly and catch up with nonadopted peers within 2–3 years after their adoption (for a review see Hwa-Froelich, 2009 and Glennen, 2009).

High-quality institutional care and early speech imitation abilities are predictive of later language outcomes. Better institutional quality may include more social interaction among adults and children resulting in the children's imitative speech skills. Imitative speech demonstrated early at the time of adoption may be a prognostic indicator of later, positive language development (Croft et al., 2007). Croft and colleagues (2007) conducted a series of studies following the development of 165 children adopted from Romania. These researchers found that 6- and 11-year-old Romanian children adopted before 6 months of age performed similarly to domestically adopted British children who were placed before 6 months of age. In contrast, Romanian children adopted after 6 months of age demonstrated greater language and cognitive developmental delays than both children adopted younger than 6 months of age and domestically adopted children. The exception to children adopted at ages older than 6 months was a group of children who: 1) were adopted between 18 and 42 months of age, 2) demonstrated verbal imitation in their L1, and 3) whose parents reported other indicators of quality institutional care. These variables predicted more advanced language development.

Although few large sample studies have been completed on articulation or phonological development in internationally adopted children, several studies provide evidence of little to no birth language interference on English speech development. Pollock (2007) reviewed single case studies and studies with small sample sizes of children adopted from Korea and China (Pollock, 1983; Pollock, Price, & Fulmer, 2003; Pollock & Schwartz, 1988; Roberts et al., 2005). From this review, she concluded that few children adopted from foreign countries display persistent articulation or phonological delays. Most internationally adopted children who were measured approximately 2 years after their adoption demonstrate common developmental error patterns similar to native English speakers without language interference from their birth language.

Speech development was studied in six girls adopted from China between 9 and 17 months of age. From speech samples collected every 3 months until the children were 3 years old, all children reached the babbling stage by 6 months of age, with babbling ratios ranging from .22 to .83. Pollock (2007) reported that syllable structure development was between .42 and .94 and the proportion of closed syllables was between 0 and .16. These proportions were within normal range for 1- to 2-year-old children.

Speech development was also reported in a nonlongitudinal study of 55 children adopted from China by U.S. families between the ages of 6 and 25 months (Roberts et al., 2005). In this study, the children's speech and language development was measured when the children were between 3 and 6 years old. The majority (93%) of the children scored within 1.25 standard deviations of the mean on the Goldman-Fristoe Test of Articulation, 2nd ed. (GFTA-2, Goldman & Fristoe, 2000). Thus, 2–3 years after adoption, children adopted from China performed similarly to English-speaking peers regarding articulation. Pollock and her colleagues (2009) analyzed the speech samples of a subset of the original sample of 55. They analyzed the speech samples for Percent Consonants Correct-Revised (PCC-R), Percent Vowels Correct-Revised (PVC-R), Phonological Mean Length of Utterance (PMLU), and phonological process usage. They reported individual variability among the 25 children, but only three children (12%) had low scores on one or more of these measures. Prosody was also assessed and only one child (4%) had problems with phrasing. Thus, in a sample of 55 children adopted from China, 88%–96% of the children performed within normal range for phonological and prosodic measures compared with same-age English-speaking peer test norms after approximately 2–3 years in adoptive care. Pollock recommends that early assessments completed within the first few months postadoption "should focus on universal aspects of speech development, such as quality of vocalizations or size and diversity of phonetic repertoire" (Pollock, 2007, p. 112).

At 1 year postadoption, similar findings of little to no L1 interference for English articulation development were found for children adopted from other countries of origin. Glennen (2007) assessed the articulation of 27 Eastern European children adopted by U.S. families between the ages of 11 and 23 months using the GFTA-2. All but three children (89%) scored within the typical range (a standard score of 80 or higher) for English-speaking peers. One child (3.7%) had an above-average score of 115 and three (11.1%) children had scores below 80. Glennen summarized her findings by stating that children who had more exposure to English had more advanced English sound system development.

In Bella's case, or for children adopted at older ages, Glennen (2009) found in a sample of 15 Eastern European children adopted between 2 and 5 years of age that the children's articulation of English sounds developed rapidly. In other words, Glennen found that most children adopted from Eastern Europe before the age of 6 years scored well within the normal range by 12–14 months following their adoption. Glennen also found that articulation abilities seemed to be moderately correlated to the amount of exposure to English. For this small sample of Eastern European children, by 9 months postadoption, the average GFTA-2 score was 95.87. At 14 months the average GFTA-2 score was 96.53 (SD = 11.22). Two of the 15 children (13%) had scores below 85. Glennen recommended that after 1 year at home, children adopted between the ages of 2 and 5 years old should score above a standard GFTA-2 score of 85. Older adopted children receiving a standard score below 85 after 1 year postadoption should be referred for early intervention speech therapy. Practitioners should exercise caution in applying these guidelines because these results are based on a sample size of 15 children adopted from Eastern Europe. Factors of cross-linguistic differences, quality of preadoption care, and other health factors can greatly affect individual children's performances.

Speech intelligibility of internationally adopted children may also be affected by other factors. Glennen (2007) observed that some of the children with average GFTA-2 articulation scores were unintelligible during conversation. Some of the children inserted prosodic or phonological place markers that were not real English or Russian words as if to increase the length of their utterances. Although their articulation was developmentally appropriate for known words, adding make-believe words when they lacked expressive vocabulary reduced intelligibility in conversation.

## POSTADOPTION FEEDING AND SWALLOWING DEVELOPMENT

Internationally adopted children may demonstrate eating and swallowing problems. Researchers and clinicians hypothesize that these problems may be related to: 1) the children being fed primarily liquid or semi-liquid foods prior to adoption, or 2) inadequate care, as with infants diagnosed with failure-to-thrive condition (infants fail to gain weight and physically grow, often associated with deprivation and poor diet). Johnson and Dole (1999) reported a range of eating and swallowing problems from clinical findings in internationally adopted children including 1) chewing problems, 2) preoccupation with food availability, 3) gorging, and 4) sometimes becoming omnivorous. Similar findings were reported from a parent-interview study of 144 children adopted from Romania between the ages of a few weeks to 43 months old (Beckett et al., 2002). Parents were interviewed when their adopted children were 6 years old and asked questions about their children's development from the time of adoption to the present. Beckett and colleagues found that 15% (21) had problems learning how to chew and swallow solid food at the age of 6 years. Children adopted after they were 1 year old or older, were more likely to have chewing and swallowing problems than children adopted at younger ages. Although older adopted children were at increased risk of having eating problems, some of the children adopted at ages younger than 6 months also demonstrated chewing and swallowing problems at 6 years of age. In addition, Beckett and colleagues reported that if the introduction of solid food was delayed beyond the first year of life, more children experienced difficulty chewing and swallowing.

Professional recommendations for treatment of chewing and swallowing problems were often inconsistent or ineffective. Beckett and colleagues (2002) reported that parents were referred to health visitors or dieticians. One recommendation was to give finger foods to chew on, such as raw vegetables. Another recommendation was a desensitization program for aversion to specific foods. Most parents, however, did not force their children to eat solid foods, opting to support nutrition first, even if it meant feeding their children pureed foods in bottles.

## ▼▼▼ IMPLICATIONS

Although individual variability should always be considered when assessing children with special learning needs, several guidelines can be followed from research evidence on internationally adopted children. A complete hearing screening including sound field, play audiometry, otoscopic examination, and tympanometry is essential to assess physical and psychometric hearing health. These screenings should be routinely and frequently completed during the first year following adoption because children who have had chronic untreated ear infections may not complain of ear pain or display warning behaviors of an infection. In addition, children who demonstrate persistent articulation errors, immature phonological processes, or errors in prosody such as disfluent speech or atypical phrasing beyond the first year postadoption, should be referred for evaluation and considered for early intervention services. Finally, initial assessments should include questions regarding eating behaviors and aversions to different kinds of food textures and types, such as substances requiring increased chewing (steak, unpeeled apples, celery), brittle foods (saltine crackers or carrots), or sticky foods (peanut butter or sticky candy). If parents report difficulties with chewing and swallowing, a feeding evaluation is recommended.

## KEY POINTS

▶ Early identification of hearing health and hearing loss is recommended.

▶ Children adopted from abroad may demonstrate delays in hearing development such as localization, speech perception, and speech processing.

▶ Preadoption speech imitation prior to an adoption age of 18 months, and positive quality institutional indicators, may be prognostic indicators for later positive language development in internationally adopted children.

▶ Assessment of articulation, phonological development, and prosody within the first year postadoption can accurately determine speech disorder in internationally adopted children.

▶ Feeding development should be explored and assessed if difficulties are reported.

## REFERRAL INDICATORS

The following are times when children should be referred to an audiologist:

▶ Upon arrival in the home country, all adopted children should receive a vision and hearing screening.

▶ For children with scarring of the tympanic membrane or showing other signs of recurrent ear infections, screenings should occur frequently during the first year following adoption.

The following are times when children should be referred to a speech-language pathologist:

▶ Children do not localize to noisemakers or sounds outside of the children's line of sight or respond to their name.

▶ Infants do not demonstrate babbling by 6 months of age.

▶ Infants do not produce age-appropriate proportions of syllable structure or closed syllables by 1 year of age.

▶ Children demonstrate little to no language comprehension or expression of words in their adopted language during the first month after arrival.

▶ Children demonstrate misarticulations, immature phonological processes, or atypical prosodic speech patterns after 12–14 months of exposure to their adopted language.

▶ Children begin to comprehend and express words and phrases in their adopted language but stop or lose comprehension or expression of these words and phrases.

▶ Children have difficulty chewing and/or swallowing, experience frequent gagging, or develop patterns of refusing to eat foods of a particular texture or consistency.

▶ Speech-language pathologists assessing articulation and phonology of older adopted children during the first year after their adoption should consider the possibility of birth language interference on productions in the adopted language.

▶ Children who do not have problems with biting, chewing, or swallowing, but demonstrate characteristics of eating disorders, should be referred to a clinical psychologist who specializes in eating disorders and has experience with internationally adopted children.

## REFERENCES

Bauman-Waengler, J. (2009). *Introduction to phonetics and phonology*. Boston: Pearson.

Beckett, C.M., Bredenkamp, D., Castle, J., Groothues, C., O'Connor T.G., Rutter, M., et al. (2002). Behavior patterns associated with institutional deprivation: A study of children adopted from Romania. *Journal of Developmental and Behavioral Pediatrics, 23*(5), 297–303.

Bledsoe, J.M., & Johnston, B.D. (2004). Preparing families for international adoption. *Pediatrics in Review, 25*(7), 241–249. Retrieved July 18, 2011, from http://www.adopt-med.org/storage/Preparing%20Families%20for%20International%20Adoption.pdf

Borras, F.M., & Christian, R.F. (1971). *Russian syntax*. Glasgow, Scotland: Oxford University Press.

Bosch, L., & Sebastian-Galles, N. (1997). Native language recognition abilities in 4-month-old infants from monolingual and bilingual environments. *Cognition.65*, 33–69.

Brodbeck, A.J., & Irwin, O.C. (1946). The speech behaviour of infants without families. *Child Development, 17*(3), 145-156. Retrieved July 18, 2011, from http://www.jstor.org/stable/3181748

Cheng, L.L. (1991). *Assessing Asian Language Performance, (2nd ed.)*. Oceanside, CA: Academic Communication Associates.

Croft, C., Beckett, C., Rutter, M., Castle, J., Colvert, E., Groothues, C., et al. (2007). Early adolescent outcomes for institutionally-deprived and non-deprived adoptees. II: Language as a protective factor and a vulnerable outcome. *Journal of Child Psychology and Psychiatry, 48*, 31–44.

Donaldson, E.B. (2002). International adoption facts. Retrieved July 18, 2011, from http://www.adoptioninstitute.org/FactOverview/international.html#6

Dulay, H., & Burt, M. (1974). Natural sequences in child second language acquisition. *Language Learning 24*, 37–53.

Ferguson, C.A., Menn, L., & Stoel-Gammon, C. (Eds.). (1992). *Phonological development: Models, research, implications*. Timonium, MD: York Press.

Friederici, A.D., & Wessles, J.M.I. (1993). Phonotactic knowledge of word boundaries and its use in infant speech perception. *Perception and Psychophysics, 54*, 287–295.

Gildersleeve-Neumann, C.E., Kester, E.S., Davis, B.L., & Pena, E.D. (2008). English speech sound development in preschool-aged children from bilingual English and Spanish environments. *Language, Speech, Hearing, Services in Schools, 39*, 314–328.

Glennen, S. (2009). Speech and language guidelines for children adopted from abroad at older ages. *Topics in Language Disorders, 29* (1), 50–64.

Goldman, R., & Fristoe, M. (2000). *Goldman-Fristoe Test of Articulation* (2nd ed.). Upper Saddle River, NJ: Pearson.

Gordon-Brannan, M. (1994). Assessing intelligibility: Children's expressive phonologies. *Topics in Language Disorders, 14*, 17–25.

Hague Conference on Private International Law. (1993). 33: *Convention on Protection of Children and Co-operation in Respect of Intercountry Adoption*. Retrieved July 18, 2011, from http://hcch.e-vision.nl/index_en.php?act=conventions.text&cid=69

Hellerstedt, W.L., Madsen, N.J., Gunnar, M.R., Grotevant, H.D., Lee, R.M., & Johnson, D.E. (2008). The international adoption project: Population-based surveillance of Minnesota parents who adopted children internationally. *Maternal Child Health Journal, 12* (2), 162–171.

Hwa-Froelich, D.A., (2009). Communication development in infants and toddlers adopted from abroad. *Topics in Language Disorders, 29* (1), 27–44.

Hwa-Froelich, D.A., Glennen, S., Pollock, K.E., Roberts, J., Scott, K., & Krakow, R. (2006). *Internationally adopted children: Evidence-based practices*. Invited presentation at the American Speech-Language-Hearing Association annual conference, Miami, FL.

James, D.G.H. (2001a). The use of phonological processes in Australian children aged 2 to 7:11 years. *Advances in Speech-Language Pathology, 3*, 109–128.

James, D., Doorn, J., van, & J., McLeod, S. (2002). Segment production in mono-, di- and polysyllabic words in children aged 3–7 years. In F. Windsor,l. Kelly, & N. Hewlett (Eds.), *Themes in clinical phonetics and linguistics* (pp. 287–298), Hillsdale, NJ: Lawrence Erlbaum.

Johnson, D.E. (2000). Medical and developmental sequelae of early childhood institutionalization in Eastern European adoptees. In C.A. Nelson (Ed.), *The Minnesota symposia on child psychology: The effects of early adversity on neurobehavioral development* (Vol. 31, pp.113–162). Minnesota Symposium on Child Psychology.

Johnson, D.E., & Dole, K. (1999). International adoptions: Implications for early intervention. *Infants and Young Children, 11*, 34–45. Retrieved July 18, 2011, from http://www.peds.umn.edu/iac/prod/groups/med/@pub/@med/documents/asset/med_49295.pdf

Klein, J.O. (1984). Otitis media and the development of speech and language. *Pediatric Infectious Disease, 3*(4), 389–391.

Mattys, S.L., Jusczyk, P.W., Luce, P.A., & Morgan, J.L. (1999). Phonotactic and prosodic effects on word segmentation in infants. *Cognitive Psychology, 38*, 465–494.

McGuinness, T.M., & Dyer, J.G. (2008). International adoption as a natural experiment. *Journal of Pediatric Nursing, 21*(4), 276–288.

McLeod, S. (2007). *The international guide to speech acquisition*. Clifton Park, NY: Thomson Delmar Learning.

Miller, L. (2005). Special regional considerations. In L.C. Miller *The handbook of international adoption medicine* (pp. 45–66). New York: Oxford University Press.

Miller, L., & Hendrie, N. (2000). Health of children adopted from China. *Pediatrics, 105*(6), 76–87. Retrieved July 18, 2011, from http://pediatrics.aappublications.org/cgi/reprint/105/6/e76

Moon, C., Cooper, R.P., & Fifer, W.P. (1993). Two-day-olds prefer their native language. *Infant behavior and development, 16*, 495–500.

Morris, S.E., & Klein, M.D. (2000). *Pre-feeding skills, second edition*. San Antonio, TX: Therapy Skill Builders.

National Eating Disorder Association (NEDA). (2009). *Learn basic terms and information on a variety of eating disorder topics*. Retrieved July 18, 2011, from http://www.nationaleatingdisorders.org/information-resources/general-information.php.

Nazzi, T. Bertonici, J., & Mehler, J. (1998). Language discrimination by newborns: Towards an understanding of the role of rhythm. *Journal of Experimental Psychology: Human Perception and Performance, 24*, 756–766. Retrieved July 18, 2011, from http://lpp.psycho.univ-paris5.fr/pdf/1387.pdf

Nazzi, T., Jusczyk, P.W., & Johnson, E.K. (2000). Language discrimination by English-learning 5-month-olds: Effects of rhythm and familiarity. *Journal of Memory and Language, 43,* 1-19.

Nelson, III, C.A., Zeanah, C.H., Fox, N.A., Marshall, P.J., Smyke, A.T., & Guthrie, D. (2007). Cognitive recovery in socially deprived young children: The Bucharest Early Intervention Project, *Science, 318*(5858), 1937–1940.

Nicoladis, E., & Grabois, H. (2002). Learning English and losing Chinese: A case study of a child adopted from China. *The International Journal of Bilingualism, 6*(4), 441–454.

Odenstad, A., Hjern, A., Lindblad, F., Rasmussen, F., Vinnerljung, B., & Dalen, M. (2008). Does age at adoption and geographic origin matter? A national cohort study of cognitive test performance in adult inter-country adoptees. *Psychological Medicine, 38,* 1803–1814.

Pallier, C., Dehaene, S., Poline, J.B., LeBihan, D., Argenti, A.M., Dupoux, E., et al. (2003). Brain imaging of language plasticity in adopted adults: Can a second language replace the first? *Cerebral Cortex, 13,* 155–161. Retrieved July 18, 2011, from http://cercor.oxfordjournals.org/cgi/reprint/13/2/155

Pollock, K.E. (2007). Speech acquisition in second first language learners (Children who were adopted internationally). In S. McLeod *International guide to speech acquisition* (pp. 107–112). New York: Thompson-Delmar Learning.

Roberts, J.A., Pollock, K.E., Krakow, R., Price, J., Fulmer, K.C., & Wang, P.P. (2005). Language development in preschool-age children adopted from China. *Journal of Speech, Language, and Hearing Research, 48*(1), 93–107.

Schulte, E.E., & Springer, S.H. (2005). Health care in the first year after international adoption. *Pediatric Clinics of North America, 52,* 1331–1349.

Shi, Y. (2002). *The establishment of Modern Chinese grammar: The formation of the resultative construction and its effects.* Philadelphia: John Bejamins Publishing.

Sininger, Y.S., Doyle, K.J., & Moore, J.K. (1999). The case for early identification of hearing loss in children. Auditory system development, experimental auditory deprivation, and development of speech perception and hearing. *Pediatric Clinics of North America, 46*(1).

So, L.K. H. (2007). Cantonese speech acquisition. In S. McLeod (Ed.), *The international guide to speech acquisition* (pp. 313–326). Clifton Park, NY: Thomson Delmar Learning.

Stach, B.A., & Ramachandran, V.S. (2008). Hearing disorders in children. In J.R. Madell & C. Flexor (Eds.), *Pediatric audiology. Diagnosis, technology, and management* (pp. 3–12). New York: Thieme.

Stauffer, W.M., Kamat, D., & Walker, P.F. (2002). Screening of international immigrants, refugees, and adoptees. *Primary Care Office Practice, 29,* 879-905.

Townsend, C. E. (1968). *Russian word formation.* New York: McGraw-Hill Book Company.

Tsao, F-M., Liu, H-M., & Kuhl, P.K. (2004). Speech perception in infancy predicts language development in the second year of life: A longitudinal study. *Child Development, 75,* 1067–1084. Retrieved July 18, 2011, from http://ilabs.washington.edu/kuhl/pdf/tsao_liu_2004.pdf

Van IJzendoorn, M.H., & Juffer, F. (2006). The Emanual Miller Memorial Lecture 2006: Adoption as intervention. Meta-analytic evidence for massive catch-up and plasticity in physical, socio-emotional, and cognitive development. *Journal of Child Psychology and Psychiatry, 47*(12), 1228–1245.

Werker, J.F., & Polka, L. (1993). Developmental changes in speech perception: New challenges and new directions. *Journal of Phonetics, 21,* 83–101. Retrieved July 18, 2011, from http://infantstudies.psych.ubc.ca/uploads/forms/1252960218WerkerPolka_1993.pdf

Werker, J.F., & Tees, R.C. (1984). Cross-language speech perception: Evidence for perceptual reorganization during the first year of life. *Infant Behavior and Development, 7,* 49-63.

Windsor, J., Glaze, L.E., Koga, S.F., & the Bucharest Early Intervention Project Core Group. (2007). Language acquisition with limited input: Romanian institution and foster care. *Journal of Speech-Language-Hearing Research, 50,* 1365–1381.

Wolf, L.S., & Glass, R.P. (1992). *Feeding and swallowing disorders in infancy: Assessment and management.* San Antonio, TX: Therapy Skill Builders.

Wright, K.L. (2005). *Typical phonological development in English: Effects of a bilingual Russian–English language environment.* Unpublished master thesis, Portland State University, Portland, Oregon.

# 7

# Prelinguistic, Receptive, and Expressive Language Development

*Deborah A. Hwa-Froelich*

*"Language exerts hidden power, like a moon on the tides."*

Rita Mae Brown, *Starting from Scratch* (1988)

Drew was adopted from a Russian orphanage when he was 3 years, 10 months old. He spent his first year of life in a Russian hospital, his second year with his grandmother, and approximately 1½ years in an orphanage. According to the medical reports from the orphanage, his mother's pregnancy and delivery were normal and no problems were reported. Drew's developmental history up to the time of adoption was not reported. Drew spoke only Russian at the time he was adopted.

For the first 5 months following Drew's adoption, his parents reported that he was healthy and developing typically. At the time he was adopted, Drew was diagnosed with scabies, which was treated and no longer a problem. He also had several cavities that were filled. His parents reported that he was generally happy, well behaved at home and preschool, and interacting well with both adults and other children. Although Drew initially spoke Russian, he was also rapidly learning English, and his parents reported having no difficulty understanding his wants and needs.

Drew was initially evaluated when he was 4 years, 3 months old, approximately 5 months after he was adopted. He passed a hearing screening and received a standard score of 85 for receptive language and 79 for expressive language on a general English language test. During a play-based assessment, Drew's play behaviors in the cognitive, social-emotional, and communication development areas were age appropriate. By 13 months postadoption, at age 5 years, both his receptive (85) and expressive language (89) scores were above a standard score of 80, with a total language score of 86. His play behaviors continued to be age appropriate. When Drew was 5 years, 10 months old—2 years with his adoptive family—his language scores were in the average range, with a total language score of 106, a receptive language score of 125, and an expressive language score of 100. On a standardized English test of articulation, Drew received a standard score of 107. His parents reported that Drew was performing well in the regular classroom and that he had no problems communicating with the teacher or his peers.

Drew, like Bella described in Chapter 6, represents one of 43% of internationally adopted children who are older than 1 year of age at the time of adoption (Evan B. Donaldson Adoption Institute, 2002). He also experienced three different kinds of preadoption care by residing first in a hospital environment, then living with his grandmother, and finally living in institutional care. His story of English language development is nothing short of amazing and exemplifies typical language development for the majority of internationally adopted children.

Language development is dependent upon several factors. Infants must have no neurological symptoms, hearing loss, recurrent ear infections, or oral motor anomalies such as cleft palate. In addition, as social interaction theorists believe, infants must be exposed to language-rich social interactions to begin to develop knowledge, social communicative functions, and receptive and expressive language (for a review see Chapter 1). Although hospital care resembles orphanage care, the year Drew spent with his grandmother may have provided him with enough stimulation and care to help him overcome the adversity of institutional life to acquire language. Children removed from institutional care prior to 15 months of age tend to catch up with community peers in receptive language after approximately 27 months of foster care (Windsor, 2007). Social interactions with his grandmother may have helped Drew comprehend and express the Russian language prior to entry into an orphanage. As described in Chapter 6, internationally adopted children who experience better quality of care and can imitate words in their birth language prior to adoption tend to develop better speech and language skills (Croft et al., 2007). Drew's preadoptive language development may have helped him adapt his language learning to learning English. These different experiences, resulting in quick acquisition of English, provide support for a dynamic systems theory of language development, in that different variables result in different nonlinear outcomes (for a review see Chapter 1).

Language learning is a developmental process affected by many variables. The purpose of this chapter is to contrast typical English language development with a different kind of English language learner (ELL). As shown in Figure 7.1, internationally adopted children may become sequential bilingual language learners or disrupted ELLs based on whether their adoptive families speak or do not speak the children's birth language. Most sequential bilingual ELLs learn their native language at home and begin learning English once they enter school. In contrast, if adoptive families provide learning experiences in their children's birth language,

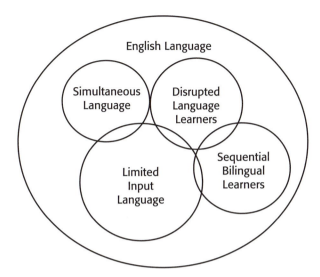

**Figure 7.1.**   English language learners (Reprinted with permission from Hwa-Froelich, D.A. [2009]. Communication development in infants and toddlers adopted from abroad. *Topics in Language Disorders, 29*[1], 27–44).

some internationally adopted children continue educational learning in their native language from a tutor or nanny and begin learning English at home through family interactions. This may not always be the case, however. Glennen and Masters (2002) reported on one case in which a parent who spoke the child's birth language adopted a child, but the child stopped speaking the birth language in spite of this situation. If the adoptive families do not speak or provide learning experiences in the children's birth language, internationally adopted children exemplify disrupted language development in that they stop listening to and expressing their birth language to focus on learning their adopted, or a second, first language (Glennen, 2005; Hwa-Froelich, 2009).

In either case of sequential or disrupted language learning, adopted children may have received limited social and linguistic input if they resided in institutions, or they may have experienced better social and language interactions if they lived with relatives or foster families prior to adoption. On the other hand, if children are adopted at younger ages from poor quality institutional care, developmental outcomes are more positive than if they are adopted at older ages (Rutter & the English and Romanian Adoptees [ERA] Study Team, 1998; Van IJzendoorn, Bakermans-Kranenburg, & Juffer, 2007; Van IJzendoorn & Juffer, 2006). Consequently, language development for internationally adopted children may differ based upon the language input they received prior to adoption, the age at which they were adopted, and the quality of language exposure they receive following adoption. For these reasons, language development for younger and older adopted children will be described, as well as later language development at school age.

## RISK FACTORS ASSOCIATED WITH LANGUAGE DELAY

From the descriptions of medical health and physical growth risk factors for internationally adopted children, it is clear that these factors can result in language delays (Ladage, 2009; Mason & Narad, 2005; Pomerleau et al., 2005). For children who are born without abnormal neurological symptoms or exposure to toxins, drugs, alcohol, or nicotine, the success of language acquisition depends on social interaction and language input from an adult caregiver. When children are exposed to inconsistent or inappropriate social interactions, or their communication is misinterpreted, they are more likely to exhibit dysfunctional or delayed communication development and social-emotional relationships (Beck, 1996; Coh, Matias, Tronick, Connell, & Lyons-Ruth, 1986; Solantus-Simlua, Punamaki, & Beardslee, 2002; Sroufe, 1997). The amount and quality of caregiver verbal stimulation have been found to strongly correlate with communication abilities in children being raised by their biological parents and for children attending a child care center (Clarke-Stewart, 1973; National Institute of Child Health and Human Development Early Child Care Research Network [NICHD], 2000; Stafford & Bayer, 1993). These studies support the premise that if children are provided "good enough care" (Odenstad et al., 2008, p. 1810), they develop skills that enable them to achieve academic and social success. Children residing in orphanages that offer poorer quality of care may experience less social interaction or language input, which may adversely affect their language acquisition.

### Institutional Risk Factors

From clinical data, Miller (2005) reported that quality and type of care vary across both Asian and Eastern European orphanages. Some countries offer foster care placement in addition to orphanage care. As in Drew's case and those of other children adopted from Eastern European, Asian, and South American countries who were seen at the International Adoption Clinic (IAC) at Saint Louis University in St. Louis, Missouri, parents have reported that their children spent some time with their biological families or spent some time in foster care before being placed in the orphanage. Parents have reported variability in preadoption experiences, ranging from foster care, institutional care, or a combination of both (Hellerstedt et al., 2008).

Quality of institutional care depends in large part on the training of orphanage caregivers. Orphanage caregivers provide care for several children at one time, may not direct their discourse directly to children, or may not have the educational knowledge or training to provide conversations with each child. In an early study of orphanage care, Tizard and Joseph (1970) compared British children living in institutions with community children living with their biological families. Children living in institutions exhibited indiscriminate friendliness with strangers, lower cognitive scores, and delayed expressive language. Later, Tizard, Cooperman, Joseph, and Tizard (1972) compared children's language comprehension and expression for two groups of children residing in orphanages providing different levels of care. One group of institutions provided excellent physical care, exposure to books and play equipment, low child–staff ratios, and increased opportunities for social interaction. Another group of children resided in orphanages that provided lower quality physical care, less exposure to books and play equipment, higher child–staff ratios, and fewer opportunities for social interaction. Although the majority of the children demonstrated at least average language abilities, the children residing in the better quality orphanages had above-average language performance (Tizard et al., 1972). The quantity of caregiver talk and daily reading sessions in the higher quality institutions were associated with more advanced child communication development, and the quality of staff talk (e.g., more talk intended to inform and not just for basic care) was highly correlated with language comprehension. Similar findings for children in U.S. foster care indicate that consistency of care and increased opportunities for social interaction have a positive impact on children's cognitive and linguistic development (Pears & Fisher, 2005). British institutional care and U.S. foster care may differ from institutional and foster care in different countries.

From a literature review of Eastern European orphanage care and educational training of the Baby Homes' (the name given to infant/toddler group care rooms or buildings) directors and staff and from personal experience, Johnson (2000) reported that the training of staff of Eastern European institutions focused on health care rather than child development. Infants and toddlers are raised in institutionalized Baby Homes, where they received basic care to meet their biological needs, but social and language stimulation were not emphasized, and children were often kept in their cribs for most of the day. Given these circumstances, internationally adopted children may be at increased risk for receptive, expressive, and social language delays.

In some cases of children living in orphanages, having a preferred caregiver may be enough to result in better language and attachment outcomes. Smyke, Dumitrescu, and Zeanah (2002) interviewed caregivers about 89 Romanian children they knew well who resided in large (3 staff to 30 children) or small (1 staff to 10–12 children) institutional groups. Their answers were compared with parents whose children attended Romanian child care centers and lived with their biological families. Children were grouped as 1) living with biological caregivers, 2) having a preferred caregiver, and 3) not having a preferred caregiver. Children residing in orphanage care without a preferred caregiver were reported to have more stereotypical behavior, indiscriminant friendliness, and language delays.

These reports of stereotypical behavior, such as rocking or head banging, were mildly to moderately related to caregiver-reported delays in language development and attachment disturbance. Children with a preferred caregiver had fewer of these behaviors compared with children without a preferred caregiver, but more of these behaviors compared with the children living with their families (Smyke et al., 2002). Thus, children living in institutions without a preferred caregiver may be at increased risk for delayed language development than children with a preferred caregiver. Children with a preferred caregiver, however, continue to demonstrate more delays than children living with their families.

Some research has shown that higher quality preadoptive care and preadoptive language development predicted better postadoption development. Romanian children adopted before 6 months of age performed similarly to domestically adopted British children who were placed before 6 months of age. In contrast, Romanian children adopted after 6 months of age demonstrated greater language and cognitive developmental delays than children adopted younger than 6 months of age and domestically adopted children (Rutter, Colvert et al., 2007; Rutter, Kreppner et al., 2007). As reported in Chapter 6, Croft et al. (2007) found that for Romanian children adopted by British families at ages 18 to 42 months who could imitate words in their birth language and their adoptive parents reported indicators that their children had received better quality of institutional care (e.g., opportunity for motor development, better psychological environments, less emotional disturbance, a higher developmental quotient at arrival), postadoption language performance at age 6 and 11 years was more advanced. Thus, parent-reported variables of institutional quality and imitative speech skills observed early after adoption may offer prognostic indicators of later positive developmental outcomes (Croft et al., 2007). In contrast, longer exposure to adverse environments and the absence of imitative speech skills may indicate an increased risk of language delay.

Some investigators have studied developmental outcomes for children in foster care in other countries compared with children residing in institutions and children raised by their biological parents. Windsor et al. (2007) studied developmental growth for 20 Romanian children who were removed from an institutionalized environment between the ages of 17 and 19 months and randomly placed in Romanian foster care for different lengths of time: 1) community foster care for less than 6 months and 2) community foster care for at least 12 months (Windsor, Glaze, Koga, & the Bucharest Early Intervention Project Core Group, 2007). Language outcomes at 30 months of age for both foster care groups were compared with an age-matched group of institutionalized Romanian children and children living with their biological families. Children in foster care for at least 12 months and those living with their biological families had more advanced cognitive and language development than children in institutional care and those in foster care for less than 6 months (Nelson et al., 2007; Windsor et al., 2007).

The 12-month foster care group was comparable to children living with their families in terms of phonological and vocabulary development but demonstrated delays in mean length of utterance. Language gains were not evident in children placed in foster care for less than 6 months. Thus, children placed in foster care for at least 12 months caught up with children living with their biological families in receptive language but continued to demonstrate some expressive language delay. Windsor reported later that there seemed to be a critical age for foster care placement, in that children placed before 15 months of age were comparable to community peers by 42 months of age. Children placed in foster care after 15 months of age demonstrated delayed language development at 42 months of age. Similar changes in cognitive development have been documented with Romanian children randomly selected to remain in institutional care or be placed in foster care (Nelson et al., 2007). These studies provide evidence that early exposure to the quantity, quality, and consistency of social interaction and language input positively impacts cognitive and language development. In these studies, language input across conditions was monolingual in the children's birth language and original culture. Language acquisition development may vary after adoption, when children experience a disruption in language exposure; that is, they stop hearing and expressing their birth language and begin hearing and expressing the language of their adoptive homes.

## Risk Factors Following Adoption

In addition to preadoptive variables having an impact on later language development, more variables are introduced after adoption as children are moved from daily exposure to their birth language and culture into different linguistic and social learning contexts. Several factors have been shown to have an impact on adaptation and development subsequent to adoption: 1) disrupted language development, 2) children's attention and activity levels, 3) disrupted attachment and relationship development, and 4) postadoption maternal sensitivity.

The process of speech-language development for internationally adopted children differs from the process for bilingual children who are exposed somewhat equally to two languages and who can use one language (L1) to assist them in learning a second one (L2). In contrast, children adopted from other countries are rarely adopted by families who speak their birth language or who have access to resources in their children's language on a consistent basis. As a result, these children quickly stop speaking and responding to their birth language and begin learning a second first language (Gindis, 1999, 2003, 2005; Nicoladis & Grabois, 2002). When the first language has not yet been established firmly, this presents a new and different challenge in learning another language.

Disrupted language development has been studied in single cases and in clinical samples. In a case study of a 17-month-old girl adopted from

China by a single parent, the degree of Chinese language retention and English language acquisition was measured (Nicholadis & Grabois, 2002). Beginning 1 month after adoption, between the ages of 18 and 20 months, she was videotaped weekly during free play with Chinese- and English-speaking adults. At the first session she produced 1) one English and three Chinese words, 2) demonstrated comprehension of one English and no Chinese words, and 3) imitated one English and no Chinese words. Within 2 weeks, she stopped producing and imitating Chinese words but responded appropriately to two Chinese words. Two months after adoption, she no longer expressed, imitated, or responded to any Chinese words. Because her adoptive parent spoke no Chinese, she had few opportunities to imitate her birth language after adoption. At the same time that her few Chinese words were disappearing, however, she continued to accelerate her English language acquisition.

Children adopted at older ages demonstrate a similar progression of birth language attrition and second first language development. From clinical data, Gindis (1999, 2003, 2005) reported that when children are adopted at older ages (4–9 years), attrition of L1 expression (tones, inflectional patterns, words, and grammar) occurred within 3–6 months after adoption. Responses to L1 decreased and stopped within 3–12 months following adoption. Because of this rapid attrition of the birth language, there may be less birth language interference when learning a second first language. Researchers have found little to no interference in articulation and phonological and early morphological development between the children's birth and second first language for children adopted by U.S. or Canadian families before 2 years of age (Glennen, Rosinsky-Grunhut, & Tracy, 2005; Pollock, 2007). These factors differentiate the language development process of internationally adopted children from sequential bilingual learners who retain access to the first language.

Additional outcomes of institutional rearing that may negatively impact children's communication development are behaviors of inattention and overactivity (Kreppner, O'Connor, Rutter, & the ERA Study Team, 2001). Kreppner et al. compared 165 six-year-old children adopted from Romania before the age of 2 years with children adopted from institutions in the United Kingdom. Data were collected on both groups at age 4; the Romanian adoptees were evaluated again at age 6. Romanian children adopted after 6 months of age were rated by parents and teachers as being significantly more inattentive and overactive than Romanian children adopted before 6 months of age and domestically adopted children. The children did not differ in conduct or in terms of having emotional difficulties, and these difficulties were not related to their age of adoption. The authors hypothesized that this type of inattention/overactivity may be an outcome of institutionalized neglect and deprivation as opposed to typical varieties of attention deficit disorder with or without the hyperactivity component (ADD, ADHD), which are hypothesized to have a genetic or neurologically based etiology. Thus, medications typically prescribed for individuals with ADD or ADHD may not have the same effect on internationally adopted children with inattention/overactivity. On the other hand, inattention/overactivity may have similar effects on learning, working memory, and social communication skills as other disorders of attention and hyperactivity (Baker & Cantwell, 1982; Cantwell, Baker, & Mattison, 1979; Fox, Long, & Langlois, 1988; Love & Thompson, 1988; Oram, Fine, & Okamoto, 1999; Ruhl, Hughes, & Camarata, 1992; Singer & Bashir, 1999). Please refer to Chapter 5 for more specific information related to attention and working memory development.

Some adopted children have difficulty forming a close, attached relationship with their adoptive parents, which could impact social interactions and language development. O'Connor, Marvin, Rutter, Olrick, and the ERA Study Team (2003) found that Romanian children adopted at ages older than 6 months compared with children adopted from British domestic orphanages displayed more frequent insecure or different kinds of attachment behaviors (avoiding or dependent behaviors directed toward a stranger, emotional exuberance, nervous excitement, silliness or coyness, and excessive playfulness similar to immature children). Rutter et al. (Rutter, Colvert, et al., 2007; Rutter, Kreppner, et al., 2007) followed 144 children adopted from Romania, measuring the children's performance at 4, 6, and 11 years of age. Head circumference and inattention/overactivity were associated with the duration of institutional care or age of adoption. At age 6, lower head circumference and higher levels of inattention/overactivity predicted indiscriminant friendliness or disinhibited attachment in the Romanian adoptees at age 11. Disinhibition was associated with what Rutter et al. (Rutter, Kreppner et al., 2007) called "quasi-autism," cognitive impairment, peer relationship problems, inattention/overactivity, and conduct problems. The authors described quasi-autism as autisticlike behaviors of obsessive, repetitive, and/or stereotypical behaviors; poor social relationships; and communication with atypical, autisticlike behaviors such as interest in social approach and flexible communication skills. Disinhibited attachment and indiscriminant friendliness may affect social-emotional development, in that children may demonstrate impulsive or antisocial behaviors and may not follow directions, or they may break rules without understanding the consequences of their behavior. Inhibition, overactivity, inattention, and quasi-autistic behaviors may reflect problems in the children's ability to regulate attention and behavior so that behaviors, such as superfluous spontaneous expression, during learning situations may interfere with attention for processing information for learning.

Temperament and maternal sensitivity differences of the adoptive parents may also play a factor in communication development. When adoptive parents demonstrated maternal sensitivity and their child had an easy temperament, this combination resulted in positive developmental adaptation following adoption. Stams, Juffer, and Van IJzendoorn (2002) measured maternal sensitivity and the temperament of 146 children from Sri Lanka (79), South Korea (48), and Columbia (19) who were adopted by Dutch families. The children were adopted before the age of 6 months; were followed at 12, 18, and 30 months; and then seen again at 7 years of age. At 12, 18, and 30 months of age, maternal sensitivity was assessed during free play in the home and during five tasks in which the parents assisted their children in completing a task such as putting together a puzzle. Child temperament was measured using a parent-report questionnaire. Parents judged temperament by how easy or difficult their children were in the areas of sociability, persistence, mood, and adaptability. The investigators found that maternal sensitivity and child temperament predicted social and cognitive development at age 7 (Stams, Juffer, & Van IJzendoorn, 2002). Because social and cognitive development influence language development, maternal sensitivity and child temperament may affect language development also.

In addition, a more stimulating and supportive adoptive home environment correlated with higher cognitive outcomes for Romanian adopted children (Morison & Ellwood, 2000). Researchers recruited 94 children from three groups: 1) 24 children adopted from Romania prior to 4 months of age, 2) 35 children adopted from Romania between 8 and 53 months of age, and 3) 35 Canadian-born gender and age-matched children. Quality of stimulation and support available in the home environment was measured with the Home Observation for Measurement of the Environment Inventory (Caldwell & Bradley, 1984). Children whose parents provided more stimulation and support scored higher on measures of cognition.

Parental sensitivity in responding and communicating with infants may contribute to the relationship between parents and children, help children learn successful ways to communicate, and provide the foundation for later successful communicative interactions in academic and social contexts. Researchers (e.g., Morison & Elwood, 2000) have theorized that a transactional relationship may exist between parents and children. Because the parents provide increased stimulation and social support at home, this stimulation may facilitate higher developmental behaviors so that children can provide more responses that may elicit more parental stimulation.

These studies provide evidence that disruption in language and relationship development, inattention, overactivity, and maternal sensitivity affect postadoption adaptation. However, more research is needed to study the relationship among genetics, temperament, attachment, attention, overactivity, and communication development as well as other unstudied variables in internationally adopted children.

## INFANT/TODDLER LANGUAGE DEVELOPMENT AFTER ADOPTION

### Communication Development Observed by Parents

For infants in the developmental stages of acquiring language, early childhood professionals may collect parent-report assessments to measure infants' prelinguistic and early linguistic behaviors that are predictive of later language development. These measures may focus on social interaction behaviors such as eye gaze, joint attention, vocalizations, gestures, and symbolic play behaviors (Wetherby, Warren, & Reichle 1998; Wetherby & Prizant, 2002). Linguistic measures typically focus on comprehension and expression of words, phrases, sentences, and morphological development in a particular language (e.g., in English: plural –s, possessive –s, verb tense –ing, -ed). These measures include 1) the Rossetti Infant-Toddler Language Scale (the Rossetti) (Rossetti, 1990), 2) the Language Development Scale (LDS) (Rescorla, 1989), and 3) the MacArthur-Bates Communicative Development Inventories-Words and Gestures (MCDI-WG) (Fenson et al., 2007).

Research on the performance of internationally adopted infants on these measures provides preliminary developmental information on children adopted from Eastern Europe and China by U.S. families (as reviewed by Hwa-Froelich, 2007 & 2009). Table 7.1 provides referral cut-off scores for English-speaking parent-report and behavior measures for internationally adopted infants and toddlers. Research on early development of children adopted from Eastern Europe on the adapted Rossetti, LDS, and the MCDI-WG has been reported by Glennen and Masters (2002) and by Glennen (2005). The majority of the Eastern European children adopted at younger ages (<12 months) had parent-reported LDS receptive and expressive language behavior comparable to English-speaking peers by 24 months of age, or 12 months postadoption. Although older adopted children (>12 months) continued to demonstrate delays at 37–40 months of age or older (14–27 months postadoption), they demonstrated rapid expressive language development. These older children should begin expressing English words quickly, have an expressive vocabulary of 50 words, and begin expressing two-word phrases by 24–28 months of age. MCDI-Words Comprehended scores for Eastern European children adopted between ages 11 and 23 months were found to be predictive of later language development for children adopted from Eastern Europe. Glennen (2007a) reported that MCDI comprehension developmental quotients (DQ = 50th percentile age equivalent/chronological age × 100) of less than 47 at 2–4 months postadoption predicted below-average language abilities 1 year later.

LDS and MCDI-WG data are also available for Chinese adopted children (Krakow & Roberts, 2003; Krakow, Tao, & Roberts, 2005; Pollock, 2005). The majority of Chinese children scored above the 15th percentile on the LDS measured between 12–16 months postadoption, when they

**Table 7.1.**  Referral guidelines for internationally adopted infants and toddlers

| Measure | Adoption age | Months postadoption | Provide service if scores are equal to or below… |
|---|---|---|---|
| LDS | <12 months and 12–16 months | 12 or 16 months | 15th percentile |
| | 13–18 months | 6–11 months | Expresses 50 words and 2-word phrases |
| | 19–24 months | 4–9 months | Expresses less than 50 English words and frequent 2-word phrases |
| | 25–30 months | 1–8 months | Express English words in first weeks; 50 words in 1 month |
| MCDI-WC DQ* | 11–23 months | 2–4 months | 47 |
| CSBS–Speech Standard Score | 11–23 months | 2–6 months | 6 |
| CSBS–Total Standard Score | 11–23 months | 2–6 months | 80 |

Note: *DQ = closest 50th percentile age equivalency/chronological age × 100.

were between 24 and 32 months of age (Krakow & Roberts, 2003; Krakow et al., 2005). From LDS data, Tan and Yang (2005) reported that children adopted from China by U.S. families between ages 3 and 25 months had expressive language comparable to English-speaking peers by 16 months postadoption. From these studies it appears that some Chinese children take a little longer (4 months) than Eastern European children to catch up with English-speaking peers.

Early postadoption, however, no differences were found in English vocabulary development between children adopted from Eastern Europe and children adopted from China. Hwa-Froelich and Matsuo (2010) found no significant differences in MCDI-Words Comprehended or MCDI-Words Expressed DQs prior to 6 months postadoption between children adopted from Eastern Europe (9) and China (11) at ages younger than 24 months. In other studies of MCDI-Words Expressed scores, Chinese adopted children demonstrated equivalent and sometimes faster expressive vocabulary development than Eastern European adopted children (Pollock, 2005).

Based on the evidence from the literature, clinical assessment decisions can be made for internationally adopted children from Eastern Europe and China younger than 24 months of age. Children adopted from Eastern Europe or China should be referred for early intervention services when they:

- have an MCDI-Words Comprehended DQ ≤ 47 by 2–4 months postadoption

- score less than a 15th percentile on the LDS or Rossetti by 12–16 months postadoption

- fail to express 50 English words by 24–28 months of age

- fail to express two-word phrases by 24–28 months of age

- fail to express English words within the first 3 months postadoption if adopted at 25–30 months of age

## Behavior Measures of Communication Development

Practitioners may use the Communication and Symbolic Behavioral Scales Developmental Profile (CSBS DP) (Wetherby & Prizant, 2002) to assess behavioral prelinguistic development in toddlers between 12 and 24 months of age. Research data on Eastern European and Chinese adopted children have been collected by Glennen (2005, 2007a) and Hwa-Froelich and Matsuo (2008, 2010). Glennen (2005) reported referral guidelines for 28 children adopted from Eastern Europe by U.S. families between 11 and 23 months of age. She found that the majority of her sample scored above a standard score of 6 on the three CSBS DP subtests and a standard CSBS DP total score of 80 within 2–4 months postadoption. In a later follow-up study of 27 of the original sample approximately 1 year after adoption, the CSBS DP total standard score of 80 or lower at 24 months postadoption was predictive of continued language delay.

During the first 6 months postadoption, Chinese adopted children demonstrated similar CSBS DP performances as children adopted from Eastern Europe (Hwa-Froelich & Matsuo, 2008, 2010). In a longitudinal study of 4 adopted Chinese girls, the children demonstrated early postadoption vocabulary comprehension and prelinguistic behaviors within the specified cutoffs reported by Glennen (2005). In another study following 20 children adopted from Eastern Europe and China, no differences on CSBS DP scores were found between 11- and 23-month-old Eastern European and Chinese adopted children measured between 1 and 6 months postadoption (Hwa-Froelich & Matsuo, 2010). In conclusion, if internationally adopted children receive a CSBS DP total score of less than 80 during the first 6 months postadoption, they should be referred for early intervention (Glennen, 2007a & b; Hwa-Froelich & Matsuo, 2008, 2010).

After approximately 1 year, receptive language for children adopted from Eastern Europe between 11 and 23 months of age should be comparable to English-speaking peers. Glennen (2007a) found that although expressive language development lagged behind receptive language development on the Preschool Language Scale, version 4 (PLS-4)

(Zimmerman, Steiner, & Pond, 2002) for children adopted from Eastern Europe seen at 12 months postadoption, her sample mean was within 1.25 standard deviations (SDs) of the standard mean. The PLS-4 is a general measure of English language comprehension and expression development. The expressive language mean on the PLS-4 for 27 children adopted from Eastern Europe approximately 1 year after adoption was 93.33 (SD=15.96). The receptive mean was 103.85 (SD=16.02).

After living with their adoptive family for 1 year, children adopted from China demonstrate similar but different patterns of English language development in comparison with children adopted from Eastern Europe. Hwa-Froelich and Matsuo (2010) followed 20 children adopted between 11 and 23 months of age from Eastern Europe and China and found that children adopted from Eastern Europe had more advanced expressive language development as measured by the PLS-4 approximately 1 year after adoption. Although not significant, qualitatively the Chinese children had more advanced receptive language performances. No differences, however, were found between total language scores. These different patterns of language development may represent typical variability within disrupted language development. The total language score may be more indicative of true language learning ability than the subtest scores of receptive and expressive language. Other studies have found that the majority of adopted children from China performed above or within 1.25 SDs of English-speaking norms on standardized English language tests 2 or 3 years postadoption (Cohen, Lojkasek, Zadeh, Pugliese, & Kiefer, 2008; Hwa-Froelich & Matsuo, 2008; Roberts et al., 2005). Roberts et al. reported that in their sample of 55 Chinese children adopted by U.S. families between 6 and 25 months of age and measured between 3 and 6 years of age, children with older adoption ages had lower language scores than children adopted at younger ages. They also reported a group of children who did not reach average language performance until after the third year of adoption. Cohen et al., (2008) found at 6 months postadoption that their sample of 70 children adopted from China by Canadian families between the ages of 8 and 21 months had average PLS-4 receptive language scores compared with a Canadian control group, but it took at least 2 years for them to be commensurate in expressive language skills. They hypothesized that for the subgroup of children who needed 3 years to catch up in expressive language, they may have language problems in later years.

In summary, practitioners should take care to avoid comparing expressive language scores of children adopted from China with children adopted from Eastern Europe. It is recommended that a referral cutoff for expressive language in infants and toddlers should be a standard CSBS DP total or PLS-4 Auditory Comprehension subtest score of 80 and the expressive language performance of internationally adopted children should be compared with local norms of other internationally adopted children instead of English-speaking peers. It is possible that it may take longer for some internationally adopted children to catch up in expressive language than in receptive language.

## PRESCHOOL LANGUAGE DEVELOPMENT AFTER ADOPTION

### Receptive Language Development

Few studies have measured postadoption receptive language development in internationally adopted children adopted at older ages. Glennen (2009) provides preliminary evidence of receptive language development in children adopted from Eastern Europe by U.S. families. From a small sample of 15 children adopted between the ages of 2 years, 1 month and 4 years, 9 months, Glennen measured English receptive vocabulary and receptive language development at 3–4 months, 9 months, and 14 months after adoption. The children demonstrated rapid receptive English language development. The Peabody Picture Vocabulary Test, version 4 (PPVT-4) (Dunn & Dunn, 2007) was administered 9 and 12–14 months postadoption. Outcomes and recommended cut-off scores for the total group were reported. As a group, the children averaged scores of 82.26 to 93.33, with only two children receiving standard scores below 85 by 14 months postadoption.

Glennen (2009) also measured general English language development. The PLS-4 was administered to 2-year-olds, and their average receptive language standard scores ranged from 80 to 95.2 and 93.8. The Clinical Evaluation of Language Fundamentals-Preschool 2 (CELF-P2) (Wiig, Secord, & Semel, 2004) was administered to the 3- and

**Table 7.2.** Referral guidelines for internationally adopted preschool-age children after 1 year

| Measure | Adoption age | Provide service if scores are equal to or below... |
|---|---|---|
| MCDI-WS | 2 years old | 340 words |
| PPVT-4 | 2 years old | Standard score 85 |
| CELF-P2 Receptive Language | 2 years old | Standard score 85 |
| CELF-P2 Expressive Language | 2 years old | Standard score 75 |
| Expressive MLU | 2 years old | 2.62 MLU |
| MCDI-WS | 3 and 4 years old | 520 words |
| PPVT-4 | 3 and 4 years old | Standard score 85 |
| CELF-P2 Receptive Language | 3 and 4 years old | Standard score 85 |
| CELF-P2 Expressive Language | 3 and 4 years old | Standard score 76 |
| Expressive MLU | 3 and 4 years old | 3.74 MLU |

Key: MLU, mean length of utterance.

4-year-olds, and their average receptive language scores ranged from 70.9 to 88.8 and 91.5. Based on these preliminary findings, Glennen suggested some early guidelines for referral, which are shown in Table 7.2. After 1 year with their adoptive families:

- Children adopted after the age of 2 years should have PPVT-4 receptive vocabulary standard scores of at least 85 or higher and PLS-4 receptive language standard scores of 85 or higher.

- Children adopted after the age of 3 and 4 years should have PPVT-4 receptive vocabulary standard scores of 85 or higher and receptive CELF-P2 language standard scores of 85 or higher.

Information on receptive language development in older adopted Chinese children is not available at this time.

## Expressive Language Development

Studies on expressive language development for preschool-age internationally adopted children provide preliminary evidence of second first language development following adoption. Geren, Snedecker, and Ax (2005) and Snedeker, Geren, and Shafto (2007) collected MCDI-2 parent-report and spontaneous language sample measures for 27 children adopted from China by U.S. families between the ages of 2 years, 7 months and 5 years, 6 months. The MCDI-2 (Fenson et al., 2007) is a vocabulary checklist of words children say and parents are asked to select examples of sentence complexity choices measuring the children's use of inflectional morphemes, for example, present progressive -ing, past tense -ed, or plural or possessive -s. The MCDI-2 sample included monolingual children between the ages of 16 and 30 months. One year after adoption, Geren et al. (2005) reported that in their sample of 14 Chinese children adopted between the ages of 2 years, 7 months and 5 years, 1 month, the children had acquired 500 words or more on the MCDI-2. In a later study with some of the same children, Snedecker et al. (2007) compared MCDI-2 performances of the older adopted children (27) with monolingual infants matched by developmental language age. The infant control group's chronological ages were between 1 year, 6 months and 2 years, 9 months. The authors found that the older adopted children acquired English vocabulary rapidly and, 3 months after adoption, were similar to 2-year-old monolingual speakers. After 3 months of exposure and rapid vocabulary learning, the Chinese children's language development was similar to typically developing infants between 24 and 30 months of age. Their process of vocabulary learning was similar to the infant group in rate and content; that is, the adopted children learned nouns before verbs. Thus, Snedeker et al. hypothesized that the children were mapping second first language vocabulary to prelinguistic mental representations (knowledge) rather than to first language labels (Chinese words).

Vocabulary was correlated with other variables. The children's mean length of utterance (MLU) was correlated with a vocabulary size of less than 550 words. Once vocabulary sizes exceeded this number, the MLU became variable. Language development correlated with amount of exposure or time spent in the United States, not age of adoption. Thus, older adopted children should begin acquiring English vocabulary rapidly during the first 3 months following adoption. MLU should also begin to increase rapidly after the first 3 months postadoption.

Preliminary information on expressive language development of older adopted children from Eastern Europe is also available. Glennen (2009) collected data on 15 preschool-age children (2 years, 1 month to 4 years, 9 months) at 3–4, 9, and 14 months following adoption into U.S. families. She collected parent-reported expressive vocabulary on the MCDI, spontaneous language samples, and PLS-4 and CELF-P2 expressive language performances. The PLS-4 was administered to the 2-year-olds and the CELF-P2 was administered to the 3- and 4-year-olds. The 2-year-old's expressive vocabulary on the MCDI grew from an average of 59 words at 3–4 months after adoption to an average of 311 and 453 words within 9 and 14 months of adoptive care. The 3- and 4-year-old children averaged 175 to 503 and 580 words in the same amount of time. At 9 and 14 months after adoption, MLUs for the 2-year-olds averaged from 2.05 to 3.50, and for the 3- and 4-year-olds the MLU averaged from 4.10 to 5.24. The PLS-4 expressive language standard scores averaged from 73.0 to 87.2 and 93.2 at 3–4, 9, and 14 months after adoption. For the 3- and 4-year-olds, their standard scores averaged from 70.5 to 75.9 and 86.3. In general, expressive language development lagged behind receptive language development, similar to monolingual typically developing children. Please refer to Table 7.2 for these guidelines. Glennen suggests the following referral guidelines 1 year after adoption:

- Children adopted after age 2 should have MCDI expressive vocabularies of 340 or more, MLUs equal to or greater than 2.62 morphemes, and CELF-P2 expressive language standard scores of 85 or greater.

- Children adopted at age 3 or 4 should have MCDI expressive vocabularies of 520 words or more, MLUs of 3.74 or higher, and CELF-P2 expressive language standard scores of 76 or higher.

Similar receptive and expressive language measures using standardized English language tests with older children adopted from China are not available at this time. However, it should be noted that the expressive vocabulary and MLU measures on older adopted Chinese children reported by Snedeker, Geren, and Shafto (2007) are similar to Glennen's data. It is recommended that until this information is available for children adopted from other countries, practitioners follow these same guidelines.

## SCHOOL-AGE LANGUAGE DEVELOPMENT AFTER ADOPTION

### Parent and/or Teacher Survey Reports

Several studies have employed survey methods to document developmental outcomes during the school-age years or adulthood, but very few of the studies document language development (for a review see Scott, 2009). Scott reviewed studies of children between the ages of 5 and older that included 1) internationally adopted children, 2) the children's adoption age and chronological age at the time of the study, 3) a clear description of methods with an outcome measure of language, and 4) explicitly described language analyses. These studies are summarized here.

Survey instrumentation was initially used with children adopted from India. Schaerlaekens, Huygelier, and Dondeyne (1988) used an unpublished survey for 25 children adopted from India by Belgium parents between the ages of 14 months and above 7 years. The survey was completed after the children had been adopted between 2 and 5 years of age. No differences in parent-reported language development were found for children adopted younger than 14 months. Consequently this age group was dropped from further analyses. Children adopted at ages older than 2 years had more language problems (i.e., sentence formulation, vocabulary, verb use, gender of words). Dalen (1995) also used survey measures with parents and teachers to study everyday, conversational language skills as compared with higher level or school language in children adopted from India to Norwegian parents. The sample included 70 children adopted from India between ages 0 and 4 years or older and data were collected when the children were between age 7 and 16 years. A weakness of the study was that approximately 46% of the sample was younger than 1 year old and 30% were older than 4 years when they were adopted. Although no relationship was found between conversational language and school achievement, a later age of adoption was negatively related to later school language skills. In other words, older age at adoption was related to poorer academic language performance.

Later, Dalen (2001) collected these survey measures with children adopted from different countries. She surveyed the parents and teachers of 193 children adopted between the ages of 0 and 81 months (6 years, 9 months) from Korea (84) and Columbia (109) and a Norwegian control group (193) matched by gender and grade level. She found that the Korean children performed as well or better than their Norwegian peers, but the children from Columbia performed more poorly than both the Korean and Norwegian peers, particularly in school language. Finally, Dalen and Rygvold (2006) administered the same survey instrument to a sample of

75 girls and 2 boys adopted from China between 2 and 52 months of age. The children were measured between 7 and 13 years of age and compared with an age- and gender-matched control group of Norwegian peers. The findings from this study indicated that although there was great variability among the adopted children, as a group their language and academic performance were not reported to be significantly different from their Norwegian peers. Other surveys of Korean adolescents and/ or adults adopted by Swedish and U.S. families supported these findings (Andresen, 1992; Berg-Kelly & Eriksson, 1997; Wickes & Slate, 1996). Although these findings seem to support the idea that language outcomes were related to country of origin, with children adopted from India and Columbia faring worse than children adopted from Korea or China, Odenstad et al. (2008) provided evidence that the variable of preadoptive care for children adopted by Norwegian families, not country of origin, predicted positive developmental outcomes. When "good enough" care (Odenstad et al., p. 1810) was provided, as in Korean orphanages and foster care described in Chapter 1, children adopted at any age from that background fared well. For children from other countries and different levels of quality care, if children were adopted before the age of 4, they had more positive developmental outcomes. Children adopted from Eastern European countries, however, were not included in these survey studies.

Other studies have focused on the school-age development of children adopted from Eastern Europe. Groze and Ileana (1996) administered a survey to 462 U.S. parents of children adopted between infancy and the age of 13 from Romania when the children were between infancy and 18 years old. The weaknesses of this study are the large range of adoption ages and the fact that some of the sample had only been in the United States for 2 months at the time of the survey. Regardless of this limitation, the authors found that approximately 30% of the sample reported language difficulties. Glennen and Bright (2005) collected survey data from U.S. parents and teachers reporting on communication and social skills on 46 children adopted at ages younger than 30 months from Eastern Europe. The children were between 6 years, 6 months and 9 years, 1 month of age at the time of the study. Although the majority of the children were reported to have average "speech, language and oral narrative skills (i.e., speech, syntax, semantics)," the authors reported that the children had weaker communication skills in "Use of context, Nonverbal Communication, and Social Relations" (p. 97). These communication behaviors are important for social communi-cation and higher level, abstract language skills such as interpretation and expression of inferential language, figurative language, and jokes. Beverly, McGuinness, and Blanton (2008) also conducted a survey study of 55 children adopted from the former Soviet Union between the ages of 13 and 35 months by U.S. parents. The survey was collected from the parents when the children were between 9 and 12 years, 9 months of age. The authors reported that 34 (62%) of the sample had the label of communication disorder. Twenty children (36%) were receiving speech therapy, and 55%–58% of girls and boys, respectively, had trouble reading. Communication disorders rarely occurred in isolation, with 31 of the 34 children with communication disorders also having additional labels of learning disabilities, ADHD, or both. From these findings, it appears that children adopted from Eastern European countries may be at risk for communication or language-based learning problems during school age. For this reason, practitioners should periodically monitor language development in internationally adopted children during the school-age years.

## Behavior Measures

Few studies have included behavior measures of language performance in internationally adopted children after they enter school. Clark and Hanisee (1982) measured receptive vocabulary performance in 25 children adopted before the age of 3 years from Korea, Cambodia, Thailand, and Vietnam into U.S. families. All of the children were measured 23 months postadoption and performed higher than the test mean for their age. Frydman and Lynn (1989) measured the verbal intelligence of 19 children adopted from Korea into Belgium families between 3 and 72 months of age. Their verbal intelligence was measured when they were between the ages of 6 years, 4 months and 13 years, 11 months. Although the children's scores were higher on the visual-spatial measures, their average verbal score was 110.6, almost 1 SD above the average. Scott, Roberts, and Krakow (2008) collected numerous language measures on 24 children adopted from China by U.S. families before the age of 24 months. The children were measured when they were between the ages of 7 years and 8 years, 8 months. The majority performed within the average to above-average range for all measures of oral and written language. An older adoption age was negatively related to language performance, and more grammatical errors correlated with lower reading comprehension scores. In other words, if children were adopted at older ages or they demonstrated more problems with syntax, they also had lower language scores or more difficulty with reading comprehension.

To summarize these studies, the current evidence on school-age language development of children adopted from Asian countries shows largely positive outcomes. Children adopted from Eastern European countries may be at increased risk of communication problems during school age. Little research is available on school-age performance for children adopted at older ages. More research is needed to follow development through the later school years, when expectations for higher language skills increase.

Most of the research with behavior measures on school-age internationally adopted children is based on children adopted from Romania. Croft et al. (2007) collected language and cognitive outcomes on 132 children adopted from Romania into U.K. families before the age of 42 months. The children were measured at ages 6 and 11 years. In general, children who were adopted prior to 6 months of age performed as well as adopted U.K. peers who were adopted before the age of 6 months. Children who endured institutional care past the age of 6 months demonstrated more delayed language and cognition than the control group and their peers who were adopted before 6 months of age. As already mentioned, when children between the ages of 18 and 42 months imitated Romanian words at the time of adoption, this was predictive of better quality institutional care and better linguistic and cognitive outcomes at age 6 and 11 years. These findings indicate mixed outcomes for language performance during school age. Hough and Kaczmarck (2011) completed a study of school-age performance for 44 Eastern European children between the ages of 5 years, 10 months and 11 years, 8 months who had been adopted by U.S. families for at least 2 years. Their sample performed lower than standardized test norms on general language (receptive and expressive language, morphology, semantics, syntax, and pragmatics) and reading. The children performed lower than age norms on all measures with about one third demonstrating language or reading problems and about 14% having impairments in both language and reading. Duration of institutional care was not related to language outcomes except for reading, in that children adopted at older ages had a poorer reading performance. This sample, however, may not represent a typically developing group of internationally adopted children, because the authors did not exclude children receiving speech or language services or children receiving medication for attention deficit problems. Thus children with communication and/or learning difficulties may have affected group performances. In a meta-analytic study, internationally adopted children, including children from Eastern European countries, were found to perform similarly to nonadopted peers in language development (Van IJzendoorn & Juffer, 2006). Children adopted from Eastern Europe were included in the meta-analytic study by Van IJzendoorn and Juffer, who found that in analyses of 14 studies with more than 15,000 participants, language performance was somewhat delayed (group differences with small effect). However, internationally adopted children had more learning problems (group differences with large effect) compared with their peers in an analysis of eight studies with more than 13,000 children. The researchers concluded that if children were adopted prior to 12 months of age, school catch-up occurred.

In contrast, in a national Swedish register study that did not include children adopted from Eastern European countries or adopted females, Odenstad et al. (2008) found that if children were adopted prior to 4 years of age, verbal intelligence scores between 16 and 19 years of age were comparable to their peers. For Korean children, age at adoption was not a factor. In other words, if children were adopted from Korea, verbal intelligence was average or above average compared with their peers, regardless of their age at adoption.

In conclusion, when children adopted from Eastern Europe are included, it appears that exposure to adverse preadoption care has negative effects in later years, more so than for children adopted from better preadoption situations. Thus, developmental outcomes at school age for children adopted from Eastern Europe appear to be mixed. Although in the case of Drew, who demonstrated rapid English language acquisition and development, children adopted from Eastern European countries may be at increased risk for learning problems in the areas of general language, reading, and phonological processing. More research is needed to determine if the variable of international adoption continues to affect language performance during the school-age years. For practitioners, it is recommended that language performance of internationally adopted children be monitored closely so that language needs are not overlooked. As children enter third and fourth grade, academic language expectations increase and children begin to use language for learning. Inferential, figurative, and pragmatic language skills are essential for continued academic success. At this point, it is relatively unknown whether internationally adopted children develop these skills. If internationally adopted children were adopted before the age of 5 years and demonstrate problems in basic language areas and/or social language during the school-age years, they should be referred for special education services. Children adopted at ages older than 5 years should receive a bilingual evaluation immediately postadoption to determine whether there is a language disorder or delay in their native language.

## ▼▼▼ IMPLICATIONS

Because internationally adopted children may have had different preadoption and postadoption linguistic experiences, it is essential that practitioners collect a thorough and detailed preadoption and postadoption history of their experiences. It is also important to consider the age of adoption in terms of amount of exposure to adverse preadoption care, family or foster care, formal schooling, and chronological age expectations in their adopted language. This chapter provides guidelines for 1) children adopted before the age of 2 years, 2) children adopted during the preschool ages of 2–5 years, and 3) performance during early elementary ages for children adopted before the age of 3–6 years. No research has been done to measure language outcomes of children adopted at ages older than 5 years. It may take children adopted at ages older than 5 years more time to become commensurate with English-speaking peers, because they have more to learn at older ages, but this is unknown at this time.

## KEY POINTS

Risk factors include the following:

▶ Poor quality of preadoptive care by parent-report and physical growth indicators

▶ Child adopted at 18 months of age or older and does not imitate birth-language words (more than *mamma* or *papa*)

▶ Observation of inattentive or overactive behaviors

▶ Insecure attachment 1 year postadoption

▶ Less or mismatched parental sensitivity and difficult child temperament

Developmentally, internationally adopted children at any age, regardless of the birth or adopted language, should demonstrate the following:

▶ Rapid growth in comprehension of words, phrases, and sentences

▶ Rapid expressive language growth in words and phrases

## REFERRAL INDICATORS

For children adopted before 2 years of age, initial assessment of language development according to parent report should be within normal range for English standardized measures. For specific English standardized measures, referral indicators include the following:

▶ LDS scores below 15th percentile

▶ MCDI-WG DQ at or below 47

▶ CSBS DP total standard scores equal to or below 80.[1]

At 1 year postadoption, for children adopted before the age of 2 years, their performance on standardized general oral language measures should be within or above approximately 1.5 SD of the average. For specific English standardized measures, referral indicators include the following:

▶ PLS-4 receptive language scores below average (85 or lower) for English-speaking peers

▶ PLS-4 expressive language lower than other children adopted from the same country of origin.[2]

---

[1]Children adopted into families who speak other languages should perform similarly on similar parent-report surveys marking typical language development. The MCDI-WG is available in other languages. Children adopted into families who speak languages other than English should perform similarly on other general prelinguistic measures of speech, social, and symbolic behavior such as the CSBS DP.

[2]Children adopted into families who speak languages other than English should perform similarly on general measures of language acquisition in the dominant language.

[3]Children adopted into families who speak languages other than English should perform similarly on general measures of language development in the dominant language.

At 1-year postadoption, for children adopted between ages 2 and 5 years, performance on general language measures and receptive and expressive vocabulary assessments should be within 1.5 SDs of the average and their MLUs should be approximately 2.62. For specific English standardized assessments, referral indicators include the following:

▶ For children adopted after the age of 2 years, PPVT-4 and CELF-P2 receptive scores less than 85, MCDI expressive vocabularies of fewer than 340 words, MLUs less than 2.62, and CELF-P2 expressive language standard scores less than 75.

▶ For children adopted after the age of 3 or 4 years, PPVT-4 and CELF-P2 receptive scores less than 85, MCDI expressive vocabularies less than 520 words, MLUs less than 3.74, and CELF-P2 expressive language standard scores less than 76.[3]

During the school years, for children adopted before the age of 6 years, assessment referral indicators include delays or below-average performance on any test of written or oral language, including tests for vocabulary, syntax, and pragmatics.

## REFERENCES

Andresen, I. -L.K. (1992). Behavioural and school adjustment of 12-13-year old internationally adopted children in Norway: A research note. *Journal of Child Psychology and Psychiatry, 33*, 427–439.

Baker, L., & Cantwell, D. (1982). Psychiatric disorder in children with different types of communication disorders. *Journal of Communication Disorders, 15*, 113–126.

Beck, C.T. (1996). Postpartum depressed mothers' experiences interacting with their children. *Nursing Research, 45*(2), 98–104.

Berg-Kelly, K., & Eriksson, J. (1997). Adaptation of adopted foreign children at mid-adolescence as indicated by aspects of health and risk taking—a population study. *European Child & Adolescent Psychiatry, 6*, 199–206.

Beverly, B.L., McGuinness, T.M., & Blanton, D.J. (2008). Communication and academic challenges in early adolescence for children who have been adopted from the former Soviet Union. *Language, Speech, and Hearing Services in Schools, 39*, 303–313.

Caldwell, B., & Bradley, R. (1984). *Home Observation for Measurement of the Environment Inventory*. Eau Claire, WI: Lorraine Coulson Home Inventory.

Cantwell, D.P., Baker, L., & Mattison, R.E. (1979). The prevalence of psychiatric disorder in children with speech and language disorder: An epidemiologic study. *Journal of the American Academy of Child Psychiatry, 18*, 450–461.

Clark, E.A., & Hanisee, J. (1982). Intellectual and adaptive performance of Asian children in adoptive American settings. *Developmental Psychology, 18*, 595–599.

Clarke-Stewart, A. (1973). Interactions between mothers and their young children: Characteristics and consequences. *Monographs of the Society of Research in Child Development, 38*(6, Serial No. 7), 1–109. Retrieved July 18, 2001, from http://www.jstor.org/pss/1165928

Coh, J.F., Matias, R., Tronick, E.Z., Connell, D., & Lyons-Ruth, K. (1986). Face-to-face interactions of depressed mothers and their infants. In E.Z. Tronick and T. Field (Eds.), *Maternal Depression and Infant Disturbance: New Directions for Child and Adolescent Development, 34*, 31–45.

Cohen, N.J., Lojkasek, M., Zadeh, Z.Y., Pugliese, M., & Kiefer, H. (2008). Children adopted from China: A prospective study of their growth and development. *Journal of Child Psychology and Psychiatry, 49*(4), 458–468.

Croft, C., Beckett, C., Rutter, M., Castle, J., Colvert, E., Groothues, C., et al. (2007). Early adolescent outcomes for institutionally-deprived and non-deprived adoptees. II: Language as a protective factor and a vulnerable outcome. *Journal of Child Psychology and Psychiatry, 48*, 31–44.

Dalen, M. (1995). Learning difficulties among inter-country adopted children. *Nordisk Pedagogikk, 15 (No. 4)*, 195–208.

Dalen, M. (2001). School performances among internationally adopted children in Norway. *Adoption Quarterly, 5*, 39–58.

Dalen, M. (2005). Psychological issues in adoption: Research and practice. In D.M. Brodzinsky and J. Palacios (Eds.), *International adoptions in Scandinavia: Research focus and main results* (pp. 211–232). Westport, CT: Greenwood Publishing.

Dalen, M., & Rygvold, A. (2006). Educational achievement in adopted children from China. *Adoption Quarterly, 9*, 45–58.

Dunn, L., & Dunn, D. (2007). *Peabody Picture Vocabulary Test–IV*. Bloomington, MN: Pearson Assessments.

Evan B. Donaldson Adoption Institute. (2002). *International adoption facts*. Retrieved July 18, 2001, from http://www.adoptioninstitute.org/FactOverview/international.html#6.

Fenson, L., Marchman, V.A., Thal, D.J., Dale, P.S., Reznick, J.S., & Bates, E. (2007). *MacArthur-Bates Communicative Development Inventories (CDIs)*. (2nd ed.). Baltimore: Paul H. Brookes Publishing Co.

Fox, L., Long, S., & Langlois, A. (1988). Patterns of language comprehension deficit in abused and neglected children. *Journal of Speech and Hearing Disorders, 53*, 239–244.

Frydman, M., & Lynn, R. (1989). The intelligence of Korean children adopted in Belgium. *Journal of Individual Differences, 10*(12), 1323–1325.

Geren, J., Snedeker, J., & Ax, L. (2005). Starting over: A preliminary study of early lexical and syntactic development in internationally adopted preschoolers. *Seminars in Speech and Language, 26*(1), 44–53.

Gindis, B. (1999). Language-related issues for international adoptees and adoptive families. In T. Tepper, L. Hannon, & D. Sandstrom (Eds.), *International adoption: Challenges and opportunities* (pp. 98–107). Meadowlands, PA: First Edition.

Gindis, B. (2003). *What should adoptive parents know about their child's language-based school difficulties?* Retrieved July 16, 2007, from http://www.adoptionarticlesdirectory.com/Article/What-should-adoptive-parents-know-about-their-children-s-language-based-school-difficulties---Part-1-/5

Gindis, B. (2005). Cognitive, language, and educational issues of children adopted from overseas orphanages. *Journal of Cognitive Education and Psychology*. Retrieved June 8, 2011, from http://www.bgcenter.com/BGPublications/Article%20in%20JCEP%20-%202005.pdf

Glennen, S. (2002). Language development and delay in internationally adopted infants and toddlers: A review. *American Journal of Speech-Language Pathology, 11*, 333–339.

Glennen, S. (2005). New arrivals: Speech and language assessments for internationally adopted infants and toddlers within the first months home. *Seminars in Speech and Language, 26*(1), 10–21.

Glennen, S. (2007a). Predicting language outcomes for internationally adopted children. *Journal of Speech, Language and Hearing Research, 50*, 529–548.

Glennen, S. (2007b). International adoption speech and language mythbusters. *Perspectives on Communication Disorders and Sciences in Culturally and Linguistically Diverse Populations, 14*(3), 3–8. Retrieved June 8, 2011, from http://div14perspectives.asha.org/cgi/reprint/14/3/3

Glennen, S. (2009). Speech and language guidelines for children adopted from abroad at older ages. *Topics in Language Disorders, 29*(1), 50–64.

Glennen, S., & Bright, B.J. (2005). Five years later: Language in school-age internationally adopted children. *Seminars in Speech and Language, 26*(1), 86–101.

Glennen, S., & Masters, G. (2002). Typical and atypical language development in infants and toddlers adopted from Eastern Europe. *American Journal of Speech-Language Pathology, 11*, 417–433.

Glennen, S., Rosinsky-Grunhut, A., & Tracy, R. (2005). Linguistic interference between L1 and L2 in internationally adopted children. *Seminars in Speech and Language, 26*(1), 64–75.

Groze, V., & Ileana, D. (1996). A follow-up study of adopted children from Romania. *Child and Adolescent Social Work Journal, 13*, 541–565.

Hellerstedt, W.L., Madsen, N.J., Gunnar, M.R., Grotevant, H.D., Lee, R.M., & Johnson, D.E. (2008). The international adoption project: Population-based surveillance of Minnesota parents who adopted children internationally. *Maternal Child Health Journal, 12*(2), 162–171.

Hough, S.D., & Kaczmarek, L. (2011). Language and reading outcomes in young children adopted from Eastern European orphanages. *Journal of Early Intervention, 33*(1), 51–74.

Hwa-Froelich, D.A. (2007). Infants and toddlers adopted abroad: Clinical practices. *Perspectives of Communication Disorders in Culturally and Linguistically Diverse Populations in Communication, 14*(3), 8–11.

Hwa-Froelich, D.A. (2009). Communication development in infants and toddlers adopted from abroad. *Topics in Language Disorders, 29*(1), 27–44.

Hwa-Froelich, D.A., & Matsuo, H. (2008). Cross-cultural adaptation of internationally adopted Chinese children: Communication and symbolic behavior development. *Communication Disorders Quarterly, 29*, 149–165.

Hwa-Froelich, D.A., & Matsuo, H. (2010). Communication development and differences in children adopted from China and Eastern Europe. *Language, Speech, and Hearing Services in Schools, 41*, 1–18.

Johnson, D.E. (2000). Medical and developmental sequelae of early childhood institutionalization in Eastern European adoptees. In C.A. Nelson (Ed.), *The Minnesota symposia on child psychology: The effects of early adversity on neurobiological development: Vol. 31. Minnesota symposium on child psychology* (pp. 113–162). Minneapolis: University of Minnesota Press.

Krakow, R.A., & Roberts, J. (2003). Acquisition of English vocabulary by young Chinese adoptees. *Journal of Multilingual Communication Disorders, 1(3)*, 169–176.

Krakow, R.A., Tao, S., & Roberts, J. (2005). Adoption age effects on English language acquisition: Infants and toddlers from China. *Seminars in Speech and Language, 26*(1), 33–43.

Kreppner, J.M., O'Connor, T.G., & Rutter, M., and the English and Romanian Adoptees Study Team (2001). Can inattention/overactivity be an institutional deprivation syndrome? *Journal of Abnormal Psychology, 29*, 513–528.

Ladage, J.S. (2009). Medical issues in international adoption and their influence on language development. *Topics in Language Disorders, 21*(1), 6–17.

Love, A.J., & Thompson, M.G. (1988). Language disorders and attention deficit disorders in young children referred for psychiatric services. *American Journal of Orthopsychiatry, 58*, 52–64.

Mason, P., & Narad, C. (2005). International adoption: A health and developmental prospective, *Seminars in Speech and Language, 26*(1), 1–9.

Miller, L. (2005). *The handbook of international adoption medicine* (pp. 45–66). New York: Oxford University Press.

Morison, S.J., & Ellwood, A.L. (2000). Resiliency in the aftermath of deprivation: A second look at the development of Romanian orphanage children. *Merrill-Palmer Quarterly, 46*, 717–737.

National Institute of Child Health and Human Development Early Child Care Research Network [NICHD]. (2000). The relation of child care to cognitive and language development. *Child Development, 71*(4), 960–980.

Nelson, III, C.A., Zeanah, C.H., Fox, N.A., Marshall, P.J., Smyke, A.T., & Guthrie, D. (2007). Cognitive recovery in socially deprived young children: The Bucharest Early Intervention Project. *Science, 318*(5858), 1937–1940.

Nicoladis, E., & Grabois, H. (2002). Learning English and losing Chinese: A case study of a child adopted from China. *The International Journal of Bilingualism, 6*(4), 441–454.

O'Connor, T.G., Marvin, R.S., Rutter, M., Olrick, J.T., & the English and Romanian Adoptees Study Team. (2003). Child-parent attachment following early institutional deprivation. *Development and Psychopathology, 15*, 19–38.

Odenstad, A., Hjern, A., Lindblad, F., Rasmussen, F., Vinnerljung, B., & Dalen, M. (2008). Does age at adoption and geographic origin matter? A national cohort study of cognitive test performance in adult inter-country adoptees. *Psychological Medicine, 38,* 1803–1814.

Oram, J., Fine, J., & Okamoto, C. (1999). Assessing the language of children with attention deficit hyperactivity disorder. *American Journal of Speech-Language Pathology, 8,* 72–80.

Pears, K., & Fisher, P.A. (2005). Developmental, cognitive and neuropsychological functioning in preschool-aged foster children: Associations with prior maltreatment and placement history. *Journal of Developmental and Behavioral Pediatrics, 26,* 112–122.

Pollock, K.E. (2005). Early language growth in children adopted from China: Preliminary normative data. *Seminars in Speech and Language, 26(1),* 22–32.

Pollock, K.E. (2007). Speech acquisition in second first language learners (Children who were adopted internationally). In S. McLeod *International guide to speech acquisition* (pp. 107–112). New York: Thompson-Delmar Learning.

Pomerleau, A., Malcuit, G., Chicoine , J. Séguin , R., Belhumeur C., Germain, P., et al. (2005). Health status, cognitive and motor development of young children adopted from China, East Asia, and Russia across the first 6 months after adoption. *International Journal of Behavioral Development, 29(5),* 445–457.

Rescorla, L. (1989). The language development survey: A screening tool for delayed language in toddlers. *Journal of Speech and Hearing Disorders, 54,* 587–599.

Roberts, J.A., Pollock, K.E., Krakow, R., Price, J., Fulmer, K.C., & Wang, P.P. (2005). Language development in preschool-age children adopted from China. *Journal of Speech, Language, and Hearing Research, 48(1),* 93–107.

Rosetti, L. (1990). *The Rosetti Infant-Toddler Language Scale.* East Moline, IL: Linguisystems.

Ruhl, K.L., Hughes, C.A., & Camarata, S.M. (1992). Analysis of the expressive and receptive language characteristics of emotionally handicapped students served in public school settings. *Journal of Childhood Communication Disorders, 14,* 165–176.

Rutter, M., Colvert, E., Kreppner, J., Beckett, C., Castle, J, Groothues, C., et al. (2007). Early adolescent outcomes for institutionally-deprived and non-deprived adoptees. I: Disinhibited attachment. *Journal of Child Psychology and Psychiatry, 48,* 17–30.

Rutter, M., & the English and Romanian Adoptees Study Team (1998). Developmental catch-up and delay, following adoption after severe global early privation. *Journal of Child Psychology and Psychiatry, 39,* 465–476.

Rutter, M., Kreppner, J., Croft, C., Murin, M., Colvert, E., Beckett, C., et al. (2007). Early adolescent outcomes of institutionally deprived and non-deprived adoptees. III. Quasi-autism. *Journal of Child Psychology and Psychiatry, 48,* 1200–1207.

Schaerlaekens, A., Huygelier, N., & Dondeyne, A. (1988). Language adjustment in international adoptions: An exploratory study. *Journal of Multilingual and Multicultural Development, 9,* 247–266.

Scott, K.A. (2009). Language outcomes of school-aged internationally adopted children. *Topics in Language Disorders, 29(1),* 65–81.

Scott, K.A., Roberts, J., & Krakow, R.A. (2008). Oral and written language development of children adopted from China. *American Journal of Speech Language Pathology, 17,* 150–160.

Singer, B.D., & Bashir, A.S. (1999). What are executive functions and self-regulation and what do they have to do with language-learning disorders? *Language, Speech, and Hearing Services in Schools, 30,* 265–273.

Smyke, A.T., Dumitrescu, A., & Zeanah, C.H. (2002). Attachment disturbances in young children. I: The continuum of caretaking casualty. *Journal of the American Academy of Child and Adolescent Psychiatry, 41,* 972–982.

Snedecker, J., Geren, J., & Shafto, C.L. (2007). Starting over. International adoption as a natural experiment in language development. *Psychological Science, 18(1),* 79–87. Retrieved June 8, 2011, from http://www.psych.unito.it/csc/cogsci05/frame/talk/f803-snedeker.pdf

Solantus-Simlua, T., Punamaki, R., & Beardslee, W.R. (2002). Children's responses to low parental mood. *Journal of the American Academy of Child and Adolescent Psychiatry, 41,* 287–295.

Sroufe, L.A. (1997). Psychopathology as an outcome of development. *Developmental and Psychopathology, 5,* 251–268.

Stafford, L., & Bayer, C.L. (1993). *Interaction between parents and children*. Newbury Park, CA: Sage.

Stams, G.J. J.M., Juffer, F., & Van IJzendoorn, M.H. (2002). Maternal sensitivity, infant attachment, and temperament in early childhood predict adjustment in middle childhood: The case of adopted children and their biologically unrelated parents. *Developmental Psychology, 38*, 806–821.

Tan, T.X., & Yang, Y. (2005). Language development of Chinese adoptees 18-35 months old. *Early Childhood Research Quarterly, 20*, 57–68.

Tizard, B., Cooperman, O., Joseph, A., & Tizard, J. (1972). Environmental effects on language development: A study of young children in long-stay residential nurseries. *Child Development, 43*, 337–358.

Tizard, B., & Joseph, A. (1970). Cognitive development of young children in residential care: A study of children aged 24 months. *Journal of Child Psychology and Psychiatry, 11*, 177–186.

Van IJzendoorn, M.H., Bakermans-Kranenburg, M.J., & Juffer, F. (2007). Plasticity of growth in height, weight, and head circumference: Meta-analytic evidence of massive catch-up after international adoption. *Journal of Developmental Behavior and Pediatrics, 28*, 334–343.

Van IJzendoorn, M.H., & Juffer, F. (2006). The Emanuel Miller Memorial Lecture 2006: Adoption as intervention. Meta-analytic evidence for massive catch-up and plasticity in physical, socio-emotional, and cognitive development. *Journal of Child Psychology and Psychiatry, 47*(12), 1228–1245.

Wetherby, A.M., & Prizant, B.M. (2002). *Communication and Symbolic Behavior Scales Developmental Profile (CSBS DP)*. Baltimore: Paul H. Brookes Publishing Co.

Wetherby, A.M., Warren, S.F., & Reichle, J. (Vol. Eds.). (1998). *Transitions in prelinguistic communication*. In S.F. Warren & J. Reichle (Series Eds.). *Communication and language intervention series*, Vol. 7. Baltimore: Paul H. Brookes Publishing Co.

Wickes, K.L., & Slate, J.R. (1996). Transracial adoption of Koreans: A preliminary study of adjustment. *International Journal for the Advancement of Counseling, 19*, 187–195.

Wiig, E., Secord, W., & Semel, E. (2004). *Clinical evaluation of language fundamentals-preschool 2*. San Antonio, TX: Psychological Corporation.

Windsor, J. (2007, November). *Language skills of Romanian children in orphanage and foster care*. Paper presented at the American Speech-Language-Hearing Annual Convention, Boston.

Windsor, J., Glaze, L.E., Koga, S.F., & the Bucharest Early Intervention Project Core Group. (2007). Language acquisition with limited input: Romanian institution and foster care. *Journal of Speech-Language-Hearing Research, 50*, 1365–1381.

Zimmerman, I.L., Steiner, V.G., & Pond, R.E. (2002). *Preschool Language Scale–4* (4th ed.). San Antonio, TX: Psychological Corporation.

# 8 ▼▼▼▼

# Social Communication Development

## Deborah A. Hwa-Froelich

---

*"To use the same words is not a sufficient guarantee of understanding; one must use the same words for the same genus of inward experience; ultimately one must have one's experiences in common."*

Friedrich Wilhelm Nietzsche. (Trans., 1989). *Beyond Good and Evil.*

*"It is wise to apply the oil of refined politeness to the mechanisms of friendship."*

Sidonie Gabrielle Colette. (1932). *The Pure and the Impure.*

---

## ▼▼▼ CHELSEA

Chelsea was found and placed in a Chinese orphanage at approximately 1 week of age. The staff reported that Chelsea was attached to her regular caregiver and called her *mother*. No other medical or developmental concerns were reported.

Chelsea's parents had previously adopted two girls from China. One of these daughters and the mother traveled to China to adopt Chelsea when she was 22 months of age. Chelsea's adoptive mother reported that Chelsea bonded with her very quickly and once home in the United States, Chelsea bonded quickly with her father. Initially, Chelsea demonstrated some mild motor delays, tantrums, biting, and sensitivity to novel noises and loud sounds. During the next year, Chelsea's parents observed her to have a high energy level and difficulty sleeping through the night.

Chelsea's parents enrolled her in a preschool program when she was 3 years old, but when Chelsea became upset when her parents left her at the preschool, they decided to wait another year before reenrolling her in preschool. Approximately 2 years after Chelsea was adopted, at the age of 4, her parents enrolled her in a preschool program located at the same elementary school Chelsea's older sisters attended. Chelsea was able to see her sisters at school and her parents volunteered consistently. Chelsea remained at this school for kindergarten and first grade. However, Chelsea continued to demonstrate inattention and impulsivity in the classroom. Her parents removed her from school and began educating Chelsea at home.

The parents described Chelsea as very social and impulsive. They reported that Chelsea was friendly, talkative, and interactive with others, but she tended to cross social boundaries by moving too close to another person, touching others too much, and speaking too loudly, and she inconsistently maintained eye contact. When angry, Chelsea yelled, stomped her feet, kicked the walls, slammed doors, and threw things. The parents tried numerous strategies, including redirecting her, removing her from the situation, or breaking the cycle of inappropriate behavior by running through a pattern of behaviors such as an obstacle course. These strategies had limited success over time. They also tried several different medications for her hyperactivity and impulsivity with little success.

During this same time period, several specialists evaluated Chelsea. The school psychologist administered tests and found that Chelsea scored above average in intelligence. A pediatrician with specialized training and experience with internationally adopted children examined Chelsea and although Chelsea was judged to be healthy, the pediatrician recommended an occupational therapy (OT) evaluation for sensory integration problems, a psychological evaluation to assess Chelsea's attention skills, and a speech-language evaluation to assess her communication development. The OT diagnosed Chelsea with sensory integration problems and recommended daily sensory stimulation at home and verbal strategies for self-regulation of anxiety and impulsive behaviors. The clinical psychologist reported that Chelsea met the criteria for ADHD-hyperactive/impulsive subtype and recommended family counseling services and future consideration of stimulant medication. The speech-language pathologist (SLP) assessed Chelsea's general language abilities, working memory, verbal processing, and social language skills. Based on her test results, Chelsea demonstrated adequate receptive and expressive language and working memory development, but she had delayed or weak performance in social-language skills. Although Chelsea was able to recognize facial expressions and identify common emotions, she had difficulty describing others' feelings or perspectives. The SLP recommended speech-language therapy focusing on nonverbal and verbal social communication as well as increasing her social cognition and skills in reading and interpreting the perspective of others or theory of mind development. It was also recommended that the SLP and OT work together to help Chelsea develop self-talk strategies to facilitate self-regulation of her emotions and impulsivity.

Chelsea's profile represents a developmental pattern for many internationally adopted children. She quickly developed a close intimate relationship with her parents and sisters and rapid acquisition of English language comprehension and expression (Cohen, Lojkasek, Zadeh, Pugliese, & Kiefer, 2007; Glennen, 2007). However, she continued to demonstrate inattentive, overactive, impulsive, and overfriendly behaviors and problems regulating her emotions. These behaviors are commonly reported for internationally adopted children (Juffer & Van IJzendoorn, 2009; Rutter et al., 2007a, 2007b; Tan, 2009; Tan & Marfo, 2006; Van IJzendoorn & Juffer, 2006) and discussed in detail in Chapter 3. Chelsea also demonstrated splintered skills in social communication in that she was able to identify facial expressions and emotions but had difficulty understanding and describing the feelings or perspectives of others. This combination of behaviors negatively affected her social interactions and relationships with others so much so that she was unable to function within a regular classroom environment and had difficulty making and maintaining friendships. Chelsea's unusual profile is an example of how multiple variables can result in unique and dynamic developmental outcomes. Dynamic Systems Theory, as explained in Chapter 1, helps provide a theoretical understanding for such diversity in international adoptee development.

Social communication development consists of the development of social competence and communication (Westby, 2010). To be socially competent, one must 1) be securely attached, 2) share experiences with others, and 3) understand the relationship between communication and outcomes. To be securely attached, a child develops a close relationship with a caregiver. This secure relationship typically develops when caregivers are sensitive to and able to read their children's behaviors and meet their needs. This attuned relationship facilitates the ability to learn that communicative behaviors result in specific outcomes, e.g., reaching toward the caregiver results in being picked up, following directions leads to successful manipulation of a toy, asking for a cookie results in receipt of the desired object, or playing with forbidden objects results in a negative consequence. These communicative relationships are learned in specific contexts in which certain behaviors may be expected and associated with consequences in particular places and times. How children learn communicative functions and social rules of communication is dependent upon social interactions with adults, as explained by social interaction theorists in Chapter 1. Through the development of attachment, children are exposed to and initially share emotions and experiences with their caregivers and siblings. Sharing emotions and experiences is one of the basic motivators for communication. In Chelsea's case, although she was securely attached to her parents and sisters, she had not learned communicative behaviors to express anger and frustration, or to negotiate choices with her parents. She also had not learned the specific communicative behaviors to use when communicating with others in various social contexts, such as outside the family home at school. These two components of social competence, using communication instrumentally and sharing emotions and experiences, are the major components of social communication and the topic of this chapter. Attachment and social and emotional development are discussed fully in Chapter 3.

To be effective in social interactions, one must be able to 1) use communication for a variety of functions, 2) predict and plan ahead for future social interactions and contexts, 3) process and interpret both nonverbal and verbal communication, and 4) flexibly respond to a dynamically changing communicative interaction. Successful social communicators interpret and express appropriate eye gaze, joint attention, facial expression, gestures, postures, proximity control, tone of voice, vocal intensity, and self-regulation and understand appropriate verbal communication or pragmatics. These skills require the development of 1) theory of mind—the knowledge of one's and others' mental states ; 2) social cognition—the knowledge that events cause people to feel particular emotions and emotions cause people to act in certain ways; 3) other cognitive skills such as working memory, selective attention, and the ability to switch attention (discussed in Chapter 5); 4) receptive and expressive language (discussed in Chapter 7); and 5) pragmatic knowledge and expression—the appropriate, effective, rule-governed employment of speech in interpersonal situations (Ninio & Snow, 1996). This chapter will focus on 1) typical development of social communication in nonadopted children, 2) influential factors affecting this development, 3) social communication development after adoption, and 4) referral indicators for intervention services.

## SOCIAL COMMUNICATION DEVELOPMENT

### Intersubjectivity and ToM

To share emotions and experiences, children must maintain interaction with another person. Trevarthen (1979; 1992) termed this face-to-face sharing of feelings and mental state as *primary intersubjectivity*. This drive for primary intersubjectivity motivates children's intentions and their intentionality is the motivation behind their need to communicate. Primary intersubjectivity also helps children learn about their own emotions and eventually, they learn how to identify and predict the emotions of other people. The ability to recognize or predict self and other people's emotions, intentions, or thought is called the development of Theory of Mind (ToM, Baldwin & Moses, 1994; Baron-Cohen, 1997; Butterworth, 1994).

ToM and intersubjectivity, the foundations for social competence and social communication development, are affected by individual (endogenous) and environmental (exogenous) factors. Intra-ToM is the ability to identify one's own thoughts and feelings; knowing what one knows and does not know and determining how to access what one does not know. Infants are initially focused on egocentric desires and needs, but they are born ready to perceive the mental states of others and prefer interactions with people rather than objects (Legerstee, 2005). Caregivers interact with infants face-to-face, meet their infants' biological needs of hunger and discomfort, and communicate positive facial expressions, touch, and tone of voice to help the infant develop primary intersubjectivity. Through these interactions, infants learn to identify and regulate their own emotional states, share emotional states with their caregivers, and draw inferences about their own and others' mental states from their caregivers' nonverbal and verbal communication (Baldwin & Moses, 1994; Butterworth, 1994; Legerstee, 2005; Moses, Baldwin, Rosicky, & Tidball, 2001; Smith, 2005; Trevarthen, 1979, 1992). The understanding of emotions is facilitated through face-to-face interactions with the caregiver. This interaction allows infants to perceive the nonverbal aspects of the communicated message, including facial expressions, tone of voice, and physical movements associated with the social context (Smith, 2005).

Infants use caregivers' mental states to resolve uncertainty about their emotional states and identify their own feelings. A caregiver's social and communicative interactions facilitate the infants' ability to develop social cognition about their own emotions, desires, and intentions (Perner, 1991; Zeedyk, 1996). As children begin to understand their feelings and intentions, they develop an emerging sense of self and intra-ToM during the first 4 to 6 months of life (Legerstee, 2005).

Caregivers include communication about the emotions, expectations, and intentions of themselves and others, and describe to infants the social cognition about objects, actions, and emotions. By 5 to 6 months old, infants follow gazes of others to see what others see and develop joint attention (look at what others look at and get others to look at what they are looking at) and secondary intersubjectivity (sharing emotional states involving an object) (Legerstee, 2005). They learn to coregulate their interactions with others through shared emotional states and social referencing, and directed and shared joint attention with caregivers between 9 and 15 months old (Baron-Cohen, 1997; Bruner, 1999; Legerstee, 2005). Initially, children perceive and infer what object, event, or being someone else sees, but as children develop secondary intersubjectivity, they learn inter-ToM. Inter-ToM is the awareness that people have thoughts and feelings. This allows a prediction to be formed of what others are thinking based on what is known about that person and the world (social cognition). Social cognition is then used to understand or act upon a particular social situation (Garfield, Peterson, & Perry, 2001). Children learn that others may have thoughts or feelings about an object causing them to act in specific ways or express particular intentions (Wellman, Phillips, & Rodriguez, 2000; Zeedyk, 1996). In typically developing children, understanding of self and others' mental states, and the ability to draw inferences about others' mental states, intentions, and perspectives (inter-ToM) as well as understanding of deception and false beliefs, develop implicitly. A false belief occurs when individuals behave because they believe something is true when unbeknownst to them, the reality of their belief has changed. For example, children can observe their mother moving their father's shoes from the floor to the closet when the father is not in the room. When the father comes back to put on his shoes, children may point to the closet (implicit ToM) because they know their father believes the shoes should be on the floor (false belief) and did not see the mother move the shoes to the closet.

Implicit knowledge of self and others' perspectives underlie a child's ability to communicate this knowledge (Low, 2010). Several studies have documented explicit communication about false beliefs in children between 3 and 4 years of age. This explicit communication of ToM is found to be correlated and predicted by expressive linguistic mastery of linguistic complementation and flexible thinking (Astington & Jenkins, 1999; Legerstee, 2005; Lewis & Osborne, 1990; Low, 2010; Perner & Lang, 1999).

## Language Development and ToM

Talk about emotions and other individuals' perspectives are embedded in complex language. To describe the thoughts and emotions of others, abstract mental-state verbs are expressed using complex syntax with independent and dependent clauses (Astington & Jenkins, 1999; Astington & Peskin, 2004; de Villiers & Pyers, 2002). For example, mental-state verbs, subordinate conjunctions, complements, and complex syntax are reflected in the following sentences: 1) The little pig was afraid that the wolf would eat him; and 2) The little girl thought her grandmother was in the bed but it was the wolf. In a study by de Villiers and Pyers (2002) and a recent meta-analysis by Milligan, Astington, and Dack (2007), syntactical development of complements predicted performance on explicit false-belief tasks. Thus, syntactical development of complex sentences is strongly related to ToM development. For example, deaf children of hearing parents or deaf children who acquired a language system (sign language) late during their development have delayed language development in comparison to deaf children of deaf parents or deaf children who acquired sign language at an early age. Deaf children with delayed language development were also significantly delayed in explicit ToM development (de Villiers, 2005; Schick, de Villiers, de Villiers, & Hoffmeister, 2007). In addition, 34 children with language impairment between the ages of 42 and 65 months were found to have developmental delays in explicit ToM. In a study by Farrar et al. (2009), general grammar and receptive vocabulary scores predicted children's explicit ToM performance. These language and ToM relationships may underlie the correlations between children with language impairment who often have problems with social skills (Baker & Cantwell, 1987; Brinton & Fujiki, 1993).

ToM ability is also related to exposure to discussions and conversations about mental states and perspectives (Cutting & Dunn, 1999; Dunn, Brown, & Beardsall, 1991; Harris, de Rosnay, & Pons, 2005; Hughes et al., 2005; Lucariello, 2004). In a large study of 1,116 5-year-old twins, Hughes et al. found that variation in ToM performances was not only accounted for by linguistic ability but also by individual variation in life experiences such as accidents or illnesses and their sibling's relationships with their parents, each other, and with peers (Hughes et al., 2005, p. 362). In other words, increased exposure to situations and discussions around self or others' emotions, and interpersonal relationships, affect ToM development.

## Pragmatic Communication Development

Throughout development, children listen to, interpret, and express themselves through nonverbal and verbal communication. Children begin to discriminate facial expressions at the age of 7 months (Caron, Caron, & Myers, 1982), and begin to understand that facial expressions have emotional meaning by 12 months of age. This is the same age at which they use joint referencing, or secondary intersubjectivity, to determine whether or not to engage with an object (Sorce, Emde, Campos, & Klinnert, 1985; Walden & Ogan, 1988). Children as young as 3 years old are able to identify common emotions from facial expressions (Verbeek, 1996). By approximately 10 years of age, children reach competency in nonverbal communication, when they are able to correctly name the emotions of happiness, sadness, anger and fear (Camras & Allison, 1985; Kirouac & Dore, 1983).

Social communication, or pragmatic communication development, includes the appropriate vocabulary, semantics, syntactical structures, and nonverbal behaviors that are expected for a particular social context or situation (Goncu, 1993; McGuigan & Salmon, 2004; Pelligrini, 1985). Pragmatic behavior is learned through the early communicative interactions with caregivers. Infants receive support, role models, information and guidance about emotions, behavior regulation, and social, linguistic, and cognitive knowledge from these shared interactions with adults. Preverbal communicative intent is demonstrated by intentional vocalization and symbolic gestures for directing attention or requesting objects or actions, and typically develops around 8 to 10 months of age (Ninio & Snow, 1996). Children begin to express words symbolically between 10 and 12 months of age. They begin to use these words for a variety of functions and intentions framed within social rules for nonverbal and verbal behavior (Ninio & Snow, 1996). Functions range from initiating an interaction, requesting, or commenting, to stating an intention. Between 1 and 2½ years of age, children know and express emotional labels, identify primary emotions in themselves, and begin to demonstrate polite social behaviors and empathy for others (Saarni, 1999). Toddlers and preschoolers also internalize their caregivers' language and use these language models (self-talk) to verbally help regulate their negative emotions and unacceptable behavior of themselves and others (Bronson, 2000). At this age, they also begin to express polite forms of greeting, parting, thanking, and response to thanking (Ninio & Snow, 1996).

Over time, self-talk becomes internalized when children begin to think in language (Barkley, 1997; Bronson, 2000; Diaz & Berk, 1992; Vygotsky, 1986). Children begin to develop an increasing variety of conversation interchanges (different types of discussion and negotiation) and functions between the ages of 2 and 3 years (Ninio & Snow, 1996). By the age of 5 years, children continue to progress in 1) emotion regulation, 2) verbal expression of internal feelings and emotional events, 3) pretend play by acting out different emotional states, intentionally misleading others about their emotional states, and 4) conversations demonstrating taking turns, topic initiation and maintenance, complex narratives, and clarification or repair behaviors (Ninio & Snow, 1996; Saarni, 1999). By early elementary grades, children continue to use adults to cope with emotional regulation, but they have emerging problem-solving skills. Children show more social skill coordination with their own and others' emotions by demonstrating the ability to be emotionally distant from peers and expressing socially appropriate emotions in pretend or other contexts (Saarni, 1999). They learn how to ask for help or information, politely order at a restaurant, inquire about someone's background, avoid hurting someone's feelings, and provide expected social-obligatory responses. At the same time, they monitor their conversational expression for rapid turn taking, overlaps, fluency, interruptions, comments that are on topic, and moments when conversational repair is needed. Emotion, social cognition, and social pragmatic communication continue to become refined across social contexts with peers in developing close relationships with others outside of the family.

In summary, children are exposed to social factors that, coupled with adequate care for biological needs, result in social communication development. Through face-to-face interactions with a caring adult who shares positive emotional states, infants learn to cope with negative feelings and identify their emotional states and the emotional states of others. These interactions and experiences facilitate development of the ability to self-regulate their own emotions, draw inferences from others' nonverbal behaviors to interpret emotions, and develop intra- and inter-ToM, social cognition, and rule-governed nonverbal and verbal pragmatic communication behaviors, which are all important for social communication development.

## PREADOPTION RISK AND ADVERSITY

As discussed in Chapters 1 and 2, there is variability in the quality of preadoption care across countries of adoption origin. Quality care includes adequate nutrition and medical care, social-emotional interaction and stimulation, and environmental opportunities for learning. Most institutions fail to provide a level of care that facilitates development comparable to children born to and living with their biological families (Johnson, 2000; Miller, 2005). Some children may have been placed in orphanages because the parents did not have the social or economic means to care for them, or the courts may have terminated parental rights because of documented abuse and/or neglect (for a review see Hwa-Froelich, 2009; Johnson, 2000). Thus, children may have experienced poor early care prior to entering an institution. As explained by Ladage (2009), poor quality of institutional care can result in psychosocial short stature, growth and developmental delays, infectious diseases, and a variety of complex medical issues for the majority of children adopted from institutions. Caregivers often care for large numbers of children and receive training on health care instead of child development. Children may receive basic care to meet biological needs, but stimulation needed for learning and interaction with a consistent caregiver is often limited (Johnson, 2000).

Children in institutions may also experience abuse and neglect, which may affect their postadoption adjustment. A survey study of 695 U.S. parents who adopted children from China, Tan and Marfo (2006) found that parental report of preadoption neglect and early postadoption behaviors of rejection toward the parents predicted negative behavioral adjustment outcomes. Thus, children living in institutions may not receive the kind of social interaction needed to facilitate development in social behaviors, ToM, social cognition, or pragmatic communication.

Some internationally adopted children may receive foster care. Although foster care is a better alternative to institutional care, children living in foster care demonstrate both catch-up and continued developmental delays (Nelson et al., 2007; Pears & Fisher, 2005; Windsor, Glaze, Koga, & the Bucharest Early Intervention Project Core Group, 2007). In a randomized control study, Ghera et al. (2009) found that 30- and 42-month-old Romanian children who were removed from institutional care and placed between an average of 7 and 19 months in foster care, dramatically improved in positive affect and attention. Using the same sample, Windsor et al. (2007) found that although 30-month-old children in foster care for at least 1 year significantly improved in language development over institutionalized peers, their expressive syntactical development remained delayed compared with Romanian community peers.

Although foster care is preferable to institutional care, transitions during foster care can negatively affect children's development. Pears and Fisher (2005) found that consistent U.S. foster care and social interaction positively affected foster children's cognitive and language development. Children who experienced more transitions during foster care, however, had more negative cognitive and language developmental outcomes. Because children experiencing foster care in different countries may experience multiple transitions prior to adoption, these transitions may adversely affect later developmental outcomes. During my clinical and research interactions with adoptive parents, they have reported wide variability in care experiences, ranging from institutional care only to foster care and institutional care, to relative care and institutional care and foster care only. The number of transitions in care and the quality of early care may have differential effects on later development of ToM, social cognition, and pragmatic communication development.

## The Impact of Stress on Neurobiological Development

The negative effects of stress on infant development have been widely reported in the literature (Fox, Levitt, & Nelson, 2010; Gunnar & Quevedo, 2007; Sánchez & Pollak, 2009; Nelson, 2007; Schore, 2001) and provide support for the connectionist theory. This states that early appropriate care and stimulation promotes neural connectivity and development (for a review, see Chapter 1). Infants who are born neurologically intact expect and depend upon environmental experiences to facilitate and refine later neurological development for several years. As Fox et al. (2010) stated, "...through a well defined developmental process, the basic connectivity of local and long distance neurons is set up to take advantage of a highly flexible organization that is both activity dependent and expectant post-natally" (p. 31). Initial learning is the foundation for later learning, and changes in the environment early in life can have major effects on later neurological development. When young children are exposed to stressful events, trauma, abuse and/or severe neglect, their physical, emotional, social, and cognitive development may be affected. Children living in stressful environments may have inadequate secretion of the growth hormone, cortisol, resulting in psychosocial short stature and an overactive hypothalamic-pituitary-adrenal (HPA) stress axis resulting in production of higher than normal cortisol levels (Mason & Narad, 2005). Cortisol levels have been associated with lower cognitive and motor performance scores. Stress responses also affect the sympathetic adrenomedullary (SAM) system responsible for activation of the fight/flight response. When the fight/flight response is triggered, children are hypervigilant to any stimuli that may pose a risk to their survival. This state increases stress and is not conducive to learning or building relationships. The limbic-hypothalamic-pituitary-adrenocortical axis is also involved and is responsible for the production of glucocorticoids that impairs processes involved in learning and memory (for a review see Gunnar & Quevedo, 2007).

Early trauma has adverse effects on right hemisphere and frontal lobe brain development that are involved in the processing and regulation of emotions and behavior. Children who do not form a secure attachment with a caregiver early in life are at risk of not developing the skills to regulate their emotions and behaviors, as well as the ability to process social, emotional, and behavior information that are primarily processed through the right hemisphere (for a review see Schore, 2001). It is the caregiver who provides sensitive, consistent care to help infants learn how to regulate their emotions. The absence of this relationship, or the substitution of multiple inconsistent or abusive and neglectful caregivers, fails to provide the infant with the experiences to facilitate typical early neurological (right hemisphere and frontal lobe) and psychosocial (flexible thinking and social competence) development. Negative experiences during the first year of life negatively affect the growth and development of the frontal lobe and higher cortico-limbic circuitry responsible for attachment, empathy, regulation of affect, problem solving, and cognitive flexibility needed for dynamic thinking (Schore, 2001).

Research on animals and children exposed to trauma or abuse and neglect provides evidence of these neurobiological outcomes (Sánchez, Hearn, Do, Rilling, & Herndon, 1998; Sánchez, Ladd, & Plotsky, 2001; Sánchez & Pollak, 2009; Teicher et al., 1997). Animal studies on rodents and nonhuman primates have found that the quality of maternal care affects the neuroendocrine and neurobiological systems involved in regulating stress, emotion, and attention. These are skills necessary for social competence, as well as for executive function used during problem solving, such as planning and execution of a plan (Sánchez et al., 1998; Sánchez et al., 2001). Studies with human infants demonstrating a disorganized attachment, often associated with children who have been abused or severely neglected, found that these children had left-sided facial tics indicative of dysfunction of the right hemisphere. Additionally electroencephalogram (EEG) abnormalities have been reported in the front temporal lobes and anterior brain regions in children exposed to physical and sexual abuse and in the frontal lobes of infants born to mothers with depression (Schore, 2001). Although infants born to mothers with depression may experience better quality of early care than infants in institutions, the fact that infants born to mothers with depression have frontal lobe EEG abnormalities renders the possibility that infants reared in institutions may be at risk of similar outcomes of right hemisphere dysfunction and/or abnormal EEGs.

## Possible Effects on ToM, Language, and Social Communication Development

Studies on children who have experienced abuse and/or neglect conclude that these children have problems regulating and recognizing emotions, engage in aggressive behavior, withdraw socially, or display inappropriate affect and behavior (Sánchez & Pollak, 2009). For example, in contrast to a control group (17), eighteen 5- and 6-year-old children who were abused or neglected associated negative emotional outcomes (anger or sadness) with positive situations, such as winning a prize or helping around the house (Perlman, Kalish, & Pollak, 2008). In other words, children who have experienced abuse and neglect may develop atypical social cognitions and theories about others' mental states affecting their ToM development and social communication.

Cicchetti, Rogosch, Maughan, Toth, and Bruce (2003) and Eigsti & Cicchetti (2004) found that early abuse and neglect resulted in later delays in ToM and expressive language development. In a sample of 518 children between 3 and 8 years old from low and middle socioeconomic (SES) backgrounds, 203 were children experiencing maltreatment and poverty. Children experiencing maltreatment demonstrated difficulty in the understanding of false beliefs. The history of maltreatment beyond SES background predicted ToM performance (Cicchetti et al., 2003). In a later study, Eigsti and Cicchetti (2004) recruited 34 children between 55 and 60 months of age from low SES backgrounds. Nineteen of the children were active cases in the Department of Social Services, had maltreatment documentation before the age of 2 years, and were living with their biological parents who were the original abusers. Thus, these children were exposed to chronic maltreatment. On measures of expressive syntax and receptive vocabulary, children who had a history of maltreatment had "less complex language and less advanced knowledge of vocabulary" (p. 96). This finding may be related to the caregivers' language productions because they were found to produce fewer utterances and fewer different types of utterances than the parents in the control group. Thus, early maltreatment and poor caregiver–child communicative interactions appear to negatively affect children's language and ToM development.

Abuse and neglect affect children's narrative descriptions of their caregivers and their emotion regulation. Measures of their narrative caregiver descriptions and emotion regulation also predicted their relationships with peers. Shields, Ryan, and Cicchetti (2001) found that in a sample of 76 maltreated and 45 nonmaltreated children between the ages of 8 and 12 years, maltreated children's narrative descriptions of their caregivers and measures of emotion regulation predicted peer nominations for aggression and rejection. Using eight story stems "designed to elicit emotionally charged themes" inherent in parent–child relationships, children were asked to complete the story stems, then trained interviewers asked a series of structured probes (Shields et al., 2001, p. 325). Narratives were coded for content (autonomy support, responsiveness, emotional coercion, and physical coercion) and organizational structure (resistance, impoverishment, tangentiality, and incoherence). The children's emotion regulation was measured using the Emotion Regulation Q-Scale (Shields & Cicchetti, 1997); those experiencing maltreatment gave more negative and constricted narratives and had poorer emotion regulation than children with no history of maltreatment. These patterns in narratives and emotion regulation scores also predicted that their peers would identify these children as aggressive and that they would not want them as a friend (rejection). The authors suggested that children's early negative social interactions with their caregivers could become internalized mental representations that may affect their ability to regulate their emotions in similar social contexts with peers, consequently affecting their social relationships.

In conclusion, early abuse and neglect and chronic abuse and neglect have long-lasting effects on children's later social development. ToM, language development, and social competence are negatively affected by exposure to adverse social experiences. Given the adverse experiences children experience in institutional care, do children adopted from institutions have similar developmental outcomes?

## SOCIAL COMMUNICATION DEVELOPMENT AFTER ADOPTION

Little research has been published on the social-communication development of internationally adopted children. Most of the research has focused on children adopted from Romania who suffered some of the worst institutional care documented. In this section, I will review studies on 1) neurobiological development, 2) ToM, and 3) social communication development on children adopted from Romania as well as preliminary data on children adopted from Eastern European and Asian countries.

## Neurobiological Development After Adoption

As described in Chapters 1 and 2, poor prenatal care, postbirth nutrition, and social neglect have negative effects on physical growth, head circumference, and weight. Children who had more positive growth and developmental outcomes had shorter duration or exposure (less than 12 months) to adverse care (Van IJzendoorn, Bakermans-Kranenburg, & Juffer, 2006). These negative physical outcomes may affect brain growth and development.

Several neurobiological studies of children adopted from Romania have documented differences in metabolism and electrical activity. Using positron–emission tomography (PET) scans, Chugani et al. (2001) compared PET scans of 17 normally functioning adults, 7 nonadopted children with a mean age of 10.7 years, and 10 Romanian children whose mean age was 8.8 years. The Romanian children had lived in institutions for approximately 38 months prior to adoption into U.S. families. The researchers found reduced metabolism in the prefrontal cortex and temporal lobe regions. These regions are responsible for higher cognitive functions, such as memory and emotion. Relative to these findings, the children also exhibited mild cognitive impairment, impulsivity, inattention, and social problems (for a review see Nelson, 2007). Eluvathingal et al. (2006) analyzed the myelinated brain regions, as a measure of connective tissue, in these same children and found reduced connectivity in the uncinate fasciculus. This region is responsible for interbrain communication for cognitive and emotional processing.

Romanian children living in institutions demonstrate different electrical brain activity than children who have never experienced institutional care. In two studies comparing institutionalized Romanian children with children who had never been institutionalized, Marshall, Fox, and the BEIP Core Group (2004) found less general electrical brain activity on the EEG and found reduced event-related potential (ERP) when the children viewed different facial expressions. Other studies by Parker, Nelson, and the Bucharest Early Intervention Project Core Group (2005, 2008) found different patterns in perceptual processing of emotional stimuli (different facial expressions and familiar and stranger faces) between 7- to 32-month-old Romanian children who were institutionalized compared with never-institutionalized groups. The institutionalized group demonstrated greater response to fear expressions and a smaller response to sad and happy expressions. In addition, the institutionalized group showed little hemispheric specialization (e.g., asymmetry in hemispheric response to the facial expressions) in comparison to the control group. This may be an indication that exposure to adverse care affected hemispheric connectivity (Parker et al. 2005). In Parker et al.'s later study (2008), differences in amplitude of the ERPs were found between groups, as well as more activation of a positive slow wave (PSW) for familiar caregivers in the institutionalized group. PSW is associated with updating memory for a partially encoded stimulus. The institutionalized children's increase in PSW may indicate that the familiar caregivers' faces were not yet encoded into their memories. This evidence may offer preliminary explanation for internationally adopted children's overly friendly behaviors toward unfamiliar adults and problems with attachment after adoption.

When children have consistent interaction with one caregiver, patterns of neurological electrical activity change. Subsequent to the studies described above, researchers compared ERPs of 42-month-old Romanian children living in institutions to an age-matched group of Romanian children who had never been institutionalized, and to Romanian children living in foster care (Moulson, Fox, Zeanah, & Nelson, 2009). The ERPs of children in foster care fell between the ERPs of institutional and never-institutionalized groups, and their facial emotion processing was similar to that of the never-institutionalized group. The authors suggested that foster care might help mediate processing of emotions. In a later randomized control study of 136 Romanian children between 6 and 31 months of age, approximately half of the children were randomly assigned to a foster care situation and followed and assessed by EEG at 18, 30 and 42 months of age (Marshall, Reeb, Fox, Nelson, & Zeanah, 2008). These researchers found small group differences in neurophysiological changes for children who entered foster care at younger ages, although evidence of foster care mediation was unclear. Thus, early foster care may provide some promise for better neurological development, but more research is needed.

In addition, hormone levels for children adopted from institutional care differ from nonadopted children. Gunnar, Morison, Chisholm, and Schuder (2001) compared saliva samples of cortisol, a hormone associated with stress, in late-adopted (18), Romanian children, early adopted (15) Romanian children, and a group of Canadian born children (27). The Romanian children had been with their adoptive families for about 6½ years. Cortisol saliva samples were taken when the children awoke, at noon, and in the evening. Gunnar et al. found that the late-adopted group (adopted after 8 months in an institution) had higher cortisol levels throughout the day than the other two groups. High levels of cortisol adversely affect the HPA and SAM axes and are associated with learning, memory, motor skills, and fight/flight responses discussed earlier in this chapter. In addition, Fries, Shirtcliff, and Pollak (2008) studied cortisol levels of 18 children adopted from Russian and Romanian institutions and 21 nonadopted children. The adopted children had lived in the institution from 7 to 42 months and had been adopted for approximately 3 years.

Control-cortisol levels were measured from urine samples taken after the children woke up on typical days in which no unusual or stressful events had occurred. Basal samples were collected prior to experimental conditions and on days between experimental sessions (playing a computer game on a parent's or an unfamiliar female's lap) and other samples were taken immediately following experimental sessions. Basal-cortisol levels and cortisol levels after playing with a stranger did not differ between children who were institutionalized and comparison children. Cortisol levels for the adopted group were higher after the session with the parent. The authors suggested that "close physical contact with a caregiver was a particular challenge …rather than a buffer against prolonged activation," (p. 595) and that this finding may be related to the children's early caregiving experiences.

Fries, Ziegler, Kurian, Jacoris, and Pollak (2005) also studied vasopressin and oxytocin neuropeptides in children who had experienced institutional care. An increase in neuropeptides is related to social bonding, being nurtured, regulation of stress, social communication, and positive emotions. Two groups of children were studied: 1) children who had been institutionalized for 7 to 42 months and in U.S. adoptive care for 10 to 48 months and, 2) an age and SES matched nonadopted group. Urine samples were gathered after each child had interacted with their parent or an unfamiliar female during a computer game with "regularly timed physical contact." (p. 17, 238). Nonadopted children had higher levels of vasopressin and oxytocin after interacting with their mothers. The authors concluded that when children do not receive the expected and needed typical care, neuropeptide development may be negatively affected and the effects may persist over time.

In summary, children experiencing extreme deprivation of quality early care, as in the case of children reared in Romanian institutions, may have persistent differences in neurological development. After several years of improved care, electrical activity and responses improved for children adopted at younger ages and for children experiencing foster care at younger ages. In contrast to these positive findings, however, levels of stress hormones and neuropeptides are different after approximately 1 to 4 years after adoption for children who experienced institutional care early in their lives.

## Measures of ToM Development After Adoption

ToM development has traditionally been measured by children's expressive responses to designed scenarios eliciting awareness of self and others' knowledge, lack of knowledge, and false beliefs (Baron-Cohen, 1997). One task involves showing children a container of a common candy with unexpected contents inside (smarties task; Perner, Leekman, & Wimmer, 1987). The child is asked, "What do you think is inside this container?" Typically the child answers, "smarties." Then the child is shown the unexpected contents of the container and is asked, "What did you think was in this container?" (Correct answer: smarties) and "What will your friend think is in this container?" (Correct answer: smarties).

Another task involves a story with pictures of the characters and their actions (Sally-Ann story; Wimmer & Perner, 1983). In this story, Sally places her marble in a basket. While Sally is away, Ann moves the marble to a box, thus, Sally is unaware the marble has been moved. Sally returns and is going to look for her marble. The child is asked, "Where will Sally look for her marble?" (Correct answer: In the basket where Sally left it). Then the child is asked, "Why will she look there?" (Correct answer: because she did not know Ann moved her marble so she must believe it is still where she left it).

A third task is a combination of the prior two tasks with the use of a puppet (explaining action; Bartsch & Wellman, 1989). The child is told that the puppet is sleeping and is shown an egg carton with plastic eggs inside. While the puppet sleeps, the examiner removes the eggs and places them in a different box. Once the puppet is awakened, the child is told, "Do you know what he likes to do when he wakes up? He likes to eat eggs." The puppet looks in the egg carton and the child is asked, "Why is he looking in there?" (Correct answer: because he thinks eggs are in there.) and, "Why isn't he looking in that (other) box?" (Correct answer: because he doesn't know that the eggs are in that box). The majority of 4-year-old typically developing children is able to answer these questions correctly (Baron-Cohen, 1997).

In a study by Yagmurlu, Berument, and Celimli (2005), tasks similar to the ones described above were used to measure ToM development in three groups: 1) 34 children living in Turkish institutions, 2) 32 children living with their Turkish parents from low SES backgrounds, and 3) 44 Turkish children living with their parents from middle SES backgrounds. Children were divided into a group of 4- to 5-year-old children and a group of 6-year-old children. Children raised in institutions performed more poorly on ToM tasks regardless of SES background, gender, language or nonverbal intelligence. The adult-to-child ratio in the children's institutional environment predicted ToM outcome, suggesting that adult-to-child interactions might be necessary for ToM development. There were some confounding variables in this study that make it difficult to generalize these findings. For example, not all children were placed in the institution at the same age, with a range of 8 to 66 months of age at the time of placement. This wide age range resulted in variability as to how long the children were exposed to institutional care ranging from 7 to 66 months. In spite of these variables, the ToM performance for children living in institutions was significantly different and the fact that this performance was predicted by adult to child staffing ratios is particularly relevant in support of the need for adult and child interaction for ToM development. False-belief development was studied in a group of 6- and

7-year-old children adopted by U.S. families from a number of different countries and compared with children raised in country of origin foster care and U.S. nonadopted children (Tarullo, Bruce, & Gunnar, 2007). Tarullo et al. recruited 120 children from three groups. Each group consisted of 40 children (10 boys) matched by age and gender. The institutional group lived in institutions for approximately 10 to 36 months and were adopted between 12 and 36 months of age. The foster-care group spent approximately 0 to 2 months in institutional care and was placed in foster care between 2 and 25 months of age. The birth-child group had never experienced institutional or foster care. The authors measured ToM using a contextualized version of the Sally-Ann story with two dolls and two locations. They repeated the story with a different object and three location possibilities. The institutionalized group performed within average range for language abilities, although their scores were lower than the foster care and birth-child groups. When language performance was controlled, the institutionalized group's ToM performance was significantly lower than the other two groups. The foster-care group scored between the institutionalized and birth-child groups. From these findings, it appears that exposure to institutional environments is related to delays in ToM development.

I have been following a group of 4-year-old children adopted from Eastern Europe and Asia prior to their 2nd birthday since 2008. These children were exposed to institutionalization for 24 months or less and have received adoptive parent care for at least 2 years. The ToM tasks described above were used to measure internationally adopted children's and nonadopted children's ToM development. All children were recruited from the same early childhood settings, were not receiving speech or language services at the time of the study, were matched by age and SES background, and had general language skills above a standard score of 90. Preliminary findings provide evidence that after approximately 2 or more years postadoption, the internationally adopted children were delayed in their ToM development in comparison to nonadopted children (Hwa-Froelich & Schuette, 2010). Although this sample of adopted children scored within normal range on general language tests, their expressive language scores were significantly lower than the control group. This lower-expressive-language performance may be related to poorer performance on the ToM tasks that are sensitive to expressive language competence. When expressive language scores were controlled, the significant differences in ToM remained. I am in the process of measuring ToM development when the children turn 6 years old to determine if adopted children's language and ToM performance improves or is equivalent to the performance of same-age peers.

For school-age children, Happé (1994) used "strange stories" to measure ToM development (p. 916; O'Hare, Bremner, Happé, and Pettigrew, 2009). These short stories are followed by questions about the characters' mental states. Answers can be scored as correct (2 points), partially correct

(1 point), or incorrect (0). O'Hare et al. provided average scores and standard deviations for children from 5 years to 12 years 11 months of age.

The stories were used to measure ToM in a comparison study of Romanian adoptees and children adopted within the United Kingdom (U.K.) (Colvert et al., 2008). The Romanian group of 165 children was split into three groups: 1) adopted before 6 months of age (58), 2) adopted between 6 and 24 months of age (59), and 3) adopted after 24 months of age (48). The comparison group consisted of 52 children who were domestically adopted. All measures were collected when the children were 11 years old. Children who had experienced institutional care beyond 6 months of age demonstrated deficits in ToM when answering questions about the *Strange Stories*. ToM performance was correlated with *quasi-autism*; these behaviors can include obsessive, repetitive, and/or stereotypical behaviors, poor social relationships, and communication with unusual behaviors such as interest in social approach and excessive communication. In their discussion, the authors concluded that "institutional deprivation often leads to an impaired ToM" (Colvert et al., 2008, p. 1066) and delayed ToM was associated with autism-like behaviors.

Although only four studies have measured ToM development in children living in Turkish institutions or adopted from institutional care, the results seem to support delayed or impaired ToM development. Continued research in this area of development, however, is needed.

## SOCIAL COMMUNICATION DEVELOPMENT AFTER ADOPTION

Social communication development includes comprehension of both nonverbal and verbal communication and pragmatics. Nonverbal communication involves the comprehension and expression of facial expressions, tone of voice, and postures. Although little research has been done on nonverbal communication development in internationally adopted children, a few studies have been published.

Nonverbal social communication measures were studied in a sample of children adopted from Romania. *The Diagnostic Analysis of Nonverbal Abilities*, version 2 (DANVA2; Nowicki & Duke, 1994) was used in a study with 165 children adopted from Romania and 52 children domestically adopted in the United Kingdom, the same sample described earlier in the Colvert et al. (2008) study (Rutter et al., 2007b). The DANVA2 includes measures of identification of different child and adult facial expressions and tone of voice. All children were 11 years of age at the time of this study. Children adopted from Romania made more errors on the DANVA2 test than domestically adopted peers. Nonverbal communication comprehension was not measured when the Romanian children were younger; therefore, it is unknown whether the children's development had improved since the time of their adoption or remained delayed across time.

In a sample of 28 children adopted from Eastern Europe (12) and Asia (16), nonverbal communication development was measured and compared with an age and SES matched nonadopted peer group (Roselman, 2010). Children in the adopted group were adopted before the age of 2 years and were between the ages of 4 years and 4 years 11 months at the time of the study. None of the children were receiving speech or language therapy services at the time of the study and all children scored above a 90 standard score on a general language measure. Significant differences were found between the adopted and nonadopted groups in reading both children's facial expressions and adult and child tone of voice. Group differences were also found between the Eastern European group and the Asian group in comprehension of children's tone of voice. However, all group differences were of small effect. Thus, after 2 or more years of living in a nurturing family, internationally adopted children interpreted adult facial expressions almost as well as their nonadopted peers. They appeared to have more difficulty interpreting children's facial expressions and tone of voice for both adults and children, but the differences were of small effect. Interpretation of tone of voice and facial expressions of peers may take longer to develop and children may need more exposure to other children to develop these skills. Children adopted from Asian countries seemed to have better skills in interpreting children's tone of voice. Interpretation of tone of voice may be affected by early exposure to Asian languages in which linguistic tones carry semantic meaning (Hwa-Froelich & Matsuo, 2010). However, more research is needed to clarify these findings.

Tarullo et al. (2007) measured emotional understanding with similar tasks. In their first task, they asked 6- and 7-year-old children to identify emotions from four facial expressions (happy, sad, mad, or scared). A second task involved vignettes with a parent and child in which the child was asked to identify how a character was feeling by pointing to a facial expression of sad, happy, mad, or scared. No differences were found among the institutional, foster care, or birth child groups for the measure of emotional understanding. Group ToM scores were not related to emotional understanding performance. The authors suggested that the measures they used were designed for younger children and may not have been sensitive to measure older children's development of emotional understanding. More research in this area is needed to document postadoption development.

The other major component of social communication is the understanding and expression of pragmatic communication. Few studies have measured this area of communication development and few standardized instruments for pragmatic language development exist. Most measures are parent–report measures such as the *Children's Communication Checklist*, 2nd edition (CCC-2; Bishop, 2006), a screening measure of general and social communication or the *Ages and Stages Questionnaire*

(ASQ; Squires & Bricker, 2009), a developmental screening instrument covering development in communication, gross and fine motor, problem solving, and social skills. The ASQ is a standardized measure of English pragmatic development and the CCC-2 is a measure of British English pragmatic development.

The ASQ was used in a longitudinal study of children adopted from Eastern Europe, Guatemala, and Asia. Wilson and Weaver (2009) followed 23 children from an original sample of 26 children adopted by U.S. families between the ages of 4 and 36 months. They asked parents to complete the ASQ questionnaire approximately 19½ months after adoption and between the ages of 23½ and 55 months. According to ASQ norms, the children were within normative range for social and motor development when they were approximately 19½ months of age. Five of the 23 (22%) children had a delay in one of the following areas: 1) communication, 2) fine motor, or 3) problem solving.

In a survey study measuring social language and social skills, Glennen and Bright (2005) followed a subset (46) of 130 children adopted by U.S. families from Eastern Europe recruited for a longitudinal study (Glennen & Masters, 2002). The original sample was recruited when the children were between 9 and 40 months of age. The authors of the study contacted parents of the original sample 5 years later when the children were 6.6 and 9.1 years of age. The parents were asked to complete the CCC-2 and another measure of social skills and behaviors. Although the children had average to above-average performance for subtests on using stereotypical language (using specific phrases or sentences inappropriately) and interests (perseverating on specific interests to the exclusion of others), the children scored below the test average for the subtests measuring social relations (may seem distant with familiar adults or may unintentionally hurt peers), use of context (misunderstanding of jokes or is too literal), and nonverbal communication (poor eye contact or doesn't read conversational overtures). The authors concluded that children adopted from Eastern Europe might need assistance with pragmatic communication development and recommended pragmatic behavioral assessments (Glennen & Bright, 2005).

To add to these studies, the current research project described earlier includes measures of pragmatic communication with the same sample. To measure pragmatic language, the *Comprehensive Assessment of Spoken Language* pragmatic subtest was administered (CASL; Carrow-Woolfolk, 1999). Preliminary findings show that in spite of group differences in ToM development, the adopted group (32) scored similarly on the CASL pragmatic language subtest in comparison to a nonadopted group (31) (Hwa-Froelich & Schuette, 2010).

In summary, only two studies could be found that report on social-communication development and both used screening parent–report measures. One unpublished thesis study (Roselman, 2010) and a study by Tarullo et al. (2007) reported on nonverbal social communication development using a behavior measure. Although more research is needed with behavior measures, these early studies provide evidence that internationally adopted children may have social delays in developing ToM and mild delays in nonverbal social communication skills, but their pragmatic communication development appears comparable to same-age peers.

## ▼▼▼ IMPLICATIONS

In spite of the evidence of negative neurobiolgocial effects of early adverse care, internationally adopted children demonstrate amazing resiliency. Although internationally adopted children may demonstrate delays in interpretation of nonverbal communication and ToM development, their social language or pragmatic language appears comparable to same-age peers. In other words, internationally adopted children who may have had negative or insufficient social interactions were able to make up for these adverse experiences and learn pragmatic communication. They may need help with development of some nonverbal communication and ToM skills, as well as with inferential and abstract language such as interpretation of jokes and nonliteral language.

As in the case of Chelsea, she demonstrated an above average cognitive level but had problems with emotion regulation, attention, and impulsivity that affected her ability to inhibit and to think flexibly and dynamically in order to deal with novel events, changing situations, and problems. Her intra-ToM (self-awareness of her mental states and knowledge) was emerging, but Chelsea needed help identifying and regulating her emotions and impulses to focus attention on learning. Her lack of social cognition about other people's feelings and perspectives (inter-ToM) negatively influenced her ability to plan her behavior for specific social contexts or draw inferences from nonverbal and verbal communication to dynamically and flexibly adapt or change her social behavior when needed. Her ToM development may have been delayed because of her early adverse experiences at the orphanage. Since Chelsea was 7 years old at the time she was seen at the clinic, we felt her nonverbal communication and pragmatic language development were delayed and negatively influencing her social relationships. Chelsea needed to improve her social knowledge about expected behaviors in specific social contexts and learn how to process and interpret social behaviors and ambiguous inferential communication flexibly and dynamically. She also needed to develop self-talk and other self-regulating strategies to help her identify and regulate her emotions and inhibit her impulsivity.

## KEY POINTS

▶ Face-to-face interactions are important for developing primary intersubjectivity and ToM.

▶ Joint attention with a third object or person is important in developing secondary intersubjectivity and inter-ToM.

▶ Talk about emotions demonstrated through facial expressions and tone of voice helps children learn to associate facial expressions and tone of voice with emotions.

▶ Talk about how events may cause emotions and how people's emotions may cause them to act in certain ways helps children learn social cognition, which is necessary for ToM development.

▶ Early adverse experiences such as abuse and/or neglect negatively affect neurobiological development, ToM, nonverbal, verbal, and pragmatic communication development.

▶ Internationally adopted children have demonstrated delays in ToM and nonverbal communication development, but not pragmatic communication development.

▶ More research is needed to determine referral indicators for delayed nonverbal communication and ToM development.

## REFERRAL INDICATORS

Internationally adopted children should be referred for special education services when the following factors apply:

▶ They receive a standard score of 80 or lower on a pragmatic test of language.

▶ They have difficulty identifying emotions of adult faces after 2 years postadoption or if the child is 4 years old or older.

▶ They have difficulty understanding nonverbal communication.

▶ They demonstrate poor eye contact.

▶ They have persistent delays in ToM development.

▶ They have problems understanding inferential or nonliteral language, or are too literal.

▶ They have persistent problems with social relationships.

## REFERENCES

Astington, J.W., & Jenkins, J.M. (1999). A longitudinal study of the relation between language and theory-of-mind development. *Developmental Psychology, 35*(5) 1311–1320.

Astington, J.W., & Peskin, J. (2004). Meaning and use: Children's acquisition of the mental lexicon. In J.M. Lucariello, J.A. Hudson, R. Fivush, & P.J. Bauer (Eds.). *The development of the mediated mind* (pp. 59–78). Mahwah, NJ: Lawrence Erlbaum.

Baker, L., & Cantwell, D.P. (1987). A prospective psychiatric follow-up of children with speech/language disorders. *Journal of the American Academy of Child and Adolescent Psychiatry, 26,* 546–553.

Baldwin, D.A., & Moses, L.J. (1994). Early understanding of referential intent and attentional focus: Evidence from language and emotion. In C. Lewis & P. Mitchell (Eds.) *Children's early understanding of mind. Origins and development* (pp. 133–156). Hillsdale, NJ: Erlbaum.

Barkley, R.A. (1997). *ADHD and the nature of self-control.* New York: Guilford.

Baron-Cohen, S. (1997). *Mindblindness. An essay on autism and theory of mind.* Cambridge, MA: MIT Press.

Bartsch, K., & Wellman, H.M. (1989). Young children's attribution of action to beliefs and desires. *Child Development, 60,* 946–964.

Bishop, D. (2006). *Children's Communication Checklist,* (2nd ed.). San Antonio: Pearson.

Brinton, B., & Fujiki, M. (1993). Language, social skills, and socioemotional behavior. *Language, Speech, and Hearing Services in Schools, 24,* 194–198.

Bronson, M.B. (2000). *Self-regulation in early childhood.* New York: Guilford.

Bruner, J.S. (1999). The intentionality of referring. In P. Zelazo & J.W. Astington (Eds.), *Developing theories of intention: Social understanding and self-control* (pp. 329–339). Mahwah, NJ: Erlbaum.

Butterworth, G. (1994). Theory of mind and the facts of embodiment. In C. Lewis & P. Mitchell (Eds.), *Children's early understanding of mind: Origins and development* (pp. 115–132). Hillsdale, NJ: Erlbaum.

Camras, L.A., & Allison, K. (1985). Children's understanding of emotional facial expressions and verbal labels. *Journal of Nonverbal Behavior, 9,* 84–94.

Caron, R., Caron, A., & Myers, R. (1982). Abstraction of invariant facial expression in infancy. *Child Development, 53,* 1008–1015.

Carrow-Woolfolk, E. (1999). *Comprehensive assessment of spoken language.* Circle Pines, MN: American Guidance Service.

Chugani, H.T., Behen, M.E., Muzik, O., Juhasz, C., Nagy, F., & Chugani, D.C. (2001). Local brain functional activity following early deprivation: A study of postinstitutionalized Romanian orphans. *Neuroimage, 14,* 1290–1301.

Cicchetti, D., Rogosch, F.A., Maughan, A., Toth, S.L., & Bruce, J. (2003). False belief understanding in maltreated children. *Development and Psychopathology, 15*(4), 1067–1091.

Cohen, N.J., Lojkasek, M., Zadeh, Z.Y., Pugliese, M., & Kiefer, H. (2008). Children adopted from China: A prospective study of their growth and development. *The Journal of Child Psychology and Psychiatry, 49*(4), 458–468.

Colvert, E., Rutter, M., Kreppner, J., Beckett, C., Castle, J., Groothues, C., et al. (2008). Do theory of mind and executive function deficits underlie the adverse outcomes associated with profound early deprivation? Findings from the English and Romanian adoptees study. *Journal of Abnormal Child Psychology, 36,* 1057–1068.

Cutting, A.L., & Dunn, J. (1999). Theory of mind, emotion understanding, language, and family background: Individual differences and interrelations. *Child Development, 70,* 853–865.

Diaz, R., & Berk, L.E. (Eds.). (1992). *Private speech: From social interaction to self- regulation.* Hillsdale, NJ: Erlbaum.

de Villiers, P. (2005). The role of language in theory-of-mind development: What deaf children tell us. In W. Astington & J.A. Baird (Eds.). *Why language matters for theory of mind* (pp. 266–297). New York: Oxford.

de Villiers, J., & Pyers, J.E. (2002). Complements to cognition: A longitudinal study of the relationship between complex syntax and false-belief-understanding. *Cognitive Development, 17,* 1037–1060.

Dunn, J., Brown, J., & Beardsall, L. (1991). Family talk about feeling states and children's later understanding of others' emotions. *Developmental Psychology, 27,* 448–455.

Eigsti, I-M., & Cicchetti, D. (2004). The impact of child maltreatment on expressive syntax at 60 months. *Developmental Science, 7*(1), 88–102.

Eluvathingal, T.J., Chugani, H.T., Behen, M.E., Juhász, C., Muzik, O., Maqbool, M., et al. (2006). Abnormal brain connectivity in children after early severe socioemotional deprivation: A diffusion tensor imaging study. *Pediatrics, 117*(6), 2093–2100.

Farrar, M.J., Johnson, B., Tompkins, V., Easters, M., Zilisi-Medus, A., & Benigno, J.P. (2009). Language and theory of mind in preschool children with specific language impairment. *Journal of Communication Disorders, 42*(6), 428–441.

Fox, S.E., Levitt, P., & Nelson, III, C.A. (2010). How timing and quality of early experiences influence the development of brain architecture. *Child Development, 81*(1), 28–40.

Fries, A.B., Shirtcliff, E.A., & Pollak, S.D. (2008). Neuroendocrine dysregulation following early social deprivation in children. *Developmental Psychobiology, 50*(6), 588–599.

Fries, A.B., Ziegler, T.E., Kurian, J.R., Jacoris, S., & Pollak, S.D. (2005). Early experience in humans is associated with changes in neuropeptides critical for regulating social behavior. (2005). *PNAS, 102*(47), 17237–17240.

Garfield, J.L., Peterson, C.C., & Perry, T. (2001). Social cognition, language acquisition, and the development of theory of mind. *Mind & Language, 16*, 494–541.

Ghera, M.M., Marshall, P.J., Fox, N.A., Zeanah, C.H., Nelson, C.A., Smyke, A.T., et al. (2009). The effects of foster care intervention on socially deprived institutionalized children's attention and positive affect: Results from the BEIP study. *The Journal of Child Psychology and Psychiatry, 50*(3), 246–253.

Glennen, S. (2007). Predicting language outcomes for internationally adopted children. *Journal of Speech, Language and Hearing Research, 50*, 529–548.

Glennen, S., & Bright, B.J. (2005). Five years later: Language in school-age internationally adopted children. *Seminars in Speech and Language, 26*(1), 86–101.

Glennen, S., & Masters, G. (2002). Typical and atypical language development in infants and toddlers adopted from Eastern Europe. *American Journal of Speech-Language Pathology, 11*, 417–433.

Goncu, A. (1993). Development of intersubjectivity in social pretend play. *Human Development, 36*, 185–198.

Gunnar, M.R., Morison, S.J., Chisholm, K., & Schuder, M. (2001). Salivary cortisol levels in children adopted from Romanian orphanages. *Development and Psychopathology, 13*, 611–628.

Gunnar, M., & Quevedo, K. (2007). The neurobiology of stress and development. *Annual Review of Psychology, 58*, 145–173.

Happé, F.G.E. (1994). An advanced test of theory of mind: Understanding of story characters' thoughts and feelings by able autistic, mentally handicapped, and normal children and adults. *Journal of Autism and Developmental Disorders, 24*, 129–154.

Harris, P.L., de Rosnay, M., & Pons, F. (2005). Language and children's understanding of mental states. *Current Directions in Psychological Science, 14*(2), 69–73.

Hughes, C., Jaffee, S.R., Happe, F., Taylor, A., Caspi, A., & Moffitt, T.E. (2005). Origins of individual differences in theory of mind: From nature to nurture? *Child Development, 76*(2), 356–370.

Hwa-Froelich, D.A. (2009). Communication development in infants and toddlers adopted from abroad. *Topics in Language Disorders, 29*(1), 32–49.

Hwa-Froelich, D.A., & Matsuo, H. (2010). Communication development and differences in children adopted from China and Eastern Europe. *Language, Speech, and Hearing Services in Schools, 41*, 1—18.

Hwa-Froelich, D.A., & Schuette, K. (2010, July 15). *Social communication outcomes in internationally adopted children.* Poster presentation at the International Conference on Adoption Research, Leiden, Netherlands.

Johnson, D.E. (2000). Medical and developmental sequelae of early childhood institutionalization in eastern European adoptees. In C.A. Nelson (Ed), *The Minnesota symposia on child psychology: The effects of early adversity on neurobehavioral development* (Vol. 31) (pp. 113–162). Minnesota Symposium on Child Psychology. Mahwah, NJ: Lawrence Erlbaum.

Juffer, F., & Van IJzendoorn, M.H. (2009). International adoption comes of age: Development of international adoptees from a longitudinal and meta-analytical perspective. In G.M. Wrobel & E. Neil (Eds), *International advances in adoption research for practice* (pp. 169–192). Malden, MA: Wiley.

Kirouac, G., & Dore, F.Y. (1983). Accuracy and latency of judgment of facial expressions of emotions. *Perceptual and Motor Skills, 57*, 683–686.

Ladage, J.S. (2009). Medical issues in international adoption and their influence on language development. *Topics in Language Disorders, 29*(1), 6–17.

Legerstee, M. (2005). *Infants' sense of people: Precursors to a theory of mind.* United Kingdom: University Press.

Lewis, C., & Osborne, A. (1990). Three-year-old's problems with false belief: Conceptual deficit or linguistic artifact? *Child Development, 61*, 1514–1519.

Low, J. (2010). Preschoolers' implicit and explicit false-belief understanding: Relations with complex syntactical mastery. *Child Development, 81*(2), 597–615.

Lucariello, J. (2004). New insights into the functions, development, and origins of theory of mind: The functional multilinear socialization (FMS) model. In J.M. Lucariello, J.A. Hudson, R. Fivush, & P.J. Bauer (Eds.), *The development of the mediated mind* (pp. 33–57). Mahwah, NJ: Lawrence Erlbaum.

Marshall, P.J., Fox, N.A., & The BEIP Core Group. (2004). A comparison of the electroencephalogram between institutionalized and community children in Romania. *Journal of Cognitive Neuroscience, 16,* 1327–1338.

Marshall, P.J., Reeb, B.C., Fox, N.A., Nelson, III, C.A., & Zeanah, C.H. (2008). Effects of early intervention on EEG power and coherence in previously institutionalized children in Romanian. *Development and Psychopathology, 20,* 861–880.

Mason, P., & Narad, C. (2005). International adoption: A health and developmental perspective. *Seminars in Speech and Language, 26*(1), 1–9.

McGuigan, F., & Salmon, K. (2004). The time to talk: The influence of the timing of adult–child talk on children's event memory. *Child Development, 75,* 669–686.

Miller, L. (2005). *The handbook of international adoption medicine.* New York: Oxford University Press.

Milligan, K., Astington, J.W., & Dack, L.A. (2007). Language and theory of mind: Meta-analysis of the relation between language ability and false-belief understanding. *Child Development, 78,* 622–646.

Moses L.J., Baldwin, D.A., Rosicky, J.G., & Tidball, G. (2001). Evidence for referential understanding in the emotions domain at twelve and eighteen months. *Child Development, 72*(3), 718–735.

Moulson, M.C., Fox, N.A., Zeanah, C.H., & Nelson, C.A. (2009). Early adverse experiences and the neurobiology of facial emotion processing. *Developmental Psychology, 45*(1), 17–30.

Nelson, III, C.A. (2007). A neurobiological perspective on early human deprivation. *Child Development Perspectives, 1*(1), 13–18.

Nelson, III, C.A., Zeanah, C.H., Fox, N.A., Marshall, P.J., Smyke, A.T., & Guthrie, D. (2007). Cognitive recovery in socially deprived young children: The Bucharest Early Intervention Project, *Science, 318*(5858), 1937–1940.

Ninio, A., & Snow, C.E. (1996). *Pragmatic development.* In J. Kagan (Series Ed.), *Essays in developmental science.* Boulder, CO: Westview Press.

Nowicki, S., Jr., & Duke, M.P. (1994). Individual differences in the nonverbal communication of affect: The diagnostic analysis of nonverbal accuracy scale. *Journal of Nonverbal Behavior, 18,* 9–35.

O'Hare, A.E., Bremmer, L., Happé, F., & Pettigrew, L.M. (2009). A clinical assessment tool for advanced theory of mid performance in 5 to 12 year olds. *Journal of Autism and Developmental Disorders, 39,* 916–928.

Parker, S.W., Nelson, C.A., & the Bucharest Early Intervention Project Core Group. (2005). The impact of early institutional rearing on the ability to discriminate facial expressions of emotion: An event-related potential study. *Child Development, 76*(1), 54–72.

Parker, S.W., Nelson, C.A., & The Bucharest Early Intervention Project Core Group. (2008). An event-potential study of the impact on institutional rearing on face recognition. *Development and Psychopathology, 17,* 621–639.

Pears, K., & Fisher, P.A. (2005). Developmental, cognitive and neuropsychological functioning in preschool-aged foster children: Associations with prior maltreatment and placement history. *Journal of Developmental and Behavioral Pediatrics, 26,* 112–122.

Pellegrini, A. (1985). Relations between preschool children's symbolic play and literate behavior. In L. Galda & A. Pellegrini (Eds.), *Play, language, and stories.* Norwood, NJ: Ablex.

Perlman, S.B., Kalish, C.W., & Pollak, S.D. (2008). The role of maltreatment experience in children's understanding of the antecedents of emotion. *Cognition and Emotion, 22*(4), 651–670.

Perner, J. (1991). *Understanding the representational mind.* Cambridge, MA: MIT Press.

Perner, J., & Lang, B. (1999). Development of theory of mind and executive control. *Trends in Cognitive Sciences, 3*(9), 337–344.

Perner, J., Leekman, S., & Wimmer, H. (1987). Three-year-olds' difficulty with false belief: The case for a conceptual deficit. *British Journal of Developmental Psychology, 5,* 125–137.

Roselman, J. (2010). *Nonverbal communication development in internationally adopted children.* Unpublished Master Thesis, Saint Louis University, St. Louis, MO.

Rutter, M., Colvert, E., Kreppner, J., Beckett, C., Castle, J., Groothues, C., et al. (2007a). Early adolescent outcomes for institutionally-deprived and non-deprived adoptees. I: Disinhibited attachment. *Journal of Child Psychology and Psychiatry, 48*(1), 17–30.

Rutter, M. Kreppner, J., Croft, C., Murin, M., Colvert, E., Beckett, C., et al. (2007b). Early adolescent outcomes of institutionally deprived and non-deprived adoptees. III: Quasi-autism. *Journal of Child Psychology and Psychiatry, 48*(12), 1200–1207.

Saarni, C. (1999). *The development of emotional competence.* New York: Guilford.

Sánchez, M.M., Hearn, E.F., Do, D., Rilling, J.K., & Herndon, J.G. (1998). Differential rearing affects corpus callosum size and cognitive function of rhesus monkeys. *Brain Research, 812,* 38–49.

Sánchez, M.M., Ladd, C.O., & Plotsky, P.M. (2001). Early adverse experience as a developmental risk factor for later psychopathology: Evidence from rodent and primate models. *Development and Psychopathology, 13,* 419–449.

Sánchez, M., & Pollak, S.D. (2009). Socioemotional development following early abuse and neglect. Challenges and insights from translational research. In M. de Hoon & M.R. Gunnar (Eds.), *Handbook of developmental social neuroscience* (pp. 497–520). New York: Guilford.

Schick, B., de Villiers, P., de Villiers, J., & Hoffmeister, R. (2007). Language and theory of mind: A study of deaf children. *Child Development, 78,* 376–396.

Schore, A. N. (2001). The effects of early relational trauma on right brain development, affect regulation, and infant mental health. *Infant Mental Health, 22*(1), 201–269.

Shields, A., & Cicchetti, D. (1997). Emotion regulation in school-age children: The development of a new criterion Q–sort scale. *Developmental Psychology, 33,* 906–916.

Shields, A., Ryan, R.M., & Cicchetti, D. (2001). Narrative representations of caregivers and emotion dysregulation as predictors of maltreated children's rejection by peers. *Developmental Psychology, 37*(3), 321–337.

Smith, A.D. (2005). The inferential transmission of language. *Adaptive Behavior, 13*(4) 311–324.

Squires, J., & Bricker, D. (2009). *Ages and stages questionnaire, 3rd ed.* Baltimore: Paul H. Brookes Publishing Co.

Sorce, J.F., Emde, R.N., Campos, J., & Klinnert, M.D. (1985). Maternal emotional signaling: Its effect on the visual cliff behavior of 1-year-olds. *Developmental Psychology, 21,* 195–200.

Tan, T. (2009). School-age adopted Chinese girls' behavioral adjustment, academic performance, and social skills: Longitudinal results. *American Journal of Orthopsychiatry, 79*(2), 244–251.

Tan, T., & Marfo, K. (2006). Parental ratings of behavioral adjustment in two samples of adopted Chinese girls: Age-related versus socioemotional correlates and predictors. *Applied Developmental Psychology, 27,* 14–30.

Tarullo, A.R., Bruce, J., & Gunnar, M.R. (2007). False belief and emotion understanding in postinstitutionalized children. *Social Development, 16*(1), 57–78.

Teicher, M.H., Ito, Y., Glod, C.A., Andersen, S.L., Dumont, N., & Ackerman, E. (1997). Preliminary evidence for abnormal cortical development in physically and sexually abused children using EEG coherence and MRI. *Annals of the New York Academy of Science, 821*(1), 160–175.

Trevarthen, C. (1979). Communication and cooperation in early infancy. A description of primary intersubjectivity. In M. Bullowa (Ed.), *Before speech: The beginning of human communication* (pp. 321–347). Cambridge: Cambridge University Press.

Trevarthen, C. (1992). An infant's motives for speaking and thinking in the culture. In A.H. Wold (Ed.), *The dialogical alternative: Towards a theory of language and mind* (pp.99–137). Oslo: Scandinavian University Press.

Van IJzendoorn, M.H., Bakermans-Kranenburg, M.J., & Juffer, F. (2006). Plasticity of growth in height, weight, and head circumference: Meta-analytic evidence of massive catch-up after international adoption. *Journal of Developmental Behavior and Pediatrics, 28*, 334–343.

Van IJzendoorn, M.H., & Juffer, F. (2006). The Emanuel Miller memorial lecture 2006: Adoption as intervention. Meta-analytic evidence for massive catch-up and plasticity in physical, socio-emotional, and cognitive development. *Journal of Child Psychology and Psychiatry, 47*(12), 1228–1245.

Verbeek, P. (1996). *Peacemaking in young children*. Unpublished doctoral dissertation, Emory University, Atlanta, GA.

Vygotsky, L. (1986). *Thought and language*. (A. Kozulin, Trans.). London: MIT Press (Original work published in 1934).

Walden, T.A., & Ogan, T.A. (1988). The development of social referencing. *Child Development, 59*, 1230–1240.

Wellman, H.M., Phillips, A.T., & Rodriguez, T. (2000). Young children's understanding of perception, desire, and emotion. *Child Development, 71*, 895–912.

Westby, C.E. (2010). Social-emotional bases of communication development. In B.B. Shulman & N.C. Capone (Eds.), *Language development: Foundations, processes, and clinical applications* (pp. 133–176). Boston: Jones & Bartlett.

Wilson, S.L., & Weaver, T.L. (2009). Follow-up of developmental attainment and behavioral adjustment of toddlers internationally adopted into the USA. *International Social Work, 52*(5), 679–684.

Wimmer, H., & Perner, J. (1983) Beliefs about beliefs: Representation and constraining function of wrong beliefs in young children's understanding of deception. *Cognition, 13*, 103–128.

Windsor, J., Glaze, L.E., Koga, S.F., & the Bucharest Early Intervention Project Core Group. (2007). Language acquisition with limited input: Romanian institution and foster care. *Journal of Speech-Language-Hearing Research, 50*, 1365–1381.

Yagmurlu, B., Berument, S.K., & Celimli, S. (2005). The role of institution and home contexts in theory of mind development. *Applied Developmental Psychology, 26*, 521–537.

Zeedyk, M.S. (1996). Developmental accounts of intentionality: Toward integration. *Developmental Review, 16*, 416–461.

# 9 ▼▼▼

# Intervention Strategies

*Deborah A. Hwa-Froelich, Samantha L. Wilson,*
*Sarah E. Harris, and Jennifer S. Ladage*

---

*"It has been a universal finding, however, in all studies of risk experiences, that there is enormous variation in children's responses...one of the potentially important features fostering resilience are happenings that end damaging experiences and open up new opportunities and a change of environment."*

(Rutter, 2000, pp. 651 & 653)

*"Having been adopted, I really have a strong sense—a necessity almost—for stability. A foundation where my family is concerned. [Success] would be meaningless without anyone to share it with." —Faith, Hill, an adopted child*

(McGuire Roche, 2000, p. 66)

---

Throughout this book we have provided case examples reflecting the variability of health and developmental outcomes of children who are adopted from various environments and diverse early experiences. When there is such variability, including genetic and environmental experiences as well as individual differences in temperament and personality, it is difficult to predict longitudinal developmental trajectories or universally needed treatment and/or educational services. Every child has the potential of presenting a unique profile of health and learning potential that may result in the delivery of different treatment regimens and/or combinations of educational services. In addition, there is little research available to show the efficacy of specific interventions with internationally adopted children.

This chapter is not reflective of all the possible interventions that may be recommended or effective for the myriad needs a child may have.

205

We will, however, describe the more common types of services that have been recommended for internationally adopted children. Three case studies reflect these common types of treatments and will be used to illustrate examples of 1) medical services and sensory motor interventions, 2) relationship development and behavioral interventions, and 3) memory and communication interventions.

## ▼▼▼ MEDICAL SERVICES AND INTERVENTION

Alayna was a 30-month-old girl adopted from Russia at 24 months of age who exhibited hyperactivity, aggression, and repetitive behaviors since adoption. Alayna's parents described her as extremely hyperactive, remaining in constant motion throughout the day and night. Alayna had trouble falling asleep and usually played until 12:00 or 1:00 AM. She also felt the need to touch everything, and at night, she had to rub either her parent's face or her own to fall sleep. Additionally, Alayna's parents described her as having an obsession with jumping and swinging. When her parents told Alayna "no" or took something away from her, she became angry and hit, kicked, or banged her head. She would also exhibit these same aggressive tendencies at times when she was overstimulated. She could become overstimulated easily and would scream or tantrum inconsolably when playing with other children and in unfamiliar situations and settings. Her parents reported that she was sensitive to sudden loud noises and would become "fretful" when loud noises were anticipated, such as her father starting the lawn mower. When Alayna was able to calm herself, she was noted to stare blankly for 5–10 minutes. During these times, her parents were unable to get her attention and stated that Alayna had to "come out by herself."

Probably most concerning to Alayna's parents was her rocking behavior that occurred frequently throughout the daytime and had been occurring since her adoption. The episodes were described as side-to-side rocking and wiggling of her hips and buttocks while lying prone with her legs in full extension. At times, the episodes were portrayed as violent. Alayna engaged in this behavior continuously for 3–10 minutes at a time, and multiple times throughout a day. While the behavior occurred when she was tired, being disciplined, and sleeping, the majority of episodes occurred without an apparent precipitating cause. Alayna's rocking behaviors became so disruptive to everyday interactions that her parents avoided trips to the supermarket and other places for fear that Alayna would become overwhelmed and "meltdown."

Alayna's past medical history was significant. She was born at term weighing 2,430 grams (2nd percentile) to a known drug abuser infected with hepatitis C. She was placed in an orphanage shortly after birth, where she received care until her adoption. She had no history of seizures, nor did she have any known or suspected history of head trauma, physical abuse, or sexual abuse. She was reported to have "low growth" but was described as otherwise healthy. Physical examination upon her arrival to the United States demonstrated her length, weight, and head circumference to be symmetric but greater than 2 standard deviations *(SD)* below the mean for her age. She demonstrated mild acceleration in growth velocity 6 months after placement, with her head plotting at the 5th percentile and her weight and length plotting just below the 2nd percentile. Her medical evaluation was found to be within normal limits, with the exception of a positive tuberculin skin test

(PPD) measured at 10 mm in duration. Her chest x ray was negative, and she was started on a 9-month course of anti-tuberculin medication. Her immunizations were found to be age appropriate and included a Bacille Calmette-Guérin (BCG) vaccination at 2 months of age. An electroencephalogram (EEG) was administered to rule out seizures and results revealed typical brain activity during both sleep and when awake.

After Alayna's weight began to reach a healthy percentile, she was referred to a therapist for an occupational therapy evaluation. The therapist had experience working with international adoptees and, after clinical observation and review of results from a parent-report questionnaire, suggested that Alayna had delays in fine and gross motor skills and that she demonstrated signs of immature sensory processing, particularly with respect to auditory, visual, and vestibular integration. Specifically, Alayna was having trouble modulating her responses to sensory information, meaning she could not control how excited or overwhelmed she would become in response to sensations. A twice-weekly therapy program was initiated that involved therapist-facilitated sensory motor experiences to help Alayna desensitize and learn to process input more effectively. Additionally, the therapist coached Alayna's parents to recognize the subtle signs she gave to signal her overstimulation. When Alayna felt overwhelmed, she often smiled and giggled, or grunted and became destructive, rather than communicate her discomfort through language. In time, Alayna's parents improved their ability to read her subtle signals and were able to help her use language to communicate when something was difficult or uncomfortable.

## INTERVENTIONS FOR HEALTH AND PHYSICAL GROWTH

Alayna's story illustrates many of the consequences of early deprivation on the physical health and development observed in internationally adopted children in the first year following adoption. This section will discuss evidence-based interventions to optimize a child's overall health and well-being. Three common parental concerns regarding the physical health of their internationally adopted child in the initial time period following adoption include 1) the child's immunization status, 2) treatment of infectious diseases, and 3) growth or stature.

In today's cultural climate, especially with prominent celebrities denouncing the value of and calling into question the safety of vaccinations, a growing number of parents are choosing to forego immunizations. The majority of parents assisted in our international adoption clinic, however, want only to make the most prudent decision to maximize their child's protection against these preventable diseases while minimizing the exposure to unnecessary inoculations and the inherent trauma associated with multiple needle sticks. To do so, parents must facilitate a careful assessment of the child's immunization record from his or her country of origin by a practitioner knowledgeable of recommendations published by the Advisory Committee on Immunization Practices (ACIP) of the Centers for Disease Control. However, as previously discussed in Chapter 2, documentation of immunizations, if given to parents, is often lacking and medical records of adopted children may merely state, "immunizations up to date" without specific vaccines or dates of administration (Miller, 2005a; Miller, Chan, Comfort, & Tirella, 2005; Miller, Tseng, Tirella, Chan, & Feig, 2008; Shulte et al., 2002; Viviano et al., 2006). Recommendations by most adoption medicine physicians for internationally adopted children immunized in their countries of origin are to verify antibody titers, or the body's immune response, to each disease vaccinated against to confirm adequate immune protection (Miller, 2005a). The titers reflect the amount of circulating antibodies in the child's blood at the time the titers are obtained and must be interpreted with regard to the number of vaccines for that disease that have been given and the timing of the vaccines. A child who was immunized for the first time to polio 6 weeks prior to obtaining antibody titers may have the same circulating antibody level as a child who has completed the series of three vaccines 2 years prior. However, the first child is unlikely to have sustained immunity and the second child should. Without any documentation of the specific vaccines and the dates given, it is impossible to interpret antibody titers; thus it becomes prudent to start over with each undocumented age-appropriate series (Miller, 2005a; Verla-Tebit, Zhu, Holsinger, & Mandalakas, 2009). Vaccination series that have been given at appropriate dosing intervals and have protective levels of antibody titers documented may be accepted (AAP, 2009a; Miller, 2005a; Verla-Tebit et al, 2009).

One vaccination that tends to raise many questions and concerns for parents is the BCG vaccine against tuberculosis. The BCG vaccine is a live, attenuated vaccine made from altered bacteria that does not cause disease but elicits the body's immune response to the disease. Usually given in the shoulder, the injection site can remain red, crusted, or oozing for weeks, even months, after receipt of the inoculation. It eventually heals with a scar in most recipients. The BCG is not given in the United States and other developed countries in which the incidence of tuberculosis infection is low, because in addition to the risk of exposure being low, many of the strains do not elicit an adequate or sustained immune response and therefore only approximates 50% efficacy in preventing tuberculosis infection (AAP, 2009b). In most countries with higher incidences of tuberculosis, the BCG is given to infants often in the first 2 months of life because children less than 4 years of age are at risk for disseminated disease. Tuberculosis will remain dormant or inactive in most individuals after initial infection. Upon activation, it generally causes disease in the lungs. In children less than 4 years of age, tuberculosis does not stay isolated in the lungs but disseminates to other organs, particularly the brain, yielding a devastating form of meningitis. The BCG has approximately 80% protective efficacy against meningeal tuberculosis in children (AAP, 2009b).

Administration of the BCG vaccine has been correlated in internationally adopted children with having a positive tuberculin skin test or PPD (Mandalakas, Kirchner, Zhu, Yeo, & Starke, 2008; Trehan, Meinzen-Derr, Jamison, & Staat, 2008). The BCG vaccine may result in a reaction upon PPD placement due to cross-reacting proteins with the tuberculin germ, so many parents and practitioners falsely believe that that previous immunization with BCG precludes screening for tuberculosis with a PPD. This potentially dangerous misconception can be devastating for young children, because the incidence of tuberculosis in internationally adopted children has been documented to be as high as 20% (Miller, 2005a), and the BCG is more effective at preventing dissemination than infection. The PPD remains the recommended screening test for tuberculosis infection in children 4 years and younger regardless of BCG status (AAP, 2009b). In children 5 years of age and older, including adults, a blood test called an interferon-gamma radioimmunoassay (IGRA) may be performed. This test is designed to detect proteins in the tuberculin germ that are not found in any of the BCG vaccines and are therefore useful in determining between infection and previous vaccination. Both IGRA and PPD are comparable in their ability to detect tuberculosis (AAP, 2009b). Testing is still needed to establish their safety and usefulness in younger children and infants. Any positive PPD or IGRA requires prompt clinical evaluation, chest radiograph, and treatment with anti-tuberculin medication (AAP, 2009b).

Internationally adopted children are at risk for a constellation of infectious diseases. These diseases are not unique to internationally adopted children, but collectively reflect the adversity of their prenatal and postnatal environments. What is unique is not the treatment of these diseases in the internationally adopted child but the necessity of appropriate screening tests. Recommended guidelines for physicians screening internationally adopted children in the postplacement period are outlined in the *American Academy of Pediatrics' Red Book: Report of the Committee on Infectious Diseases, 28th Edition* (AAP, 2009a). Treatment for each specific disease identified through screening should follow recommendations for children in the general population and should also take into account varying practices for certain infections in immigrants based on emerging resistance patterns in their country of origin. Such recommendations for most infectious diseases are also found in the *AAP Red Book*.

Beyond infectious diseases, a leading parental concern is the child's physical stature. As is true with Alayna, many international adoptees from various countries and preadoption backgrounds are physically stunted when initially evaluated postplacement. Most adopted children will demonstrate rapid growth and will often completely catch up in growth in the years immediately following adoption (Van IJzendoorn, Bakersmans-Kranenburg, & Juffer, 2007; Van IJzendoorn, & Juffer, 2006). In fact, Van IJzendoorn and Juffer found physical growth is usually the first area of catch-up attained, but this is not always the case. Internationally adopted children who have completed catch-up growth and continue to have short stature, defined as a height-for-age 2 *SD* below the mean or greater, may be candidates for growth hormone therapy. To date, growth hormone therapy, specifically for the treatment of internationally adopted children, has not been studied except as an adjunct therapy for the treatment of internationally adopted children with precious puberty.

Upon research of possible benefits of treatment with growth hormone for children with short stature alone, two populations emerge that provide some comparison with internationally adopted children: children born small for gestational age (SGA) and those with idiopathic short stature (ISS), defined as stature 2 *SD* below the mean or greater with normal growth hormone levels. According to the International Small for Gestational Age Advisory Board Consensus Development Conference Statement: Management of Short Children Born Small for Gestational Age (Lee, Chernausek, Hokken-Koelega, & Czernichow, 2003), an assessment for use of growth hormone therapy is warranted for children born SGA who remain 2 or more *SD* below the mean at 3 years of age or older, because these children are not likely to demonstrate any additional catch-up growth. The milestones of growth hormone therapy should be catch-up growth in early childhood, maintenance of normal growth in childhood, and achievement of normal adult height defined as a final height in the normal range. Growth hormone therapy is documented to be safe and effective in the SGA population. The frequency and intensity of monitoring for glucose homeostasis, lipids, and blood pressure may vary based on family history. Van Pareren, Duivenvoorden, Slijper, Koot, and Hokken-Koelega (2004) examined adolescents who exhibited short stature secondary to being born SGA and were also found to have lower intelligence, poor academic performance, lower social competence, and behavior problems associated with being born SGA. They reported findings that in addition to GH-induced catch-up growth, these adolescents demonstrated significant improvement over time in the additional areas of deficiency; they were able to improve from low-average scores to scores comparable to their Dutch peers in intelligence quotients (IQ), self-perception, and problem behaviors.

Bryant, Baxter, Cave, and Milne (2007) compared the results of 10 randomized control trials of recombinant growth hormone therapy given to children with ISS and found improved short-term growth as well as improved final growth or, in some studies, meeting near-final height. They concluded that studies addressing quality of life and cost issues are lacking. Richmond and Rogol (2010) published indications for use of growth hormone therapy and included its use in non–GH deficient children with significant short stature. They report that the U.S. Food and Drug Administration (FDA)–approved indications are GH deficiency, Turner syndrome, chronic kidney disease, and SGA with failure to catch up to typical height percentiles. Recombinant growth hormone therapy, if used for an unapproved indication, may require out-of-pocket payment and can be exceedingly costly. The decision to initiate growth hormone therapy should be directed by a pediatric endocrinologist.

## Sensory Motor Interventions

When a child exhibits delays in sensory motor function that inhibit the ability to participate in daily functional activities, a referral to occupational and/or physical therapy is generally appropriate. This approach is a standard for internationally adopted children too. A therapist with a background in sensory processing, and with experience working with children who have psychosocial issues, is the ideal team member to offer sensory motor interventions for the internationally adopted child (Haradon, 2001).

There is a scarcity of literature that investigates specific sensory motor interventions using a sample of internationally adopted children. Although referrals to occupational and physical therapy are commonly cited by adoption medicine specialists (Beverly, McGuinness, & Blanton, 2008; Haradon, 2001; Johnson & Dole, 1999; Nalven, 2005), there is less understanding about particularly effective intervention strategies or techniques that are discrete from the general therapy intervention process. For the area of sensory motor development, it is necessary to examine evidence-based interventions that are effective for children with similar histories and similar clinical presentations. In general, most families can benefit from recommendations about developmentally appropriate activities to support the sensory motor function of their adopted child (Haradon, 2001).

## Evidence-Based Sensory Motor Interventions

For children who demonstrate general motor delays, neuromuscular facilitation and therapist-guided skills practice can help a child's body develop and achieve motor milestones they would be unable to accomplish without treatment (Ketelaar, Vermeer, Hart, Van Petegem-van Beek, & Helders, 2001; Larin, 2000). Valvano (2004) described the therapeutic process in the following way: "Activity focused interventions involve structured practice and repetition of functional actions and are directed toward the learning of motor tasks that will increase independence and participation in daily routines" (p. 79). Valvano described the occupational or physical therapist as a change agent whose role is to guide the child toward solving a movement problem. Guidance is given through verbal and/or physical assistance and is only provided as long as the child needs it to succeed in performing or refining a movement skill.

One example of activity-focused intervention is therapeutic facilitation of trunk muscle strength and cocontraction for children with weaknesses in their core muscles from a lack of tummy time during early infancy. It is documented that internationally adopted children raised in institutions or in countries in which it is common for children to be carried or tightly bundled often show this pattern of motor delay (Miller, 2005b). In cases such as these, the therapist can facilitate the desired pattern of muscle contraction by presenting toys or other objects of interest in a way that requires the child to move to the toy in the desired fashion. The movement is voluntary, intrinsically motivated, and therefore, child-centered and sensory driven.

Interventions based on the theory of sensory integration are becoming increasingly popular as evidence grows in support of the theoretical concepts and the efficacy of treatment programs. There is evidence of sensory processing differences within the population of internationally adopted children in the form of tactile defensiveness (Wilbarger, Gunnar, Schneider, & Pollak, 2010), neuroendocrine dysregulation (Wismer Fries, Shirtcliff, & Pollak, 2008), sensory-seeking behaviors (Cermak & Daunhauer, 1997), and atypical sensory discrimination, praxis, and sensory modulation (Lin, Cermak, Coster, & Miller, 2005). Therapeutic treatment approaches to address sensory processing abilities can be modeled to resemble unstructured play and include activities such as obstacle courses, finger paints, and swings. With these play items, the therapist accomplishes specific goals to help the child discriminate sensations, modulate excitement level, and demonstrate an integrated, adaptive response to sensory information by successfully completing a task. Most experiences an infant encounters include a variety of sensory challenges. Most children independently learn to cope with these challenges over time, or they use communication to alert a caregiver that they are over-stimulated. Some children, however, have trouble making this adaptive response on their own. In Alayna's case, she likely did not experience a range of sensory experiences in her early life, allowing her to develop this coping mechanism, and she also did not have a constant caregiver to help her learn how to mentally code sensations as ones that are pleasurable, uncomfortable, or even dangerous.

One noninvasive strategy guided by sensory integration theory is to redirect compulsive and/or self-stimulatory behaviors to seek sensory input by offering socially acceptable alternatives. To illustrate this point, a child who seeks oral proprioceptive input by chewing on toys, school supplies, or even fingers may be given chewable rubber tubing or a chewable pencil topper to keep during the day. Scheerer (1992) presented case studies of nonadopted children documenting the effectiveness of this strategy by providing a substitute to mouthing of nonedible items to help school children stay calm and focused during the day. In the presented cases, the children who chose to use the "chewies" and had documented episodes of overactivity, distractibility, tactile defensiveness, and autistic-like self-stimulatory tendencies, all experienced a decrease in frequency and/or intensity after initiated use of the chewie.

Another example of a noninvasive strategy is the implementation of a daily program of active sensory motor activities, known as a sensory diet. Common sensory diet activities involve swinging, spinning, jumping, crawling, and climbing. This type of program is most applicable to the child who seeks movement sensations and subsequently has a difficult time maintaining attention when sitting in the classroom or at the dinner table. Sensory diets have been effective treatments for children diagnosed with autism (Anzalone & Williamson, 2000) and children receiving occupational therapy for sensory processing disorder and delays in visual-motor function (Hall & Case-Smith, 2007). Implementing a sensory diet program proved successful for Alayna and her family. Alayna's father installed a small swing in a doorway of their home and she could voluntarily use it when she desired. After presenting this option to her, Alayna's parents noted that Alayna would swing quickly but quietly for a while each day, especially when she came home from school. Her parents reported that, as a result, she had fewer episodes of withdrawal and seemed better able to cope with her attention and cognitive processing challenges because she had the extra vestibular input from the swinging.

The aforementioned sensory motor interventions represent some of the most common approaches that are used by occupational and physical therapists working with internationally adopted children. Although many children adopted from institutional environments may have a history of sensory deprivation and may show signs of sensory processing disorder, parents and professionals should use discretion when considering engaging a strict treatment regimen that has not yet been subject to scientific inquiry with a sample group of internationally adopted children (Gunner, Bruce, & Grotevant, 2000). Intensive attachment therapies that involve holding and other forms of imposed physical touch, have not been proven to be effective with internationally adopted children and may actually cause further trauma to children (Pignotti & Mercer, 2007; Van IJzendoorn & Juffer, 2006). This is especially true of a child who has tactile defensiveness. All efforts should be made to avoid the risk of retraumatizing the child with interventions that may be uncomfortable, frightening, and imposed. Parent coaching techniques offer an alternate choice by focusing on a child- and family-centered option for intervention (Graham, Rodger, & Ziviani, 2009). The first step to creating a safe and comfortable treatment regimen is completing a Sensory Profile (Dunn, 1999; Dunn, 2002; Dunn & Bennett, 2002; Dunn & Westman, 1997). This will likely illuminate the child's sensory processing abilities and shortcomings and can be helpful for parents to better understand their child's unique needs and preferences when direct intervention is not necessary or possible.

## KEY POINTS

▶ Immunization records with documented vaccines, dates of administration, and laboratory evidence of protective immunity are essential before a practitioner can accept vaccinations given to most internationally adopted children from their country of origin.

▶ Appropriate screening for infectious diseases and other medical conditions such as short stature are best completed by a practitioner experienced with addressing the medical issues common to internationally adopted children. Children exhibiting these medical conditions should then be monitored closely until their growth, development, and general health are within the range considered normal for their age-related peers.

▶ Rigid treatment protocols that involve imposed touch should be used with caution and after careful assessment of the benefits of the intervention compared to the potential risk of retraumatizing the child.

▶ A therapist with experience in sensory integration and in working with children with psychosocial problems is best suited to provide sensory motor interventions for internationally adopted children.

## ▼▼▼ RELATIONSHIP DEVELOPMENT INTERVENTION

Libby was 7 years, 4 months old and in second grade. She resided with both parents and a 4-year-old sister. Libby and her sister were simultaneously adopted from an orphanage in Ukraine when Libby was about 4 years of age. Preadoption information indicated that Libby had resided with her biological family for about 18 months prior to entering orphanage care. She was removed from her family due to neglect. Her sister (not biologically related) had reportedly entered the orphanage following birth and was about 10 months old at the time of adoption.

Postadoption physical and developmental growth occurred rapidly. Receptive and expressive English skills emerged rapidly, but spontaneous communication remained low. Within 1 year of adoption, Libby was socially proficient in English and had sufficient preacademic skills to enter a prekindergarten classroom. Within the classroom, Libby was noted to be quiet and passive, though attentive. She rarely initiated social interactions, preferring to watch her peers with interest from a distance. She readily responded to peer requests for play and was perceived to be an agreeable (yet passive) child. Teachers noted that Libby tended to follow her peers and rarely made a request or demand of them. Her parents observed this tendency as well. Within her home, Libby never requested food, rarely acknowledged a preference (for toys, food, clothes, etc.), and she was exceptionally slow to respond to verbal questions. Her parents viewed her as highly compliant and were distressed by her overall passivity and low verbal discourse.

During the course of her academic progress, Libby had attained age-appropriate academic skills. It was noted that she was nearly always the last one to complete tasks, she required increased time to formulate verbal responses, and she was always a follower on the playground. Her language and auditory skills were assessed twice and were deemed to be within the average range (relative to U.S.-based norms). The difficulty with her verbal narrative appeared to be related in part to poor emotional regulation, such as increased anxiety.

After assessment, it was determined that Libby was highly susceptible to stress. Her predominant response was to withdraw and shut down. This manifested in hypercompliance and low spontaneous social language. Libby had learned that the best way to keep safe in the face of distress and to cope with stress was to become invisible.

Her parents were highly distressed by this withdrawal. Home-based interactions with Libby were typically tense. Frustrated by Libby's minimal response and passivity within the home, her parents often resorted to yelling in hopes of stimulating a response. This approach increased Libby's distress and she withdrew even further. The cycle of interaction was continually reinforced and spiraled into increased negativity. Her parents, exasperated by Libby's withdrawal, would angrily send her to her room to remain alone. It might be hours before her parents would welcome her back into family interactions due to their own anger at the perceived rejection from their daughter. Relational repairs were limited, resulting in Libby and her parents feeling continually disconnected from each other.

Children with unusual behaviors or atypical social and emotional functioning can create stress for parents, especially those parents who have less experience with early childhood behavior or have inappropriate expectations for their children's adjustment to the family. As exemplified with Libby, when parents are distressed by their children's behavior, a cyclical pattern of tense caregiver–child interactions can further reduce a child's capacity to develop optimal social-emotional skills. Postadoption services are addressing this negative synergistic influence by offering support to families to reduce the risk of adoption dissolution or disruption (North American Council on Adoptable Children, 2007) and addressing this with families before a crisis emerges.

In promoting the emerging relationship between a child and his or her new caregiver, the individual components that come from the parent or the child may be less critical than the interactive "goodness of fit" (Thomas & Chess, 1977) between the two. Goodness of fit refers to the concordance between the environmental expectations and the child's abilities, characteristics, and style of behaving. As noted with Libby, mismatch (or dissonance) within this interactive context is thought to underlie problematic behaviors and interactions (Seifer, 2000).

## SUPPORTING EMERGING RELATIONSHIPS

Interactive factors are believed to be the most critical in promoting optimal child development and resiliency. Dyadic, relationship-focused treatments (e.g., infant and parent psychotherapy or child and parent psychotherapy) can be effective in ameliorating disordered attachments or disruptive behaviors (Lieberman, 2003). Children adopted with a history of early adversity often fail to signal their needs to caregivers (Stovall

& Dozier, 2000). It can be difficult for the caregiver to interpret subtle, contradictory, or minimized behavior signals that facilitate emerging attachment relationships (Dozier, 2003). To promote social-emotional development, effective interventions should help parents understand their child's behavior (Marvin & Whelan, 2003) and understand the child's unique history. Doing so has proven to reduce the stress response of children living in foster care (Fisher, Gunnar, Dozier, Bruce, & Pears, 2006) and is thought to underlie subsequent behavior improvement. In most cases, caregivers serve as an extension of their children's regulatory system, supporting new physiological patterns and promoting resiliency through supportive relationships.

Infant/Early Childhood Mental Health refers to an emerging specialty area of practice that focuses on the strength of the young child, assesses and intervenes within a relational perspective, attends to developmental trajectories, and focuses on prevention (Zeanah & Zeanah, 2009). Though the majority of these specialty-trained clinicians aim to support children under 5 years old, the principles of Infant/Early Childhood Mental Health complement work with older children, especially those who have experienced relational disruption because these children emphasize the centrality of the parent–child relationship for social-emotional development. These empirically supported treatments have been increasingly used with young and school-age children to support optimal emotional and behavior health. Though efficacy studies specific to internationally adopted children are limited, treatment protocols that are effective within similar cohorts (e.g., young children in foster care) will be reviewed.

## Video-Feedback Intervention to Promote Positive Parenting

Video-Feedback Intervention to Promote Positive Parenting (VIPP; Juffer, Bakermans-Kranenburg, & Van IJzendoorn, 2008) aims to promote early social-emotional development in young children to reduce later problematic behaviors. The VIPP program is gaining recognition as an effective prevention and treatment program for families. Since 2000, VIPP has been implemented as part of a government-supported prevention program for adoptive families within the Netherlands (Juffer, 2009). For a nominal fee (about 100 euro), families receive four home-based visits during which video footage is taped. Video-feedback guidance is provided back to the family to promote the emerging parent–child relationship, promote parental sensitivity to subtle behavior cues, and highlight moments of positive parent–child engagement.

VIPP intervention is grounded in attachment theory (Bowlby, 1969: 1988) and has been expanded by new research on early relationships within the field of Infant/Early Childhood Mental Health. Home-based parent–child interactions are recorded and reviewed collaboratively during 90-minute sessions within the family home. During review of the video interactions, parents are encouraged to 1) increase awareness of the child's alternating needs for comfort and exploration and 2) consider their own behavior, the child's behavior, and the impact of historical relationships on their interactions with their child. Parental understanding of relational disruption and repair (Tronick, 1989) is a key component to intervention. Parents are taught that the ability to repair relational disruptions (not the lack of disruptions) is the core of positive parent–child relationships. Video-supported feedback promotes parent–child relationships through parental understanding of and responsiveness to the child's signals (e.g., for play or comfort) and increased competence to repair relational disruptions.

Published data suggest that VIPP is effective in increasing maternal sensitivity (Kalinauskiene et al., 2009), lowering rates of externalizing preschool behaviors (Velderman et al., 2006), and reducing daily cortisol production for some groups of high-risk children (Bakermans-Kranenburg, Van IJzendoorn, Mesman, Alink, & Juffer, 2009). Specific to families who have adopted internationally, participation in VIPP is related to reduced rates of problematic parent–child relationships (i.e., disorganized attachment) within families who adopted from Sri Lanka, South Korea, Colombia, and the Netherlands (Juffer, Bakermans-Kranenburg, & Van IJzendoorn, 2005).

VIPP intervention is one of the earliest to explore intervention effects based on genetic differences (Bakermans-Kranenburg, Van IJzendoorn, Pijlman, Mesman, & Juffer, 2008). By exploring the differential impact of VIPP, Bakermans-Kranenburg, Van IJzendoorn, Pijlman, et al. noted that positive effects of VIPP were largest for children who had a specific variation of the dopamine D4 receptor in conjunction with the increased use of positive discipline by their parents. Specifically, children with the seven repeat allele (a genetic variation that has been linked to increased sensory seeking) showed the largest *decrease* of externalizing behaviors after the intervention, especially within the context of positive discipline practices. The complexity and impact of gene x environmental interactions is in its early stages, but continued knowledge about this dynamic relationship will likely shape future intervention efforts.

## Attachment and Biobehavioral Catch-Up

VIPP appears to be effective as a preventive program for infants and their new parents. Attachment and Biobehavioral Catch-up (ABC; Dozier, Lindheim, & Ackerman, 2005) shows promise in ameliorating relational concerns for children who may be adopted at older ages and have a history of relational trauma. ABC was developed for children in U.S.-based foster care and seeks to intervene with four empirically identified needs of children in foster care: 1) some foster parents have difficulty providing nurturance to children in their care, 2) children in foster care often fail to signal a need for nurturance, 3) children in foster care tend to be physiologically, behaviorally, and emotionally dysregulated, and 4) children in foster care often perceive relational threat from actions or words of the foster parent. Some internationally adopted children and their new families have similar needs to these identified for foster children, and though ABC has yet to be implemented specifically for internationally adopted children, using ABC may be therapeutically valuable in some situations.

The ABC intervention consists of 10 home-based sessions, with some portions of dyadic interactions recorded for later review. The initial sessions highlight generalized child behaviors (e.g., avoidance or withdrawal) that reduce receipt of nurturing care. Caregivers are supported to evaluate their child's behavior, especially with regards to the child's response to distress. Middle sessions discuss child-directed play by using prerecorded clips of unknown children responding in various ways to play and distress. The clips are shown to promote caregiver's understanding of the various meanings of child behavior. Later sessions allow caregivers to reflect on their own ability to provide nurturance and how their own state of mind impacts their perception of their child's behavior. Final sessions encourage positive touch with the foster parent–child dyad and seek to increase the child's capacity to express emotions.

Randomized control trials have indicated that ABC supports increased positive caregiver–child relationships (Dozier et al., 2009), reduces problematic behavior for children in foster care (Dozier et al., 2006), and decreases physiological reactivity of participating children (Dozier, Peloso, Lewis, Laurenceau, & Levine, 2008). Given the similarities between children in foster care and some groups of internationally adopted children (e.g., disrupted relationships, experience of adverse early care), ABC may be an appropriate intervention protocol for higher risk dyads.

## Circle of Security

Circle of Security (Marvin, Cooper, Hoffman, & Powell, 2002) is a group-based intervention developed especially for high-risk toddlers, preschoolers, and their families. Parents participate in small groups of six who collectively observe and discuss previous recordings of the participating parent and child interactions. Similar to VIPP, a large component of Circle of Security is parental understanding of relational repair. This requires accurate perception and appropriate response to the child's alternating signals for comfort and shared exploration. As with VIPP, the basis of change is presumed to be the development of relational capacities rather than parental knowledge of specific techniques to manage their children's behavior (Cooper, Hoffman, Powell, & Marvin, 2005).

During 20 weeks of group-based intervention, parents are supported to: 1) reflect on their parenting (including missteps in parent–child communication), 2) improve observational skills of their child's behaviors, 3) more accurately perceive the child's intended behavioral communication, and 4) increase empathy for the child's worldview. Initial weeks are used to highlight dyadic strengths and relational connection for all participating parents. During weeks 3 through 8, parents alternately watch clips from each participating dyad in which times of disconnect and repair are highlighted and acknowledged. Weeks 10 through 15 more closely support parental reflection on areas of dyadic difficulty and encourage parents to explore areas of potential change. The final weeks are used for review and group-based acknowledgement of dyadic changes and relational improvements. In an initial outcome study with 65 families attending Head Start (Hoffman, Marvin, Cooper, & Powell, 2006), Circle of Security led to significant improvement in the quality of the parent–child relationship. Specifically, 70 percent of children rated before the intervention as having a disorganized attachment pattern in the context of their primary relationship moved toward a more organized attachment pattern (and in a majority of cases were classified as having a secure pattern). Though this longitudinal study lacked a comparison group, this is an impressive change. The developers of Circle of Security indicated that the change in relationship quality was attributable to a new parental capacity to recognize and reflect on previous behaviors that had historically hindered their ability to respond to their child's needs for nurturance (Hoffman et al. 2006).

Although there are obvious financial differences between families who participate in Head Start services and those families with the resources to adopt internationally, it is prudent to consider that Circle of Security could provide a potential resource for families adopting children who may have confusing or dysregulated behavior.

## Dyadic Developmental Psychotherapy

Dyadic Developmental Psychotherapy (DDP) is a family-centered treatment approach based on attachment theory. It attends to various levels of impairment commonly noted for children with experiences of complex trauma (Becker-Weidman & Hughes, 2008). Specifically, DDP seeks to support a child's capacity to self-regulate, relate interpersonally, form meaningful relationships with his or her parent (attachment), reduce physiological arousal, regulate affect and attention, and increase a positive sense of self. DDP highlights a therapeutic stance, rather than a manualized treatment (as exemplified by VIPP, ABC, or Circle of Security). As such, content for treatment sessions (which are not time-limited) are not delineated but rather emerge from the family's immediate therapeutic concerns. DDP seeks to incorporate parents into the creation of the therapeutic experience for the child. This is created through an emphasis on shared affect (i.e., attunement), joint attention, and social reciprocity. Children are typically seen in the context of their primary relationship and parents are encouraged to focus on PLACE—being Playful, Loving, Accepting, Curious, and Empathic. The therapist models PLACE through his or her own in-session attention to PACE—being Playful, Accepting, Curious, and Empathic. Interactive relational repair is emphasized to reduce the child's feelings of shame and fear. The parent is supported by the therapist's presence to explore verbal and nonverbal meanings of the child's previous experience of maltreatment to cocreate new meanings of previous traumatic events.

The therapeutic process begins with identification of a behavior (either recent or historical) and exploring that behavior with curiosity and acceptance to discover the meaning of the behavior for the child. Empathy is used to reduce the child's sense of shame and increase his or her perception of being accepted and understood (Becker-Weidman, 2006a). The child and parent are both taught to accept the behavior as a somewhat normative reaction to aspects of the child's previous experiences.

In one study, after an average of 23 sessions over 11 months, DDP was shown to be more effective than standard outpatient care in increasing levels of positive interpersonal relatedness and reducing levels of emotional and behavioral distress (to nonclinical levels) with a group of 34 children (age 5 years to 16 years old at the onset of treatment) with significant experiences of maltreatment and relational disturbances (Becker-Weidman, 2006a). Clinical improvements were maintained after a year of completing DDP. The 30 children in the comparison group who were clinically similar to the DDP participating children in pretreatment level of emotional-behavioral distress but were seen for an average of 25 sessions over 7 months in other clinics showed no clinical change in relationships or reduction of emotional distress at conclusion of treatment, or 1 year later. Differences in the DDP groups versus the comparison group remained similar on average after years posttreatment (Becker-Weidman, 2006b).

## CONCLUSION

Though specific modalities vary, the best available evidence indicates that problems in social-emotional development and behavior regulation for young children are best ameliorated through sensitive and responsive parenting and a focus on dyadic interactions. Libby's parents, recognizing the need to alter her behavior patterns, sought help from a clinician trained in the field of Infant/Early Childhood Mental Health, which values relationships as the bedrock of social-emotional development. The clinician highlighted Libby's coping response as an adaptive legacy of her early institutional care and provided intellectual understanding of the pattern that maintained negative interactions and contributed to simultaneous perceptions of rejection. Though her parents intellectually understood the pattern, their ability to perceive Libby's subtle cues of distress, and subsequently reduced verbal demands, was limited. The clinician moved to dyadic therapy so Libby was seen in the context of one parent for play-based interactions. The clinician observed all sessions via a one-way mirror and prompted the parent's awareness and behavioral response via use of a "bug in the ear." The clinician supported the parent's recognition of Libby's increased distress by directly coaching and prompting empathic parental responses and allowing the parents to experience a new type of interaction.

The clinician worked to highlight the myriad subtle ways that Libby sought connection and shared positive affect with her parents by explaining them and pointing them out as they occurred. With her quiet signals of distress, her cues for engagement were equally tentative, and easily missed. As the parents increasingly became aware of such signals and responded in ways that did not elevate Libby's emotional distress, they began to notice an increase in spontaneous language and assertive comments—making a choice or stating preferences. At first, these moments of therapeutic victory were limited to the weekly therapeutic sessions led by the coaching therapist, but with practice, such moments of positive engagement and empathic parental response became more frequent. Consequently, Libby's parents were able to directly experience (and later review with the clinician) the powerful change that occurred when they provided increased "wait time" to Libby during informal interactions. Consistent with changes noted in the aforementioned treatment modalities, this increased parental awareness and promoted out-of-session change. With support, her parents acknowledged how their own perception of rejection contributed to a pattern of negative interaction. They bravely sought individual therapy to complement dyadic therapy to allow them the space to understand the basis of their own fears of rejection. This combined approach facilitated a new pattern of family interactions and provided a more secure base from which Libby's future social-emotional development could proceed.

## KEY POINTS

▶ Adopted children bring previous experiences with them when they enter new family environments. Past experiences impact their engagement and behavior within a new family.

▶ Children with unusual behaviors, or atypical social-emotional functioning, can create stress for parents, especially for those parents who are unfamiliar with early childhood behavior or have inappropriate developmental and behavioral expectations.

▶ When parents are distressed by their child's behavior, a cyclical pattern of tense caregiver–child interactions can develop and further reduce a child's capacity to develop optimal social-emotional skills.

▶ The best available evidence indicates that social-emotional development and behavior regulation for young children are promoted through sensitive and responsive parenting.

▶ A focus on dyadic interactions should be provided for families seeking therapeutic support.

▶ Treatment programs that have been developed for children with problems in behavior regulation, trauma, and/or relational disruption may provide appropriate starting points for families who have adopted internationally and who are seeking support.

## ▼▼▼ ATTENTION, MEMORY, AND COMMUNICATION INTERVENTIONS

Yana lived with her biological Russian family and attended local Russian schools. When she was 8 years old, she and two other siblings were removed from the home and placed in an orphanage. At the orphanage, Yana did not attend school, but she was trained in life skills including cooking and cleaning. After approximately 2 years in the orphanage, when Yana was 11 years old, an American couple, Mr. and Mrs. Brown, adopted her. Another family from the United States adopted Yana's biological siblings.

Soon after Yana's adoption, Mr. and Mrs. Brown began helping Yana adjust to life in the United States. They spent the first few months teaching Yana the English alphabet and functional English words. They hired a Russian interpreter to continue Yana's education in Russian. The interpreter informed Mr. and Mrs. Brown that Yana's Russian language was not well developed for her age and Yana was not literate in the Russian language. The Brown's enrolled Yana in public school with English as a second languge services. She attended both fourth and fifth grade, then the Browns decided to teach Yana at home. Her parents reported that Yana was functioning at a fourth-grade level in history and reading at a sixth-grade level. She had difficulty with spelling, puns, multiple meanings of words, memory of mathematical problems, sequential information, people's names, phone numbers, and daily activities.

Yana was evaluated at a developmental clinic for internationally adopted children when she was 15 years old, approximately 4 years after she was adopted. Yana passed a hearing screening and a test of nonverbal communication comprehension (reading facial expressions and tone of voice). In addition, examination of her mouth and oral musculature was typical. Although Yana did not meet the criteria for auditory processing disorder, she demonstrated some weaknesses in auditory processing that overlapped with her linguistic development and skills. Yana had difficulty with auditory decoding, binaural integration—one ear processes sounds less well than the other—and auditory closure (words with missing parts can be decoded). Given Yana's disrupted experiences with language development and formal schooling, she performed amazingly well on several English language measures scoring within 2 *SD* below the average score. Her strengths were expressive language, phonological awareness, and visual memory. The areas that fell below 2 *SDs* were receptive language, language memory, and interpreting nonliteral and ambiguous language. Her reading comprehension was measured at a fifth-grade level for both narrative and expository texts with particular difficulty in drawing inferences from information that was implied in the text. Yana also demonstrated difficulty with English long and short vowels and English inflectional endings, most likely due to the influence of Russian-on-English-language learning. The primary areas of concern for both Yana and her parents were her: 1) social language skills, particularly her anxiety with remembering other people's names and other social skills such as ordering from a menu, 2) the need for individualized literacy strategies to improve reading comprehension and spelling, and 3) the need for consultation and strategies to individualize the home-school program.

All of Yana's resulting intervention was purposefully framed within a relationship development model (Gutstein, 2009). Initially, speech and language clinicians focused on creating an environment in which Yana felt safe and comfortable. Specific therapeutic strategies included providing visual supports to facilitate social communication and to reduce the stress on her auditory and working memory systems. As Yana improved her name recall in these environments, stressors were added one by one until she was able to maintain name recall and have conversations with strangers. This progress facilitated confidence and learning in other areas such as reading comprehension. Yana began with auditory discrimination of syllables and vowels that improved her decoding skills. Joint book reading helped Yana learn the strategies of using understood context to assist her comprehension and her ability to infer from ambiguous text. By the end of the year, Yana was reading for enjoyment and selecting narrative books at an upper-middle-school level (eighth to ninth grade). Mr. and Mrs. Brown learned how to use visual supports to adapt and individualize the home-school curriculum and their own communication. This enabled Yana to become more independent in remembering homework, routines, and her responsibilities for behavior and chores at home. Yana demonstrated a new level of confidence and reported that she felt ready to attend high school and wanted to begin studies to acquire her driver's license.

Research and documentation provide extensive evidence that the majority of internationally adopted children develop and catch up with nonadopted peers, but some differences remain. Several meta-analytic studies have shown that when adopted before 1 year of age, internationally adopted children not only fare better than peers who remain in institutional care, they also demonstrate little difference in cognitive IQ scores from nonadopted peers and siblings (Van IJzendoorn & Juffer, 2010; Van IJzendoorn, Juffer, & Poelhuis, 2005). In spite of little difference in IQ scores, internationally adopted children tend to have more learning problems as well as lower school achievement levels and language abilities (Van IJzendoorn & Juffer). The meta-analyses found that group differences for school achievement and language delays were of small effect size ($d = .19$ and $.09$ respectively) largely due to the large sample sizes (78,662 children and 15,418 children). Internationally adopted children had more learning problems than nonadopted peers with statistically significant differences with a moderate effect size ($d = .55$ for 13,291 participants in eight studies) (Van IJzendoorn & Juffer). Van IJzendoorn and Juffer suggested that these discrepancies between IQ and school achievement might be due to "adoption décolage" (a gap between the children's potential and their actual performance) (p. 328). Factors such as severity of adverse early care and social-emotional demands may influence the child's school performance, especially in the areas of executive function, working memory, and social cognition because these are cognitive skills that are integrally linked with complex cognitive, linguistic, and social thinking skills.

The previous chapters have provided evidence that internationally adopted children demonstrate outstanding resilience and developmental progress, but they may also demonstrate residual delays or weaknesses in several areas. These areas include problems with attention, inhibition, memory, theory of mind development, and social communication. Yana exemplifies how some of these weaknesses can affect a child's behavior and academic performance.

## RELATIONSHIP-BASED SOCIAL COMMUNICATION INTERVENTIONS

Every child presents a unique profile of strengths and weaknesses. Professionals must provide a unique combination of intervention strategies instead of a one-size-fits-all approach to help facilitate improvement in the areas of delay or weakness (Grotevant, Dunbar, Kohler, & Lash Esau, 2000). What is offered in this section is a brief description of some of the possible intervention models and strategies that may be recommended for internationally adopted children. This description is not exhaustive nor inclusive of all the possible interventions that may prove helpful.

Young children who have experienced disruption in relationship development need special effort devoted to building strong and secure relationships to help them regulate and cope with external stressors. For children who demonstrate difficulty focusing their attention and inhibiting their impulses, and who have memory and/or communication problems, it is recommended to develop communicative interventions that are relationship based. By building strong, close relationships with parents, children learn how to attend to nonverbal communication and emotions, regulate their emotions, and interpret and respond to the communication and emotions of other people (for a review see Chapters 3, 5 and 8) (Barth, Crea, John, Thoburn, & Quinton, 2005; Juffer, Bakermans-Kranenburg, & Van IJzendoorn, 2005; Nickman et al., 2005). It is from these strong early relationships that children develop a framework for successful future relationships with people outside of their family.

Most relationship-based communication interventions have been developed for children with social communication problems such as children with autism spectrum disorders (ASD). Relationship-based models with evidence that demonstrates effectiveness include the Social Communication, Emotion Regulation and Transactional Support Model (SCERTS Model; Prizant, Wetherby, Rubin, Laurent, & Rydell, 2006), the Developmental, Individual Difference, Relationship-based: Floortime Model (DIR: Floortime, Greenspan & Wieder, 1997), and Relationship

Development Intervention (RDI; Gutstein, 2000). In a meta-analysis of intervention programs for children with ASD, Odom and colleagues (2010) found both the SCERTS and DIR Floortime models to be most effective in improving social communication skills. In a small nonrandomized study, Gutstein and colleagues found improved social communication performance in children with a diagnosis of Aspergers or high-functioning autism after 1 to 2 years of RDI (Gutstein, Burgess, & Montfort, 2007). Although no studies have been published demonstrating the effectiveness of these programs with adopted children, the SCERTS, DIR: Floortime, and RDI models support play-based facilitation of shared nonverbal emotions through face-to-face interactions, joint attention, emotion regulation and inhibition, memory and recall, and social communication—all skills that would benefit internationally adopted children.

In general, these intervention models are based on a developmental hierarchy that begins with play-based activities during which parent and child share positive emotions face-to-face through both nonverbal and verbal communicative interactions. This strategy can be adapted and individualized for use with older children who demonstrate similar problems in relationship development. Once parents and children successfully read and interpret each other's communication, they move to a level where they share perspectives or joint attention with a third entity: either an inanimate or animate object. Refined relationship and communication development proceeds through stages of coordinated interactions, often during play-based activities in which children learn how to coordinate their actions and communication with another person. Once they achieve coordinated nonverbal and verbal communication skills, they learn how to think dynamically and flexibly when new or unexpected events occur, eventually learning how to reflect upon and interpret the exchange of actions between two people. The progression of understanding continues until children are able to recall and reflect upon events from multiple perspectives. Helping children achieve these stages of development facilitates growth and progress in attention, inhibition, memory, and social communication. Some children may need additional support in any one of these developmental areas.

## ATTENTION, INHIBITION, AND MEMORY INTERVENTIONS

Inhibition, attention, self-regulation, memory development, and executive function refer to a set of mental processes where inhibition and selective attention enable an individual to set goals, plan, solve problems, and multitask. These skills are essential for learning and memory. Inhibition and selective attention in typically developing, nonadopted, preschool children predict working memory at 6 years of age and reading and math achievement in high school (Breslau et al., 2009; Brocki, Eninger,

Thorell, & Bohlin, 2010). Interventions aimed at improving inhibition and selective attention may facilitate improved executive function and working memory. No evidence has yet been published reporting the effectiveness of such interventions with internationally adopted children.

Several new programs and intervention strategies show early evidence of effective practices facilitating inhibition and selective attention in young children. A randomized controlled study applying the Tools Curriculum improved executive skills in preschool children (Bodrove, & Leong, 2007; Diamond, Barnett, Thomas, & Munro, 2007). This program includes instruction for preschool teachers on how to create, implement, and monitor preschool activities to promote inhibition, regulation, inner speech, and selective attention. Some of the approaches of the Tools Curriculum include placing children in small and large groups and facilitating activities where children must inhibit one behavior to focus on another. For example, children may be asked to play games such as Simon Says. They must inhibit following one kind of direction and follow a different kind of direction.

Facilitation of higher levels of play also promotes self-regulation. During pretend play, children learn to take on the role of someone else and regulate their own personalities to act and talk like someone else (Berk, Mann, & Ogan, 2006). Goal-directed play, particularly in fantasy play during which children learn to play within the rules of the play scenario, facilitates children's selective attention, and their complex, flexible thinking and problem solving. These higher levels of play are achieved more easily when adults mediate and support play as opposed to directing the children (Berk, Mann, & Ogan). Mediation and support can include asking questions to encourage creativity or expand play ideas as well as suggesting a potential problem to encourage dynamic, flexible thinking. For example, adults can mediate children pretending to play doctor and patient by taking an imaginary role as an individual with a rare kind of ailment and then facilitate emerging literacy activities by asking the child playing nurse or doctor to check his or her medical file. As with many intervention strategies, these play strategies have not been studied in internationally adopted children.

Executive-function strategies for older children are proposed by Dawson and Guare (2009). Visual charts, diagrams, and graphic organizers have been suggested as ways to facilitate visual and verbal problem solving and planning for elementary-age or middle-school-age children. Some of these strategies were successfully implemented with Yana during clinical sessions and at home. Although these strategies have been tried with clinical cases, they have not been studied systematically, and none have been studied with internationally adopted children.

## ▼▼▼ *CASE STUDY APPLICATION*

In Yana's case, there was a strong, close relationship between parent and child, but Yana struggled with anxiety in social situations. Her auditory memory was underdeveloped or weak for both social and routine tasks. Yana needed strategies to 1) strengthen her selective attention, 2) reduce her anxiety in new or stressful situations, 3) improve working memory for name recall and following directions, and 4) improve reading comprehension and inferential language. By framing all intervention activities around a relationship-based intervention, Yana learned to increase her comfort level and reduce her anxiety when meeting and talking with new people. By increasing the use of visual strategies to help facilitate memory, Yana gained confidence with her social skills that in turn helped facilitate improved auditory memory of names and other social communication tools. To increase selective attention and motivation, intervention focused on topics Yana found interesting, such as popular music entertainers, movie stars, and popular adolescent fiction. Using a combination of a relationship-based hierarchy, a framework with compensatory visual strategies, individualized instruction, and practice activities to learn to communicate dynamically and flexibly, Yana made significant progress with developing her attention, decreasing her anxiety, and increasing her working memory and reading comprehension.

## ▼▼▼ *IMPLICATIONS*

It is important for parents to seek help as soon as they become aware of any learning problems. It is also important for professionals to complete a thorough, indepth assessment to guide future interventions. Each child represents a different profile of strengths and weaknesses often requiring a unique mix of interventions. These interventions may or may not include medical, sensory or motor, psychological, communicative, and developmental strategies and services. Although rare, there have been cases in which children initially demonstrate no indications of delay or developmental weaknesses, only to develop later learning problems. For these reasons, it is recommended that internationally adopted children receive regular follow-up assessments to ensure continued developmental catch up and progress.

## *KEY POINTS*

▶ Treatment should be framed within a relationship-based model.

▶ Strategies focused on improving inhibition, selective attention, and higher-level symbolic play may benefit internationally adopted children.

▶ Interventions focused on facilitating the understanding of the perspective of other people are recommended.

## REFERENCES

American Academy of Pediatrics. (2009a). Medical evaluation of internationally adopted children for infectious diseases. In L.K. Pickering, C.J. Baker, D.W. Kimberlin, & S.S. Long (Eds.), *Red book: 2009 Report of the Committee on Infectious Diseases*, 28th ed. (pp. 177–184). Elk Grove Village, IL: American Academy of Pediatrics.

American Academy of Pediatrics. (2009b). Tuberculosis. In L.K. Pickering, C.J. Baker, D.W. Kimberlin, S.S. Long (Eds.), *Red book: 2009 Report of the Committee on Infectious Diseases*, 28th ed. (pp. 680–701). Elk Grove Village, IL: American Academy of Pediatrics.

Anzalone, M.E., & Williamson, G. (2000). Sensory processing and motor performance in autism spectrum disorders. In A.M. Wetherby & B.M. Prizant (Eds.), *Autism spectrum disorders: A transactional developmental perspective* (pp. 143–166). Baltimore: Paul H. Brookes Publishing Co.

Bakermans-Kranenburg, M.J., Van IJzendoorn, M.H., Mesman, J., Alink, L.R.A., & Juffer, F. (2008). Effects of an attachment-based intervention on daily cortisol moderated by dopamine receptor D4: A randomized control trial on 1- to 3-year-olds screened for externalizing behavior. *Development and Psychopathology, 20*, 805–820.

Bakermans-Kranenburg, M.J., IJzendoorn, M.H., van, Pilman, F.T.A., Mesman, J., & Juffer, F. (2008). Experimental evidence for differential susceptibility: Dopamine D4 receptor polymorphism (DRD4 VNTR) moderates intervention effects on toddlers' externalizing behavior in a randomized control trial. *Developmental Psychology, 44*, 293–300.

Barth, R.P., Crea, T.M., John, K., Thoburn, J., & Quinton, D. (2005). Beyond attachment theory and therapy: Toward sensitive and evidence-based interventions with foster and adoptive families in distress. *Child and Family Social Work, 10*, 237–268.

Becker-Weidman, A. (2006a). Treatment for children with trauma-attachment disorders: Dyadic Developmental Psychotherapy. *Child and Adolescent Social Work Journal, 23*, 147–171.

Becker-Weidman, A. (2006b). Dyadic developmental psychotherapy: A multiyear follow-up. In S. Sturt (Ed.), *New Developments in Child Abuse Research* (pp. 43–60). New York: Nova Science.

Becker-Weidman, A., & Hughes, D. (2008). Dyadic Developmental Psychotherapy: An evidence based treatment for children with complex trauma and disorders of attachment. *Child and Family Social Work, 13*, 329–337.

Berk, L.E., Mann, T.D., & Ogan, A.T. (2006). Make-believe play: Wellspring for development of self-regulation. In D.G. Singer, R.M. Golinkoff, & K. Hirsh-Pasek (Eds.). *Play = learning.* Oxford: Oxford University Press.

Beverly, B.L., McGuinness, T.M., & Blanton, D.J. (2008). Communication and academic challenges in early adolescence for children who have been adopted from the former Soviet Union. *Language, Speech, and Hearing Services in Schools, 39*, 303–313.

Bodrove, E., & Leong, D.J. (2007). *Tools of the mind: The Vygotskian approach to early childhood education.* New York: Merrill/Prentice-Hall.

Bowlby, J. (1969). *Attachment and loss* (Vol. 1). New York: Basic Books.

Bowlby, (1988). *A secure base: Parent-child attachment and healthy human development.* New York: Basic Books.

Breslau, J., Miller, E., Breslau, N., Bohnert, K., Lucia, V., & Schweitzer, J. (2009). The impact of early behavior disturbances on academic achievement in high school. *Pediatrics, 123*(6), 1472–1476.

Brocki, K.C., Eninger, L., Thorell, L.B., & Bohlin, G. (2010). Interrelations between executive function and symptoms of hyperactivity, impulsivity and inattention in preschoolers: A two year longitudinal study. *Journal of Abnormal Child Psychology, 38*, 163–171.

Bryant J., Baxter L., Cave, C.B., & Milne R. (2007). Recombinant growth hormone for idiopathic short stature in children and adolescents. *Cochrane Database of Systematic Reviews*, (3), 1–7.

Cermak, S.A., & Daunhauer, L.A. (1997). Sensory processing in the post-institutionalized child, *American Journal of Occupational Therapy, 51*, 500–507. Retrieved July 18, 2011, from http://people.bu.edu/cermak/pdfs/senseprocessinstchild.pdf

Cooper, G., Hoffman, K., Powell, B., & Marvin, R. (2005). The Circle of Security Intervention. In L.J. Berlin, Y. Ziv, L. Amaya-Jackson, & M.T. Greenberg (Eds.), *Enhancing early attachments: Theory, research, intervention, and policy* (pp. 127–151). New York: Guilford.

Dawson, P., & Guare, R. (2009). *Smart but scattered*. New York: The Guilford Press.

Diamond, A., Barnett, W.S., Thomas, J., & Munro, S. (2007). Preschool program improves cognitive control. *Science, 317*, 1387–1388.

Dozier, M. (2003). Attachment-based treatment for vulnerable children. *Attachment and Human Development, 5*, 253–257.

Dozier, M. Lindhiem, O., & Ackerman, J. P. (2005). Attachment and biobehavioral catch-up: An intervention targeting empirically identified needs of foster infants. In L. J. Berlin, Y.Ziv, L. Amaya-Jackson, & M.T. Greenberg (Eds.), *Enhancing early attachments: Theory, research, intervention, and policy* (pp. 178–194). New York: Guilford.

Dozier, M., Lindhiem, O., Lewis, E., Bick, J., Bernard, K., & Peloso, E. (2009). Effects of a foster parent training program on young children's attachment behaviors: Preliminary evidence from a randomized clinical trial. *Child and Adolescent Social Work Journal, 26*, 321–332.

Dozier, M., Peloso, E., Lewis, E., Laurenceau, J.P., & Levine, S. (2008). Effects of an attachment-based intervention on the cortisol production of infants and toddlers in fostercare. *Development and Psychopathology, 20*, 845–859.

Dozier, M., Peloso, E., Lindhiem, O., Gordon, M.K., Manni, M., & Sepulveda, S. (2006). Developing evidence-based interventions for foster children: An example of a randomized clinical trial with infants and toddlers. *Journal of Social Issues, 62*, 767–785.

Dunn, W. (1999). *The Sensory Profile*. San Antonio, TX: The Psychological Corporation.

Dunn, W. (2002). *The infant toddler sensory profile*. San Antonio, TX: The Psychological Corporation.

Dunn, W., & Bennett, D. (2002). Patterns of sensory processing in children with attention-deficit/hyperactivity disorder. *The Occupational Therapy Journal of Research, 22(1)*, 27–41.

Dunn, W., & Westman, K. (1997). The Sensory Profile: The performance of a national sample of children without disabilities. *American Journal of Occupational Therapy, 51*, 25–34.

Fisher, P.A., Gunnar, M.R., Dozier, M., Bruce, J., & Pears, K. C. (2006). Effects of therapeutic interventions for foster children on behavioral problems, caregiver attachment, and stress regulatory neural systems. *Annals New York Academy of Science, 1094*, 215–225.

Graham, F., Rodger, S., & Ziviani, J. (2009). Coaching parents to enable children's participation: An approach for working with parents and their children. *Australian Occupational Therapy Journal, 56*, 16–23.

Greenspan, S.I., & Wider, S. (1997). *Engaging Autism: The Floortime approach to helping children to relate, communicate, and think*. New York: Perseus Books.

Grotevant, H.D., Dunbar, N., Kohler, J.K., & Lash Esau, A.M. (2000). Adoptive identity: How contexts within and beyond the family shape developmental pathways. *Family Relations, 49(4)*, 379–387.

Gunner, M. R., Bruce, J., & Grotevant, H. D. (2000). International adoption of institutionally reared children: Research and policy. *Development and Psychopathology, 12*, 677–693.

Gutstein, S.E. (2000). *Autism Aspergers: Solving the relationship puzzle*. Arlington, TX: Future Horizons.

Gutstein, S.E., Burgess, A.F., & Montfort, K. (2007). Evaluation of the relationship development intervention program. Autism. *The International Journal of Research and Practice, 11*, 397–411.

Hall, L., & Case-Smith, J. (2007). The effect of sound-based intervention on children with sensory processing disorders and visual and motor delays. *American Journal of Occupational Therapy, 61*, 209–215.

Haradon, G. (2001). Facilitating successful international adoptions: An occupational therapy community practice innovation. *Community Occupational Therapy Education and Practice, 13*, 85–99.

Hoffman, K.T., Marvin, R., Copper, G., & Powell, B. (2006). Changing toddlers' and preschoolers' attachment classifications: The Circle of Security intervention. *Journal of Consulting and Clinical Psychology, 74*, 1017–1026.

Johnson, D.E., & Dole, K. (1999). International adoptions: Implications for early intervention. *Infants and Young Children, 11*, 34–45. Retrieved July 18, 2011, from http://www.peds.umn.edu/iac/prod/groups/med/@pub/@med/documents/asset/med_49295.pdf

Juffer, F. (2009, February). *Family matters: Supporting adoptive families with an attachment-based intervention.* Paper presented at the first Annual New Worlds of Adoption Conference, Amherst, MA.

Juffer, F., Bakermans-Kranenburg, M.J., & Van IJzendoorn, M.H., (2005). The importance of parenting in the development of disorganized attachment: Evidence from a preventive intervention study in adoptive families. *Journal of Child Psychology and Psychiatry, 46*, 263–274.

Juffer, F., Bakermans-Kranenburg, M.J., & Van IJzendoorn, M.H., (2008). *Promoting positive parenting: An attachment-based intervention.* London: Lawrence Erlbaum/Taylor & Francis.

Kalinauskiene, L., Cekuoliene, D., Van IJzendoorn, M.H., Bakermans-Kranenburg, M.J., Juffer, F., & Kusakovskaja, I. (2009). Supporting insensitive mothers: The Vilnius randomized control trial of video feedback intervention to promote maternal sensitivity and infant attachment security. *Child Care, Health, and Development, 35*, 613–623.

Ketelaar, M., Vermer, A., Hart, H., Petegen-van Beek, E., van, & Helders, P.J. (2001). Effects of a functional therapeutic program on motor abilities of children with cerebral palsy. *Physical Therapy, 8*, 1534–1545. Retrieved July 18, 2011, at http://ptjournal.apta.org/content/81/9/1534.full.pdf+html

Larin, H. (2000). Motor learning: Theories and strategies for the practitioner. In S.K. Campbell (Ed.), *Physical therapy for children, 2nd edition* (pp. 170–195). Philadelphia: W.B. Saunders Co.

Lee, P.A., Chernausek, S.D., Hokken-Koelega, A.C.S., & Czernichow, P. (2003). International small for gestational age advisory board consensus development conference statement: Management of short children born small for gestational age. *Pediatrics, 111*, 1253–1261.

Lieberman, A.F. (2003). The treatment of attachment disorder in infancy and early childhood reflections from clinical intervention with later-adopted foster care children. *Attachment and Human Development, 5*, 279–282.

Lin, S.H., Cermak, S., Coster, W.J., & Miller, L. (2005). The relationship between length of institutionalization and sensory integration in children adopted from Eastern Europe. *American Journal of Occupational Therapy, 59*, 139–147.

Mandalakas, A.M., Kirchner, H.L., Zhu, X., Yeo, K.T., & Starke, J.R. (2008). Interpretation of repeat tuberculin skin testing in international adoptees. *The Pediatric Infectious Disease Journal, 27*, 913–919.

Marvin, R., Cooper, G., Hoffman, K., & Powell, B. (2002). The Circle of Security project: Attachment-based intervention with caregiver-preschool child dyads. *Attachment and Human Development, 4*, 107–124.

Marvin, R.S., & Whelan, W.F. (2003). Disordered attachments: Toward evidence-based clinical practice. *Attachment and Human Development, 5*, 283–288.

McGuire Roche, N. (2000). *Adoption is another word for love.* White Plains, NY: Peter Pauper Press.

Miller, L.C. (2005a). International adoption: Infectious diseases issues. *Clinical Infectious Diseases, 40*, 286–293.

Miller, L.C. (2005b). *The handbook of international adoption medicine.* New York: Oxford University Press.

Miller, L.C., Chan, W., Comfort, K., & Tirella, L. (2005). Health of children adopted from Guatemala: Comparison of orphanage and foster care. *Pediatrics, 115*, e710–e717.

Miller, L.C., Tseng, B., Tirella, L.G., Chan, W., & Feig, E. (2008). Health of children adopted from Ethiopia. *Maternal Child Health Journal, 12*, 599–605.

Nalven, L. (2005). Strategies for addressing long-term issues after institutionalization. *Pediatric Clinics of North America, 52*, 1421–1444.

Nickman, S.L., Rosenfeld, A.A., Fine, P., Macintyre, J.C., Pilowsky, D. J., Howe, R.A., et al. (2005). Children in adoptive families: Overview and update. *Journal of the American Academy of Child Adolescent Psychiatry, 44*(10), 987–995.

North American Council on Adoptable Children. (2007). *Postadoption services: Meeting the mental health needs of children adopted from foster care.* St. Paul, MN; Author. Retrieved July 18, 2011, from http://www.nacac.org/adoptalk/postadoptpaper.pdf

Odom, S.L., Boyd, B.A., Hall, L.J., & Hume, K. (2010). Evaluation of comprehensive treatment models for individuals with Autism Spectrum disorders. *Journal of Autism Developmental Disorders, 40,* 425–436.

Pareren, Y.K., van, Duivenvoorden, H.J., Slijper, F.S.M., Koot, H.M., & Hokken-Koelega, A.C.S. (2004). Intelligence and psychosocial functioning during long-term growth hormone therapy in children born small for gestational age. *The Journal of Clinical Endocrinology & Metabolism, 89,* 5295–5302.

Pignotti, M., & Mercer, J. (2007). Holding therapy and dyadic developmental psychotherapy are not supported and acceptable social work interventions: A systematic research synthesis revisited. *Research on Social Work Practice, 17,* 513–519.

Prizant, B., Wetherby, A., Rubin, E., Laurent, A., & Rydell, P. (2006). *The SCERTS Model: A comprehensive educational approach for children with autism spectrum disorders.* Baltimore, MD: Paul H. Brookes Publishing Co.

Richmond, E., & Rogol, A. (2010). Revised indications for growth hormone therapy for children and adolescents. *Endocrine Development, 18,* 92–108.

Rutter, M. (2000). Resilience reconsidered: Conceptual considerations, empirical findings, and policy implications. In J.P. Shonkoff & S. S. Meisels (Eds.). *Handbook of early childhood intervention,* 2nd ed. (pp. 651–682). New York: Cambridge University Press.

Scheerer, C. (1992). Perspectives on an oral motor activity: The use of rubber tubing as a "chewy." *The American Journal of Occupational Therapy, 46,* 344–352.

Schulte, J.M., Maloney, S., Aronson, J., San Gabriel, P., Zhou, J., & Saiman, L. (2002). Evaluating acceptability and completeness of overseas immunization records of internationally adopted children. *Pediatrics, 109*(2), 1–5, E22.

Seifer, R. (2000). Temperament and goodness of fit: Implications for developmental psychopathology. In A.J. Sameroff, M. Lewis, & S. Miller (Eds.), *Handbook of developmental psychopathology* (pp. 257–276). New York: Plenum.

Stovall, K.C., & Dozier, M. (2000). The development of attachment in new relationships: Single subject analyses for 10 foster infants. *Development and Psychopathology, 12,* 133–156.

Thomas, A., & Chess, S. (1977). *Temperament and development.* New York: Brunner/Mazel.

Trehan, I., Meinzen-Derr, J.K., Jamison, L., & Staat, M. A. (2008). Tuberculosis screening in internationally adopted children: The need for initial and repeat testing. *Pediatrics, 122,* e7–14.

Tronick, E. (1989). Emotions and emotional communication in infants. *American Psychologist, 44,* 112–119.

Valvano, J. (2004). Activity-focused motor interventions for children with neurological conditions. *Physical & Occupational Therapy in Pediatrics, 24,* 79–107.

Van Ijzendoorn, M.H., Bakersman-Kranenburg, M.J., & Juffer, F. (2007). Plasticity of growth in height, weight, and head circumference: Meta-analytic evidence for massive catch up and plasticity in physical, socio-emotional, and cognitive development. *Journal of Developmental & Behavioral Pediatrics, 28,* 334–343.

Van IJzendoorn, M.H., & Juffer, F. (2010). Adoption is a successful natural intervention enhancing adopted children's IQ and school performance. *Current Directions in Psychological Science, 14,* 326–330.

Van IJzendoorn, M.H., Juffer, F., & Klein Poelhuis, C.W. (2005). Adoption and cognitive development: A meta-analytic comparison of adopted and non adopted children's IQ and school performance. *Psychological Bulletin, 131,* 301–316.

Van IJzendoorn, M.H., & Juffer, F. (2006). The Emanuel Miller memorial lecture 2006: Adoption as intervention. Meta-analytic evidence for massive catch up and plasticity in physical, socio-emotional, and cognitive development. *Journal of Child Psychology and Psychiatry, 47,* 1228–1245.

Velderman, M.K., Bakermans-Kranenburg, M.J., Juffer, F., Van IJzendoorn, M.H., Mangelsdorf, S.C., & Zevalkink, J. (2006). Preventing preschool externalizing behavior problems through video feedback intervention in infancy. *Infant Mental Health Journal, 27*, 466–493.

Verla-Tebit, E., Zhu, X., Holsinger, E., & Mandalakas, A.M. (2009). Predictive value of immunization records and risk factors for immunization failure in internationally adopted children. *Archives of Pediatric Adolescent Medicine, 163*, 473–479. Retrieved July 18, 2011, from http://archpedi.ama-assn.org/cgi/reprint/163/5/473.pdf

Viviano, E., Cataldo, F., Accomando, S., Firenze, A., Valenti, R.M., & Romano, N. (2006). Immunization status of internationally adopted children in Italy. *Vaccine, 24*(19), 4138–4143.

Wismer Fries, A.B., Shirtcliff, E.A., & Pollak, S.D. (2008). Neuroendocrine dysregulation following early social deprivation in children. *Developmental Psychobiology, 50*, 588–599.

Wilbarger, J., Gunnar, M., Schneider, M., & Pollak, S. (2010). Sensory processing in internationally adopted, and postinstitutionalized children. *Journal of Child Psychology and Psychiatry 51*, 1105–1114.

Zeanah, C.H., & Zeanah, P.D. (2009). Three decades of growth in infant mental health. *Journal of Zero to Three, 30*, 22–27.

# INDEX

Tables and figures are indicated by *t* and *f*, respectively.

AAP, *see* American Academy of Pediatrics
ACIP, *see* Advisory Committee on Immunization Practices
Adoptee profiles
    Alayna (Russia), 206–207
    Andrew (Kazakhstan), 1–2, 3–4, 10, 12
    Bella (China), 133–135, 143
    Caitlyn (China), 22–23
    Chelsea (China), 177–179, 197
    Drew (Russia), 149–150
    Eric (Ethiopia), 23–24
    Libby (Ukraine), 214–215, 220–221
    Patrick (Russia), 59–60, 76–79
    Robbie (Russia), 107–109, 128
    Sophie (China), 85–86, 99–100
    Stephen (Russia), 21–22
    Yana (Russia), 222–223, 227
Advisory Committee on Immunization Practices (ACIP), 207
Africa, adoptions from, 40
Age at adoption
    catch-up after adoption, 7–10, 15
    duration of institutional stay, 121–122
    older children, language and, 150, 156, 163–165
    older children, outcomes, 133–135, 143, 222–223
    predictor of problems, 128
    younger children, outcomes, 118–119
Age determination, *see* Growth and development
Ages and Stages Questionnaire (ASQ), 195–196
AMA, *see* American Medical Association
American Academy of Pediatrics (AAP), 15, 36, 50, 97n, 208, 209
American Medical Association (AMA), 3
American Speech-Language-Hearing Association (ASHA), 3
ASD, *see* Autism Spectrum Disorders
Asperger's Syndrome, 224–225
ASQ, *see* Ages and Stages Questionnaire
Attachment and Biobehavioral Catch-up (ABC), 217–218

Attachments, *see* Social-emotional development
Attention, development of, *see* Executive function
Autism Spectrum Disorders (ASD), 46, 75, 157, 213, 224–225

Bacille Calmette-Guérin (BCG) vaccination, *see* Tuberculosis
Behavior interventions
    auditory integration therapy (AIT), 2–3
    nontraditional treatments, 1–3
    sensory integration therapy (SIT), 1, 3, 211–214
BEIP, *see* Bucharest Early Intervention Project
Birth parents
    health issues affecting fetus, 27, 33–37
    ignorance of, 5, 34
    prenatal care, lack of, 5
    termination of parental rights, 34–35
    *see also* Health issues of adoptees
Bucharest Early Intervention Project (BEIP), 89–90, 154, 185, 189

Cambodia, adoptions from, 36
Cambridge Neuropsychological Test and Automated Battery (CANTAB), 123–124
Caregivers
    attachment, effect on development of communication, 186
    brain development and institutional setting, 86–91
    communication, pragmatic, 182–184
    communication, social, 180
    foster care quality, 67
    negative effects of orphanage care, 66
CASL, *see* Comprehensive Assessment of Spoken Language
CBCL, *see* Child Behavior Checklist
CCC-2, *see* Children's Communication Checklist
Center for Disease Control (CDC), 207
Central Nervous System (CNS), 26
    *see also* Growth and development: neurobiological development

Child Behavior Checklist (CBCL), 108, 121–122, 124
Children's Communication Checklist (CCC-2), 195–196
China, adoptions from
  adoptee profile: Bella, 133–135, 143
  adoptee profile: Caitlin, 22–23
  adoptee profile: Chelsea, 177–179, 197
  adoptee profile: Sophie, 85–86, 99–100
  attention problems, 122–123
  delays, developmental, 42–43
  foster care, 89
  health issues, 35–36, 39–40, 92
  language and speech, 155–156, 159–162
  preadoption treatment, 4–6, 184–185
Circle of Security, 218–219
Clinical Evaluation of Language Fundamentals-Preschool 2 (CLEF-P2), 163t–165
Clinics, *see* Health issues of adoptees
CNS (central nervous system), *see* Growth and development: neurobiological development
Cognitive development
  adoptive parent influence, 96–97
  caregiver influences, 87–90
  comparisons, country and environment, 94–96
  environmental influences, 88–90
  language and memory, 114, 123–125
  malnutrition, effect of, 40
  postadoption catch-up, 49, 92–94, 96–97, 101, 118–119
  prenatal and early childhood brain development, 86–91, 101
  special education, learning problems and, 8
  specialized clinics for, 97–98
  stress hormones, effects of, 39, 65–66, 91, 217
  *see also* Comparisons with nonadoptees; Executive function; Language and speech
Cognitive development, theories of
  cognitive and social constructivism, 12
  connectionist theory, 117, 185
  dynamic systems theory (DST), 10–12, 15, 24, 30, 95, 119, 135, 150, 179
  epigenetic theory, 10–11
  information processing theory, 13
  sensory integration stages in infants, 30–33
Communication and Symbolic Behavioral Scales Development Profile (CSBS DP), 160t–162, 171
Communication development, *see* Language and speech
Communicative behaviors
  attachment and development of communication, 179
  caregiver role in development, 180–181
  institutional care, effect on development, 185
  instrumental use of communication, 179–180
  postadoption success and challenges, 188–197

progression of language development, 183–184
  requirements for efficacy, 179
  resilience after adoption, 197
  *see also* Theory of Mind
Communicative behaviors, emotional and social
  facial expressions and, 182–183
  nonverbal communication and, 194–195
  tone of voice, 195
Communicative behaviors, pragmatic understanding, 182–184
  postadoption studies, 195–197
  shared understanding, 180
Comparisons with nonadoptees
  academic performance and services, 8, 122–123
  executive function and environment, 117–121
  nonverbal communication, 194–195
  postadoption cognitive development, 92–93, 95–96
  preadoption quality of care, 5, 9
  stress hormone levels effect on communication, 190–191
Comprehensive Assessment of Spoken Language (CASL), 196
Cortisol, *see* Cognitive development: stress hormones; Growth and development: stress hormones
Countries of origin
  cognitive development and, 95
  executive function and, 120–121
  history of adoptions from, 3–5
  language development and, 166
  quality of care, 184–185
  *see also* Africa; China; Eastern Europe; Ethiopia; Guatemala; Korea; Romania; Vietnam
CSBS DP, *see* Language and speech: Communication and Symbolic Behavioral Scales Development Profile

DANVA2, *see* Diagnostic Analysis of Nonverbal Abilities
DDP, *see* Dyadic Developmental Psychotherapy
Developmental, Individual Difference, Relationship-based Model (DIR), 224–225
The Diagnostic Analysis of Nonverbal Abilities (DANVA2), 194
Disrupted language development, *see under* Language and speech
DST, *see* Cognitive development, theories of: dynamic systems theory
Dyadic Developmental Psychotherapy (DDP), 219–220
Dynamic systems theory (DST), *see under* Cognitive development, theories of

Eastern Europe, adoptions from, 1–2, 5–6, 41, 92, 167, 214–215
  *see also* Romania; Russia

Emotion Regulation Q-Scale, 188
English and Romanian Adoptees Study (ERA),
    6, 45, 47–48, 68, 70–71, 92–94, 96–97, 125,
    151, 156–157
Epigenetic theory, *see* Cognitive development,
    theories of
ERA, *see* English and Romanian Adoptees
    Study
Ethiopia, adoptions from, 23–24, 34, 37, 44
Executive function
    academic performance and services study,
        122–123
    attention and self-regulation, 111–113,
        117–119, 128–129, 224
    Child Behavior Checklist (CBCL), 108,
        121–122, 124
    definition of, 109
    expressive language development, 179
    inhibition and self-regulation, 110–111,
        121
    interventions to promote selective attention
        and memory, 226
    language development problems, 156
    maternal care quality, effect on, 187
    play, development of, 115–116, 118, 125,
        126f–127f
    postadoption catch-up, 118–119, 124–125
    quasi-autistic behavior and age of adoption,
        157
    Stroop test, 119
    *see also* Mental and emotional development;
        Theory of Mind

Feeding and swallowing development, 139, 144
Fetal alcohol spectrum disorder (FASD), 22,
    33, 52, 98
Food and Drug Administration (FDA), 210
Foster care
    communication, social and emotion, 190
    developmental benefits over orphanages,
        67, 89
    older children, attachment issues, 217–218
    pragmatic communication development, 185
    speech development and, 152, 154–155

Growth and development
    age at adoption, postadoption effects of,
        7–10, 15
    age dependent catch-up, 6–8
    delays, developmental, 42–44, 66, 69
    determination of birth date, 37–38
    early screening of new adoptees, 50–52
    growth hormone therapy, 210–211
    height and weight, postadoption catch-up,
        209–210
    hypothalamic pituitary adrenal (HPA) stress
        axis, 38
    infectious disease, impact of, 35–36

institutional care, effects of, 5–6, 8–9, 13–15,
    36
milestones, developmental, 28–32
motor skill development, 28–30, 32, 40–44
multiple settings prior to adoption, 6–7
neurobiological development, 13–14, 27–28,
    113, 116–117, 185–187, 189–191
physical development, adoptees and orphans,
    49
preadoption variables, effect of, 25, 33, 97,
    184–185
prenatal growth, importance of, 25–27
resilience and, 8, 10, 47–49
sensory motor development, problems of,
    211–214
stress hormones, effects of, 38–39, 65–66,
    91, 185–187
*see also* Cognitive development; Compari-
    sons with nonadoptees; Social-emotional
    development
Guatemala, adoptions from, 4, 6–7, 37, 43–44,
    92

Hague Adoption Convention (1993), 134
Health issues of adoptees
    early screening for medical conditions,
        49–52, 97–99, 208, 214
    immunization records and vaccinations, 38,
        207–209, 214
    infectious diseases, 35, 140, 208
    iron deficiencies and anemia, 23, 34, 39–40
    malnutrition, 39–40
    prenatal and perinatal problems, 33–37
    sexually transmitted infections of birth
        mothers, 22, 34–36
    *see also* Fetal alcohol spectrum disorder;
        International adoption clinics
Hearing and hearing loss, 135–136, 140,
    144–145
Hepatitis, *see* Health issues of adoptees: sexually
    transmitted infections
HIV infection, *see* Birth parents: health issues
    affecting fetus
Human development, *see* Growth and development
Hypothalamic pituitary adrenal (HPA) stress
    axis, 38

Impulse control, *see* Mental and emotional
    development: inhibition and self-regulation
Institutional care
    attachment behavior, orphanages and adopt-
        ees, 67–68
    brain development and institutional setting,
        86–91, 95–96, 101
    bundling and restraints, effects of, 41–42
    cognition and growth, orphanages and
        adoptees, 7–8
    executive function, effect on development,
        120

feeding practices, effects of, 41
memory, effect on development, 123–124, 129
negative effects of, 5–7, 140–141
postadoption effect on Theory of mind, 191–194
resilience after adoption, 48
sensory processing dysfunction, 44–47
speech and language development, 137, 140–141, 150–155
staff training, 6, 152
state resources and, 6
Interferon-gamma radioimmunoassay (IGRA), see Tuberculosis, vaccination for
International adoption clinics, 2, 36, 50, 97–98, 141, 207
International adoption, history of
comparison of U.S. with other countries, 4
live birth to adoption ratios, 4
International Small for Gestational Age Advisory Board, 210
Intersubjectivity, see Theory of Mind

Kazakhstan, see Eastern Europe
Korea, adoptions from, 4, 7–9, 40, 94–95

Language and speech
age at adoption, postadoption effect on, 166–168
birth and adopted language, 141–143
Clinical Evaluation of Language Fundamentals-Preschool 2 (CLEF-P2), 163t–165
Communication and Symbolic Behavioral Scales Development Profile (CSBS DP), 160t–162, 171–172
comparisons, country and environment, 161–162, 166–169
disrupted or sequential language learners, 150–151f, 155–156
expressive language development, 164–166, 179, 183–184, 187
Goldman-Fristoe Test of Articulation, 142
hearing impairment, effect on, 182
infant development, 136–138
influence of caregiver and setting, 150–155, 156
intervention guidelines for postadoption language development, 159–160t, 163t, 167, 170, 224
Language Development Scale (LDS), 159, 160t, 172
linguistic measures of comprehension and expression, 159–163t, 171–172
MacArthur Communicative Development Inventories (MCDI-WG), 159, 160t, 163t, 171–172
Peabody Picture Vocabulary Test (PPVT-4), 163t
Preschool Language Scale (PLS-4), 161

Rossetti Infant-Toddler Language Scale (Rosetti), 159
school-age development, 165–168
speech disorder screening, 145–146
temperament and maternal sensitivity and, 157–158
Language Development Scale (LDS), 159, 160t, 171

MacArthur Communicative Development Inventories (MCDI-WG), 159, 160t, 163t, 171–172
Memory
Cambridge Neuropsychological Test and Automated Battery, 123–124
definition of, 113–114
NEPSY Developmental Neuropsychological Assessment, 124
Mental and emotional development
inhibition and self-regulation, 109–113
play, development of, 115–116, 118
stress, effect on neurobiological development, 116–117
NEPSY Developmental Neuropsychological Assessment, 124
Neurobiological development, see Growth and development: neurobiological development

Orphanages, see Institutional care

Peabody Developmental Motor Scales, 43
Peabody Picture Vocabulary Test (PPVT-4), 163
Physical development, see Growth and development
Preschool Language Scale (PLS-4), 161
Primary intersubjectivity, see Theory of Mind

Resilience, see Growth and development
Romania, adoptions from, 4–5, 187–188
health issues, 36, 42
neurobiological developmental studies, 13–14, 188–191
orphanage conditions, 4
preadoption treatment in, 45–47, 91, 119–120, 123, 128, 141–143, 144, 153–158, 168–170
see also Bucharest Early Intervention Project (BEIP); English and Romanian Adoptees Study
Rossetti Infant-Toddler Language Scale (Rosetti), 161
Russia, adoptions from, 4
adoptee profile: Alayna, 206–207
adoptee profile: Drew, 149–150
adoptee profile: Patrick, 59–60
adoptee profile: Robbie, 107–109
adoptee profile: Stephen, 21–22
adoptee profile: Yana, 222–223

duration of institutional stay, 45
health issues, 33–36, 40
preadoption treatment in, 9

Sensory processing dysfunction
effects of institutional care, 44–47
*see also* Growth and development
Sensory Profile, *see* Growth and development: sensory motor development
Sexually transmitted diseases, *see under* Birth parents
Social cognition, 180–181, 184–185, 187, 197
*see also* Communicative behaviors
Social Communication, Emotion Regulation and Transactional Support Model (SCERTS), 224–225
Social-emotional development
abused and neglected children, effects, 187–188
assessment issues for professionals, 75, 79, 178–179
attachment, adoptee parental success, 73–74
attachment, preadoption experience and, 72
attachment, secure and insecure, 61–64, 67–68, 74–75, 79, 215–218
caregiver role in development, 64–66, 180–181
cause and effect of emotions, 179
Developmental, Individual Difference, Relationship-based Model (DIR), 224–225
interventions for social communication problems, 178–179, 224–225
orphanages, effects on development, 66
parental stress and depression in adoptive families, 73
parental understanding and repair therapies, 216–222
persistent behavioral concerns, 69–71, 76–79
psychological arousal, effect on babies, 64f, 65f
Social Communication, Emotion Regulation and Transactional Support Model (SCERTS), 224–225

"Strange Situation," 74–75
stress, anxiety and withdrawal, 215
Special education, *see* Growth and development
"Strange Situation," 74–75
Stroop test, 119
Syphilis, *see* Health issues of adoptees: sexually transmitted infections of birth mothers

Theory of Mind (ToM), 119–120, 197–198
complex language and emotions of others, 182
expressive language development, 180
postadoption development studies, 191–194
primary intersubjectivity and, 180
secondary intersubjectivity, 181
Therapies, 217–218
Attachment and Biobehavioral Catch-up (ABC), 217–218
auditory integration therapy (AIT), 2–3
Circle of Security, 218–219
Dyadic Developmental Psychotherapy (DDP), 219–220
psychotherapy for attachment disorders, 215–217
sensory diet, 213
sensory integration therapy (SIT), 1–3, 178, 211–214
Video-Feedback Intervention to Promote Positive Parenting (VIPP), 216–217
ToM, *see* Theory of Mind
Tools Curriculum, *see* Executive function: interventions
Tuberculosis
Bacille Calmette-Guérin (BCG) vaccination for, 207, 208–209
Interferon-gamma radioimmunoassay (IGRA), 209

Video-Feedback Intervention to Promote Positive Parenting (VIPP), 216–217
Vietnam, adoptions from, 36